Professor Jolowicz's analysis of civil procedure concentrates on the purposes served by the institution of litigation rather than the intentions of those who litigate. Stressing that those purposes go far beyond mere dispute resolution by non-violent means, Jolowicz surveys a variety of topics of procedural law, making substantial use of the comparative method, in the attempt to examine and explain the ideas which underlie some of the most important of its constituent elements. In the final section, he deals with the reform of English law and ventures a prediction of the consequences that the new Civil Procedure Rules, together with the reforms which more or less immediately preceded them, will have on the character of English procedural law.

CAMBRIDGE STUDIES IN INTERNATIONAL AND COMPARATIVE LAW

This series (established in 1946 by Professors Gutteridge, Hersch Lauterpacht and McNair) is a forum for studies of high quality in the fields of public and private international law and comparative law. Although these are distinct legal sub-disciplines, developments since 1946 confirm their interrelationship. Comparative law is increasingly used as a tool in the making of law at national, regional and international levels. Private international law is increasingly affected by international conventions, and the issues faced by classical conflicts rules are increasingly dealt with by substantive harmonisation of law under international auspices. Mixed international arbitrations, especially those involving state economic activity, raise mixed questions of public and private international law. In many fields (such as the protection of human rights and democratic standards, investment guarantees, international criminal law) international and national systems interact. National constitutional arangements relating to 'foreign affairs', and to the implementation of international norms, are a focus of attention.

Professor Sir Robert Jennings edited the series from 1981. Following his retirement as General Editor, an editorial board has been created and Cambridge University Press has recommitted itself to the series, affirming its broad scope.

The Board welcomes works of a theoretical or interdisciplinary character, and those focusing on new approaches to international or comparative law or conflicts of law. Studies of particular institutions or problems are equally welcome, as are translations of the best work published in other languages.

A list of books in the series can be found at the end of this volume

J. A. JOLOWICZ is Professor Emeritus of Comparative Law in the University of Cambridge and a Fellow of Trinity College. His publications include several editions of *Winfield and Jolowicz on Tort*, *Droit Anglais* (with others), *Public Interest Parties and the Active Role of the Judge in Civil Litigation* (with M. Cappelletti) and numerous articles in English and foreign periodicals.

On Civil Procedure

J. A. Jolowicz

CAMBRIDGE
UNIVERSITY PRESS

CAMBRIDGE UNIVERSITY PRESS
Cambridge, New York, Melbourne, Madrid, Cape Town, Singapore, São Paulo

Cambridge University Press
The Edinburgh Building, Cambridge CB2 8RU, UK

Published in the United States of America by Cambridge University Press, New York

www.cambridge.org
Information on this title: www.cambridge.org/9780521584197

First published 2000

A catalogue record for this publication is available from the British Library

Library of Congress Cataloguing in Publication data

Jolowicz, J. A. (John Anthony)
On civil procedure / J. A. Jolowicz.
   p.   cm.
ISBN 0 521 58419 1
1. Civil procedure – Great Britain.   I. Title.
KD7325.J65   2000   347.41′05 – dc21   99–15852   CIP

ISBN 978-0-521-58419-7 hardback

Transferred to digital printing 2008

Contents

Preface

The new Civil Procedure Rules, which are based on and broadly follow the recommendations made by Lord Woolf in his Reports of 1995 and 1996, came into force on 26 April 1999. They are supposed to give a completely new start to English civil procedure, and Lord Woolf himself is reported as having said, in a speech made in February 1999, that the White Book would be of 'historic interest' only, that looking back to old cases would 'mislead rather than inform on the new position' and even that 'all learning should be forgotten' (*Law Society Gazette*, Guardian Issue, 24 February 1999, p. 4).

It is only fair to Lord Woolf to suppose that he did not intend his words to be taken literally, but, be that as it may, this book reflects the conviction that the slate was not, and could not have been, wiped clean and a completely new system introduced in April 1999. Reformers are men and women of their time. They can learn from their past, but they cannot wholly escape from it. Even the French Revolution could not produce a truly radical civil code: its draftsmen were, inevitably, lawyers and judges of the pre-Revolutionary era who 'could not be expected to forget their education, experience, and preconceptions' (René David, *French Law* (1972), p. 12). In fact, though the new rules have introduced a number of significant innovations and have changed the style and language of our procedural law, what we have now is clearly recognisable as a development, not a rejection and replacement, of what went before. That this development, in conjunction with some earlier changes, may have long-term unintended consequences for the character of our procedure, is another matter.

The Woolf reforms are with us and they receive attention in this book, but they are not central to it. Behind much that is written here lies the belief that we have concentrated almost exclusively and for far too long on the 'nuts and bolts' of litigation and, in particular, on its costs and its delays. What is needed, if the institution of civil litigation is to meet the needs of the twenty-first century, is that we should give more attention to the purposes it serves, and should serve, in society, as distinct from

the purposes of those who choose to use it. It must not be assumed, as it
so often seems to be, that the whole panoply of (civil) courts, judges and
lawyers amounts to no more than one out of a number of institutions
whose business is simply to settle those disputes which fail to settle
themselves, and that the only question is how courts and judges can deal
with the cases that reach them as quickly and as economically as
possible. We must seek answers not only to 'How?', but to 'What?' and
'Why?' – questions that should precede 'How?' but commonly do not
even get asked.

The explanation of this failing is the assumption just mentioned,
which leads people to suppose that the answers are self-evident: courts
exist to settle disputes, and that's that. As everyone appreciates when
thinking about the law rather than litigation, however, the answers are
not self-evident at all. They demand the examination and exposition of
the principles of our procedure and, so far as possible, of the inarticulate
premises from which our conscious thoughts proceed. A comparative, as
well as a historical, approach is essential. At this stage of our history no
one could write a code of procedure from scratch and, of course, Lord
Woolf did not attempt to do so.

With three exceptions, the chapters of this book are based on papers
which have been previously published and which have been adapted
and, within limits, updated, for their present purpose. Many of them are
overtly comparative and of those which are not almost all were originally
prepared for a non-common law readership. They are published here in
the hope that they will encourage and assist the kind of study of
procedural law which goes beyond 'How?' The book does not, of
course, attempt to be comprehensive, but the adaptations of the originals, each of which deals with a distinct topic in procedural law, have
been made with an eye to their ordered presentation. It is nevertheless
intended that each chapter can stand on its own, at least with the aid of
the cross-referencing that has been provided.

My thanks are due to many, including, of course, Finola O'Sullivan,
Katy Cooper, Maureen MacGlashan – for the index – and others at
Cambridge University Press, but the help given by Laura Cordy at
Trinity College, whose skills in transferring originals to computer disk
are remarkable, and her labours in that and other technical ways, call for
special mention. Mauro Cappelletti, with whom I first collaborated
more than twenty-five years ago, inspired my interest in the comparative
study of civil procedure. I owe much to him, as I do also to so many
other colleagues in so many countries that it is impossible to name them
here. As my wife knows only too well, without her encouragement and

her patience with my periodical moodiness, this book could never have appeared. If it had a dedication it would have been to her.

The law is, in general, stated in the light of information available to me in April 1999.

Abbreviations

Am.Jo.Comp. Law	American Journal of Comparative Law
Bowman	Review of the Court of Appeal (Civil Division): Report to the Lord Chancellor September 1997
Calif.L.R.	California Law Review
C.J.Q.	Civil Justice Quarterly
C.L.J.	Cambridge Law Journal
C.p.c.	Codice di procedura civile (Italian)
C.p.p.	Code de procédure pénale (French) or Codice di procedura penale (Italian) according to context
C.P.R.	Civil Procedure Rules 1998 made under the Civil Procedure Act 1997. Where appropriate, references are given to both the R.S.C. and the C.P.R.
C.P.R., r. (rr.)	Civil Procedure Rules 1998, rule (rules)
Cappelletti *et al.*	Mauro Cappelletti, J. H. Merryman and J. M. Perillo, *The Italian Legal System* (1967)
Cappelletti and Garth	Mauro Cappelletti and Bryant Garth (eds.), *Access to Justice* (1978–1979)
Cappelletti and Jolowicz	Mauro Cappelletti and J. A. Jolowicz, *Public Interest Parties and the Active Role of the Judge in Civil Litigation* (1975)
Carey Miller	D. L. Carey Miller and Paul Beaumont (eds.), *The Option of Litigating in Europe* (1993)
Certoma	G. L. Certoma, *The Italian Legal System* (1985)
Colum.L.R.	Columbia Law Review
D.	Dalloz
D.S.	Dalloz Sirey
D.P.	Dalloz périodique
David, *Grands Systèmes*	René David and Camille Jauffret-Spinosi, *Les Grands Systèmes de droit contemporains*, 10th edn (1992)
Debbasch	C. Debbasch and J. C. Ricci, *Contentieux administratif*, 6th edn (1994)

De Smith	Stanley De Smith, H. Woolf and J. Jowell, *Judicial Review of Administrative Action*, 5th edn (1995)
Ecrits	Henri Motulsky, *Ecrits: études et notes de procédure civile* (1973)
Evershed	Final Report of the Committee on Supreme Court Practice and Procedure, Cmd 8878 (1953)
F.R.D.	Federal Rules Decisions
Fed.R.Civ.P.	Federal Rules of Civil Procedure (U.S.)
Glasson and Tissier	E. Glasson and A. Tissier, *Traité théorique et pratique d'organisation judiciaire, de compétence et de procédure civile*, 3rd edn (1926)
Harv.L.R.	Harvard Law Review
History	Arthur Engelmann *et al.*, *History of Continental Civil Procedure* (trans. and ed. Robert Millar) (1928)
Jacob, *Fabric*	I. H. Jacob, *The Fabric of English Civil Justice* (1987)
Jacob, *Reform*	I. H. Jacob, *The Reform of Civil Procedural Law and Other Essays in Civil Procedure* (1982)
James and Hazard	Fleming James, Jr and Geoffrey C. Hazard, Jr, *Civil Procedure*, 2nd edn (1977)
J.C.P.	Jurisclasseur périodique (La semaine juridique)
L.Q.R.	Law Quarterly Review
L.S.	Legal Studies
Liebman	Enrico Tullio Liebman, *Manuale di diritto processuale civile*, 4th edn (1981)
Mazeaud	H. Mazeaud, L. Mazeaud and Chabas, *Traité théorique et pratique de la responsabilité civile, III*, 6th edn (1978)
M.L.R.	Modern Law Review
Mich.L.R.	Michigan Law Review
N.c.p.c.	Nouveau code de procédure civile (French)
N.L.J.	New Law Journal
N.Z.L.J.	New Zealand Law Journal
N.Z.L.R.	New Zealand Law Reports
O.J.L.S.	Oxford Journal of Legal Studies
P.L.	Public Law
Rec.	Recueil des décisions du Conseil d'Etat statuant au Contentieux
Rev.int.dr.comp.	Revue internationale de droit comparé
Rev.trim.dr.civ.	Revue trimestrielle de droit civil

R.S.C.	Rules of the Supreme Court (1965) (Under the C.P.R., certain Orders of the R.S.C. are continued in force as scheduled to the C.P.R.)
S.	Sirey
Solus and Perrot	H. Solus and R. Perrot, *Droit Judiciaire Privé, Tome 3, Procédure de Première Instance* (1991)
U. of Chi.L.R.	University of Chicago Law Review
Vincent	Jean Vincent and Serge Guinchard, *Procédure civile*, 22nd edn (1991)
Wade	H. W. R. Wade and C. Forsyth, *Administrative Law*, 7th edn (1994)
Winn	Report of the Committee on Personal Injuries Litigation, Cmnd 3691 (1968)
Woolf Final	H. Woolf, *Access to Justice, Final Report to the Lord Chancellor on the Civil Justice System in England and Wales* (1996)
Woolf Interim	H. Woolf, *Access to Justice, Interim Report to the Lord Chancellor on the Civil Justice System in England and Wales* (1995)
Woolf reforms	The reforms introduced and to be introduced following Lord Woolf's Report (Woolf Interim and Woolf Final)
Yeazell	Stephen Yeazell, *From Medieval Group Litigation to the Modern Class Action* (1987)
Zamir and Woolf	I. Zamir and H. and J. Woolf, *The Declaratory Judgment*, 2nd edn (1993)

Introduction[1]

I keep six honest serving-men
(They taught me all I knew);
Their names are What and Why and When
And How and Where and Who.
I send them over land and sea,
I send them East and West;
But after they have worked for me
I give them all a rest.

I let them rest from nine till five,
For I am busy then,
As well as breakfast, lunch and tea,
For they are hungry men;
But different folk have different views;
I know a person small
She keeps ten million serving men,
Who get no rest at all!
She sends 'em abroad on her own affairs,
From the second she opens her eyes
One million Hows, two million Wheres,
And seven million Whys![2]

The usual moral of Kipling's poem is 'Don't ask too many questions.' An equally important moral, however, is that reasonable use of all six questions should be made on occasion, and especially if an institution of our society is to be understood, let alone reformed. No doubt different emphases on the different questions are appropriate to different endeavours, and it is natural enough that our procedural reformers, who are today more active than at any time since the Judicature Acts, should concentrate on 'How?' Is it not obvious, some may say, that the whole of the law of procedure boils down to a set of answers to 'How?' and its

---

[1] Based in part on a presidential address delivered to the Annual Meeting of the Society of Public Teachers of Law, Cambridge, 17 September 1987 and published in [1988] L.S. 1.
[2] Rudyard Kipling, 'I keep six honest serving-men'.

1

companions 'When?' (e.g. time limits), 'Who?' (e.g. judicial organisation, joinder of parties and even the appointment of judges) and
'Where?' (e.g. territorial jurisdiction of some courts and the doctrine of
forum non conveniens). 'What?' and 'Why?', however, are absentees.
Hardly ever do we direct either question to the elements of what we
recognise as the process of civil litigation or, indeed, to the process itself
as a whole.

To the innocent observer, and even to one who is not entirely
innocent, this is strange. Surely, if we are contemplating change in the
established order of things, these two questions come first. 'What?' and
'Why?' – taken separately or together – should be asked at various levels
and in various ways before it becomes sensible to move on to questions
such as 'How?'; but if we look for answers to 'What?' and 'Why?', those
that we find, are, at best, broad and general statements bordering on the
platitudinous and inserted by way of introduction to discussion of a
system of dispute settlement. Lord Woolf himself recognises at the
beginning of his Interim Report of 1995 that a system of civil justice is
essential to the maintenance of a civilised society because it safeguards
the rights of individuals, regulates their dealings with others and enforces the duties of government. He then states a number of principles
to be met by a system of civil justice: it should be just in its results and
fair in its procedures; it should deal with cases with reasonable speed
and at a cost proportionate to the issues involved; it should be understandable to and responsive to the needs of those who use it; and it
should be effective and adequately resourced. All this within two pages,
and the report then turns without more ado to dispute resolution in the
civil courts.[3] It is assumed, and not only by Lord Woolf,[4] that a system
of civil justice is about the settlement of disputes between the parties to
litigation and little if anything else. It is also assumed that what is usually
called the adversary process is the best way for us to go about it.[5]

These assumptions may or may not be valid, but both are widely
accepted, not altogether without justification. It is generally understood

---

[3] Woolf Interim, pp. 2, 3, 4.

[4] The 'General Issues Paper' issued in 1987 by the Lord Chancellor's Department as
Consultation Paper No. 6 of the Civil Justice Review states, at para. 55, that 'the
primary aim in all branches of Civil Justice is the pursuit of high quality justice which
includes the following elements: (i) fairness of procedures and methods of adjudication
such as to ensure to each party an opportunity to present his case, to have it impartially
considered, and to know and challenge the case against him; (ii) quality, fairness and
consistency of judicial decisions.' See also Review of Civil Justice and Legal Aid: Report
to the Lord Chancellor by Sir Peter Middleton GCB (September 1997), paras. 1.1, 1.4.
Cf. para. 1.3.

[5] This is reflected in Lord Woolf's Report, notwithstanding his desire to get rid of the
'adversarial culture': Interim, p. 7; below, p. 5.

that what we now call civil litigation emerged in society when governmental organisations of some sort acquired both the power and the will to substitute non-violent for violent methods of dispute settlement.[6] In a neat and often quoted sentence, the Uruguayan scholar, Edouardo Couture, said that 'the civil action is civilisation's substitute for vengeance'.[7] That may well be true, but at the end of the twentieth century can it really be regarded as the whole truth?

Probably, if they thought about it, most lawyers would agree that it is not the whole truth. Indeed, the development of what is unfortunately called 'alternative dispute resolution', and the official encouragement now given to it,[8] demonstrates an official view that civil litigation may actually be unnecessary where nothing but the settlement of the parties' dispute is in question. Yet, paradoxically, use of the phrase '*alternative* dispute resolution' perpetuates the view that civil litigation in the courts is simply one mechanism amongst others for the resolution of disputes.

The metaphor of the court as a non-violent duelling ground is thus maintained and its other functions – even its role as guardian of both law and legality – are overlooked. We do not normally enter into 'What?' and 'Why?' because we assume that we know the answers to them; we take it for granted that we know what we are working with, what we are trying to do and why we are trying to do it. Unhappily, the assumptions that we make – the inarticulate premises on which we base our thinking – provide increasingly unsure ground on which to build reform. This is particularly the case when, as once again today, we concentrate our attention on the presumed twin evils of cost and delay. 'It is difficult to avoid the conclusion that a great deal of effort has been directed to the reduction of costs and delay, but little if any to an understanding of what it is that should be done more expeditiously and more cheaply.'[9]

It may be that one of the principal reasons why we do not try to examine what it is we take for granted is that it is an uncomfortably difficult thing to do. All conscious thought has to start from somewhere, but, though thought about detail may have an explicit starting point, thought about generalities commonly does not. Such thought may

---

[6] This is even accepted judicially: *D. v. NSPCC* [1977] A.C. 171, 230, *per* Lord Simon of Glaisdale.

[7] 'The Nature of Judicial Process' (1950) 25 Tulane L.R. 1, 7.

[8] Chap. 19, below, p. 392.

[9] Chap. 17, below, p. 359. These words were originally written in 1983, before the Civil Justice Review and long before Lord Woolf's Report, but, with all respect to the many able people who have been active in procedural reform since then, they remain essentially true, and they remain true because we take so much of 'What?' and 'Why?' for granted.

sometimes start from particular instances and proceed by a process of induction and it may sometimes start from conscious acceptance of a particular religion or philosophy. In most cases, however, it stems from the things we take for granted and which we rarely, if ever, bring up to the level of conscious explicit recognition.

Comparative legal study provides a tool for lawyers to gain some insight about the things they themselves take for granted about their legal system and which they do not articulate. When they find something in a foreign legal system which to them seems inexplicable, they can come to realise that its underlying explanation is an assumption – an inarticulate premise of the foreign system – which their own system does not share. And so, by revealing what are the assumptions of the foreign legal system, they can work backwards and learn what are their own. This process is of particular value when it comes to 'What?' and 'Why?'

There is no suggestion here that comparative study in the field of procedure will provide us with solutions to particular problems which we can simply transplant into our own law.[10] On the contrary, even for the practical purposes of reform, there is more to be learned from the study of the procedural law of developed countries whose legal traditions are different from our own than from those whose legal traditions are the same. It is questions for which we should be looking, not for answers. Once we know what are the questions, we can and must work out the answers for ourselves.

The idea of the civil action as civilisation's substitute for vengeance represents essentially the contest or judicial duel concept of litigation, and that concept lies behind our own adversary process, with which the supposedly inquisitorial procedures of the continent are so unfavourably contrasted. Of course, we want the contest to be fair, we have elaborate rules of court to which the parties must conform as they prepare themselves for battle, and the contest itself is held before an impartial judge who decides, at the end of the day, which of the contestants is the winner. He – the judge – is supposed to reach his decision in the light only of the evidence presented to him and the admissions of the parties; it is even doubtful whether and how far he may introduce into his decision his own knowledge of the law as distinct from the legal argument presented to him by counsel.[11]

---

[10] This is not to say that the comparative study of two systems that belong to the same legal family may not reveal a solution to a practical problem of procedure which can be transplanted from one system to the other, but where this is the case the solution in question will relate to 'How?', not to 'What?' or 'Why?'

[11] See C. Yates, 'The Use of Judicial Knowledge' in E. K. Banakas (ed.), *UK Law in the 1980s: Comparative and Common Law Studies for the XIIth International Congress of Comparative Law* (1988), p. 320 at p. 341; chap. 10, below, p. 192.

It is at least plausible that when we find virtue in this vision of litigation as a fight which uses words instead of swords as weapons, we are finding virtue in necessity. When civil trials were regularly conducted before juries there was no alternative to exclusive party preparation for trial and trial before a court which, until the case was opened, knew nothing of what it was to hear. Now, however, the civil jury has virtually disappeared from the scene; much happened before and much more has happened since Lord Woolf's Report, which has the tendency to undermine the concept of litigation as a contest. For the time being, the procedural law of this country is in a state of flux and it is unclear whether we are in the process of moving away from the basic concept of litigation as a contest or not.

Some evidence of this kind of uncertainty lies in Lord Woolf's stated objective of giving a more interventionist management role to the court to discourage the 'adversarial culture' while explicitly rejecting any idea that 'our adversarial and oral tradition in England and Wales' might be abandoned,[12] but it can be seen also in the cases. In 1983, in the *Air Canada* case,[13] for example, Lord Wilberforce was content that a decision might be given that is known to be wrong if that was the result of the way the parties had conducted *their* battle. This could happen as a consequence of the imperfection of the evidence or the withholding of it, for there is no duty on the court to ascertain some independent truth. Yet, a mere four years later, in the *Eli Lilly* case in 1987,[14] the language of the Master of the Rolls is different. In answer to the question which might be asked by a litigant about discovery, namely, why he should be expected to supply his opponent with the means of defeating him, Sir John Donaldson replied that 'litigation is not a war or even a game. It is designed to do real justice between opposing parties and if the court does not have *all*[15] the relevant information, it cannot achieve this object.'

Not the least interesting aspect of Sir John Donaldson's words is his insistence that the court must be informed. From one point of view, no doubt, this is a truism – an uninformed court can decide nothing – but it is unusual in England to pay attention directly to that. We do not normally think about informing the court; we think about evidence and admissions and we could, indeed, hardly have done otherwise in the age

[12] Woolf Interim, pp. 7, 29. See J. A. Jolowicz, 'The Woolf Report and the Adversary System' (1996) 13 C.J.Q. 198.
[13] *Air Canada* v. *Secretary of State for Trade* [1983] 2 A.C. 394, 438. Chap. 18, below, p. 376.
[14] *Davies* v. *Eli Lilly & Co.* [1987] 1 W.L.R. 428, 431–2.
[15] Emphasis in the original.

of jury trial. On the continent, however, the civil jury never came into existence and there is no real equivalent to the concept of evidence. What there is is a stage in the proceedings – the *instruction* – the whole purpose of which is to build up the body of information on which the court's decision will be founded. A somewhat simplified comparative observation might be that continental procedures concentrate on preparation for decision while ours concentrate on preparation for trial.

There is nothing inconsistent with the contest notion in the continental idea of preparation for *decision*. The body of information built up during the *instruction* need contain nothing that is not put in by the parties, but because the process goes on over a period of time, not at a single concentrated trial, it is possible as a practical matter for the court to see the information as it becomes available and to make suggestions for additions to it and so on. Today, in France, for example, the process has been brought under the control of a judge[16] who has the power not only to disallow the use of certain methods of information gathering[17] but also to order the use of at least some of them of his own motion.

In the past, the necessities of jury trial made such a thing impossible in England, but changes in procedural rules over the last thirty years – changes which were only made possible by the virtual disappearance of the civil jury – have made a great volume of information in documentary form available to the judge before the trial.[18] If, as he is encouraged to do, the judge makes use of the opportunity he now has to inform himself before the trial, he puts himself in a position to take an active role in the preparation of the case. Though its importance may not always be recognised, this involves a dramatic change in the character of our procedure; it is impossible that a jury can know anything about the case it is to try before the trial itself begins, but the modern judge can and should know a great deal. We may now be on the way towards an English model of the continental idea that a case should be prepared for decision rather than for trial.

If this should happen, there is no more reason here than on the continent why the freedom of the parties to determine the subject matter of the litigation should be restricted, but the contest concept would be on its way out. That might or might not be a good thing, but if it did happen it would happen because of changes introduced with a view to improved procedural economy. The character of civil litigation

[16] The juge de la mise en état: n.c.p.c., arts. 763–81.
[17] It is his duty to limit them to what is necessary and to ensure the use only of those which are the least burdensome and expensive: n.c.p.c., art. 147.
[18] See chaps. 18, 19, below.

would be transformed, and the transformation would have come about by accident rather than design.

Even a fundamental but accidental change such as this is unobjectionable if it comes through the evolutionary processes of common law development. Slow change, on a case-by-case basis, maintains continuity between the new and the old; changes in value come gradually and a change, if seen to be erroneous, can be reversed. Change by report and legislation, on the other hand, risks the accidental destruction of values which the system as a whole cannot or cannot yet afford to lose. Reforms introduced to promote economy are capable of bringing fundamental change to the character of our civil process and so of changing the role which it fulfils in our society. That is not necessarily undesirable, but we must not throw the baby out with the bath water, and we must learn how to distinguish the one from the other.

Our choices, when choices have to be made, may not be those made elsewhere, but we must know what are the values we wish to preserve and, to change the metaphor, what are no more than sacred cows. For that, comparative study is essential.[19] In an article published in *The Times* as long ago as 1949[20] it was observed that:

it is in its legal institutions that the characteristics of a civilised country are most clearly revealed, not only and not so much in its substantive law as in the practice and procedure of its courts. Legal procedure is a . . . ritual of extreme social significance. If we can appreciate the meaning of this ritual in the case of our own and even one other community, we obtain a remarkable insight into the fundamental and largely unformulated beliefs accepted by, and acceptable to, those societies; we begin to understand their collective and perhaps contrasted social sense of what is just and fair.

The purpose of the article when written was to encourage understanding of foreign systems in the interests of the then-embryonic proposals for European union. The present purpose is to urge that we should seek to understand our own 'fundamental and largely unformulated beliefs' so that deliberate change in our procedures can be informed by that understanding.

Now that we are embarked upon extensive and far-reaching procedural reform, the need for this understanding is urgent. It is time that our procedural reformers brought to their task not only the expertise of management consultants and the like who can make valuable proposals on efficiency – they can no doubt help in answering 'How?' type questions – but also a greater appreciation of the importance and the

[19] Above, p. 4.
[20] C. J. Hamson, 'In Court in Two Countries: Civil Procedure in England and France', *The Times*, 15 November 1949.

difficulty of 'What?' and 'Why?'[21] Comparative study will not reveal answers to these questions, but it will reveal the issues to be faced.

More now, perhaps, than ever before, the traditional English view that procedure is not a subject for academic writing, still less for teaching in university law schools, must be changed. Thanks largely to the pioneering work of Sir Jack Jacob and one or two others, there is now a growing body of high-quality literature on the English law of civil procedure. Publication in England of comparative work on civil procedure, on the other hand, is still quite rare. This is unfortunate, and it is a principal objective of the present collection of papers, many of which seek to make use of the comparative method, to help fill the gap.

[21] In one major field of procedural law – appeals – there are at last signs that those charged with reform are beginning to consider these questions. In Woolf Final a short paragraph identifies two different purposes served by appeals (p. 153) and this is taken up briefly in Bowman, p. 25. See below, chaps. 14, 15 and 16.

Part I

The litigation process

1   Civil litigation

It is one thing to say what civil litigation is; it is another to say what are the purposes which the institution of civil litigation exists to serve. It is interest in the latter – which are not the same as the purposes of those who engage in litigation – that is one of the principal factors connecting the succeeding chapters of this book. This chapter looks to what civil litigation is.

It might be thought that the phrase 'civil litigation' and its companions, 'civil proceedings' and 'civil procedure', are well enough known to stand without explanation. All three form part of the everyday language of lawyers, and even Parliament has been prepared to use an unbroken circle by way of definition, as it did, for example, in the Civil Evidence Act 1968: 'civil proceedings', it is said, 'includes in addition to civil proceedings in any of the ordinary courts of law', certain other 'civil proceedings'.[1]

This kind of thing may be harmless when only one legal system is in contemplation; it is unlikely that a French lawyer would have any more trouble within his own system with the phrase 'procédure civile' than his English counterpart has with 'civil procedure'. Indeed, the French lawyer has a code of civil procedure, now the nouveau code de procédure civile, and for him civil procedure is the subject matter of that code. What is more, an English lawyer would almost certainly recognise as civil the kind of proceedings regulated by that code and recognised as such in France. This does not mean, however, that the English and the French understandings of what is civil are co-extensive. On the contrary, the English idea is by far the wider; there is much which an English lawyer regards as civil which a French lawyer would see quite differently.

In several of the chapters of this book comparisons are drawn between the civil procedure of this country and that of France and other continental countries. Those chapters do not, however, routinely warn the reader that 'civil procedure' does not mean the same for all. It is the

---

[1] Civil Evidence Act 1968, s. 18(1). See also the Evidence (Proceedings in Other Jurisdictions) Act 1975, below, p. 13.

object of this opening chapter, therefore, to give an account of the most important of those differences and to supply a working description – not a definition – of civil litigation which, it is hoped, is capable of use in more than one jurisdiction, whether it coincides with the classification used in a given jurisdiction or not.[2]

The English system

In comparison with most continental systems, which are decentralised on a regional basis at all levels except that of the Supreme Court, the English judicial system is highly centralised. It is true that the House of Lords in its appellate capacity forms no part of what is called the Supreme Court, but this has little if any practical significance.[3] It is also true that neither the magistrates' courts nor the county courts are part of the Supreme Court[4] and that there are numerous specialist tribunals. However, an appeal from such courts or tribunals may lie, and in appropriate circumstances an application for the judicial review of their decisions does lie, to the Supreme Court.[5] That Court, which consists of the Court of Appeal, the High Court of Justice and the Crown Court, does, of course, have its subdivisions,[6] but it is a single whole; it is a unique jurisdiction of first instance and of appeal for the whole country.

This centralisation may explain and certainly assisted development of

[2] As will appear, certain institutions developed for the purposes of 'civil litigation', as described, have come to be used also for purposes which fall outside it. They are, perhaps, best regarded as sui generis, but, being neither criminal proceedings according to the English classification nor administrative according to the continental, they are treated as falling within the broad category of civil litigation. See chaps. 5, 6 and 7.

[3] Its orders are made orders of the High Court and thus of the Supreme Court under R.S.C., Ord. 32, r. 10.

[4] Proposals equivalent to proposals for the transfer to the Supreme Court of the jurisdiction of the county courts and the amalgamation of the two sets of courts, such as those made in Jacob, *Reform*, p. 7 and Jacob, *Fabric*, p. 259 were not accepted by the Civil Justice Review (Report of the Review Body on Civil Justice, Cm 394 (1988) paras. 82–115) and have not been implemented by the Courts and Legal Services Act 1990. By that Act, however, the jurisdiction of the county courts was greatly enlarged and the co-ordinate jurisdiction of both expanded: High Court and County Courts Jurisdiction Order 1991 (SI 1991 No. 724 (L.5)); High Court and County Courts Jurisdiction (Amendment) Order 1995 (SI 1995 No. 205 (L.1)). The new Civil Procedure Rules do not result in amalgamation but do give greater alignment of the two jurisdictions.

[5] For the variety of appeals see H. Woolf, 'A Hotchpotch of Appeals – The Need for a Blender' (1988) 7 C.J.Q. 44.

[6] The Court of Appeal has its Civil and its Criminal Divisions, the High Court has its Chancery, Queen's Bench and Family Divisions, not to mention the specialised Patents Court within the Chancery Division and the Admiralty and Commercial Courts within the Queen's Bench Division. The jurisdiction of the Crown Court varies with its constitution: Supreme Court Act 1981, ss. 8 and 73–5.

the prevailing English view that the most important and overriding division of proceedings before the courts of law is that between the criminal and the civil: any proceedings that are not criminal are civil. So, for example, subject to one exception,[7] no appeal lies to the Court of Appeal from a judgment of the High Court 'in any criminal cause or matter';[8] the Attorney-General, by the entry of a *nolle prosequi*,[9] can bring criminal but not civil proceedings to an end regardless of the wishes of the parties;[10] the rules of procedure for civil and for criminal cases are quite distinct.

In *Re Norway's Application (Nos. 1 and 2)*,[11] it was necessary for the House of Lords to decide whether proceedings in a Norwegian court in respect of an assessment to tax raised in Norway against the estate of a deceased Norwegian citizen qualified as civil proceedings within the meaning of an English statute.[12] Following the familiar language derived from various international conventions,[13] civil proceedings are defined as 'proceedings in any civil or commercial matter', and it was argued that this required that 'civil proceedings' should be interpreted as that phrase would be interpreted in countries which, unlike England, recognise that 'civil' does not necessarily include 'commercial'.[14] The argument was rejected. Lord Goff had no doubt that 'under English law the words . . . should be given their ordinary meaning, so that proceedings in any civil matter should include all proceedings other than criminal proceedings, and proceedings in any commercial matter should be treated as falling within proceedings in civil matters'.[15]

Both the negative and the positive aspects of this statement call for attention.

(a) *Negative.* Proceedings which are criminal in nature are, ipso facto, not civil proceedings. This is not to say that it is always easy to decide whether particular proceedings are criminal or civil. On the contrary,

---

[7] Certain cases of contempt of court: Administration of Justice Act 1960, s. 13(2)(b). By the same Act, appeal lies directly to the House of Lords from the decisions of certain courts 'in a criminal cause or matter': *ibid.*, s. 1.
[8] Supreme Court Act 1981, s. 18(1). The jurisdiction of the High Court in criminal matters is exceptional. There is, of course, nothing exceptional in an appeal in a 'criminal cause or matter' from the Crown Court to the Court of Appeal (Criminal Division).
[9] See J. Ll. J. Edwards, *The Law Officers of the Crown* (1964), pp. 227–37.
[10] *Gouriet* v. *U.P.W.* [1978] A.C. 435, 477, *per* Lord Wilberforce.
[11] [1990] 1 A.C. 723.
[12] The Evidence (Proceedings in other Jurisdictions) Act 1975.
[13] At the time, the Convention on the Taking of Evidence Abroad in Civil or Commercial Matters 1970.
[14] This argument, had it succeeded, would probably have had the effect of excluding tax cases from the scope of the Act as being neither 'civil' nor 'commercial'.
[15] [1990] 1 A.C. 723, 806.

the question has sometimes proved controversial[16] and there is no agreed definition of a crime.[17] It is, however, to say that English law does not envisage the possibility that proceedings may, at one and the same time, be both criminal and civil.[18]

It is true that criminal courts are now possessed of quite extensive powers to order a convicted person to pay compensation for personal injury or loss or damage suffered as a result of the offence of which he is convicted[19] and also to order the restitution of stolen property.[20] The exercise of such powers does not, however, amount to the disposal of a civil claim which the victim might have against the person convicted of the offence. The victim is not a party to the criminal proceedings, and the making of a compensation order in his favour does not affect his right to bring a civil claim in respect of the loss or damage to which the compensation order relates.[21] The procedure is not comparable to one in which a civil claim is joined to a criminal prosecution, as is possible in many continental systems.[22]

(b) *Positive.* All cases which are not criminal are civil: there is no other category of proceedings. Reference has already been made to *Re Norway's Application*[23] as showing that a tax case is civil; so also is any other litigation raising a matter of public law, whether introduced by action or by application for judicial review. It has actually been held that a vexatious litigant, subject to an order that 'no civil legal proceedings

[16] *Amand* v. *Home Secretary* [1943] A.C. 147 is, probably, still the best-known case.

[17] See, e.g. C. S. Kenny, *Outlines of Criminal Law*, 16th edn, Appendix I (subsequent editions omit this appendix); Glanville Williams, 'The Definition of Crime' (1955) 8 Curr.Leg.Prob. 107.

[18] In *Re Smalley* [1985] A.C. 622, where it was unclear whether the proceedings should be classified as criminal or as civil, a Divisional Court of the High Court granted two alternative certificates, one appropriate to a criminal cause or matter and the other appropriate to civil proceedings, so that the case could go directly to the House of Lords whatever the correct classification. Otherwise there would have been the risk, on appeal to the Court of Appeal, Civil Division, that that court might hold that the case involved a criminal cause or matter and thus that it had no jurisdiction.

[19] Powers of Criminal Courts Act 1973, s. 35. The court is encouraged to use these powers by the requirement that, where it refrains from doing so in an apparently proper case for an order, it should explain its reasons: *ibid.*, as amended by the Criminal Justice Act 1988, s. 104.

[20] Theft Act 1968, s. 28 as substituted by the Criminal Justice Act 1972, Sched. 5.

[21] The damages in the civil action, if successful, are assessed without regard to the order, save that the plaintiff may not recover in total more than the aggregate of the amount by which the damages assessed exceed the amount of the order, and any unrecovered portion of the amount ordered by the criminal court to be paid as compensation: Powers of Criminal Courts Act 1973, s. 38 as substituted by the Criminal Justice Act 1988, s. 105. In so far as the damages awarded include an unpaid part of a compensation order, the judgment may not be enforced in respect of that part without the leave of the court.

[22] Below, pp. 15–16.

[23] [1990] 1 A.C. 723, above, p. 13.

shall be instituted by him without the leave of the court',[24] cannot even make an application for leave to apply for judicial review until he has independently obtained leave to institute civil proceedings.[25] It was taken for granted by the Court of Appeal, and formed part of the reasoning of Nicholls L.J.,[26] that the application for judicial review was itself a form of civil proceedings.

Continental systems

For the continental systems, neither the negative nor the positive aspects of Lord Goff's statement hold true.

(a) *Negative.* In English law the same conduct may attract both civil and criminal liability, but where this is so, it is the result not of legal equivalence but of the coincidence of two distinct legal rules.[27] In Italy the precise converse is stated by the penal code. This provides that 'every crime gives rise to an obligation of restitution in accordance with the civil law. Every crime which has occasioned pecuniary or non-pecuniary damage obliges the guilty person, and persons who, according to the civil law should answer for his act, to make compensation.'[28] As a matter of substance, therefore, conduct which constitutes a criminal offence is, for that reason, capable of giving rise to civil liability. In France the position is less clearly stated in legislation, but the civil code contains a general provision imposing liability for 'fault'[29] and 'fault' includes a criminal offence.[30] In both countries crime and tort can coincide, and provision is accordingly made in the code of *criminal procedure* for the criminal and the civil questions arising out of a single act or course of conduct to be dealt with at one and the same time in the court of criminal jurisdiction.

The victim of a crime is not obliged to join the prosecution, but, in contrast with the position in England, if he brings proceedings in the civil court those proceedings will be stayed until the criminal proceed-

---

[24] Supreme Court Act 1981, s. 42.
[25] *Ex parte Ewing* [1991] 1 W.L.R. 388; *Ex parte Ewing (No. 2)* [1994] 1 W.L.R. 1553, distinguishing *Ex parte Waldron* [1986] Q.B. 824.
[26] *Ex parte Ewing* [1991] 1 W.L.R. 388, 394.
[27] See, e.g. *Hollington* v. *F. Hewthorn and Co. Ltd* [1943] K.B. 587, where it was held that the fact of a conviction could not even be used as evidence in a civil action for damages arising out of the same events. Proof of a conviction is now admissible in civil proceedings as (normally) rebuttable evidence that the person convicted committed the offence of which he was convicted: Civil Evidence Act 1968, ss. 11 and 12. Proof of an acquittal remains inadmissible.
[28] Art. 185. Note that this provision is contained in the *penal*, not the civil, code.
[29] Arts. 1382, 1383.
[30] See J. A. Jolowicz, 'Procedural Questions' in *International Encyclopaedia of Comparative Law*, Vol. XI (ed. A. Tunc) (1986), chap. 13, no. 7.

ings have been concluded.[31] It is normally both easier and cheaper for him to bring what is actually called a 'civil action' in conjunction with the prosecution,[32] and he can even take the initiative himself thereby, in effect, compelling the public prosecutor to act.[33] His action may be civil, but it is brought in the criminal court and in accordance with the code of criminal procedure.

It is unnecessary, for present purposes, to enter into detail on this matter.[34] In some countries, including Germany, the combination of the civil with the criminal in a single set of proceedings is little used.[35] In others, including Belgium, France and Italy, it is routine and, indeed, the modern tendency there is to expand rather than to reduce its scope.[36] The important point is, however, that where a prosecution and a civil claim are combined in a single set of proceedings before a criminal court – where there is a prosecutor and also a 'civil plaintiff' – not to mention a 'civil defendant', it is impossible to classify the proceedings as a whole as either criminal or civil. It is not a general truth that proceedings which are criminal are not also civil.

(b) *Positive*. The fundamental distinction for continental systems is that between private and public law,[37] but even within private law a

---

[31] C.p.p., art. 4, al. 2; Italy, c.p.p., art. 3. Note that if civil proceedings are instituted or continue after the criminal proceedings have concluded, the civil court is bound by the decision of the criminal court. For Italy, see c.p.p., arts. 25, 27, 28 and, e.g. Certoma, 262–4. In France no law actually carries the rule 'le criminel emporte le civil', but it is clearly settled in the cases: e.g. J. Pradel, *Procédure pénale*, 3rd edn (1985), no. 665. In England civil proceedings against a person accused of crime may be stayed if justice so demands having regard to concurrent criminal proceedings against the accused in respect of the same subject matter, but such a stay is discretionary, not automatic: *Jefferson Ltd* v. *Bhetcha* [1979] 1 W.L.R. 899.

[32] France, c.p.p., art. 2; Italy, c.p.p, art. 22; Certoma, pp. 265–6.

[33] C.p.p. arts. 85, 86. In Italy the public prosecutor is obliged to act whenever an offence is brought to his attention (Italian Constitution, art. 112; c.p.p., art. 74), so the result, from this point of view is similar.

[34] See Jolowicz, 'Procedural Questions', nos. 5–40.

[35] The criminal court in that country, if seised of a civil claim, is entitled to and commonly does refuse to decide it: Strafprozessordnung, para. 405.

[36] So, for example, in countries such as France and Italy, a variety of persons such as the accused's employer and even, sometimes, his insurer can be joined as defendants to the civil action: France, code pénal, art. 69; Italy, Codice penale, art. 185, cited above, p. 15. In certain cases the criminal court can proceed to consider whether the accused is civilly liable even if he is acquitted on the criminal charge: France, c.p.p., arts. 470–1, introduced in 1983. See, e.g. C. Roca, 'De la dissociation entre la réparation et la répression', D.S. 1991, Chron. 85.

[37] The distinction goes back to the Greeks and is placed in the forefront of both the Digest and Justinian's Institutes: 'Publicum ius est, quod ad statutum rei Romanae pertinet: privatum, quod ad singulorum utilitatem': See H. F. Jolowicz, *Lectures on Jurisprudence* (1963), chap. XXI and also his *Roman Foundations of Modern Law* (1957), chap. 6. The distinction is not uniformly applied. See C. Szladits, *International Encyclopaedia of Comparative Law*, Vol. II, chap. 2.

distinction is often taken between the civil law, which is contained in the civil code, and commercial law, which is, or was, contained in the commercial code.[38] For present purposes, however, the most important matter is that in many countries there is more than one hierarchy of courts[39] and, in particular, there are ordinary courts and administrative courts – the 'ordre judiciaire', which is competent in matters both criminal and 'civil', and the 'ordre administratif', which, in broad and general terms, deals with public law. It is not true, as it is true in England, that there is but one supreme court, and it is not true that cases coming within the jurisdiction of the *ordre administratif* are civil.

In some countries with a separate administrative jurisdiction, the ordinary courts are competent to deal with litigation involving the State or other public authority where the plaintiff's claim relates to an alleged infringement of a right for which he seeks compensation in damages. That is the position, for example, in Belgium.[40] Where, on the other hand, the plaintiff seeks the annulment of an administrative act or order, he must proceed in the administrative jurisdiction.[41] In Italy, the ordinary courts have jurisdiction where the case concerns a person's

---

[38] France still has a commercial code even though much that can be considered as commercial law is now to be found in special statutes: D. Tallon, 'Reforming the Codes in a Civil Law Country' (1980) XV J.S.P.T.L. (N.S.) 33, 34–5. In Germany, too, much commercial law is the subject of special enactments and it has been said that the commercial code (Handelsgesetzbuch) can only be understood in the light of the civil code (Bürgerliches Gesetzbuch): N. Horn, H. Kötz and H. G. Leser, *German Private and Commercial Law*, trans. Tony Weir, 217–18. In Italy, commercial law has been brought within the civil code since 1942. For a full discussion of the relationship between civil and commercial law, see D. Tallon, *International Encyclopaedia of Comparative Law*, Vol. VIII, chap. 2. The traditional distinction between civil and commercial law probably explains the use of the phrase 'civil or commercial matter' to which reference has already been made (above, p. 13). If the word 'civil' stood alone it could be read as excluding 'commercial'. See also G. Samuel, 'Civil and Commerial Law: A Distinction Worth Making?' (1986) 102 L.Q.R. 569.

[39] In some countries there are several hierarchies of courts, each of a more or less specialised nature. In Germany, for example, there are, in addition to the Federal Constitutional Court, separate hierarchies of courts dealing respectively with 'ordinary' cases, that is 'civil' and criminal cases; with labour cases; with administrative law cases; with social insurance cases and related matters; and, finally, with tax cases. (For a convenient short exposition see Horn, Kötz and Leser, *German Private and Commercial Law*.) In Italy there is a Constitutional Court, a Court of Accounts and a distinct hierarchy of administrative courts as well as the ordinary courts of 'civil' and criminal jurisdiction: Certoma, pp. 158–63.

[40] Cass. 3 December 1920 (*Pasicrise Belge* 1920, I, 193), opinion of the premier avocat général Paul Leclerq. See A. Mast, *Précis de Droit Administratif Belge* (1966), nos. 459–77. See also M. A. Flamme, *Droit Administratif* (1989), Vol. II, nos. 502 *et seq.*

[41] In Belgium, the 'Section d'administration' of the Conseil d'Etat. The jurisdiction of this body is conveniently set out in an abbreviated form in Mast, *Précis*, no. 495.

subjective right,[42] but the administrative courts alone are competent where it concerns his legitimate interest.[43]

The Belgian and the Italian systems have departed significantly from their original French model and in France also a few claims against public authorities are today brought in the ordinary courts.[44] In that country, however, the distinction between the ordinary and the administrative courts retains almost all its original importance.

The origin of the distinction lies in a law of 1790,[45] which reflects the Revolutionary concept of the separation of powers and which is still in force; it forbids the judges, on pain of forfeiture of their office, from interfering in any way with the actions of administrative bodies and it forbids them from calling administrators before them in connection with the performance of their official functions. Until an administrative jurisdiction came to be established, therefore, a claim against the administration could be resolved only within the administration itself, and at the discretion, in the last resort, of the Head of State.

In 1799 Napoleon created the Conseil d'Etat,[46] a body whose principal function was to assist with and advise on the drafting of legislation.[47] It was envisaged, however, that the Conseil would also resolve disputes arising in administrative matters, and in 1806 a special commission within the Conseil was created to enquire into and report on such disputes. In 1849, for the first time, a special section of the Conseil, the Section du Contentieux, was created, and that section, though not quite in its original form, continues to exist.[48] Like other sections, it is manned by members of the Conseil, who are themselves members of the administration, not members of the regular judiciary, and, though it came to use procedures appropriate to a judicial body

[42] Art. 24(1) of the Constitution provides that 'Everyone may proceed at law for the protection of his rights and legitimate interests.' Translation from Cappelletti et al., p. 285.

[43] The distinction between 'subjective right' and 'legitimate interest' is complex and the subject of a considerable literature. For brief descriptions see, e.g. Certoma, pp. 20–4, 151; Cappelletti et al., p. 81. Conflicts of jurisdiction are resolved by the Corte di Cassazione, the highest of the 'ordinary' courts.

[44] See, e.g. law no. 57–1424 of 31 December 1957 (damage caused by a vehicle).

[45] Art. 13 of the law of 16–24 August 1790. The law was preceded by a decree to similar effect of 22 December 1789 and was reaffirmed by another decree of 16 Fructidor an III (1794).

[46] Constitution of 22 Frimaire an VIII (1799). At one time considered as an entirely new conception, it is now recognised that the Conseil d'Etat has a link to the pre-Revolutionary institution of the Conseil du Roi, itself abolished in 1790. See the collective work, *Le Conseil d'Etat, son histoire à travers les documents d'époque 1799–1974* (1974), chap. 1.

[47] This function it still retains. See, e.g. B. Ducamin, 'The Role of the Conseil d'Etat in Drafting Legislation' (1981) I.C.L.Q. 882.

[48] For the history, see *Le Conseil d'Etat*, Annexe V, p. 945.

and though its advice came to be invariably accepted, until 1872 it only advised: it was not a court of law.

Insistence on the advisory character of the Conseil d'Etat conformed to the principle of 'justice retenue', namely that in administrative matters it must be for the administration actually to make the decision, a principle which was finally removed by a law of 1872.[49] That law gave power to the Conseil to deliver its own enforceable decisions and so put an end to the principle of *justice retenue*. Another principle was, however, left untouched – 'le ministre juge' – the effect of which was to deny the aggrieved citizen the right of direct recourse to the Conseil. He had, first, to seek redress from the Government department or public authority concerned, and the Conseil, in effect, heard his appeal from the decision made on his complaint. Such a rule was, perhaps, acceptable for so long as the Conseil d'Etat only advised, but, once it acquired the power of final decision, adherence to the principle of *ministre juge* confused the administrative and the judicial function. The confusion was ended by the Conseil d'Etat itself, which, in a celebrated decision of 1889, held that if a dispute arose out of an executory administrative decision the Conseil could be directly seised.[50]

Since that decision, the Conseil d'Etat statuant au contentieux has had all the characteristics of a court of law, but expansion in the volume of administrative litigation has led to the creation of regional administrative courts of first instance and of appeal. Today, therefore, like its ordinary counterpart, the Cour de cassation, the Conseil stands at the head of a three-tiered hierarchy of courts, but it is a hierarchy which is separate from and independent of the hierarchy of the ordinary courts. A special court known as the Tribunal des conflits has existed since 1872 to deal with conflicts of jurisdiction.[51]

In most cases it is clear whether a case falls within the jurisdiction of the administrative or of the ordinary courts, but the criteria for decision have varied over time and there can be controversy in borderline cases. What is, however, abundantly clear is that the distinction between the civil and the administrative case, and so that between civil and administrative proceedings, is fundamental to French law. That between civil and criminal proceedings is not.

---

[49] Law of 24 May 1872, art. 9. The principle had been abandoned after the Revolution of 1848 (law of 3 March 1849), but was restored by the Constitution of 1852.

[50] *Cadot* C.E. 13 December 1889, concl. Jagerschmidt, S. 1892, 3.17, note Hauriou.

[51] Law of 24 May 1872, art. 25. It is composed of the Minister of Justice, 'Garde des sceaux', President, three members of the Conseil d'Etat, elected by their colleagues, three members of the Cour de cassation, nominated by their colleagues, and two others elected by the other members of the Tribunal.

Civil litigation: a working description

In the light of what has been said, it is obviously impossible to devise a generally valid definition of 'civil' litigation which is capable of solving technical puzzles about what is or is not civil within the meaning of specific legislation. On the other hand, as already indicated, there is a need for a description which is capable of use for comparative purposes. It is now suggested that the following four characteristics indicate the essential attributes of civil litigation and that, taken together, they provide a description of civil litigation which is generally sufficient, at least for the purposes of this book.

Civil litigation involves proceedings before a court of law

The first and most important purpose of this statement is to exclude decision-making processes, even those such as arbitration in which an *inter partes* dispute may be settled in accordance with law, let alone other forms of alternative dispute resolution in which the decision is not that of a *court*. What, then, is a court of law?

For constitutional lawyers and political scientists this question is complex. It requires consideration of the separation of powers, of the character of a 'judicial', as opposed to a 'political' or 'administrative', decision and even of the very nature of law itself. It is sufficient here, however, to stress just two characteristics that are possessed by courts:

(a) Courts are established by and exercise their jurisdiction under the authority of the State but independently of Government, and, in the last resort, the power of the State may be invoked to ensure that their orders are complied with.

(b) Unlike the legislative and the administrative arms of the State, courts as such have no power to initiate action of their own motion. They have no self-starter. This is not to say that judges or other judicial officers may not also act as legislators or administrators,[52] but if litigation is to occur an original initiative must

---

[52] The Lord Chancellor combines in himself elements of all three branches of government and increasing use is made by the courts of their power to issue 'Practice Directions' which may, in reality, amount to legislation. This is perhaps most evident in the House of Lords Practice Statement of 1966 whereby the House assumed power to depart from its own decisions: *Practice Statement (Judicial Precedent)* [1966] 1 W.L.R. 1234. In addition, it may be noted, there are cases in which there is no defendant as, for example, where an unopposed application is made for an adoption order. In such cases, though there is a judicial element, the court acts more as an administrative than as a judicial authority.

come from outside. Quite exceptional cases apart,[53] no court can itself initiate litigation of any kind.

The initiation of civil proceedings is a voluntary act

Nemo agere cogatur is a familiar adage which may be said to apply as much to the initiation of a criminal prosecution as to civil litigation however defined, at least where the prosecutor is allowed a measure of discretion to be exercised in each case. There is, however, an unbridgeable gulf between the kind of freedom of choice allowed to a prosecutor and that allowed to a potential civil litigant. At its crudest, the latter can please himself while the former cannot.[54] No creditor is obliged to call in the debt owed to him; no victim of a legal wrong is denied the right, if he so chooses, to accept as compensation a sum of money less than that to which he is legally entitled or to abandon or forego his claim before the court. Such, indeed, is the nature of the settlement of a potential civil action and settlements are normally well thought of by authority and actively encouraged.[55] On the other hand, a criminal prosecutor who accepted money in exchange for abandoning the prosecution would be in grave dereliction of his duty, to say the least.

The plaintiff acts in his own interest

This proposition follows largely from what has just been said. If I am not obliged to initiate litigation against another then it is, at least, unlikely that I shall do so unless I expect to gain an advantage from my action. Ordinarily that advantage will be personal to me or to those for whose well-being I am directly responsible, but occasionally I may wish to pursue what I see to be a wider, even a public, interest. The extent to which a person should be able to invoke the processes of the law for unselfish reasons is controversial and, in modern conditions, raises

[53] In England a judge may commit a person for contempt in the face of the court without awaiting an application for committal: R.S.C., Ord. 52, r. 5; *Morris v. Crown Office* [1970] 2 Q.B. 114. Article 2907 of the Italian civil code provides that 'legal protection of rights is provided by the judicial authorities on the demand of the parties, and, where the law so provides, on the application of the Public Ministry or *ex officio*' (emphasis added), but there appears to be only one class of case where proceedings (for insolvency) can be instituted *ex officio* by the court: R.D. (Royal Decree), 16 March 1942, art. 6.

[54] This is true even in England where a wide prosecutorial discretion is allowed: *R. v. Commissioner of the Police of the Metropolis, ex parte Blackburn* [1968] 2 Q.B. 118.

[55] R.S.C., Ord. 22 (payment into court), now replaced by the more extensive C.P.R., r. 36, provides a strong incentive to settle. Judicial activism in conciliation is encouraged elsewhere: e.g. Code judiciaire belge, arts. 731–4; n.c.p.c., arts. 21, 127–31 and law of 8 February 1995, arts. 21–6; Italy, c.p.c., art. 185.

important questions.[56] For the time being it will be assumed that litigation is not only voluntary but selfish.

Civil litigation does not occur without the will of the defendant

There are some cases in which the plaintiff cannot obtain what he wants without an order or decree from the court. Such is the case, for example, where he wants a divorce in order to be able to remarry: this is an obvious example of a case in which it can be said that the defendant does not have the power to dispose of the right to which the proceedings relate. Ordinarily, however, a person is free, if he so wishes, to accede to the claim made against him without demur: if I demand that you pay me £1,000 you are at liberty to do so, however unreasonable and unjustified my demand. If you comply with my demand, no litigation will occur. In a criminal case, on the other hand, even if the accused pleads guilty, his plea can be accepted only in properly constituted proceedings and only a court can pass sentence.

For the purposes of most of this book, therefore, ordinary civil litigation may be generally described as a process before a court of law, voluntarily initiated by a plaintiff acting in what he sees as his own interest and opposed by a defendant who refuses, in what he, in his turn, sees as his interest, to meet the plaintiff's claim against him.

[56] It is this subject, considered below, chaps. 5, 6 and 7, which cannot be accommodated easily within 'civil proceedings' as here described, above, p. 12.

2   Some twentieth-century developments in Anglo-American civil procedure[1]

Introduction

Professor René David has drawn to the attention of every comparative lawyer that the common law 'est un système marqué profondément par son histoire' and that 'cette histoire est de façon exclusive, jusqu'au XVIIIe siècle, l'histoire du droit anglais'.[2] This observation is as true for procedural as it is for substantive law; indeed, as Professor David has also pointed out, for most of its history English law was dominated by procedural considerations: remedies precede rights. 'Toute l'attention des juristes anglais s'est concentrée pendant longtemps sur les pro-cédures variées, très formalistes, qui étaient engagées par les differents writs . . . La common law ne se présente pas comme un système visant à protéger des droits; elle consiste essentiellement en des règles de procédures jugées propres à assurer, dans des cas de plus en plus nombreux, la solution des litiges conformément à la justice.'[3] Sir Henry Maine's famous statement, 'So great is the ascendancy of the Law of Actions in the infancy of Courts of Justice, that substantive law has at first the look of being gradually secreted in the interstices of procedure',[4] is true for the law of England for much of its history.

In the course of the nineteenth century most of the worst technicalities of procedure to which a long history of formalism had given rise were swept away and, so far as the superior courts of England are concerned, the Judicature Acts of 1873–5 created the system which, in its essentials, endures to the present day. An account of the develop-

[1] Based on part of a report to an international colloquium under the title 'LXXV Años de evolución jurídica en el mundo', held in Mexico in 1976. Published in Spanish in *LXXV Años de evolución jurídica en el mundo*, Vol. III, p. 99, translation by Lic. Lucio Cabrera Acevedo (1978). Also published in English ((1979) *Studi in onore di Enrico Tullio Liebman* 1, 217 and (1978) 7 *Anglo-American Law Review* 163). The English law is stated as it was prior to introduction of the C.P.R. Relevant changes under the new rules are described in the postscript to this chapter.
[2] David, *Grands Systèmes*, p. 251.   [3] *Ibid.*, p. 261.
[4] *Early Law and Custom* (1861), p. 389.

ments in civil procedure in England since 1900 might, therefore, take the organisation of courts and the principles of procedure laid down by those Acts as given and proceed from there. It was, however, the unreformed English law which was received in those parts of the world that are described as 'common law countries', and, even though there are today few if any such countries which have not adopted reforms more or less equivalent to those introduced in England during the nineteenth century, there are several important jurisdictions which did not do so until well after 1900; it was not until the late 1930s that all traces of the old system were eliminated from the procedure of the federal courts of the United States of America.[5] On the other hand, the earliest example of a modernised system in the common law world is probably provided by the state of New York where a code of civil procedure instituting a unified court of general jurisdiction was adopted in 1848.

This is sufficient to require a brief description of some of the features of the unreformed English system and to rule out the adoption, as a starting point, of the state of procedural law as it was at the beginning of the century. Even a limited comparative account must proceed from a point that is defined rather by reference to a set of ideas more or less shared by all than to a particular date. There is, however, an additional reason for going back to the state of English procedural law as it was in or about 1800, that is before any substantial changes to its basic structure had been introduced anywhere in the world. It calls for exceptional genius and wide comparative experience for a man to stand aside from his own environment and training and to distinguish between those elements in his own legal system which are 'natural' to it and those which, though familiar through centuries of existence are, in the ultimate analysis, 'artificial'.

The contrast drawn here between the natural and the artificial may not appeal to positivists, but received ideas persist in men's minds long after their underlying fallacies have been exposed; challenges to the accepted order of things, even though only challenges to method or to form, often appear as challenges to the natural order of things itself. The common law of England as administered in the king's courts developed piecemeal through the system of writs and forms of action and against the background of the idea that residual jurisdiction was retained by the jurisdictional institutions of the local communities. In course of time the royal courts achieved, to all intents and purposes, both universal and exclusive jurisdiction, but well before the eighteenth century the writ

[5] See, e.g. James and Hazard, pp. 18–22.

system had given birth to a highly formalistic approach. 'The common law writs came to be seen as somehow basic, almost like the Ten Commandments or the Twelve Tables, the data from which the law itself was derived.'[6]

One feature of English civil procedure that was received overseas was, therefore, its formalism – for different classes of action, different procedures were not merely appropriate but mandatory. The use of an inappropriate form of action could and frequently did lead to the dismissal of the action without any consideration of the merits of the plaintiff's claim.

Even more significant and even more difficult to eradicate than the idea that different classes of action belong to different legal categories calling for different procedures was, and remains, the distinction between law and equity. Though theoretically and, at least for a time, actually, having different areas of competence, the three superior courts of common law – the Court of King's Bench, the Court of Exchequer and the Court of Common Pleas – all administered the common law. The Court of Chancery, however, which grew out of the administrative practice of referring to the Chancellor, as a high officer of State, individual petitions addressed personally to the King or his Council, came in course of time to co-exist as a court alongside the courts of common law, but it was a court of equity, not a court of law. Early equity was flexible and founded upon conscience, but the increase in the judicial work of the Court of Chancery led to regularisation of the rules of equity with the result that English law as a whole came to consist of two distinct elements – law and equity – which were separately administered in separate courts. In a well-known passage in a judgment delivered in 1818, Lord Eldon[7] reflected the desire for uniformity of decision as much in equity as in law:

The doctrines of this Court ought to be as well settled and made as uniform almost as those of the common law, laying down fixed principles, but taking care that they are to be applied according to the circumstances of each case. I cannot agree that the doctrines of this Court are to be changed with every succeeding judge. Nothing would inflict on me greater pain, in quitting this place, than the recollection that I had done anything to justify the reproach that the equity of this Court varies like the Chancellor's foot.[8]

Whatever the earlier conflicts between the courts of common law, on the one hand, and the Court of Chancery, on the other, during the

---

[6] S. F. C. Milsom, *Historical Foundations of the Common Law* (1969), p. 25.

[7] Lord Chancellor 1801–5 and 1807–27.

[8] *Gee v. Pritchard* (1818) 2 Swans. 403, 414. The allusion is to the *Table Talk* of John Selden (first printed in 1689, thirty-five years after Selden's death). See the edition produced by the Selden Society (ed. F. Pollock) in 1927, p. 43.

period of their joint and several existences, by the end of the eighteenth century, at the latest, it had become clear that there were certain matters that fell within the purview of equity and equally clear that there were other matters with which equity had nothing to do. There were, for example, rights of various kinds such as those arising under a trust which were (and are) recognised only in equity. This gave rise to the idea that is still essential to an understanding of the substantive law of common law countries, namely, that law and equity are distinct bodies of law and that it may be only through the application of the relevant rules of both that the complete solution to a case can be reached.

The separate existence of law and equity as components of the substantive law does not necessarily lead to any special difficulty from the procedural point of view. A major problem of the past was, however, that their separate administration in separate courts quite frequently led to a situation in which a single case could only be disposed of completely if proceedings were brought before a court of common law and also, independently, before a court of equity: in some circumstances it might even be that the plaintiff before one court would be the defendant before the other. One simple illustration will suffice for present purposes: the victim of a wrong recognised as such at common law could, of course, take proceedings before a court of common law and obtain from that court the remedy to which he was entitled at common law – normally an award of damages in compensation for the damage suffered. Where, however, the wrong was a continuing one or where its repetition by the defendant was threatened, an award of damages in respect of the past might not be sufficient. The plaintiff might need, additionally, an order from the court that the defendant refrain from further infringements of his right, but no such order could issue out of a court of common law. Equity, on the other hand, acts *in personam*, and developed certain forms of specific redress, one of which, the prohibitory injunction, adequately meets the needs of the case supposed. But a plaintiff seeking both damages and an injunction had to bring separate actions in law and in equity.

To an English lawyer more than a century after the combined administration of law and equity in a single court was finally achieved, the solution adopted by the Judicature Acts seems, in general terms, an obvious one; the surprising thing is only that it was so long delayed. It has to be appreciated, however, that no generation of lawyers for whom the separation of law and equity was the established system of centuries, could be expected to take this view. On the contrary, if the common law system of writs had come to seem as basic as the Ten Commandments, the division between law and equity must have seemed as natural as the division between land and sea. They were different things calling for different tribunals and different procedural techniques that could not sensibly be combined. It was only as a result of the valiant efforts of farsighted reformers that change ultimately came about.

By the year 1900, the abolition of the old forms of action had been achieved in a majority of common law jurisdictions, and a unified system of courts administering both law and equity had been created. It is unnecessary, therefore, to describe the steps by which these basic reforms were brought about. For the purposes of what follows, it is generally assumed that there is a court of universal jurisdiction for civil cases and that the task of that court is to resolve in their entirety the issues brought into controversy by the parties. It must, however, be borne in mind that in 1900, and for a good many years thereafter, there was still a substantial number of jurisdictions in which no such court actually existed. It must also be borne in mind that even if the writ system of the ancient common law is now of antiquarian interest only, from the procedural as well as from the substantive point of view the division between law and equity is not. Many courts administering both law and equity conjointly retain, under one name or another, equity divisions and common law divisions; lawyers in many countries special-ise in one field or the other, and there remains in the subconscious minds of most of them the conviction that there are still two systems of rules. This cannot fail to be reflected in both the manner and the style of developments in the civil procedure of the countries of the common law.[9]

The reforms which were introduced to rid the law of civil procedure of its rigid formalistic structure and to bring about the conjoint admin-istration of law and equity, however long they may have been delayed in particular jurisdictions, were essentially the product of nineteenth-century thinking. They had as their overall objective the improvement of the judicial machinery made available by the State to the parties to a dispute: the administration of civil justice meant essentially the resolu-tion of those controversies which arise between individual members of society and which the parties choose to bring before the court; it could mean little else. What is more, although certain elements of the procedure of the old courts of equity were incorporated into the procedure of the new, unified, court of law and equity, and although special equity procedures may still be available today, the basic pattern of modern civil procedure reflects more of its common law than of its equity inheritance.

[9] Even today there is generally, in the United States, a constitutional right to jury trial in actions at law, but not in equity.

It is this, as much as anything else, which explains the sharp cleavage between the trial of the action – the single, public, oral hearing at which the evidence and argument of the parties is presented to the court for the first and only time – on the one hand, and everything which precedes the trial – the interlocutory or pretrial stages of the action – on the other. It also explains continued adherence to the adversary system, according to which it is for the parties to determine not only the issues which the court is to decide, but also the material on which the decision will be based. The evidence presented to the court will be that which the parties choose to present and none other. The judge may not require that a particular witness be summoned to give evidence or that a particular document be produced; he may not even question the witnesses himself except for the purpose of clarifying some doubt as to the meaning of what a witness has said under examination by counsel. If he intervenes too much in counsel's examination of a witness he will incur the censure of an appellate court and, in an extreme case, a new trial may actually be ordered.[10]

Civil litigation is, therefore, still seen as essentially the exclusive concern of the parties who are entitled to make use of whatever lawful means may be at their disposal in order to 'win' the action. Much of the development in procedural law thus has its origin in the desire to improve the rules of the game. It is not fair that a wealthy or powerful litigant should be able to engage experienced counsel to present his case in opposition to a poor litigant who cannot, and so one finds the introduction of schemes for providing some form of legal aid. It is not fair that one litigant should take his opponent by surprise at the trial, and so one finds developments in the rules governing discovery and the like.

Interlocutory procedures in England and the United States

Given the cleavage between the interlocutory stage of an action and the trial, the primary function of the interlocutory stage must be to prepare the case for trial, and most of the developments to be mentioned have been directed to the achievement of improvements in trial fairness and efficiency. It is, however, increasingly appreciated that a second function should be the early disposal of cases without trial where this is possible. As will appear, English and American attitudes to the three most important features of the interlocutory stage have diverged from one

[10] *Jones* v. *National Coal Board* [1957] 2 Q.B. 55. For developments in England tending to derogate from the adversary system as thus understood, see below, chaps. 18 and 19.

another, and, although these divergences can probably be explained (at least superficially) without reference to important differences in the structure of the English and the American jurisdictions, it is at least likely that those structural differences have played a part. It is necessary to begin, therefore, with a brief account of the more important of them.

The civil jury

By the late seventeenth century the common law – not equity – had reached the stage of development at which all issues of fact arising in civil actions as well as in criminal proceedings had to be decided by a jury, under instruction from a judge, in the light of the evidence presented at the trial. In other words, virtually the only mode of trial known to the common law was trial by judge and jury.

This remained the position in England until 1854, when provision was made for trial by judge alone if the parties so agreed in writing and the court gave its consent;[11] but the most significant change was in 1883, when it became the rule, subject to certain exceptions, that, unless an application for a jury was made by one of the parties, trial should be by judge alone:[12] this had the effect of making trial by judge alone appear to be the norm. Since then the use of the civil jury in England has steadily declined; in 1933[13] it became the general principle that, again subject to certain exceptions, the decision as to the mode of trial should be made by the court in the exercise of an unfettered discretion,[14] and in 1966 the Court of Appeal ruled that the court should exercise its discretion in favour of jury trial in exceptional cases only.[15] Today, and for a considerable period in the past, the number of civil cases tried by jury is an extremely small proportion of the whole: the normal assumption, on which ideas for procedural change are usually founded, is that a civil trial will take place before a judge alone, whose task it is to decide all questions, both of fact and law.

In the United States, despite the fact that waiver of jury trial has been possible, at least in some jurisdictions,[16] for longer than in England, the decline in the number of trials by jury has been less marked: the Constitution of the United States,[17] and the constitutions of the over-whelming majority of the states, preserve the right to trial by jury as it existed in England in 1791, in the federal jurisdiction, and at the date of

---

[11] Common Law Procedure Act 1854.   [12] R.S.C. 1883, Ord. 36, r. 2.
[13] Administration of Justice Act 1933, s. 6.
[14] *Hope* v. *G.W.R.* [1937] 2 K.B. 130.
[15] *Ward* v. *James* [1966] 1 Q.B. 273. See further, chap. 18, p. 378.
[16] Waiver of jury trial was possible under the original 'Field' Code as adopted in New York in 1848.
[17] Seventh Amendment of the U.S. Constitution. See James and Hazard, chap. 8.

the adoption of the state constitutions in the several states. There is no right to trial by jury in an equity case, and difficult questions may arise where a case has both equitable and legal implications, but nevertheless, speaking generally and despite the number of cases actually tried by judge alone, in the United States jury trial still presents itself as the normal mode of trial in civil cases.

Masters

The English 'Master of the Supreme Court', or 'district judge' as he is known in the Family Division of the High Court, is a judicial officer of the court whose principal business is the conduct of the interlocutory stages of an action. There is no equivalent in the United States: the Master referred to, for example, in the Federal Rules of Civil Procedure has a different function.

Before the nineteenth-century reforms in England, each of the three common law courts consisted of four judges and they conducted their business as full courts ('in banc') except when a single judge presided over a trial before a jury, in which case the jury's verdict was recorded and judgment entered subsequently by the full court. It follows that applications concerned with interlocutory questions should at that time have been made to the full court (when at least three of its judges were assembled), but during the eighteenth century the practice developed of making such applications to a single judge at his private house or private rooms ('Chambers').[18] This was unofficial – a party dissatisfied with the judge's order could always go to the full court, and if any form of execution for the enforcement of the order was required then an order of the full court was essential. In course of time, however, the convenience and cheapness of dealing with interlocutory applications in Chambers led to a great increase in its use, to its regularisation in a form of procedure known as 'summons and order', and, eventually, to its statutory recognition: certain matters were expressly given for decision to a 'judge in chambers'. By 1860 virtually all procedural questions could be decided by a single judge.

With this development Masters had, originally, no connection for, at least outside the Court of Chancery,[19] their office did not exist. The offices of the courts, other than those of the judges themselves, were administrative in character and, in many cases, had become valuable saleable sinecures: most office-holders drew their fees but appointed

[18] See A. S. Diamond, 'The Queen's Bench Master' (1960) 76 L.Q.R. 504, from which much of what follows is derived.

[19] For the Masters of the Court of Chancery, see R. E. Ball, 'The Chancery Master' (1961) 77 L.Q.R. 331.

deputies to do the actual work for a small salary. This was in part a survival of the ancient notion that an office-holder has a right of property in his office and in part simply the survival of an abuse hallowed by custom. In 1837 virtually all the ancient offices were swept away and it was provided that for each common law court there should be five principal salaried officers, appointed from amongst the legal profession, and known as Masters. At first the duties of the Masters were mainly of a non-judicial kind, but they might be called upon to report on certain matters referred to them by the court, and they might even be called upon to assess the damages in a case once liability had been established.

In the period leading up to the Judicature Acts of 1873–5, the Masters' duties became both more onerous and more responsible; since the Judicature Acts, their position in the judicial hierarchy has been firmly established. Under current legislation, they are appointed from persons who have had the right of audience in any part of the Supreme Court or in county courts or magistrates' courts for at least seven years,[20] and it is they who hear and determine, at first instance, all interlocutory applications except those involving the liberty of the subject. From the decisions of the Masters in the Queen's Bench Division appeal lies, as of right, to a judge in chambers and from the judge, with leave, to the Court of Appeal and even to the House of Lords. In the Chancery Division, on the other hand, the Masters do not constitute a separate level in the judicial hierarchy; they are deputies of the judges to whom applications may be adjourned rather than appealed.

Though not unimportant to the internal working of the English legal system, from the comparative point of view the existence of a difference between the Masters of one Division of the High Court and the Masters of another is insignificant. The important point is that the English legal system has, as the American systems do not, a corps of specialised and experienced judicial officers other than the judges themselves to deal with the interlocutory stages of the action. Appeals from the interlocutory decisions of Masters are few in number, interlocutory applications are dealt with relatively informally and normally with despatch, and the time of the judges can be devoted to the trial of actions. On the other hand, and again in contrast with the United States, until the introduction of case management it was unlikely that the judge who tried a case would have had any contact with it during the pre-trial stage.[21]

[20] Supreme Court Act 1981, Sched. 2, as substituted by the Courts and Legal Services Act 1990, Sched. 10.
[21] See chap. 19, p. 390.

The legal profession

The final point of difference in the legal structures of the English and American jurisdictions to be mentioned here concerns the legal profession itself. In the United States, as in most other countries, there is a single legal profession, but in England a divided profession, consisting of barristers and solicitors, has existed since long before 1900. This has had its effect on the way in which procedural law has developed.[22]

The division of function between the two branches of the profession, though not in all respects a rigid one, can be explained by two propositions: first, the solicitor is the general practitioner while the barrister is the specialist; secondly, in litigation the solicitor is his client's representative throughout the proceedings while the barrister is instructed by the solicitor (on behalf of the client) ad hoc to perform those services for which a specialist is required, typically the giving of specialist legal advice and the supply of advocacy in the higher courts where, formerly, members of the Bar alone had the right of audience.

Although the Bar has never had an exclusive right to give legal advice,[23] and although solicitors have for long had the right of audience in the lower courts, until now all attempts to achieve fusion of the two branches of the profession have failed. In 1979 it was actually recommended by a Royal Commission that no change should be made.[24] Today, the barristers' and the solicitors' branches of the profession still continue their separate existence, but in 1990, in Part II of the Courts and Legal Services Act, Parliament set in motion a process which tends to reduce the practical significance of the separation and which is designed to make it possible for members of other professions to perform functions in connection with litigation that were formerly reserved to barristers and solicitors.[25]

So far as litigation is concerned, the Act distinguishes between the

---

[22] So, to take just one example, in 1953 an important committee on civil procedure declined to recommend the adoption in England of the American style of pre-trial conference on the ground that 'the *economical* utility of the pre-trial conference procedure is closely related to the fact of the fusion, in the United States, of the two branches of the profession': Evershed, para. 217. See below, p. 47. It was also the fact until recently that the judges of the superior courts in England could be appointed only from members of the Bar, not from the legal profession as a whole.

[23] Indeed, many of the larger firms of solicitors now have departments specialising in particular branches of the law such as commercial law, taxation and so on.

[24] Final Report of the Royal Commission on Legal Services, Cmnd 7648 (1979), para. 17.46.

[25] It is the 'statutory objective' of Part II to develop legal services 'by making provision for new or better ways of providing such services and a wider choice of persons providing them, while maintaining the proper and efficient administration of justice': s. 17(1).

right of audience before a court[26] on the one hand, and the right to conduct litigation[27] on the other. Historically, the former belongs to the Bar, the latter to the solicitors, and it remains the case that those who qualify as barristers enjoy a right of audience in all courts while those who qualify as solicitors enjoy the right to conduct litigation and the right of audience in those courts in which, formerly, solicitors did have the right of audience: vested rights are preserved. The law itself is, however, both more complex and more flexible than that.

The basic scheme introduced by the Act is that full or restricted rights of audience and full or restricted rights to conduct litigation may be granted by an 'authorised body'. The original authorised bodies are the General Council of the Bar and the Law Society, each being authorised to confer such rights of audience or to conduct litigation as it could confer before the Act came into operation. Other authorised bodies may, however, be designated by Order in Council if they survive an elaborate system of checks designed to ensure that their regulations for the qualification of their members to act in litigation and their rules of conduct meet the requirements of the Act.[28]

It may be expected that in the future certain professional organisations will apply to become authorised bodies – accountants may wish to have the right to act in tax cases, for example, or architects in cases arising out of the construction industry – but so far this has not happened. On the other hand, the Law Society has successfully applied so to enlarge its own powers as to be able to grant to its members the right of audience in all courts and at all levels. Solicitors having such an extensive right of audience are still relatively few, though their number may grow, and it is not expected that the distinction between barristers and solicitors will disappear. It will be necessary, however, for the Bar, as a profession to whose members other professionals refer their clients, to rely on its members' specialist abilities, and especially on their skills as advocates, for its survival.

Substantial differences will, no doubt, remain between the English and the American legal professions, but the affinity between the English barrister and the American trial lawyer,[29] to whom other lawyers refer

---

[26] This includes not only the right to be heard but the right to call and examine witnesses: s. 119(1).

[27] This includes the right to begin proceedings before a court and to perform ancillary functions in connection with such proceedings: s. 119(1).

[28] Section 29 and Sched. 4. For proposals for change to this scheme, enlarging the rights of audience of solicitors and increasing the powers of the Lord Chancellor, see the Consultation Paper on Rights of Audience and Rights to Conduct Litigation of June 1998, the Government's White Paper on Modernising Justice of 2 December 1998 and the Access to Justice Bill 1998, especially clauses 29–36.

[29] A 'trial lawyer' is not a member of a distinct profession, but there are associations for

their clients' cases when the services of a specialist advocate are required, may become rather closer. England does not have a fused profession, but the structure of the legal profession is unlikely to have the same effect on procedural law in the future as it did in the past.

Interlocutory proceedings

If the trial of an action under the Anglo-American system is to be conducted with even a modicum of efficiency, let alone fairness, the parties cannot be allowed to go into court without some prior identification of the subject matter of their dispute and with each in total ignorance of the case to be presented by the other. Where the trial is by jury it is even more necessary than where it is by judge alone that the questions to be answered should so far as possible be clarified before the trial begins. There must, therefore, be a process whereby the subject matter of the action is specified and the range of the evidence to be presented by each party at the trial is kept within the limits of relevance which the parties know in advance – both in the interests of trial efficiency and for the purpose of avoiding surprise and unpreparedness. And, if substantial injustice is to be avoided, each party must disclose to the other such facts as are in his exclusive knowledge and on which the case of that other depends. The extent to which the interlocutory stage must provide for more than this depends largely upon the extent to which it is thought appropriate that each party should be informed in advance of the details of the other's case and of the evidence he proposes to adduce.

Pleadings[30]

The common law system as it was before the reforms of the nineteenth century relied heavily on the pleadings – written documents exchanged between the parties – for the fulfilment of these objectives; it paid little or no regard to the need for disclosure of evidence. The underlying idea of common law pleading was that it should culminate in the emergence of a single issue between the parties, either of fact or of law: if the issue was one of fact, the case would go to a jury; if it was one of law, the decision was for the court. By the nineteenth century, however, common law pleading had developed into a monstrous 'science' of an extremely technical character and resulted in the decision of a large proportion of cases on technical pleading points, not on their merits.

lawyers whose practices have so developed that they have in fact become specialist advocates.

[30] See below, p. 55.

One of the major sources of this technicality, though not the only one, was the persistence into the nineteenth century of the common law forms of action, each of which had its own specialised rules of pleading. This was never an attribute of equity, and the ideal of equity pleading, which was not intended to produce an issue for trial, was that all the facts should be brought before the court so that the entirety of the matters in controversy could be finally disposed of. By the nineteenth century, equity pleading had also become complex, time-consuming and expensive, but nevertheless it was to its underlying idea that the nineteenth-century reformers turned when they sought to substitute for the *issue* pleading of the common law the *fact* pleading of the new system of judicature under which the administration of law and equity was combined in a single court.[31]

Fact pleading was first introduced into the common law world by the 'Field' Code adopted by the state of New York in 1848. Within twenty-five years it had spread to a total of twenty-four American states[32] and it came fully into operation in England under the rules brought in by the Judicature Act 1875. The basic concept is an apparently simple one: in his pleading the plaintiff must state, in a series of allegations, the facts on which he relies for his claim – not the evidence whereby he intends to prove those facts nor the legal conclusions to be drawn from them – and the defendant must answer this statement of claim (or complaint) by denying those of the plaintiff's allegations which he wishes to put in controversy and by alleging any additional facts on which he wishes to rely by way of defence; provision is made for further pleading whereby the plaintiff may reply to the defence pleading – clearly necessary where the defendant raises a counterclaim – but in a straightforward case that is all that should be necessary or allowed.[33]

Under ideal conditions, and if carried out as it should be, the simple exchange of pleadings will achieve a number of important purposes. A comparison between the pleadings will reveal what are the factual differences between the parties; the rule that evidence may be admitted at the trial only if it is directed to the proof or disproof of a fact alleged in the pleadings suitably limits the permissible range of the evidence; each party will know from reading the other's pleading what is the case that he will have to meet and so will be in a position to prepare for the trial. What is more, if a pleading is defective in the sense that, even on the assumption that the facts alleged are true, it does not, as a matter of law,

---

[31] C. Clark, 'The Code Cause of Action' (1924) 33 Yale L.J. 817.

[32] C. Clark, *Handbook of the Law of Code Pleading*, 2nd edn (1947), pp. 16 and 24.

[33] In England, pleading beyond the reply is permissible only with the prior leave of the court: R.S.C., Ord. 18, r. 4. Such leave is rarely sought or given.

entitle the party to succeed in his claim or defence (as the case may be), then the opportunity exists of disposing of the case without incurring the expense of a trial on the facts.

In practice, of course, matters are rarely so simple, and a number of disadvantages may be thought to arise if too much attention is given to the pleadings, many or most of which derive from the fact that the pleadings are documents drawn up by the lawyers engaged by the parties and are not the raw material of the case upon which the judicial determination of disputes should be based.[34] It is not possible to mention all these potential disadvantages, but the following are amongst the more important.

(1) The pleadings are bound to be drawn at an early stage of the action. If, as originally drawn, they control the evidence presented at the trial then it is likely that, in many cases, important evidence will be excluded because it will not be until after the pleadings have been completed that the existence or relevance of this evidence will be appreciated. On the other hand, if amendments to the pleadings are freely allowed, then much of their value will be destroyed.

(2) The requirement that a pleading state legally complete grounds of claim or defence – essential if the possibility of judgment on the pleadings is to be retained – may lead to expensive and time-consuming hearings before the court which achieve nothing of substance, only analysis of the content of the pleadings.

(3) A pleading may succeed in stating enough by way of facts to constitute a legally complete claim or defence and yet fail to give the other party adequate notice of the case he has to meet because the facts are stated too generally. This too may lead to court hearings at which the other party seeks 'further and better particulars' of the facts alleged. Since the distinction between facts, evidence and conclusions of law is one of degree not of kind,[35] there can be no readily applied criterion for determining when such particulars should be given, and this too may lead to hearings devoted to nothing more useful than discussion of the pleadings.

(4) Even well-drawn pleadings obviate surprise at the trial only to the extent that they inform the other party of the bare outline of the case he has to meet. They do not enable him to judge the strength

---

[34] Further disadvantages may derive from the parties' failure to use the pleading process – and particularly the defence – as it should be used. See, e.g. Winn, paras. 248–70.

[35] Clark, *Handbook*, pp. 231 *et seq.*; James and Hazard, pp. 67 *et seq.*

of that case and they create no opportunity for either party to prepare his evidence in the light of even a minimum of information from the other about the evidence he proposes to adduce. If, as the Supreme Court of the United States has said, 'mutual knowledge of all the relevant facts gathered by the parties is essential to proper litigation',[36] pleadings cannot be relied upon to supply such mutual knowledge. What is more, since there is little incentive for a defendant to admit facts necessary to the plaintiff's claim, and since there is a tradition of long standing that the defendant is entitled, if he so chooses, to put the plaintiff to the proof of the whole of his case,[37] it may be inevitable that the plaintiff incurs expense in preparing evidence to prove facts which, as he finally discovers at the trial, the defendant does not seriously contest.

(5) The drawing of pleadings calls for the expenditure of time and trouble on the part of the parties' lawyers, and this in itself is a cause of expense. The less the importance attached to the pleadings the less the costs should be, for the less time and skill is called for in their preparation.

The experience of code pleading, that is, fact pleading, in the United States has not on the whole been a happy one; it seems to have given rise to numerous applications to the court in connection with the pleadings with the parties – or, rather, their lawyers – seeking to gain procedural advantages or even outright victory on more or less technical grounds. In his famous address of 1906[38] Roscoe Pound castigated the 'sporting theory of justice', observing that it creates vested rights in errors of procedure. 'The inquiry is not, what do substantive law and justice require? Instead the inquiry is, have the rules of the game been carried out strictly?' Though not restricted to problems of pleading, there can be no doubt that one of the matters which Pound had in mind was what another and later writer described as the opportunity afforded by the rules of pleading for 'haggling and delay in deciding objections to mere form'.[39]

The result in the United States has been a widespread tendency to reduce the importance of the pleadings. Though some writers have

---

[36] *Hickman* v. *Taylor*, 329 U.S. 495, 507 (1947).
[37] Winn, para. 260.
[38] 'Causes of Popular Dissatisfaction with the Administration of Justice' (1906) 40 *American Law Review* 729.
[39] E. M. Morgan, *Some Problems of Proof under the Anglo-American System of Litigation* (1950), p. 26.

stressed the values of relatively strict rules of pleading,[40] others have gone so far as to propose a deliberate change to 'notice pleading', which would reduce the role of the pleadings to that of simply giving early indication to the other party of the general sequence of events or the transaction relied on.[41] Nowhere save in some municipal courts have matters been taken quite so far,[42] but in most American jurisdictions the law now looks to the other main procedural techniques – discovery and the pre-trial conference – to do most of the work of defining the issues and limiting the evidence. In other words, the movement has been in favour of allowing general pleadings, which are less susceptible to challenge, to replace special pleadings in which the parties are required to state their cases accurately and in some detail and then, subject only to the possibility of amendment, to adhere at the trial to their cases as formulated in the pleadings.

The Federal Rules of Civil Procedure, which were introduced in 1938 and which have had extensive influence on the procedures of the state courts as well as governing proceedings in the federal courts, actually avoid altogether use of the words 'fact' and 'cause of action', both of which are important to code pleading and both of which have given rise to considerable litigation. Instead, all that is required by the Federal Rules is a 'short and plain statement of the claim showing that the pleader is entitled to relief'.[43]

In the United States, then, the emphasis has shifted from the pleadings to discovery and the pre-trial conference, both of which are discussed below. In England, though to a lesser extent, discovery has also been developed as has the hearing of the so-called 'Summons for Directions', which is an analogue to, but much less significant than, the American pre-trial conference. Notwithstanding some difficulties and some early complaints about fact pleading,[44] however, England has seen no decline in the importance of pleadings but, rather, a continuing effort to overcome the problems by way of detailed attention to the rules

[40] E.g. N. Isaacs, 'Logic and Commonsense in Pleading: The Necessity of Fact Pleading' (1918) 16 Mich.L.R. 589; J. A. Fee, 'The Lost Horizon in Pleading and the Federal Rules of Civil Procedure' (1948) 48 Colum.L.R. 491.
[41] W. B. Whittier, 'Notice Pleading' (1918) 31 Harv.L.Rev. 501.
[42] See, however, the New Zealand Code of Civil Procedure, rule 112 and *Dawson v. Warren* (1884) N.Z.L.R. 2 C.A. 255. G. P. Barton, 'Reform of Procedure' [1966] N.Z.L.J. 219.
[43] Fed.R.Civ.P. 8(a)(2). See James and Hazard, para. 2.11, n. 1. The language quoted remains unchanged but the pleading requirements have been indirectly tightened by amendments in 1983 and 1993 to Fed.R.Civ.P. 11. See also R. H. Marcus, 'The Revival of Fact Pleading under the Federal Rules of Civil Procedure' (1986) 86 Colum. L.R. 433. For the cited and other recent amendments to the Federal Rules, see M. E. Aspen, 'Procedural Reform in United States Courts' (1995) 14 C.J.Q. 107.
[44] C. S. C. Bowen, 'The Law Courts and the Judicature Acts' (1886) 2 L.Q.R. 1, 8.

of pleading themselves, so as to give a degree of flexibility under the control of the court, and by way of exhortations to the Bar to adhere more conscientiously to the rules. The Winn Report, published in 1968,[45] for example, bemoans the failure of the Bar to adhere to the rules of pleading, but does not therefore recommend that pleadings be de-emphasised as in the United States. On the contrary, it urges that the pleadings 'could and should be made a far more useful aid to the prompt and efficient determination of disputes. It is, of course, essential that a party should have adequate time and proper discovery, but provided these conditions are fulfilled we feel that he should then be bound by his pleading.' Even a radical set of proposals produced in 1974 for the reform of English civil procedure[46] did not seek to reduce the importance of the pleadings; it actually proposed more stringent rules under which, for example, the parties would be required not only to allege facts but also to make 'offers of proof' – that is, indications of the nature and sources of the evidence they intend to use – such offers of proof, subject to possible additions as the case progresses towards trial, to be binding: no other method of proving a pleaded fact would be allowed at the trial unless very good cause were shown.

In an article published in 1971,[47] a distinguished American commentator wrote that 'the big difference is that the English still take their pleadings seriously, while we, despite our occasional protestations to the contrary, have become quite cavalier about them. Symptomatically, the Federal Rules have retreated from the position of the Field Codes and no longer require the pleader to set forth "facts".' There are, no doubt, various reasons for this divergence between the English and the American practice that is reflected also in their respective attitudes to discovery. One factor may be the existence in England of the Masters, for in England applications to the court on pleading as on other interlocutory matters can normally be dealt with more speedily and informally than in the United States, where an appearance before a judge is generally required.

More significant would seem to be the fact that in England, unlike the United States, the abolition of the common law forms of action has not led to a more or less inflexible rule that there shall be only one form of originating process and only one form of procedure.[48] In addition to the

---

[45] Winn, paras. 237 and 245.
[46] Justice Report, *Going to Law, a Critique of English Civil Procedure* (1974), paras. 165–81.
[47] B. Kaplan, 'An American Lawyer in the Queen's Courts' (1971) 69(2) Mich.L.R. 821, 823.
[48] As Kaplan puts it, 'the English have made less of a fetish of one form of action than we have' (*ibid.*).

procedure initiated by writ, in which the use of pleadings is the normal rule, there is also a distinct procedure initiated by originating summons, the scope of which has been steadily enlarged since it was first introduced into the procedure of the High Court in 1883 and which dispenses with pleadings altogether. In addition, pleadings may occasionally be dispensed with even in an action started by writ. In both cases it is essential either that there be no substantial issue of fact between the parties as, for example, where the dispute concerns exclusively the interpretation of legislation or of a private document such as a will or written contract, or that the issues are clearly defined in some other way so that the use of pleadings is unnecessary.[49] The survival of the popularity of pleadings in England may, therefore, be due at least in part to the fact that where they are unnecessary they do not have to be used.

Finally, and on a somewhat speculative basis, mention should be made here of an apparent difference in the attitude to the technicalities of pleading of the English and American legal professions. It seems that one reason for the unpopularity of fact pleading in the United States during most of the twentieth century has been the proliferation of litigation on formal points of pleading to which it has led. In 1918[50] Whittier pointed out that in England in 1830 one decision in six concerned a point of pleading; in 1846, following an unsuccessful attempt at reform,[51] the number rose to one decision in four, but in what were then recent years it had fallen to one in seventy-six and is probably now a good deal lower even than that: the equivalent figure for the United States in 1918 was one in twenty.

Whittier appears to attribute this comparative success of the English procedure to a difference in the rules of pleading; he seems to have thought that the English rules approximated more closely than the American rules then in force to the notice pleading he advocated. In this, however, it is respectfully suggested that he was mistaken: there was no very significant difference in the actual rules of pleading in England and in the code states of the United States. But in England the main responsibility for pleadings and for the conduct of litigation rested, and still rests to a large extent, with the relatively small number of lawyers who practise as barristers, while the judges and the Masters, a small and homogeneous group of people, were, and to a large extent still are, former members of the Bar. However strong the adversary idea may

[49] See R.S.C., Ord. 5, r. 4(2)(b); Ord. 18, r. 21.
[50] Whittier, 'Notice Pleading' at 507.
[51] The so-called 'Hilary Rules' of 1834. See W. S. Holdsworth, 'The New Rules of Pleading of the Hilary Term, 1834' (1923) 1 C.L.J. 261.

be, within such a context there are social and professional pressures whose tendency is to discourage excessive and unreasonable attempts to take advantage of an opponent's technical or formal mistakes.

Discovery[52]

Broadly used, the word 'discovery' denotes any form of interlocutory procedure whereby a party may compel his opponent or a third party to disclose information which is in his possession or control and which is relevant to the action. To the old common law, discovery was unknown; the pleadings fixed the limits of the evidence to be given at the trial and were supposed to give sufficient advance information to the parties.[53] Equity, on the other hand, did provide for a form of inter-party interrogation as an integral part of its procedure, and this became available – by way of separate proceedings – to the parties to a common law action where one party needed the evidence of his opponent in order to prove his own case.

In both England and the United States discovery became part of the procedure of the single court of combined jurisdiction in both law and equity, but in the United States both the role and the scope of discovery became much greater than in England. This is at least in part related to the decline in the importance of pleadings: as Morgan pointed out,[54] the general pleading allowed by the Federal Rules would be unworkable without adequate discovery. It is, however, also due to other causes, foremost amongst which the following may be mentioned: the idea that each party should go to trial knowing, so far as possible, the evidence which his opponent will present; the idea that full interlocutory disclosure of evidence will eliminate unreal issues and, by revealing, in a way that pleadings cannot, the actual strengths and weaknesses of each party's case, will encourage settlements; the idea that the risk of either party being taken by surprise at the trial should so far as possible be eliminated; and the idea that, to secure a just result at the trial, each party should be able to make use, both for attack and for defence, of any relevant information known to or perhaps only discoverable by the other. Almost the only material now protected from disclosure on discovery is the so-called 'work product' of the lawyers engaged in the case; even facts and opinions of experts employed by a party may be subject to discovery under certain conditions, and so may particulars of

---

[52] See below, p. 56.
[53] They more often failed than succeeded: 'The old system of pleading at common law was to conceal as much as possible what was going to be proved at the trial': *Spedding* v. *Fitzpatrick* (1888) 38 Ch.D. 410, 414, *per* Cotton L.J.
[54] *Problems of Proof*, at p. 29.

liability insurance held by a party, whether or not such particulars would themselves be admissible in evidence at the trial.[55]

The most significant expansions in the scope of discovery, which came with the adoption of the Federal Rules in 1938, are to be found in the disappearance of the rule against 'fishing' discovery – that is, discovery whose object is basically to find out whether the other party has information or material which will help to support, or even to make out, a case or defence for the party seeking discovery[56] – and in the development of depositions upon oral examination or written questions whereby the witnesses to be called by one party may, before the trial, be examined upon oath by the other.[57] It is this technique, in particular, which enables each party to obtain full discovery of the other's evidence.

Wide though discovery under the Federal Rules seems to English eyes to have been before, an important change introduced in 1993 increased its scope still further. Unless the contrary is specified by local rule or order, each party is now required to disclose to the others, without prior request, a wide variety of information. This includes, for example, the name (and address and telephone number if known) of persons likely to have discoverable information as well as copies, or descriptions by category and location, of all documents in the possession, custody or control of the party.[58] In each case the only qualification is that the information or the documents must be relevant to disputed facts alleged with particularity in the pleadings. In the absence of contrary rule or order, the parties must meet to discuss the case and formulate their proposals on a number of matters including the management of the discovery process; their report must be sent to the court at least fourteen days before the scheduling conference or order. The disclosures required by the 1993 amendment must be made no more than ten days after the parties' meeting.[59]

In England the scope of discovery is less and the law is closer to its origins than it is in the United States.[60] Under the Federal Rules for depositions just mentioned, 'any party may take the testimony of any person, including a party', and normally may do so without the prior

---

[55] Fed.R.Civ.P. 26, as amended 1 July 1970. See 'Federal Discovery Rules: Effects of 1970 Amendments' (1971–2) 8 *Columbia Journal of Law and Social Problems*, 623.

[56] *Hickman* v. *Taylor* 329 U.S. 495 (1947). See generally 'Developments in the Law of Discovery' (1960–1) 74 Harv.L.R. 940.

[57] Fed.R.Civ.P. 30 and 31.   [58] *Ibid.*, 26(a)(1)A and B.

[59] *Ibid.*, 26(f). For the scheduling conference or order, see below, p. 49.

[60] R.S.C., Ord. 24. The modern requirements for the exchange of expert reports and witness statements (below, chap. 18, pp. 379–81), though not part of discovery, do have the effect that one party obtains information from his opponent which would otherwise not be forthcoming until the trial. See also *Khannay* v. *Lovell White Durrant* [1995] 1 W.L.R. 121.

leave of the court. The origin of this lies in an old equitable procedure, the purpose of which was to make available at the trial the evidence of a witness who was prevented, by illness or absence abroad, from attending, and in England this is still the purpose of the modern equivalent. Although the court has power 'where it appears necessary for the purposes of justice' to order the examination of any person, in practice the power is exercised only where the person to be examined is unable to attend the trial, and the procedure is not regarded as forming a part of discovery at all; it is a means of securing testimony for use at the trial which would otherwise be unavailable.[61]

A similar restrictive approach by comparison with the United States is, or was, adopted with regard to interrogatories,[62] that is, written questions addressed by one party to the other which must be answered on oath. In the United States interrogatories to parties may be freely used, may be wide-ranging in content[63] and, both because they provide a useful source of information preparatory to the use of depositions and because they are normally cheaper than depositions, have proved popular; it is also the case that in answering an interrogatory a party may sometimes be called upon actually to make investigations himself while, obviously, when under oral examination he can answer only from his personal knowledge.[64]

In the leading case of *Hickman* v. *Taylor*,[65] an action arising out of the accidental death of a seaman, the defendant objected to an interrogatory enquiring whether statements had been taken of witnesses and concluding, 'attach hereto exact copies of all such statements if in writing, and if oral, set forth in detail the exact provisions of any such oral statements or reports'. The question raised before, and decided by, the United States Supreme Court was whether the particular statements were privileged from disclosure – it was eventually decided that they were covered by a novel kind of qualified privilege – but it is virtually certain that such an interrogatory would have been disallowed in England on the twin grounds that it was directed to the evidence, not the facts, and that it was fishing.[66]

At one time, interrogatories were freely allowed in England, but it was found that this caused wasteful and unnecessary expense,[67] and the rule was changed in 1893. Thereafter, until 1990, leave had to be obtained in respect of each interrogatory a party wished to administer to his

---

[61] R.S.C., Ord. 39.   [62] *Ibid.*, Ord. 26.   [63] Fed.R.Civ.P. 33.
[64] James and Hazard, p. 186.   [65] 329 U.S. 495 (1947).
[66] See, e.g. *Lever Bros.* v. *Associated Newspapers* [1907] 2 K.B. 626; *Sebright* v. *Hanbury* [1916] 2 Ch. 245.
[67] *Aste* v. *Stumore* (1883) 13 Q.B.D. 326, 328, *per* Brett M.R. See also Evershed, paras. 297–8 and Winn, para. 363.

opponent.[68] With effect from 1990, however, the rule was changed again. A party may still apply for leave to administer interrogatories, and his opponent must answer those interrogatories in respect of which leave is given, but interrogatories may also be administered without prior leave, subject to the right of the other party to apply for the interrogatories to be varied or withdrawn.[69] In neither case may an interrogatory be administered unless it relates to a matter in question in the litigation (which excludes interrogatories as to evidence) and unless it is necessary either for disposing fairly of the case or for saving costs.

In one respect alone – disclosure of documents – discovery in England may have been more extensive than in the United States. In England it has for long been possible for each party to require that the other produce a list of all relevant documents which are or have been in his possession, custody or control and now, since 1962, in most categories of case each party must produce such a list without order or even request.[70] This means that a party can obtain discovery of a document of whose existence he would have been unaware had it not been disclosed in his opponent's list of documents. Under the Federal Rules, on the other hand, discovery of documents could originally be obtained only under an order of the court for which 'good cause' had to be shown and only in respect of 'designated' documents. The requirement of good cause has not existed since 1948. The requirement that documents be designated remains. Since 1993, however, the new requirement of spontaneous disclosure[71] means that a party is in a position to 'designate' a document of which he knew nothing prior to disclosure by his opponent and of which he would have known nothing but for that disclosure. Discovery of documents under the Federal Rules is now as wide as it is in England.

Before leaving discovery there is one final point concerning American practice to which reference should be made. As mentioned briefly in the discussion of pleadings, where reliance is placed upon the pleadings for the definition of the issues and for the giving of adequate notice to each party of the case he has to meet, the need may arise for one party to seek 'further and better particulars' of the other's pleading. This is, in fact, a regular feature of English practice; in the first instance the party seeking the particulars simply applies to the other by letter, and only if the particulars are refused is an application to the court required. Notwithstanding the absence of any clear-cut distinction between facts, of which

---

[68] R.S.C., Ord. 26, prior to its amendment in 1989.
[69] R.S.C., Ord. 26, version introduced in 1989, which came into force in 1990. Leave is always required for interrogatories to be administered to the Crown.
[70] R.S.C., Ord. 24, r. 2.   [71] Above, p. 42.

adequate particulars must be given, and evidence, of which no particulars will be ordered, in the English practice little serious difficulty seems to have arisen: the Rules themselves give some guidance,[72] and otherwise the test is pragmatic.[73] In the United States the rules for code pleading allowed for 'bills of particulars' and the Federal Rules originally made 'grudging provision' for them.[74] Bills of particulars did, however, give rise to substantial litigation, and the idea behind them is obviously disliked by those who are hostile to the existence of strict rules of pleading: they were abolished in the federal jurisdiction in 1948.

Since 1948, however, a practice has developed of using interrogatories, a form of discovery, to narrow the issues by seeking answers concerning the allegations of fact or the denials made by the pleadings. This, as Professor Fleming James has observed,[75] is to reintroduce the bill of particulars in another guise and to attempt to tie down a party to his pleaded allegations of fact as is done by special pleading and in the manner repudiated by the Federal Rules. Despite this, however, the practice of using interrogatories for the purpose of making the pleadings more precise does have the support of some at least of the judges.[76] It may, perhaps, be suggested that this development shows that, if the issues are not sufficiently defined by the pleadings, then another way has to be found to give a degree of precision to the allegations of the parties. Without that, an adversary system cannot be operated successfully.

The summons for directions and the pre-trial hearing[77]

Both the English summons for directions and the American pre-trial conference provide opportunities for at least one and perhaps several interlocutory hearings before the court in the course of the preparation for trial. There is, of course, nothing novel in the common law world about an appearance in court before the trial takes place for, originally, the process of pleading itself was conducted by way of verbal altercation between counsel under the control of the judges.[78] The immediate origins of the two institutions are, however, different, and although their functions do to some extent coincide they are by no means identical either in their purposes or in their operation. Indeed, at least two

---

[72] R.S.C., Ord. 18, r. 12.
[73] See *Phillipps* v. *Phillipps* (1878) 4 Q.B.D. 127, 139, *per* Cotton L.J.
[74] Fleming James, 'The Revival of Bills of Particulars under the Federal Rules' (1958) 71 Harv.L.Rev. 1473.
[75] *Ibid.*; C. Clark, 'To an Understanding Use of Pre-trial' (1962) 29 F.R.D. 454.
[76] E.g. *Alaska* v. *Arctic Maid*, 135 F.Supp. 164 (D. Alaska 1955).
[77] See below, p. 57.
[78] See Morgan, *Problems of Proof*; A. S. Diamond, 'The Summons for Directions' (1959) 75 L.Q.R. 43 points to an even earlier analogy.

English committees have given consideration to and have declined to recommend the adoption of the American institution by English law.[79]

The first appearance of the summons for directions in a recognisable form came in the Rules of 1883, following the recommendations of a Legal Procedure Committee published two years earlier. The main purpose of the summons then, and the main purpose that has informed most of the later changes in its timing and structure, was that all necessary interlocutory applications should be brought before the court on a single occasion, with a view to eliminating the wasteful expenditure to which numerous separate applications give rise. In 1936, however, the Peel Commission[80] recommended that the object of the summons should be 'a general stocktaking of the case with the object of arriving at the essentials of the dispute and arranging for proof of the necessary facts in the shortest and cheapest manner . . . The Master should intervene actively and should use his influence on the parties to be reasonable and accommodating.'

Little by way of positive action followed the Peel Commission's report, but its ideas were taken up and developed by the Committee on Supreme Court Practice and Procedure, which reported in 1953. In conformity with its general purpose of instilling a new approach to the process of litigation, especially in relation to costs, the Committee recommended a strengthening of the summons for directions, a removal of the atmosphere of secrecy in which the parties prepared themselves for trial and a genuine stocktaking of the action under a 'robust' Master who should, if necessary of his own motion, give directions not only as to purely interlocutory matters such as the amendment of pleadings, but also as to admissions, evidence and modes of proof of particular facts. Parties were not, of course, to be compelled to make admissions, but a refusal to make an admission that the Master considered should be made would be recorded with a view to an appropriate sanction being imposed after the trial and in the order for costs.[81]

The Rules governing the summons for directions introduced following this report, and those in force until recently,[82] which differ only in detail, reflect the objectives of the Committee. Significantly, they begin with the words, 'With a view to providing . . . an occasion for the consideration by the court of the preparations for the trial of the action' so that, *inter alia*, 'such directions may be given as to the future course of the action as appear best adapted to secure the just, expeditious and

---

[79] Evershed, para. 218; Winn, para. 355.

[80] Report of the Royal Commission on the Despatch of Business at Common Law, Cmd 5065 (1934–6).

[81] Evershed, paras. 209–46.   [82] R.S.C., Ord. 25.

economical disposal thereof', the plaintiff must, at a stated time, take out the summons for directions and arrange for its hearing. Both parties have the opportunity to make such applications as they see fit, but it is the court's duty to take all matters into account, if necessary of its own motion, and to consider such questions as whether particular evidence might be given in documentary form rather than by the more costly oral testimony. The court is also to endeavour to secure that the parties make all admissions and agreements which ought reasonably to be made by them, and, to enable the court to perform its functions, the parties are placed under a duty to produce all such documents and provide all such information at the hearing as the court may reasonably require.

The attempt to secure that all interlocutory applications are disposed of at a single hearing was in large measure successful. The attempt to provide for a general stocktaking of the action and to obtain significant admissions and agreements from the parties concerning the conduct of the trial was not. Its success depended not only on the co-operation of the Bar, but on the full preparation of the parties and their lawyers for the hearing, and this, essentially, was the rock on which the project foundered. Even if an elaborate stocktaking followed by suitable directions were to succeed in reducing the cost of the trial itself, it could not fail to increase substantially those of the interlocutory stage. The statistics show that, taking into consideration only those actions which are not disposed of by settlement or default judgment before the hearing of the summons, only about 10 per cent actually go through to trial. In 90 per cent of such cases, therefore, the additional expense of full preparation for the hearing of the summons for directions would be unnecessary.

In complex cases and, especially, perhaps, in commercial cases where the summons comes before the commercial judge, a hearing such as was envisaged by the Committee in 1953 may serve a useful purpose. Ordinarily, however, there is little preparation for the hearing, the parties' representatives are rarely authorised to make worthwhile admissions, only routine directions are given and the whole business is concluded in a matter of minutes.[83] In 1980, following a recommendation made by the Winn Committee in 1968,[84] the summons was effectively abolished for actions for personal injuries by the introduction of 'automatic' directions.[85]

---

[83] See the description in the Justice Report, *Going to Law*, para. 55.
[84] Winn, para. 352.
[85] R.S.C., Ord. 25, rr. 1(j) and 8. Application can be made for further or different orders. Since 1983, standard directions can be applied by consent in actions in the Chancery Division: *ibid.*, r. 9. For other exceptions to the general rule that a Summons for Directions must be used in all actions begun by writ, see R.S.C., Ord. 25, r. 1(2).

Although a hearing of the summons for directions is still generally required in other actions begun by writ, in 1995 the renewed call for reduction in cost and delay led to the introduction, by judicial decree, of a pre-trial review for cases in which the trial was expected to last more than ten days.[86] The review should be held between eight and four weeks before the trial and should be conducted, if possible, by the designated trial judge and attended by the advocates who will appear at the trial. In addition, for all cases in the Queen's Bench and Chancery Divisions, what approximates to a pre-trial review *inter absentes* must take place no later than two months before the trial. Each party must lodge in court, with copy to the other parties, his responses to a standard checklist designed, primarily, to ensure that necessary pre-trial action has been or is being taken and to assist preparation for the trial itself: each party is required, for example, to name the witnesses and expert witnesses he proposes to call and to provide counsels' estimates of the minimum and maximum lengths of the trial.

The origin of the American pre-trial conference lies in a practice developed in the late 1920s in the Circuit Court of Wayne County, Michigan, sitting in Detroit. Faced with a serious backlog of cases and finding that 50 per cent of the cases set for trial were ultimately settled, the judges of that court concluded that a pre-trial examination of cases could promote earlier settlement, thereby reducing the number of cases set for trial, and could reduce the issues in those which came to trial. Events proved them right,[87] and some other jurisdictions were quick to follow suit. The major impetus to the spread of the pre-trial conference came, however, with its adoption in the Federal Rules in 1938.[88]

The rule that was introduced in 1938 survived unchanged until a major revision in 1983. Its emphasis was on the forthcoming trial, and it gave as the first objective of the conference 'the simplification of the issues'. While it was said that the judge should not coerce the parties into submission, it was also said that much depended on his skill in 'shaping the case to present its actual problems and in leading counsel to define the issues with him':[89] the conference had to be seen against

---

[86] *Practice Direction (Civil Litigation: Case Management)* [1995] 1 W.L.R. 262 (Q.B.D. and Ch.D.); *Practice Direction (Family Proceedings: Case Management)* [1995] 1 W.L.R. 332 (Fam.D.) In the Family Division the review should be held where the trial is expected to last more than five days.

[87] E. R. Sunderland, 'The Theory and Practice of Pre-trial Procedure' (1937) 36 Mich.L.R. 215.

[88] Fed.R.Civ.P. 16. See D. L. Shapiro, 'Federal Rule 16: A Look at the Theory and Practice of Rulemaking' (1989) 137 U. of Pennsylvania L.R. 1969.

[89] C. Clark, 'Objectives of Pre-trial Procedure' (1956) 17 Ohio St.L.J. 163, 165.

the objective of litigation itself, namely 'a judgment settling rights after the process of fair trial'.[90]

In its original form the rule made no reference to the achievement of settlements as an objective of the conference, and one of its architects said that the omission was deliberate: the conference should be 'informational and factual', and, while it might well lead to settlement as the parties came to know the case better, 'that must remain an uncoerced by-product'.[91] Nevertheless, against opposition and notwithstanding the view expressed by some that the objectives of improving trial preparation and of promoting settlements cannot be satisfactorily pursued at the same time,[92] the use of the conference for the promotion of settlements became commonplace. In the revised rule, 'facilitating the settlement of the case' is therefore included as one of the objectives of the conference.[93]

The overall effect of the 1983 revision was to shift the main focus of the rule from trial preparation to a system of case management covering all stages of the litigation. The holding of an actual pre-trial conference or conferences[94] remains, as it always has been, at the discretion of the court. On the other hand, unless there is a local rule or an order of the court to the contrary, a scheduling order fixing the time allowed for such matters as the amendment of pleadings, the joinder of parties and the completion of discovery, is now mandatory. The court will have received the parties' report of their meeting on discovery,[95] and the scheduling order must be entered after receipt of that report or after consultation with the parties.[96] The order should issue as soon as practicable and in any event within 90 days from the defendant's appearance and 120 days from service of the complaint upon him.[97]

Despite the change in emphasis in 1983, the objective of improving

[90] C. Clark, 'To an Understanding Use of Pre-trial'(1962) 29 F.R.D. 454.

[91] *Ibid.*, at 456.

[92] M. Rosenberg, *The Pre-trial Conference and Effective Justice* (1964), pp. 9 and 113–17.

[93] Rule 16(a)(5) in the amended version of 1983. See also rule 16(c)(9) in the reamended version of 1993 which includes, as a 'subject for consideration' both settlement and the use of special procedures to assist in resolving the dispute when authorised by statute or local rule.

[94] A 'final' pre-trial conference, if held, should take place as close to the time of trial as possible, should be attended by at least one of the lawyers who will conduct the trial for each party, and the parties should formulate a plan for the conduct of the trial: rule 16(d). At any other conference at least one of the lawyers participating must have authority to commit his client on matters which may reasonably be anticipated as likely to be discussed: rule 16(c) *in fine.*

[95] Above, p. 42.

[96] Consultation may be by conference, telephone, mail or 'other suitable means': rule 16(b), 1993 version.

[97] *Ibid.* The schedule may be modified only with leave and on a showing of good cause.

trial preparation is not superseded; on the contrary, the reduced importance of pleadings and the extensive discovery allowed mean that the conference is as necessary as ever to clarify what precisely are the issues to be tried. Each conference results in an order that recites the action taken and controls the subsequent conduct of the action unless modified by later order.[98] The order issued after the final conference, which may be modified only to prevent 'manifest injustice', is often the product of agreement by the parties to which they will normally be held at the trial. It determines the course of proceedings at the trial and supersedes the pleadings to the extent that it eliminates, simplifies, or even adds to the issues to be tried.

From time to time voices have been raised to argue that the pre-trial conference undermines the adversary tradition and reduces the power of the lawyer to conduct his client's case as he judges best. The argument may be justified, but given the increase in the complexity of much modern litigation and the growth in costs and delay, the advent of judicial case management is hard to resist.[99] It has, however, also been argued that the pre-trial conference leads to over-regulation in ordinary cases with consequent waste of time and money.[100] The Advisory Committee responsible for the amendments to the rule of 1983 stressed the value of early judicial intervention to schedule dates for the performance by the parties of the principal pre-trial steps they must take, and for this reason a pre-trial scheduling order is normally mandatory. On the other hand, though scheduling and pre-trial conferences are encouraged, they are not mandatory.

In the result much depends on judicial discretion and, importantly, on rules made locally within each district. The Federal Rules themselves allow for a degree of local variation,[101] and the Civil Justice Reform Act of 1990 requires that each district court should implement a 'civil justice expense and delay reduction plan' with the objects, amongst others, of monitoring discovery, of improving litigation management and of ensuring 'just, speedy, and inexpensive resolutions of civil

[98] Fed.R.Civ.P. 16(e).
[99] See, for England, above, p. 48 and below, p. 57. For a general account of case management in the U.S. Federal Courts, see W. W. Schwarzer, 'Case Management in the Federal Courts' (1996) 15 C.J.Q. 141.
[100] M. Pollack, 'Pre-trial Conferences' (1971) 50 F.R.D. 451; also his 'Pre-trial Procedures More Effectively Handled' (1974) 65 F.R.D. 475. See also the same author's 'Cutting Fat from Pre-trial Proceedings' (1983) 97 F.R.D. 319. Cf. W. H. Becker, 'A Modern, Efficient Use of the Bar and other Parajudicial Personnel in Pre-trial of Ordinary Actions' (1971) 53 F.R.D. 195; S. Burbury, 'Modern Pre-trial Civil Procedure in the U.S.A. A New Philosophy of Litigation' (1965) 2 Univ. of Tasmania L.R. 111.
[101] Fed.R.Civ.P. 83.

disputes'.[102] Though guidelines and even models for such plans exist,[103] detailed differences from one district to another are clearly contemplated.

Conclusion

If the preceding pages do nothing else, they at least demonstrate the extent to which, during this century, English and American law have diverged from one another in their treatment of the interlocutory stages of an action. Both systems have developed from the same historical origin – namely, the English law as it was before the great reforms of the nineteenth century; both systems retain as the objective of their inter-locutory procedures the same ultimate end – the determination of litigation by a judgment based upon material presented, and mainly presented orally, at a single session trial; both systems know the three institutions of pleadings, discovery and a form of pre-trial hearing. Yet, in relation to each of these institutions, and perhaps even to the under-lying conception of preparation for trial itself, to a lawyer trained in one of them the differences between them are more striking than the similarities.

Attention has been drawn in this chapter to some underlying struc-tural differences in the two systems, which may go some way to explain this divergence. The following two reflections are now offered by way of conclusion.

(1) However much one may deplore the sporting theory of justice, the use of the single session trial demands that the questions at issue between the parties be reasonably well defined before the trial. The English system continues to pursue this objective through the pleadings; the American prefers to minimise the importance of the pleadings and to leave the final formulation of the issues to the pre-trial conference.

On the face of things, it would seem that the American system is better adapted than the English to achieve a formulation of the issues which accurately identifies the substance of the controversy between the parties, but it does so at the cost of even more elaborate and expensive interlocutory procedures. The English system is expensive enough, the American even more so and not only in money terms: the more elaborate the interlocutory

---

[102] Pubic Law, 101–650, Title 1, para. 103(a); 28 U.S.C.A. Chapter 23, para. 471. See J. Plotnikoff, 'Case Control as Social Policy: Civil Case Management Legislation in the United States' (1991) 10 C.J.Q. 230.
[103] 28 U.S.C.A. Chapter 23, paras. 473, 477.

procedures, the greater are the opportunities for harassment, delay and haggling over matters of form. In the United States efforts were made to avoid such haggling over the pleadings by reducing their importance, but that led to complaints that 'motion maneuvers formerly directed to the pleadings have been transferred to discovery',[104] complaints which in turn have led to development of case-management techniques and devices for controlling the excesses of discovery.

The Civil Procedure Rules, which were introduced following Lord Woolf's Report and which are intended to counter the adversarial culture said to have developed,[105] bring to the English system more elaborate case-management procedures than those previously in place,[106] and such procedures may now be necessary. Nevertheless, at least on an impressionistic basis, it seems that the conduct of opposing lawyers in England has for long been less adversarial or competitive than that of their American counterparts.

One reason for this may be that the legal profession in England is smaller and more homogeneous than it can be in the United States with its numerous separate jurisdictions. There is, however, another factor which may tend to encourage American competitiveness, namely the widespread use in that country of the contingent fee, something which was wholly excluded from English practice until quite recently.

In its basic form the American contingency fee system remunerates the lawyer by payment to him of a proportion of the damages recovered by his client if the claim succeeds; he receives nothing if it fails. This system is widely used, especially in claims for damages for personal injury, and although it means that the lawyer is not separately remunerated for action taken during the interlocutory stages, it also means that he has an incentive to try to win by any legal means, including the manipulation of the available procedural devices. And if one lawyer adopts a competitive approach, so, almost inevitably, will his opponent.

In England, until the Courts and Legal Services Act 1990,[107] any form of contingency fee arrangement would have been, at best, unenforceable. Now, however, the door has been opened to 'conditional fee agreements' – that is, agreements providing for a

---

[104] W. H. Speck, 'The Use of Discovery in U.S. District Courts' (1951) 60 Yale L.J. 1132 – an article generally favourable to liberal rules for discovery.
[105] Chap. 19, p. 388.   [106] Above, p. 47.   [107] Section 58.

fee to be payable only in specified circumstances.[108] Normally, it may be supposed, the circumstances will be that the proceedings for which the lawyer was engaged are terminated in a way favourable to his client, but even so, though an augmented fee may be payable, it may not be more than double the fee that would have been payable had there been no conditional fee agreement.[109] There is no possibility that the agreement should provide for remuneration by way of a proportion of any damages recovered. At first, conditional fee agreements were permissible only in limited classes of case.[110] Now, however, with the exception of cases under a variety of Acts dealing with family or domestic law, they are permissible in all civil cases.[111] Only the future can tell whether they will come to have the same consequences for the conduct of litigation in England as the contingency fee seems to have had in the United States.[112]

(2) Both English and American law maintain an overt hostility to the risk of surprise at the trial. The different rules of discovery operating in the two countries suggest, however, that they have different ideas of what amounts to surprise and perhaps, therefore, even of what the trial itself is intended to achieve. Here, it is suggested, the survival of the civil jury in the United States and its virtual disappearance in England are significant. An English reader of even a small proportion of the American literature[113] may without excessive cynicism be led to suppose that the American procedures which are intended to improve trial preparation are aimed at putting on a performance before the jury which, if not actually rehearsed, has still been carefully planned by the parties and the judge acting in collaboration.

---

[108] Such agreements must be in writing and must comply with a number of other requirements: Conditional Fee Agreements Regulations 1995 (SI 1995 No. 1675).

[109] The Act allows the fee to be increased by a specified percentage (s. 58(2)) which is fixed by regulation at a maximum of 100 per cent: Conditional Fee Agreements Order 1998 (SI 1998 No. 1860), art. 4. The client is entitled to have his bill of costs taxed, and on a taxation both what are called the 'base costs' and the percentage increase are subject to control: R.S.C., Ord. 62, r. 15A; C.P.R., r. 48.9.

[110] Most importantly, actions for damages for personal injuries or death.

[111] Act of 1990, s. 58(1)(a), (3) and (10); Conditional Fee Agreements Order 1998, art. 3. Legal aid is being withdrawn from personal injury and some other forms of civil litigation, which may be expected to increase the use of conditional fee agreements. See Access to Justice Bill 1998 and M. Zander, 'The Government's Plans on Legal Aid and Conditional Fees' (1998) 61 M.L.R. 538, 546–50.

[112] See, e.g. V. Tunkel, 'Improving Access to Justice – 3' [1998] N.L.J. 245.

[113] The American literature on procedural topics is vast; the English, though now beginning to develop, is still small – a further point of difference between the two countries which may have a bearing on the development of the law.

In England, where trial is almost invariably by judge alone, it was, until comparatively recently, regarded as a positive value that the judge should have no knowledge of the evidence before it was presented at the trial. It also continued to be widely believed that the truth will be best revealed if the witnesses are examined and, most importantly, cross-examined with the minimum of preparation. Both of these ideas are inherent in the adversary system in its traditional sense, but neither can survive judicial case management and American-style discovery unscathed. Now English law too is moving to judicial case management and it already has procedures involving the pre-trial disclosure of evidence such as the exchange of witness statements.[114] The result, at least in cases of any complexity, is that it has ceased to be true that the judge enters the courtroom knowing little or nothing about the case he is about to try. This cannot fail to undermine certain aspects of the adversary system as hitherto understood.[115] Nevertheless, for so long as the scope of discovery remains narrower in England than in the United States, it will continue to be the fact that the opportunities afforded to each party to explore every avenue before trial, and so to protect himself against surprise, are greater in the United States than in this country.

Postscript

Occasional references have already been made to Lord Woolf's Report, and the predictable impact of the consequent reforms on the general character of civil litigation in England is the subject of a later chapter.[116] Included in the reforms, however, are provisions bearing directly on three of the topics considered in this chapter – pleadings, discovery and the pre-trial hearing – and these must be mentioned here. By way of introduction all that need be said is that a fundamental shift in responsibility for the management of civil litigation from the parties to the courts is envisaged, as is the allocation of every case to one of three 'tracks' according to its importance and complexity. The tracks are, respectively, the 'small claims' track, which uses an informal procedure at the discretion of the court, the 'fast track', which uses a simplified form of procedure and a fixed timetable for each case, and the 'multi-track', which allows the use of different methods of case management as each case individually may require.

---

[114] See above, n. 60.   [115] See chap. 18, p. 383.   [116] Chap. 19.

Pleadings[117]

Under the new rules, every claim is to be started by the issue of a 'claim form', for service on the defendant, which must contain a concise statement of the nature of the claim, must specify the remedy sought and, in the case of a claim for money, must also contain a statement of value.[118] If particulars of the claim are not contained in, or served with, the claim form they must be served on the defendant within fourteen days.[119] The claim form thus replaces the writ or other form of originating process and the particulars of claim replace the statement of claim. Save for the reduction of the number of forms of originating process to one, the basic structure thus remains much as it was.

So far as the pleading process itself is concerned, the intention is that it should be simplified, but there is no suggestion of a move to mere notice pleading.[120] On the contrary, the importance of fact pleading is enhanced, at least in the early stages of litigation, since the pleadings provide the basis for a variety of case-management decisions, including the allocation of a case to a given track and the initial directions to be issued to the parties.[121] The pleadings also retain their importance for matters such as summary judgment and possible orders for the summary trial of, or the exclusion from further consideration of, identified issues. The particulars of claim must, therefore, contain specified particulars of the claim, including 'a concise statement of the facts' on which the claimant relies.[122] The defendant, in his turn, must file his defence within a further fourteen days, unless an extension is agreed or allowed.[123]

One of the most significant changes in the rules of pleading is the introduction of a requirement that both claim and defence must contain a statement, signed by the party or his legal representative, that the party believes that the facts stated are true.[124] Another, relating to the defence, requires defendants to do more than simply deny the allegations in the claim: the defendant must say which of the allegations in the

---

[117] Above, p. 34. Woolf Interim, pp. 153–63; Woolf Final, pp. 116–20; C.P.R., rr. 16.2 and 16.4. For simplicity, the word 'pleading' is replaced by 'Statement of Case' and 'Statement of Claim' by 'Claim'; 'Defence' and 'Reply' survive.

[118] C.P.R., r. 16.3. The statement of value provides essential information for allocation of the case to its appropriate track.

[119] C.P.R., r. 7.4.   [120] Above, p. 38.

[121] For most classes of case, 'allocation questionnaires' are to be issued to the parties once a defence has been put in: C.P.R., r. 26.3. Before reaching a decision, the court may call on a party to clarify his pleading or his answers to the questionnaire or otherwise to provide further information; if necessary, an 'allocation hearing' may be held: C.P.R., r. 26.5.

[122] C.P.R., r. 16.4.   [123] *Ibid.*, rr. 9 and 15.   [124] *Ibid.*, r. 22.

particulars of claim he denies and which he wishes the claimant to prove because he is unable to deny or admit them. What is more, where the defendant denies an allegation he must give his reasons for doing so, and if he intends to put forward a different version of events from that stated in the claim he must specify in the defence what that version is.[125] These provisions should ensure that the pleadings do more than hitherto to reveal the questions really at issue between the parties. Nevertheless, if the defendant has set out his case in relation to an issue without dealing specifically with an allegation in the claim which is relevant to that issue, he is not taken to admit the allegation but to require it to be proved.[126]

The details of any claim to interest and the grounds for any claim to aggravated or exemplary damages must be specifically pleaded, and so too must such other matters 'as may be set out in a practice direction'.[127] This leaves open the possibility, originally raised by Lord Woolf, that parties might eventually be required to plead both law and evidence,[128] but it is to be hoped that so unfortunate a departure from the principles of fact pleading will not be introduced.[129]

Discovery[130]

Until comparatively recently, few would have been ready to criticise the generous English rules on discovery of documents, but it has become evident, especially in the more complex cases, that discovery may constitute a major cause of expense and delay.[131] The problem is compounded by the rule, itself of respectable antiquity, that even documents which provide no more than possible trains of enquiry capable of revealing information of value to an opponent must be disclosed.[132]

To preserve the principle of compulsory disclosure of adverse, as well as favourable, documents while reducing the scope of discovery, the duty of disclosure (by way of a list of documents, as before) is limited to

---

[125] *Ibid.*, r. 16.5.   [126] *Ibid.*, r. 16.5(3).   [127] *Ibid.*, r. 16.2(1)(d).
[128] Woolf Interim, pp. 159 and 161.
[129] See below, chap. 4, p. 83. The existing Practice Direction (para. 11.3) permits, but does not require, such matters to be pleaded.
[130] Above, p. 41. Woolf Interim, pp. 164–74; Woolf Final, pp. 124–8, C.P.R., r. 31, where the subject becomes 'Disclosure and Inspection of Documents'. 'Document' means 'anything in which information of any description is recorded' (C.P.R., r. 31.4) and 'disclosure' is effected by revealing that a document exists or has existed: C.P.R., r. 31.2. Interrogatories are not covered, but the court may order a party to give further information: C.P.R., r. 18.
[131] There is even a suggestion that discovery may be used as a weapon to bring pressure on the other side: Woolf Interim, p. 164.
[132] *Compagnie Financière du Pacifique* v. *Peruvian Guano Company* (1882) 11 Q.B.D. 55, 62–3, *per* Brett L.J.

'standard disclosure' unless the court otherwise orders.[133] This requires disclosure only of two categories of documents, namely, first, those on which the party relies and, secondly, documents which support another party's case or which adversely affect his own or that of a party acting with him. So-called 'relevant documents', that is, documents which are relevant as part of the background but do not obviously support or undermine a case being put forward, and 'train of enquiry' documents, are excluded.

Subject to this, though the rules for discovery are rewritten, the substance of the law is little changed: unless privilege is claimed, the person to whom a document is disclosed has a right to inspect it,[134] as he has to inspect any document referred to in a pleading or in a witness statement, affidavit or expert's report,[135] but he must give written notice of his wish to do so.[136] It is, usefully, now specified that the duty of disclosure includes a duty to make a reasonable search for documents belonging to the second category,[137] and that the duty is a continuing one: if documents covered by the duty come to a party's notice during the proceedings, he must immediately notify every other party.[138] So far as claims for privilege – now known as claims 'to withhold inspection or disclosure' of a document – are concerned, it is made clear that production of the document to the court itself may be required so as to enable it to decide whether the claim is justified.[139]

The summons for directions and the pre-trial hearing[140]

The new system of case management overtakes or absorbs both the summons for directions and the pre-trial review that was introduced for complex cases in 1995.[141] Case management is clearly intended to be a continuous process which begins with the allocation of a case to its appropriate track; at that time directions are to be given for the future conduct of the case unless, on the multi-track, the court decides instead to fix a case-management conference or a pre-trial review, or both.[142] It

---

[133] C.P.R., r. 31.5. An application can be made for an order for disclosure of specific documents or classes of document outside standard disclosure: *ibid.*, r. 31.12.

[134] *Ibid.*, r. 31.3.   [135] *Ibid.*, r. 31.14.

[136] *Ibid.*, r. 31.15. Documents no longer in the control of the party making disclosure are excluded.

[137] *Ibid.*, r. 31.7. A party's list of documents must include a 'disclosure statement' setting out, amongst other matters, the extent of the search made to locate documents which should be disclosed: *ibid.*, r. 31.10(5) and (6).

[138] *Ibid.*, r. 31.11.   [139] *Ibid.*, r. 31.19(6).

[140] Above, p. 45.   [141] Above, p. 48.

[142] C.P.R., r. 29.2. Even so, directions may be given as the court sees fit. For the fast track, see *ibid.*, r. 28.2 and for the small claims track, see *ibid.*, r. 27.4.

is the court's duty to manage cases actively in furtherance of the 'overriding objective', which is for the court 'to deal with cases justly'.[143]

For the purposes of case management the court is endowed with substantial and wide-ranging powers,[144] and provision is made for a variety of pre-trial hearings which may be held as necessary, starting with an allocation hearing[145] and culminating with a pre-trial review.[146] None of these is compulsory, however, and the court may reach its decisions on the directions to be given, whether standard or not, on the papers. If it needs more information it may ask for it, and the Rules indicate that a case may be dealt with 'without the parties needing to attend at court';[147] use of the telephone or other method of direct oral communication is explicitly authorised.[148]

The court may make case-management orders or directions on application or of its own initiative, and if the matter is urgent it may even make a provisional order without giving the parties an opportunity to make representations. Ordinarily, however, affected parties have an explicit right to be heard, and if a provisional order is made, they may apply for the order to be set aside, varied or stayed.[149]

Most of the court's powers of case management relate directly to the conduct of the case in court, and it is given formal power to encourage the parties to co-operate with one another.[150] That kind of thing apart, most of the orders or directions which are envisaged are such as could have been made on a summons for directions or pre-trial review under the previous law, but, in addition, the court may encourage and facilitate the use of an alternative dispute resolution procedure if it considers that appropriate; it may also help the parties to settle the whole or part of the case.[151] So far as is known, no debate has taken place in this country, as it has in the United States,[152] on the compatibility of the objectives of promoting settlement, on the one hand, and of improving trial preparation, on the other. Nevertheless, at least on this point, English law now takes the same view as do the Federal Rules.

---

[143] *Ibid.*, r. 1.1(1). Some substance is given in *ibid.*, r. 1.1 (2).
[144] *Ibid.*, rr. 1.4, 5.   [145] *Ibid.*, r. 26.5(4).
[146] *Ibid.*, r. 29.3. On the multi-track the court may call a case-management conference at any time: *ibid.* On the fast track, where a pre-trial review as such is not envisaged, the court may fix a listing hearing if this is necessary for it to give adequate directions for preparation of the case for trial: *ibid.*, r. 28.5.
[147] *Ibid.*, r. 1.4(2)(j).   [148] *Ibid.*, r. 3.1(2)(d).   [149] *Ibid.*, r. 3.3(4)(5).
[150] *Ibid.*, r. 1.4(2)(a).   [151] *Ibid.*, r. 1.4(2)(e) and (f).
[152] Above, p. 50. But see Woolf Final, p. 15, where it is said that the aim of case-management conferences in multi-track cases 'is that fewer cases should need to come to a final trial'.

3 On the nature and purposes of civil procedural law[1]

Introduction

In his masterly Hamlyn Lectures,[2] Sir Jack Jacob proposes that 'the true relation between substantive and procedural law should be redefined in terms of the primacy of substantive law and the supremacy of procedure. . . The supremacy of procedure is the practical way of securing the rule of law, for the law is ultimately to be found and applied in the decisions of the courts in actual cases.'[3] This proposal is of interest for two reasons in particular.

The first of these reasons is, simply, that the proposal should have been made at all. It is true that writers on jurisprudence devote a few pages to the relationship between substantive and procedural law[4] and educated English lawyers are aware of Maine's statement that 'substantive law has at first the look of being gradually secreted in the interstices of procedure',[5] but in general most people are content to adopt, knowingly or not, Bentham's description of procedure as the course taken for the execution of the laws,[6] and Collins M.R.'s statement that 'the relation of the rules of practice to the work of justice is intended to be that of handmaid rather than mistress'.[7] Something more is, no doubt, required in certain specific contexts, for example where it is necessary to classify a rule as procedural or not for the purposes of the conflict of

[1] Based on an article written as a contribution to the volume published in honour of Sir Jack I. H. Jacob Q.C.: I. R. Scott (ed.), *International Perspectives on Civil Justice* (1990). Also published under the same title in (1990) 9 C.J.Q. 262.
[2] Jacob, *Fabric*.   [3] *Ibid.*, pp. 63–7.
[4] Including T. E. Holland, who considered that the rules of procedure 'have attracted a share of attention perhaps in excess of their real importance': *Jurisprudence*, 13th edn (1924), p. 359. See also, e.g. Glanville Williams, *Salmond on Jurisprudence*, 11th edn (1957), pp. 503 *et seq.*; G. W. Paton, *A Textbook of Jurisprudence* (1946) pp. 443 *et seq.*; H. F. Jolowicz, *Lectures on Jurisprudence* (1963), pp. 359 *et seq.*
[5] Sir Henry Maine, *Early Law and Custom* (1861), p. 389.
[6] *Principles of Judicial Procedure*, p. 5, cited in Jacob, *Fabric*, p. 64, where Bentham's way of thinking is said to have been 'the traditional English and even common law view of the place of civil procedural law in the legal system'.
[7] *Re Coles and Ravenshear* [1907] 1 K.B. 1, 4.

laws, or where the validity of a rule of court made under the general rule-making power[8] is in question. There is no reason to expect, however, that judicial decisions or even academic writings in these contexts should throw any light on the subject as a whole. On the contrary, what is procedural for one purpose may well not be so for another. Thus, for example, rules of evidence are procedural for the purposes of the conflict of laws,[9] but no one supposes that they fall within 'practice and procedure' for the purposes of the rule-making power.[10]

The second point of interest in Sir Jack's proposal is the importance that he attaches to procedure as the means through which proceedings are brought before the courts *and the law thereby determined.*

That Sir Jack should thus give supremacy to procedure on the particular ground that it provides the means whereby decisions on the substantive law are obtained, may be thought surprising in the light of his suggestion elsewhere that the rules of procedure should be reframed on the premise that most of the actions that are started will not proceed to trial: 'The emphasis of the rules or codes should be on methods of the disposal of proceedings without trial or without a final determination by the courts.'[11] Any inconsistency is, however, more apparent than real. Sometimes, it is true, an innovative decision, a decision which runs counter to the expectations of the profession, may lead to a spate of litigation.[12] More usually, however, judicial decisions which do not turn exclusively on the relative credibility of the evidence produced by the opposing parties and which amount to more than mere necessary preliminaries to forcible execution, serve to clarify uncertain points of law or else to give guidance on the application of flexible rules of law or judicial discretion in particular circumstances. It may be that a compromise settlement is more advantageous to the parties than a judgment strictly in accordance with the law, but such a settlement is more difficult to achieve where the law or its application in the circumstances is unclear than where it is straightforward: an adequate flow of judicial

---

[8] Supreme Court Act 1981, s. 84(1); Civil Procedure Act 1997, s. 1.
[9] *Leroux* v. *Brown* (1852) 12 C.B. 801.
[10] See *Re Grosvenor Hotel, London (No. 2)* [1965] Ch. 1210, 1243, *per* Lord Denning M.R.; *Comfort Hotels* v. *Wembley Stadium* [1988] 1 W.L.R. 872. Nor can the rules governing the limitation of actions be altered by rule, but it is only since the Foreign Limitation Periods Act 1984 that they are treated as 'substantive' for the purposes of the conflict of laws. See, e.g. *British Linen Co.* v. *Drummond* (1830) 10 B. and C. 903; *Harris* v. *Quine* (1869) L.R. 4 Q.B. 653.
[11] 'Accelerating the Process of Law' in Jacob, *Reform*, pp. 91, 100.
[12] As occurred following the decision of the House of Lords in *Anns* v. *Merton LBC* [1978] A.C. 728.

decisions adequately reported is essential if most cases are to be disposed of without trial.

It is the object of this chapter to respond to the invitation implicit in Sir Jack's proposal and to consider some aspects of the relationship between substantive and procedural law and of the purposes to which the latter should have regard, using Sir Jack's observations as a text. Before turning to that, however, it is necessary, first, to draw attention to the distinction between procedural law on the one hand and actual proceedings on the other, and, secondly, to raise the question of the meaning of a civil action and the right to invoke the jurisdiction of the court.[13]

Proceedings and procedural law

As is implied in what has already been said, questions of classification such as those that arise in the conflict of laws are of peripheral if any importance for present purposes. It matters not whether a given rule is held by private international law to be substantive or procedural. What does matter – though the point is obvious as soon as made – is that it is proceedings in actual cases that lead to the kind of results which Sir Jack has in mind, not procedural law as such. Procedural law, in its most basic and elementary sense, is the law which governs the conduct of proceedings before the court – 'the mode of proceeding by which a legal right is enforced, as distinguished from the law which gives or defines the right'[14] – but it also governs what can properly be called 'procedural rights', including not only such rights as the right to discovery but also the right of appeal and, most importantly, the right to invoke the jurisdiction of the court.[15] Procedural law does not, or, rather, does not ostensibly, produce results which are unconnected with the process of litigation itself, but actual proceedings do so, and in more than one way.

'Action' and the right to invoke the jurisdiction

In the technical terminology of English law, 'action' is not only defined but is given a restricted meaning: it means 'civil proceedings

---

[13] For the separation of 'action' from 'right', see chap 4, p. 82.

[14] *Poyser* v. *Minors* (1881) L.R. 7 Q.B.D. 329, 333, *per* Lush L.J.

[15] E. J. Couture describes the 'right of action, or action in justice' as a '*species* within the *genus* of the right of petition' and attributes constitutional value to it: 'The Nature of Judicial Process' (1950) 25 Tulane L.R. 1, 9–10. This emphasises the importance of the right to invoke the jurisdiction but does not detract from its procedural nature.

commenced by writ or in any other manner prescribed by rules of court'.[16] In accordance with this it has been held, for example, that a petition for the compulsory winding up of a company is not an 'action' because the procedure for that is not prescribed by rules of court but by the Companies Act.[17] On the other hand, the application for judicial review is governed by rules of court and is therefore an 'action', notwithstanding that no one can apply for judicial review without first having obtained the leave of the court, and so too, presumably, is the application for leave itself.[18]

This kind of technical approach to the meaning of 'action' is useless in the wider context, but it has helped to conceal from English lawyers the critical distinction between the right to invoke the jurisdiction of the court, on the one hand, and the substantive right which will be recognised by a favourable judgment, on the other.[19] Be this as it may, there is a widespread and long-standing view that a person always has the right to invoke the jurisdiction of the court because the issue of originating process is not a judicial act but his own.[20] Indeed, Sir Jack himself argues on that ground that the requirement of leave to apply for judicial review should be abolished.[21]

The idea that leave might have to be obtained for the issue of originating process is as alien to the civilian legal systems as it is said to be for England, but that has not prevented those systems from developing a concept of the action which contemplates that a person does not always have the right to invoke the jurisdiction of the court. In France, for example, and only after a long period of controversy,[22] a definition of action was eventually introduced into the new code of civil procedure which came into force in 1975.

The action is the right, for the person making a claim, to be heard on the substance of the claim so that the judge can pronounce it well- or ill-founded.

For the opposing party, the action is the right to challenge the well-foundedness of the claim.[23]

It is, of course, no more possible in France than in England for a person to be prevented from taking whatever may be the prescribed

---

[16] Supreme Court Act 1981, s. 151(1).
[17] *Re Simpkin, Marshall Ltd* [1959] Ch. 229.
[18] If the making of the application is not the 'commencement' of proceedings it is nothing. The procedure is prescribed by R.S.C., Ord. 53, r. 3(2).
[19] The habitual use of the phrase 'cause of action' or, worse, 'right of action' to signify the existence of grounds for a favourable judgment is another contributory factor. See, e.g. *Letang* v. *Cooper* [1965] 1 Q.B. 232, 242–5, *per* Diplock L.J.
[20] *Clarke* v. *Bradlaugh* (1881) 8 Q.B.D. 63, 69, *per* Brett L.J.
[21] Jacob, *Fabric*, p. 183.
[22] See, e.g. Motulsky, 'Le droit subjectif et l'action en justice' in *Ecrits*, p. 85.
[23] N.c.p.c., art. 30.

initial step towards invocation of the jurisdiction of the court,[24] and, if he takes that step and does not withdraw it, the court is inevitably seised of something. It does not follow, however, that that person has an action or that he has invoked the jurisdiction of the court on the substance of his claim. French law recognises a number of 'fins de non-recevoir', the effect of which is to render the claim inadmissible, and the most important of these, for present purposes, is that the claimant lacks 'interest'.[25] If, therefore, the claimant is found to lack interest in the claim he has put forward, he cannot invoke the jurisdiction of the court with regard to that claim even though he can, of course, invoke the jurisdiction with regard to his (implicit) contention that he does have interest.[26]

In the application for judicial review the application for leave plays a role analogous to that of the French *fin de non-recevoir* but with a reversed burden. In France a litigant can proceed unless the court holds that he lacks interest; in the application for judicial review the applicant cannot proceed beyond his application for leave unless the court finds that he has sufficient interest. That no application for leave is necessary in ordinary civil cases does not mean, however, that in all such cases the court is obliged to consider the substance of a claim once the claimant has taken the initial steps of serving a writ and statement of claim. He cannot ordinarily be prevented from doing that, but a successful application to strike out under R.S.C. Order 18, rule 19 on the ground that the statement of claim discloses no reasonable cause of action will bring the proceedings to an abrupt end.

It is true that a party who fails to state a reasonable cause of action is not in all respects the same as a party who lacks interest in the French sense. It is also true that the hearing of an application to strike out is,

---

[24] It may be said to be even less so in France. In England, in addition to cases in which leave to issue a writ is required *ratione personae* (e.g. vexatious litigants or by virtue of a special statutory rule such as that contained in the Mental Health Act 1983, s. 139(2)) leave is also required, subject to the Civil Jurisdiction and Judgments Act 1982, where the writ is intended to be served out of the jurisdiction (R.S.C., Ord. 11, r. 1). In France no question of 'leave' arises, only that of the competence of the French court once process has been served, and those courts are always competent, even in 'international' civil litigation, provided that one of the parties is a French national: code civil, arts. 14 and 15. See, e.g. Solus and Perrot, *Droit Judiciaire Privé, Tome 2, La Compétence* (1973), nos. 386–93. Special rules for 'service' outside France are prescribed: n.c.p.c., arts. 683–8.

[25] N.c.p.c., art. 122. If the claimant lacks interest the court may take the point and declare the claim inadmissible of its own motion: *ibid.*, art. 125, al. 2.

[26] See n.c.p.c., art. 31, and, for the meaning of 'interest', e.g. L. Cadiet, *Droit Judiciaire Privé* (1992), nos. 715–33. A person who has himself suffered no damage will not have 'interest' to claim damages whatever the wrong allegedly done by the proposed defendant. See also c.p.c., art. 2.

theoretically, a hearing on the substance of the claim taking the facts alleged as true. A decision to strike out is thus a decision that, as a matter of law, the party is bound to fail on the substance of his claim even if he can prove the truth of the facts relied on: a pleading by a party whom French law would regard as having interest might still be struck out.[27] The fact remains, however, that a claim made by a party whose statement of claim does not allege that he has suffered damage recognised as such by the law, will, when damage is the gist of the action, have failed to state a reasonable cause of action and his pleading will be struck out: neither the legal consequences nor the truth of his allegations of fact will be considered by the court. The practical result is the same as if his claim had been pronounced inadmissible for lack of interest; he will no more succeed in invoking the jurisdiction of the court than will a French litigant who lacks interest.[28]

If this is right, it follows that it is not only in the application for judicial review[29] that the right to invoke the jurisdiction is not unfettered. There are, in reality, not two but three possibilities once a party has taken the first step in initiating ordinary civil proceedings. It may be that his pleading is struck out, in which case the court will not consider the substance of his allegations and it makes little sense to say either that he has the right to invoke the jurisdiction of the court or that he has an action. It may be that the proceedings run their full course and end in judgment for the plaintiff, in which case he has both an action and a substantive right. It may be that the proceedings run their full course and end with judgment against him, in which case it can, indeed, be said that he has no substantive right; it can even be said, giving the phrase its accepted, but unfortunate, English meaning, that he has no cause of action. But he has successfully invoked the jurisdiction of the court and it would be absurd to say that he had no action.[30]

---

[27] In the elaborate consideration of the application to strike out the statement of claim in *Rondel* v. *Worsley* [1969] 1 A.C. 191, for example, the plaintiff's 'interest' was neither in issue nor in doubt.

[28] *Gouriet* v. *Union of Post Office Workers* [1978] A.C. 435, provides an apt illustration. It was the absence of damage personal to himself – his lack of 'interest' – that deprived the plaintiff of the right to have the court pronounce on the substance of his allegations of unlawful conduct on the part of the defendants. He did not have an 'action'. It is not wholly inaccurate to say that, *mutatis mutandis*, the French brocard, 'pas d'intérêt, pas d'action' is as true in England as it is in France.

[29] And in those special cases in which leave to issue a writ is required. If a court lacks jurisdiction in a given matter, no one has the right to invoke its jurisdiction in relation to that matter.

[30] This follows the view, convincingly sustained, of Motulsky, 'Le droit subjectif': the action is 'la faculté d'obtenir d'un juge une décision sur le fond de la prétention à lui soumise'.

Substantive and procedural law

It seems to be little more than a matter of definition to say that procedural law affects only those who litigate. As will appear, this is less than the truth, but it does have sufficient truth to support two broad propositions that help to differentiate procedural from substantive law.

> *Subjection to substantive law is, subjection to civil procedural law is not, involuntary*

In some circumstances, as, for example, under certain contracts of insurance, a person may be unable to prevent litigation from being undertaken in his name. Even these cases, however, are not true exceptions to the voluntary character of civil litigation;[31] the element of compulsion comes not from the general law but from the particular relationship between the parties. In the overwhelming majority of cases, the person who supposes, or who knows, himself to be possessed of a substantive right is not compelled to enforce it through litigation, and the person against whom a claim is made is free to concede it, if he so wishes, without demur. Even where a particular result can be obtained only by judicial decree, as is the case, for example, with certain changes of personal status, the initiation of proceedings remains voluntary: one is not obliged to petition for divorce merely because grounds for divorce exist. It follows, since civil procedural law applies only to the process of litigation, that no one need be subjected to it against his will.

From this point of view, substantive law is different. Even if subjection to some parts of substantive law follows a voluntary act – the law governing marital relations is an example[32] – subjection to substantive law in general derives from the fact of being born and living in society. A person may be able to exercise an element of choice in the system of substantive law to which he is subject – temporarily by travel or more permanently by change of residence, domicile or nationality – but only the person who finds himself in virtual isolation on an island which forms part of the territory of no state can claim to be subject to no substantive law whatever.

> *Substantive law is, procedural law is not, 'self-executing'*

Substantive law

Although Sir Jack goes so far as to say that 'what is the law applicable in any given circumstances or events is not that which it is thought to be or

---

[31] See chap. 1, p. 21.
[32] Subjection to the law of contract is, at least theoretically, another.

any person has been advised that it is, but it is that which is duly laid down by the appropriate court of law in actual proceedings dealing with those circumstances or events',[33] it is not to be supposed that he denies the existence of law outside the courts. There is nothing in his writings to suggest that he espouses the view, so well and so scornfully described by Cardozo, that 'law never *is*, but is always about to be. It is realized only when embodied in a judgment, and in being realized, expires.'[34] The thrust of Sir Jack's words and, indeed, of his argument for the supremacy of procedure is that the courts have the last word on questions of law when they are raised in litigation that is pursued to judgment.

This, for all practical purposes, recognises that judges make law. It is, however, necessary also to recognise the truth of Maine's observation that we 'habitually employ a double language and entertain . . . a double and inconsistent set of ideas'.[35] We accept that judicial decisions may develop or change as well as declare the law, but at the same time we speak and act on the hypothesis that the legal consequences of our actions are determined directly by self-executing law, not by judicial decisions. Where counsel's opinion has been obtained on a point of law and it transpires in subsequent litigation that the judge's decision is to the opposite effect, we may say that counsel was mistaken or that he was proved wrong, but we never say that his opinion *became* wrong. In other words, though we recognise the fiction involved in the declaratory theory of judicial decision, we act on that theory most of the time[36] and we are encouraged to do so by the style in which most judgments are delivered.

The importance of this is not simply that a law-abiding society works on the assumption that the law exists. It is that such a society accepts that the law, or at least the civil law, is self-executing – that is, it normally produces its results of its own force without more. If I make a will in proper form, my property vests in my executors on my death; if I borrow money I incur, automatically, the obligations of a debtor; if a child is born in the United Kingdom to parents one at least of whom is a British citizen, the child is a British citizen.[37] Even if the legal consequences of

---

[33] Jacob, *Fabric*, p. 65.

[34] B. Cardozo, *The Nature of the Judicial Process* (1922), p. 126.

[35] Sir Henry Maine, *Ancient Law*, 10th edn (1905), p. 28.

[36] The hypothesis of the declaratory theory is certainly no worse as a guide to everyday behaviour than the hypothesis that the earth is flat, on which most of our daily movements are based. The force of the declaratory theory has now been confirmed. In *Kleinwort Benson Ltd* v. *Lincoln C.C.* [1998] 3 W.L.R. 1095, the House of Lords, by a majority, held that money had been paid under a mistake of law even though it had in fact been paid on an understanding of the law as it was generally supposed to be at the time but which had subsequently been held to be wrong.

[37] British Nationality Act 1981, s. 1.

an event depend on facts which remain in dispute until they are determined authoritatively by a judge, those consequences are still taken to follow the event, not the judgment. If this were not so it would be arguably wrong to award damages for loss suffered prior to judgment as a result of personal injury and it would certainly be wrong to award interest on such damages;[38] it is not wrong precisely because the liability of the defendant – that is, the legal consequence of his negligence or other tortious conduct – is understood to have accrued when the injury occurred, whether subsequent litigation was necessary to establish that or not.

This is not to say that there are no situations in which the consequences of substantive law are not seen as following automatically upon events,[39] or that forcible execution is never necessary to give those consequences practical effect; it is to say that such cases form the exception, not the rule, and that, typically, substantive law is self-executing.

Procedural law

It might be possible to construct a similar description of procedural law,[40] and to regard decisions on questions of procedure as declaratory, but to make the attempt would be useless as well as artificial. The importance of judicial discretion in procedural matters is, alone, enough to deprive the declaratory theory of value in this field; it does not explain the conduct of those involved in litigation and it is contrary to their ordinary understanding.

Rules of procedure typically permit or require certain specified acts on the part of one or other of the litigants. They also, commonly, permit and occasionally require certain action on the part of the court. It is, no doubt, possible to say that a party actually required to perform some act

---

[38] The rules about the award of interest on damages have become complex. It is sufficient here to refer simply to the idea that interest is awarded for the loss which is suffered 'by being kept out of money to which one is entitled': *Pickett* v. *British Rail Engineering Ltd* [1980] A.C. 13, 173, *per* Lord Scarman.

[39] Sometimes a judicial decree is necessary, as in the case of divorce, and sometimes positive action by one of the parties, as where one party 'accepts' the repudiation of it by the other: *Heyman* v. *Darwins* [1942] A.C. 356; *Howard* v. *Pickford Tool Co. Ltd* [1951] 1 K.B. 417, 421, *per* Asquith L.J. Cf. *Vitol S.A.* v. *Norelf Ltd* [1996] A.C. 800.

[40] A few rules do operate 'automatically', e.g. the ('deemed') close of pleadings and the consequent 'implied' joinder of issue under the former R.S.C., Ord. 18, rr. 14(2)(a) and 20, but perhaps the use of 'deemed' is significant. The 'nullity' of a procedural act, which may be considered 'automatic', is more common in France than in this country where it is virtually ruled out by R.S.C., Ord. 2, r. 1; C.P.R., rr. 3.9 and 3.10 (for a strong case see *Singh* v. *Atombrook Ltd* [1989] 1 All E.R. 385). Even in France, however, rectification can often cure a nullity: n.c.p.c., art. 115.

is under a duty to perform it,[41] but no question arises of the enforcement of such a duty in accordance with its terms,[42] and no question arises of compensating the other party for its breach. On the contrary, the Court of Appeal has held that an order for the payment of money into court by a party who had failed over a long period of time to comply with his 'duty' to give discovery was 'wholly inappropriate and quite wrong'.[43] Even an 'unless' order (that is, an order that, unless the required act is carried out by a specified date, the claim or defence, as the case may be, will be struck out) does not necessarily mean what it says: after the date has passed, the court still has jurisdiction to extend the time allowed.[44]

The fact is that the rules of procedural law usually do little more than create choices or a sequence of choices. This is obviously so where a rule simply permits a party to do something[45] or permits him to do it with the leave of the court,[46] but the position is not really different where a rule is mandatory in form. If the party to whom such a rule applies chooses to disregard it, the normal outcome is that a choice accrues to the other party: he may do nothing or he may seek an appropriate order from the court. If he chooses to do nothing, nothing will happen; if he chooses to bring the matter before the court, a choice accrues to the Master or the judge: in contrast to substantive law, procedural law rarely purports to dictate what the court's order must be, even after the facts have been established.

That procedural law merely creates choices in this way is most evident in the common law style of procedure where the court's power to act of its own motion is restricted and to which the idea that a judge should be assigned to a case from the beginning to take charge of its preparation is alien.[47] In a modern continental system such as that of France, every case is assigned from its inception to a judge – the juge de la mise en état – whose duties are to supervise and control the progress of the case, in particular the proper and timely exchange of pleadings

---

[41] There is nothing wrong in saying that a defendant on whom a statement of claim has been served is under a duty to serve his defence within fourteen days: R.S.C., Ord. 18, r. 2(1), C.P.R., r. 15.4.

[42] A summons calling on the defendant to serve his defence within the fourteen days allowed, which would have to be served before the expiry of that period, would, at best, be dismissed as premature.

[43] *Husband's of Marchwood v. Drummond Ltd* [1975] 1 W.L.R. 603, 605, *per* Russell L.J.

[44] *Samuels v. Linzi Ltd* [1981] Q.B. 115. The position is similar in France: n.c.p.c., art. 764. In Italy, in certain circumstances, the *giudice istruttore* can fix peremptory time limits which do mean what they say: c.p.c., art. 152.

[45] E.g. R.S.C., Ord. 20, r. 3(1); C.P.R., r. 17.1.

[46] E.g. R.S.C., Ord. 26, r. 1(2); C.P.R., r. 18.1. Examples of this kind of rule are legion.

[47] What was until recently alien has become commonplace in England under the C.P.R.

and documentary evidence.[48] There is much, for example by way of fact-finding procedures, that can be done only by order of the juge de la mise en état[49] and he has substantial power to act of his own motion.[50] It is, however, rare that the law deprives him of choice, and when it does so it is usually for reasons of public policy. The judge himself must, for example, take the point that an action is inadmissible if the *fin de non-recevoir*[51] applicable is one of *ordre public*,[52] but in nearly all cases the word used by the law is not 'doit', which imposes an obligation on the judge, but 'peut', which gives him a power and thus a choice.

It does not follow from the fact that procedural law creates choices that judicial decisions on procedural questions are necessarily unpredictable: an experienced practitioner may well be able to advise with virtual certainty what order will be made in given circumstances. To say that a rule of procedural law can lead to predictable decisions is, however, by no means to say that it is self-executing. In the first place, an order is often required even where there can be no doubt that it will be made, as where a party seeks leave to amend his pleading to correct a simple error only a short time after the close of pleadings. In the second and more important place, the ultimate sanction for breach of a mandatory procedural rule is usually that the claim or the defence, as the case may be, should be struck out and judgment entered accordingly.[53] The threat of such a sanction is, no doubt, effective in securing obedience to the rule, but to put it into effect is not to execute the rule itself. On the contrary, by bringing the proceedings to an end, it renders the whole of procedural law inapplicable save for those parts of it which deal with costs and the execution of judgments.

The purposes of civil procedural law

Legal proceedings cannot come into existence without party initiative, and it is a safe assumption that no party brings or defends proceedings unless he sees advantage in their successful conclusion. Usually the advantage he seeks is personal to himself, but those who bring proceedings unselfishly in what they see as the public interest, or the interest of a group or section of society, are no less anxious than are their selfish

---

[48] N.c.p.c., art. 763.   [49] *Ibid.*, arts. 143 and 144.

[50] E.g. 'Les faits dont dépend la solution du litige peuvent, à la demande des parties *ou d'office*, être l'objet de toute mesure d'instruction légalement admissible': *ibid.*, art. 143 (emphasis added).

[51] Above, p. 63.   [52] N.c.p.c., art. 125.

[53] Disobedience to an actual order may render the offender liable to committal, R.S.C., Ord. 24, r. 16(2), but this is a liability based on contempt of court and, in any case, actual committal is extremely rare.

counterparts to succeed in their litigation: rightly or wrongly they believe that the interest they seek to serve will be best served if they obtain from the court the judgment for which they ask.

It is natural, therefore, that civil litigation should be seen primarily as a process for the resolution of disputes. As presently written, the English rules and those of many other countries[54] scarcely seem even to contemplate that more than one case will be proceeding at any one time,[55] let alone that more may be at stake than the interests of the parties to each case.

This sort of approach leads to the idea that the purposes of procedural law are restricted to the provision of the institutions and rules of procedure best fitted to the fair, economical and expeditious adjudication, in accordance with law, of those disputes which the parties choose to submit to the courts. Subsidiary rules seek to protect defendants against harassment by actions which the plaintiff has no right to institute[56] or which have no prospect of success[57] and to protect plaintiffs against dilatory tactics on the part of defendants.[58] There are also rules designed to encourage settlements,[59] but even these seem to look primarily to the interests of the parties: it is widely held that the parties to a dispute are better served by an accommodation between them than by formal adjudication.[60]

It is appropriate that the interests of the parties, as defined by law, should be seen as paramount when attention is directed to proceedings in an individual case. It does not follow, however, that procedural law as such can be based on the single hypothesis that its business is no more than to provide for the resolution of a sequence of disputes, one after the other. The importance of achieving justice between individual litigants is in no way diminished by recognition that the process of

---

[54] But not those of the former socialist countries. See, e.g. Principles of Civil Procedure of the Soviet Union and the Union Republics, art. 2, trans. A. K. R. Kiralfy in (1963) 7 *Law in Eastern Europe* 299; Cappelletti and Jolowicz, pp. 174–7.

[55] The rules and directions about listing do, of course, contemplate that more than one action will be proceeding at one time, but there are few, if any, others that do so. Even the 'rule' that an application for habeas corpus takes precedence over all other proceedings on the same day seems to be a matter of practice rather than rule strictly so-called: statements of the 'rule' are easy to find, but not formal authority for it. See, e.g. *Supreme Court Practice 1999*, para. 54/1/3.

[56] E.g. n.c.p.c., arts. 122 *et seq.* See p. 63, above.

[57] E.g. R.S.C., Ord. 18, r. 19; C.P.R., r. 3.4.

[58] E.g. R.S.C., Ord. 14; C.P.R., r. 24.

[59] E.g. R.S.C., Ord. 22; C.P.R., r. 36, and the many rules in other jurisdictions for conciliation such as n.c.p.c., art. 21.

[60] See, e.g. M. Galanter, 'Justice in Many Rooms' in M. Cappelletti (ed.), *Access to Justice and the Welfare State* (1981), p. 147 at p. 151; Baur, cited in Cappelletti and Jolowicz, p. 267. Cf. O. M. Fiss, 'Against Settlement' (1984) 93 Yale L.J. 1073.

litigation, considered as a whole, serves at least two other ends, connected but distinct, and that their attainment should be included in the purposes of procedural law. First, civil proceedings serve to demonstrate the effectiveness of the law; secondly they provide the opportunity for the judges to perform their function of interpreting, clarifying, developing and, of course, applying the law.

The effectiveness of the law

In a country whose law is well developed the law is, by most people for most of the time, simply accepted as being there. They act on the hypothesis that the civil law is self-executing, they respect the legal rights of others and they comply with their legal obligations. This is not, however, universally the case, and in the past the effectiveness of the law in this sense was much less. 'Primitive man's reaction to injustice appears in the form of vengeance . . . The first impulse of a rudimentary soul is to do justice by his own hand. Only at the cost of mighty historical efforts has it been possible to supplant in the human soul the idea of self-obtained justice by the idea of justice entrusted to authorities.'[61]

Civil procedural law cannot afford to overlook the tendency of some people even today to take the law into their own hands. It cannot be safely assumed that, whatever the failings of civil justice, the criminal law can always take care of those who resort to violent self-help, but there is more to it than that. There have always been, and there always will be, victims of injustice – or of supposed injustice – who are quite incapable of resort to self-help for the simple reason that their adversary is much the stronger. The civil action must be not only civilisation's substitute for vengeance, it must also be civilisation's substitute for injustice.

It is this kind of thinking which leads to the development of legal aid and other devices aimed at opening the doors of the court to those who cannot afford to finance their litigation from their own pockets,[62] and also to the perennial modern concern with cost and delay. It is, however, essential to maintain a balance. If litigation is too costly and if the resolution of litigated disputes is too long delayed, the law will not be effective; self-help and injustice may result. On the other hand, if litigation is too easy – if, to all intents and purposes, there is no disincentive to litigation – then the volume of litigation will rise and

---

[61] Couture, 'Judicial Process', p. 7. See also *ibid.*, 21; *D.* v. *NSPCC* [1978] A.C. 171, 230–1, *per* Lord Simon of Glaisdale; F. Pollock and F. W. Maitland, *History of English Law*, Vol. II, 2nd edn (1898), p. 574.

[62] Not to mention the entire 'access to justice movement'. See Cappelletti and Garth.

delay, if not also cost, will once more increase and the law's effectiveness will be correspondingly reduced.

In England this may not, as yet, be seen to be a problem, but it is certainly a problem in some other countries. A comparison of some simple statistics from this country and Italy makes the point even after all allowances are made for differences between the two legal systems and differences of national characteristics. No figures are available of the number of disputes disposed of by settlement or otherwise before proceedings are ever begun, but it appears that in Italy, where, if the inordinate delay is overlooked, litigation is both easier and cheaper than in England, over 40 per cent of the total of all civil actions started run their full course, while in this country the equivalent figure is barely 3 per cent.[63]

As Professor Galanter has observed, 'Courts produce not only decisions but also messages. These messages are resources which parties use in envisioning, devising, negotiating and vindicating claims (and in avoiding, defending and defeating them).'[64] It is by no means only a person's estimate of the chances of ultimate success that controls his determination to initiate or to resist proceedings before the court but also such factors as cost, delay, the need to disclose matters he would prefer to keep to himself, and even the strain and sheer unpleasantness of being dragged through the courts. The potential litigant's information about these factors comes from what he learns from the media or from professional advisers about the litigation that actually comes before the courts. If the messages that he receives are too discouraging, justice will be denied and the law will be ineffective; if they are too encouraging the courts will become overloaded and even if the consequent increase in delay will itself have some correcting effect, what Sir Jack Jacob holds to be two of the fundamental features of English civil justice, namely, the adversary system and the principle of orality,[65] will be put at risk. Both are inherently expensive and time-consuming.

Bearing in mind that far more disputes are, and must continue to be,

---

[63] Figures taken from J. A. Jolowicz, 'Comparative Law and the Reform of Civil Procedure' (1988) 8 *Legal Studies* 1, 8. See also Gimena Sendra, 'Causas historicas de la ineficacia de la justicia'; P. Julien, 'Causes et origines des problèmes actuels de l'arrière judiciaire: aperçu procédural'; M. Borucka-Arstowa, 'Causes et origines des problèmes actuels de surcharge; aperçu sociologique', all in W. Wedekind (ed.), *Justice and Efficiency* (1989), pp. 17, 39 and 45, respectively.

More recent figures for England indicate a reduction in overall numbers and a slight increase in the proportion of cases running their full course to something over 4 per cent: *Judicial Statistics 1997*. For Italy the figures are little changed: (1999) 3 *Guida al diritto* 13.

[64] 'Justice in Many Rooms', p. 158.

[65] Jacob, *Fabric*, pp. 5 *et seq*. See chaps. 18 and 19, below.

disposed of without trial and even without proceedings of any kind, the effectiveness of law in society may well depend more on society's understanding of what the courts do – giving that expression the widest possible meaning – than on anything else, and that understanding depends on the messages that come from the courts, especially as they relate to the balance of incentives and disincentives to litigation. It must be one of the purposes of procedural law to maintain that balance.

The interpretation, clarification, development and application of the law

While the English version of the doctrine of precedent may be the strictest of any,[66] most developed countries recognise the importance to the substantive law of judicial decisions in actual cases, at least those of the highest courts.[67] The courts cannot, however, meet their responsibility to the law unless certain conditions are fulfilled. These conditions fall, broadly, into two categories. First, if a satisfactory body of jurisprudence is to be produced the question of law at issue must be well defined, well researched and well presented by counsel, whether the judges are allowed or encouraged to do their own research or not, and the judges must have adequate time for reflection and for the formulation of their judgments. Secondly, the courts must be given the opportunity to pronounce on questions of law of general interest and importance.

(a) If attention is directed only at the House of Lords, it can safely be said that the first of these conditions is fulfilled. For whatever reason – and the cost and delay of an appeal to the House of Lords may well be factors – it has to deal with only very few cases and it has the ability to protect itself against appeals which raise no point of law of importance by simply refusing leave to appeal.[68] It may, indeed, be the fact that the number of judgments given by the House of Lords in English civil cases

---

[66] A. Tunc, 'The Not so Common Common Law' (1984) 47 M.L.R. 150.
[67] E.g. A. Tunc, 'La Cour de cassation en crise' (1985) 30 *Archives de philosophie du droit* 157, 159; A. Touffait and A. Tunc, 'Pour une motivation plus explicite des décisions de justice, notamment de celles de la Cour de cassation': 1974 Rev.trim.dr.civ. 487. The subject has generated a vast literature of which a valuable selection may be found in O. Kahn Freund *et al.*, *A Source-book on French Law*, 3rd edn by B. Rudden (1991), pp. 241–58.
[68] See *Re Wilson* [1985] A.C. 750, 756, *per* Lord Roskill. No doubt Lord Roskill's words are borne in mind when the Court of Appeal considers an application for leave. It is, nevertheless, unfortunate that reasons for the grant or refusal of leave to appeal are not made more explicit: Jacob, *Fabric*, p. 233. For the position in some other countries see chap. 16, pp. 335 and 336.

could usefully be increased from its present level of around fifty or less a year, but the dangers of overload in supreme courts is graphically illustrated by the experience of courts of cassation such as those of France and Italy.[69] The case-loads of those courts are measured in thousands, not in tens, and as Professor Tunc has said of the French court, 'however conscientious its members, it is idle to pretend that it can produce work of the desired quality'.[70] Paradoxically, what Calamandrei once said seems to bear more relation today to the House of Lords than to the Italian Court of cassation, to which he referred: 'the state makes use of the private self-interested initiative of the disappointed party by putting it to the wider interests of society':[71] though the appellant hopes to gain an advantage from his appeal, if he is given the chance of gaining that advantage it is with a view less to protection of his personal interest than to improvement of the law.

The position in the Court of Appeal is different for that court is normally a court of second instance[72] and it is widely accepted that justice between the parties requires that a defeated litigant shall be entitled to have his case considered a second time.[73] It is, however, impossible, at least in common law countries, that the law-making function is left to the ultimate court of appeal alone: even decisions at first instance constitute authority,[74] but 'the Court of Appeal exercises an outstanding and crucial influence over the whole body of the law'.[75]

The dual role thus exercised by the Court of Appeal is bound to produce tensions. It is true that some of the devices introduced for the saving of judicial time, such as the lodging of skeleton arguments in time for them to be studied by the judges in advance of the hearing,[76] assist

[69] Jolowicz, 'Comparative Law', pp. 81–5; see n. 63.

[70] 'La Cour de cassation en crise', p. 162. See also the observations of the President of an Italian ministerial commission reporting in 1986, cited Jolowicz, 'Comparative Law', p. 84.

[71] La Cassazione Civile, Vol. II, chap. 6, no. 64 in Piero Calamandrei, Opere Giuridiche (a cura di Mauro Cappelletti), Vol. VII, p. 133. See also J. A. Jolowicz, 'Appellate Proceedings' in M. Storme and H. Casman (eds.), Towards a Justice with a Human Face (1978), p. 127 at p. 154.

[72] It is a court of third instance when it hears appeals on interlocutory questions decided originally by a Master. This provides a better justification for the rule that leave must be obtained to appeal to the Court of Appeal against an interlocutory decision than that based on the nature of interlocutory decisions as such: Jacob, Fabric, p. 223.

[73] Evershed, para. 473. Many countries recognise a right to a 'double degré de juridiction' but have nevertheless been obliged to admit some exceptions to it, e.g. by excluding a right of appeal (but not of recourse to cassation) in small cases. See chap. 16, p. 334; 'L'appel et l'Europe' [1989] Revue Juridique de l'Ouest, Special Issue, 29–41 and chaps. 15 and 16.

[74] Colchester Estates v. Carlton Industries [1986] Ch. 80.   [75] Jacob, Fabric, p. 222.

[76] Of a series of Practice Notes and Directions, the most recent is that of [1999] 1 W.L.R. 2.

the Court in its consideration of difficult questions of law, but on the whole the demands of the two functions of the Court are not easy to reconcile. So, for example, the increased use of a court of two judges is unobjectionable where no more is involved than the resolution of an individual dispute, but it is less satisfactory when an important point of law is raised. Yet it is for the parties to request a hearing before three judges in cases in which a court of two has jurisdiction,[77] and it would not be proper for counsel to advise the making of such a request unless he thought it to be in the interests of his client to do so. When Oliver L.J. stressed that it is open to counsel to request a hearing before a court of three if they consider that points of difficulty arise,[78] he cannot have intended to suggest that counsel acting in a particular case should put his client's interest in the expeditious hearing of his appeal at risk on the ground that the law itself would thereby be better served.

It is, no doubt, essential to avoid waste of judicial time so that judges are able to give adequate attention to the jurisprudence of the court, as well as to reduce delays in the hearing of appeals. Here too, however, the dual role of the court gives rise to conflict of principle, first because of the dangers inherent in attempting to speed up the processes of the court,[79] and, secondly, because it leads to self-imposed limitations to the scope of an appeal. The point emerges in the approach to appeals from the exercise by a judge of his discretion. Lord Diplock has, to all intents and purposes, made it clear that an appellate court should entertain an appeal only if it is necessary in the interest of the law,[80] but this places a serious restriction on the right of a defeated litigant to a reconsideration of the decision against him.[81]

There is reason to believe that the English Court of Appeal considers that it suffers from overload, though its case-load is much lighter than that of equivalent courts in many other countries. There is also reason to believe not only that it is conscious of its dual role, but that it is seeking methods for reconciling them without, thus far, being compelled to resort to some of the more radical efficiency devices that have been introduced elsewhere.[82] On the other hand, there is even now relatively

---

[77] *Supreme Court Practice 1999*, para. 20A-409.

[78] *Coldunell Ltd v. Gallon* [1986] Q.B. 1184, 1202.

[79] Sir Jack Jacob himself has stressed that 'the acceleration of the legal process should be treated as a means to the attainment of justice and not as an end in itself': 'Accelerating the Process of Law' in Jacob, *Reform*, pp. 91 and 95.

[80] *Birkett v. James* [1978] A.C. 297, 317.

[81] Sir Jack Jacob raises, but without answering, the question whether the policy and principle of discouraging rather than encouraging appeals is right: Jacob, *Fabric*, p. 232. It does, certainly, help in securing the normal finality of the decision at first instance, but it is possible to take that too far.

[82] See chap. 16, p. 346.

little explicit recognition in procedural law of the courts' crucial law-making role. It is time for this to be changed if the continuing search for the necessary compromise solutions to conflicts of principle and policy are to succeed.

(b) The production of jurisprudence at any level depends on the initiative of litigants, and it requires a persistent litigant to carry his case to the Court of Appeal, let alone the House of Lords. Lord Devlin once said, extra-judicially, that 'half a century is not an unreasonable estimate of the time that is likely to elapse before a doubtful point is settled'.[83] This may be unduly pessimistic, and there are some litigants with a continuing interest in some branch of the law, such as the Revenue authorities, who will seek or seize an opportunity to obtain a decision on a point of law even if the actual subject matter of the dispute which raises that point is of minimal importance. Nevertheless, it is normally little more than accident which determines whether questions calling for the attention of the courts are actually presented to them.

In continental legal systems it is open to a public authority – in France the ministère public – to bring before the Court of cassation, 'in the interest of the law', a decision of a lower court which is considered to be wrong in law.[84] This is, however, little used[85] and it is not suggested that anything similar should be adopted here. Nevertheless, it is not un-common that situations arise in which there is a wide general interest in the application of the law to particular circumstances or in which a question of law arises on which an authoritative answer is necessary. One example is provided by *Gillick* v. *West Norfolk AHA*.[86] The plaintiff in that case no doubt felt strongly that contraceptive advice and treatment should not be given to girls under sixteen without the knowledge of their parents, and it is a safe assumption that her failure to persuade the majority of the House of Lords to pronounce such treatment and advice unlawful was seen by her as resulting in a decision contrary to the public interest. The actual decision is, however, not important for present purposes. What is important is that by her action Mrs Gillick obtained clarification of an important question of law and thereby, herself, performed a useful public service.

There is no possibility – nor should there be – of introducing into civil procedural law a process whereby a question can be put to the court in

---

[83] P. Devlin, *Samples of Lawmaking* (1962), p. 14.

[84] French law no. 67–523 of 3 July 1967, art. 17; n.c.p.c., art. 618–1.

[85] But see the important decision on surrogate motherhood, Ass. Plén. 13 May 1991 D.S. 1991, 417; J.C.P. 1991, II, 21752, noted J. C. Hall and J. A. Jolowicz [1992] C.L.J. 37.

[86] [1986] A.C. 112. See especially at 206–7, *per* Lord Templeman.

the abstract for a purely consultative opinion.[87] Nevertheless, it can be suggested that English law is unnecessarily hostile to what may loosely be called public interest litigation. Rules that are tantamount to rules of standing are strictly enforced[88] in what is, unfortunately, now called private law even if they are more relaxed in administrative law;[89] no legal aid is available for a relator action, and the class action, which plays so large a role in the United States, is virtually unknown in this country.

It is not, however, only in the United States that the path is sometimes eased for litigation of a kind which should be brought for the sake of interests wider than those of the parties to a given dispute. In Germany, for example, special statutes reduce the financial risk to plaintiffs in certain classes of litigation,[90] and in France various associations are given special standing to take proceedings for the protection of the group or public interests with which they are particularly associated.[91] If it is one of the purposes of procedural law to promote the interpretation, clarification and development of the law; if, as Sir Jack Jacob says, it is the contribution of judicial decisions to the substantive law that gives procedural law its 'supremacy', some attention should be given to ways not only of excluding worthless cases, especially from appeal, but also of encouraging litigants whose cases raise questions the adjudication of which will be of public benefit.

Conclusion

If civil procedural law is to serve any purpose in society, even if only that of supplying civilisation's substitute for vengeance, the law which provides the necessary institutions and which regulates the actual process of litigation must start from the proposition that civil litigation is voluntary. It is possible, and in certain circumstances it is desirable, to deny the right to invoke the jurisdiction of the court, and there is more than one way in which this can be done. The denial may be absolute and general, as where a given kind of question is declared non-justiciable; it

[87] See *Baker* v. *Carr* 369 U.S. 186, 204 (1962), *per* Brennan J., cited in chap. 6, p. 110.
[88] *Gouriet* v. *Union of Post Office Workers* [1978] A.C. 435; *Ashby* v. *Ebdon* [1985] Ch. 394.
[89] *R.* v. *IRC, ex parte Fed. of Self-employed* [1982] A.C. 617. See also *R.* v. *Secretary of State* [1989] 1 All E.R. 1047 where, for all practical purposes, they were ignored.
[90] See H. Kötz, 'Civil Litigation and the Public Interest' (1982) 1 C.J.Q. 237, 248. In Sweden, consideration was actually given to ways in which the Supreme Court's contribution to the law might be enlarged: Report of the Judicial Procedure Commission 1986, cited P. H. Lindblom, 'Regional Report: Scandinavian Countries' in P. Yessiou-Faltsi (ed.), *The Role of the Supreme Courts at the National and International Level* (1998), p. 223 at p. 263.
[91] Chap. 6, below, p. 117.

may be absolute but particular, as where jurisdiction is possessed exclusively by a special tribunal, not the ordinary courts;[92] it may be conditional, as where leave is required to initiate proceedings; and it may also be conditional in the different sense that the plaintiff must have an action.[93] It is impossible, on the other hand, that a person should be compelled, save by virtue of a special relationship with another person, to invoke the jurisdiction of the court.

It follows from this that rules of procedure operate mainly by the creation of choices for the parties, and the court's power of decision or order – which itself involves choice – is, in a liberal procedure, exercised only on the application of a party. There is, however, no logical necessity that this should be so. On the contrary, there is nothing illogical in the view that, *once the jurisdiction of the court has been invoked*, 'there stands over and above the parties a benefit in law ('Rechtsgut') to which they are both subordinated'.[94] The allocation of the power of choice between the parties, on the one hand, and the court, on the other, comes from tradition and from prevailing views of principle and policy, not from the nature of things.

The traditional rule in most legal systems – not only the common law – is that the power of choice rests largely with the parties. This is an aspect of the 'dispositive' principle, which holds that the parties have the power of disposition of their rights, procedural as well as substantive.[95] That principle has, however, been modified to varying extents in different legal systems since the nineteenth century or before.[96] In France, where a judge is regularly appointed to oversee and control the preparation of a case from its inception,[97] the Conseil d'Etat has clearly distinguished the dispositive principle from the principle of contradiction, namely the principle that no element of either fact or law may be used by the judge in his determination of the case unless the parties

---

[92] Or, as in France, where there is an administrative jurisdiction quite distinct from the 'judicial'. No one has the right to invoke the jurisdiction of the 'judicial' courts in a matter classified as administrative.

[93] Above, p. 62.

[94] A. Engelmann, 'Der Civilprozess: Allgemeiner Theil', trans. Millar in *History*, p. 13. See also Z. Stalev, 'El proceso civil en los estados socialistas' in *LXXV Años de evolución jurídica en el mundo*, III (1978); Cappelletti and Jolowicz, pp. 221 *et seq.* and pp. 275 *et seq.*

[95] Millar, *History*, p. 14.

[96] An early example is provided by the Prussian code of Frederick II. Considerable power was conferred on the court by the Austrian code of 1895 (*History*, p. 636) and by the German code of 1877 as amended in 1924 (*History*, p. 617). The active role of the court is particularly marked under the so-called 'Stuttgarter Modell' in Germany: R. Bender, in Cappelletti and Garth, Vol. II, p. 431.

[97] N.c.p.c., arts. 763 *et seq.*

have had the opportunity to be heard upon it.[98] French civil procedure, it was said, is traditionally characterised by its adherence to both principles,[99] but it was held that while the principle of contradiction admits of no qualification, power can be transferred from the parties to the judge, and the dispositive principle thus modified, for the purpose, amongst others, of reducing delay.

In this country, devotion to the very idea that our system is the adversary system tends to inhibit open discussion of the relative value of the different principles which that system embraces, but here too there are the beginnings of an enlargement of the court's power to act of its own motion.[100] Is it not, therefore, time to abandon our inhibitions and to give theoretical as well as practical consideration to the most suitable allocation of power between the parties and the court, bearing in mind that the suitability of any allocation must be assessed by reference to the purposes of procedural law as a whole, not only to that of the resolution of a sequence of individual disputes?[101]

Whatever the future allocation of power between parties and judge, it is both inevitable and right that a substantial power of choice will remain with the parties. Their exercise of their choices is influenced by their perception of their own interest, informed by the messages sent by the courts through other litigation and by the threat of a sanction in costs or otherwise if the other party exercises his choice of making an application to the court. If, however, the wider purposes of procedural law, of which those mentioned in this paper are no more than examples, are brought into account, it may be found useful that the rules of procedure should contain some carrots as well as sticks.

In the penultimate paragraph of his Hamlyn Lectures[102] Sir Jack Jacob cites from a speech of Mr Quintin Hogg, as he then was, in which it is stressed that although litigation is an evil, its ultimate objective is justice. This must not be thought to mean justice only for those who take part in actual proceedings before the court. That litigation should take place is essential to maintenance of the rule of law and to the achievement of justice for the mass of people who are never, themselves, involved in actual proceedings before the court. If civil procedural law is to achieve its purposes, a choice in favour of litigation or a choice in

---

[98] C.E. 12 October 1979. D. 1979, 606, note Bénabent; J.C.P. 1980, 19288, concl. Franc, note Boré.

[99] J.C.P. 1980, 19228 at no. 10(a).

[100] The court's power to act of its own motion is further and substantially enlarged under the C.P.R.

[101] The purpose of making the civil action civilisation's substitute for injustice may, in particular, require an 'active' court.

[102] Jacob, *Fabric*, p. 285.

favour of an appeal, to say nothing of lesser matters on which litigants have a choice, should sometimes be encouraged, especially when a question of general importance is at issue. The process of civil litigation serves purposes other than that of doing justice to those who appear before the courts, and the achievement of those purposes must be an objective of procedural law.

4   The dilemmas of civil litigation[1]

Action and right

In a famous passage in the Institutes of Justinian, the 'action' is defined as 'nothing other than the right of pursuing *in judicio* that which is due to one',[2] and when it eventually became necessary for European lawyers to find a link between the substantive law which had for so long been studied in the universities, on the one hand, and the procedures of the courts, on the other, it was natural for them to turn to that. The action became 'the law in motion', the 'law in a state of war'[3] or, in the less exciting but more precise language of Glasson and Tissier's treatise on French civil procedure 'the action is the power which a person possessed of a right has of obtaining from a judge the protection of that right'.[4] In other words – and the words were used – if there is no right, there is no action.

In England the starting point was different, for in England, so far as proceedings in the royal courts were concerned, the formulary system of the forms of action was the basis of the law for centuries. Substantive law, as such, could not really be said to exist: only if a writ and a form of action adapted to his case was available to a would-be plaintiff could he invoke the jurisdiction of the king's courts at all. What is more, even if a suitable form of action existed, if the plaintiff had mistakenly used not that form but a different one, his claim would fail.[5] In the well-known phrase, 'Remedies precede rights'; and that is the same as saying that if I have no action I have no right. This proposition, the apparent converse of that used on the continent, comes to the same thing. In the common law and the civil law alike, action and right are two sides of the same coin.

[1] Based on the Lionel Cohen Lecture for 1983, published (1983) 18 *Israel Law Review* 161.
[2] Inst. 4, 6, pr.
[3] C. Demolombes, *Cours de code Napoléon*, 4th edn (1870), Vol. IX, no. 338.
[4] Glasson and Tissier, Vol. I, p. 423.
[5] This continued to be true even after extensive joinder of causes of action was permitted by the Common Law Procedure Act 1852: *Bracegirdle* v. *Hinks* (1854) 9 Ex. 361.

The conceptual identity of action and right may or may not have been productive of, but it certainly is consistent with, the idea that civil litigation is little more than the private affair of the parties. The institutions of civil litigation – the judges, the courts and so on – may be put at the disposal of the parties in order to minimise recourse to violent self-help and even, perhaps, to help the weak against the strong; but the court will not intervene of its own motion. And when it is called upon to lend its authority and even its powers of coercion to a claim made by one person upon another, its task is neither more nor less than to decide which of the two parties before it has the better of the argument between them.

The relatively simple and traditional view of civil litigation as a private contest conducted before a judge whose decision, subject to appeal, the parties are obliged to accept is still very much with us,[6] and it is not a view of civil litigation that creates no dilemmas. For years the search has gone on for acceptable compromises between, for example, the need to provide adequate procedures for the honest defendant to resist a claim made against him and the need to ensure that the dishonest or unscrupulous defendant does not make use of those procedures to avoid or delay an unfavourable judgment. This is essentially the dilemma of uncertainty, for the outcome of a contest cannot be known until the contest has run its course; it cannot be known whether a party to litigation is a villain or a saint until the case is over.

Problems of this kind are familiar to anyone with experience of any system of procedure, and, while they are far from unimportant, discussion of them is bound to be technical and closely directed to the detailed rules of particular systems. They are not the subject matter of this chapter, whose intention is, rather, to draw attention to two new dilemmas which now face the institution of civil litigation, dilemmas which are the product of new demands made upon it. These may be called, respectively, the 'demand for correct decisions' and the 'demand for legality'. Neither demand could have arisen if the identity of action and right – the idea that they are different sides of the same coin – had not virtually disappeared.

The separation of right and action

In England it was the Judicature Acts 1873–5 that finally severed the link between right and action. Although partial reform of the legal system had been achieved in the earlier years of the nineteenth century,

---

[6] *Air Canada* v. *Secretary of State for Trade* [1983] 2 A.C. 394. It may not, however, survive indefinitely. See chap. 18, p. 385, chap. 19, p. 389.

it was only the enactment of that legislation which brought to an end the system of the forms of action and at the same time created a single court of universal jurisdiction in place of the variety of more or less specialised courts which had existed until then. Once the Acts had been passed, the plaintiff's choice of form or choice of court ceased to have any critical effect upon the outcome of his claim – indeed, in no important sense did he have to make a choice at all except whether to sue or not.[7] All that he had to do was to plead the facts on which he relied; it was then for the defendant to plead his response, admitting and denying the plaintiff's allegations as he chose and introducing new allegations of his own. This remains, in its essentials, the position to this day, and it was and is for the court to pronounce upon the legal consequences of the facts as alleged and as admitted or proved.

Such a system is not inconsistent with the traditional view of litigation as a private contest, and it has taken time for the full significance of the changes effected by the Judicature Acts to penetrate into and become part of our general manner of thinking about the law; but what those Acts did was to secure the separation of substantive law from procedure and so to enable us to think of substantive law, and thus of substantive rights and substantive duties, as existing, and, indeed, as existing independently of judicial decision. Substantive law is now commonly understood to operate in society of its own force; it produces legal consequences, and those consequences are taken to have occurred even if it sometimes requires litigation and a judicial decision to discover what they were. If I buy a tin of meat from my grocer and the meat proves to be unfit for human consumption, anyone with any knowledge of the law will tell me that I have a right to compensation, not that I have an action. Indeed, unless I have eaten the meat and become ill in consequence, a sensible lawyer will tell me that I do not have a worthwhile action, for the costs of litigation would exceed the amount I would recover if I sought to enforce my right. It is a useful indication of the way in which we now think about the operation of the law, that, when we find that practical advice of that kind is necessary, we see it not as a denial of the existence of the right but as a procedural imperfection, though not necessarily one to be corrected.

No equivalent legislative change led to the separation of action and right on the continent of Europe, and, in any case, no one there questioned the existence of substantive law or substantive or subjective rights. What did happen – and it happened through the work of scholars

---

[7] An exception, now much reduced in scope, was introduced when the House of Lords insisted that only the application for judicial review might be used for 'public law litigation': *O'Reilly* v. *Mackman* [1983] 2 A.C. 236. See chap. 8, p. 160.

rather than legislators – was recognition that procedure could and should be separated from substance, that an action could exist without a right. In 1885 the German scholar A. Wach wrote of the action as itself an autonomous right, as a means to permit a substantive right to be enforced rather than the right itself,[8] but the most important advances were made by bringing into the discussion the common phenomenon that a plaintiff can pursue his claim through all its stages in the courts and on appeal without ever persuading a judge of the existence of his right.[9] He may, no doubt, sometimes be told that his claim is inadmissible, in which case its substance will never be considered, and if that happens it can be said that he has no action; but to say that he has no action merely because at the end of the litigation the court finds that he has no right is absurd. As the French code recognises, to say that a person has an action is to say no more than that he is entitled to a judicial determination of the validity or otherwise of his claim.[10]

On both sides of the divide between the common and the civil law, therefore, we have come to a view of substantive law and procedure as two different things; and the separation between them has led those who belong to both legal cultures to accept that legal rights and duties exist as such. In these circumstances, it is, perhaps, not too fanciful to speak of substantive law as being supposed to create a kind of legal environment in which we live, in much the same way as we also live in a natural environment. No doubt the law is normative in character and rules of law which purport to dictate how people should behave can be disobeyed. Nevertheless, though law expressed in the form of commands will not always produce its intended consequences in the physical world, our present conception is that the law as a whole does, of its own force, give rise directly to legal consequences. The law is there, it exists, and certain acts, certain events, have certain legal consequences whether intended or unintended.

It follows from this approach – this supposition that the law is there and all-pervasive in the form of a legal environment – that it is facts, not law, which are the source of particular legal rights and duties, and this has been said by distinguished lawyers on both sides of the divide.[11] Now facts are facts: they may be obscure, they may be in controversy, they may even be unknown, but they exist – or such, at any rate, is the

[8] Cited in Edouardo Couture, 'The Nature of Judicial Process' (1950) 25 Tulane L.R. 1. Compare the well-known statement of Lush L.J. in *Poyser v. Minors* (1881) L.R. 7 Q.B.D. 329, 333.
[9] Couture, 'Judicial Process'.   [10] N.c.p.c., art. 30. See chap. 3, p. 62.
[11] E.g. *Letang v. Cooper* [1965] 1 Q.B. 232, 242–3, *per* Diplock L.J.; Motulsky, 'La cause de la demande dans la délimitation de l'office du juge', in *Ecrits*, p. 101 at p. 106.

belief of most ordinary men. It follows, if law and facts both exist, that so also do the legal consequences which flow from the facts.

There is, of course, a substantial element of fiction in all this. As appears from our ordinary modes of speech, however, the fiction is generally sustained by lawyers and non-lawyers alike, and they are encouraged by the way in which judges explain their decisions. Judges do not say – they virtually never say – how in their personal opinion the legal relationships between the parties to litigation ought to be regulated. They declare what those relationships *are*, though they may, of course, go on to say what ought to be done by one or both parties, given the nature of their relationship as it is found to be. In any case, the element of fiction should not be overstated. It is, after all, true in the vast majority of cases that no one entertains any doubt at all that certain legal consequences have followed upon the occurrence of certain events or the performance of certain acts.

It is this widespread belief in the independent existence of a substantive law which operates automatically – a belief that could not have been entertained so long as action and right were identified with each other – that has given rise to the two new demands made on civil litigation or, at least, has created conditions in which they could be made. Each demand has brought with it serious dilemmas which can be resolved only by compromise, and if satisfactory solutions are to be found the nature of those dilemmas must be understood.

The demand for correct decisions

It may seem strange to describe as 'new' the demand that the decisions of the courts should be correct, but it must be borne in mind that under a formulary system no decision can be either correct or incorrect save in the context of the particular form employed. A decision refusing to the plaintiff who has sued in debt the authority and assistance of the court in pursuit of his claim on the ground that he should have sued in assumpsit, may be perfectly correct even if, in assumpsit, the outcome of the litigation would have been different. It is only when substantive law is understood to exist on its own that it is possible to say, as a matter of substance, that a decision is correct or incorrect. On the other hand, when, as we now habitually say, judicial decisions are made by the application of *the law* – not of some particular part of the law but of *the law* – to the facts, then it is natural for us to demand that the exercise of applying the law to the facts be performed correctly. What we want of our courts is that they should tell us, in case of doubt, what the legal consequences of certain facts actually *are*, and, of course, we want them to be correct. Indeed, in the former socialist countries this was actually demanded of them by the legislature. The Principles of Civil Procedure of the Soviet Union and the Union Republics, for example, stated that the tasks of civil procedure are the *correct* and expeditious trial and *decision* of civil cases.[12]

The principal difficulty about the demand for correct decisions, that is for decisions which declare correctly the legal consequences that have come about through the operation of existing law on facts which have already occurred, is that when we speak of law existing and operating in society we use the language of metaphor. Or, if that be too sceptical a view, at least it is true that the results of the operation of law cannot be independently observed and verified. So far as the parties to litigation are concerned, the judge has the last word, subject only to appeal to other judges, and we are schooled to accept as correct decisions which are not reversed, especially if they are affirmed in appellate courts. The fact is, however, that no judicial decision, though final and binding on the parties, can be more than an expression of opinion on a matter not susceptible of proof: there are no objective or external criteria capable of establishing the correctness or otherwise of a decision.

In these circumstances, and however unfortunate some may consider the conclusion to be, it has to be accepted that the nearest thing to a correct decision that it is possible to achieve is a decision reached by a judge who has all the information at his disposal that he personally considers necessary concerning both the facts – which means the facts that he considers to be relevant – and the law. Or, to put the same point negatively, the dangers of an incorrect decision are much greater where the parties have control of the information which the judge may use when he comes to his decision than where the judge has that control himself.

Other things being equal, an inquisitorial type of procedure is, there-fore, more likely to produce the correct decision than an accusatorial or adversarial procedure, where the judge's role is only to decide between the rival contentions of the parties. Whatever we may ultimately mean by a correct decision, it would be odd to describe as correct a decision that the judge himself believes to be wrong because he was deprived of information he considered he should have had, or was debarred from applying the rule of law he thought appropriate to the case.

In the former socialist system the law specified that the court was not limited to consideration only of the materials produced and the explana-tions given by the parties. It was formally required itself to take all lawful

---

[12] Article 2. Translation by A. K. R. Kiralfy in (1963) 7 *Law in Eastern Europe* 299. Emphasis added.

steps for 'overall, complete and objective clarification of the true facts of every case'.[13] Elsewhere, however, the transfer to the court of control over the preparation and presentation of a case for decision has not gone so far, but in some countries it has gone quite a long way. In France, for example, it is for the juge de la mise en état to decide what methods for collecting information – such as the taking of oral testimony or the obtaining of an expert's report, if any – shall be employed.[14] What is more, although his power to refuse an application for, say, an expert's report, can be explained by the need for economy,[15] his power to order one even if neither party makes an application, cannot. It can only be explained on the ground that if the judge considers such a report to be necessary to enable him to come to a correct decision, then he should have it, whether either party wants it or not. On the legal side of things the judge's control is even more clearly stated – he must decide the case in accordance with the applicable rules of law and he must qualify the facts correctly, whatever the parties may have contended.[16]

The movement towards what is sometimes called the more active court which has undoubtedly taken place on the continent and also, though to a lesser extent, in common law countries,[17] is in part attributable to realisation that for a correct decision to be achieved, the court must be able to obtain and to use the information which it considers necessary, rather than that it should base its decision only on the information which the parties are willing that it should have. However, any movement to increase the powers of the judge is seen as a restriction on the freedom of the parties to structure what is still regarded as *their* litigation as they see fit and, perhaps most importantly, as a curtailment of a man's freedom to abandon in whole or in part his legal rights. He is not compelled to bring proceedings; he is not, if a claim is made against him, compelled to resist it. He must, therefore, be free also to decide for himself what will and what will not be put before the judge.[18] This is a significant aspect of the so-called 'dispositive principle'.

It is the natural resistance of most systems to the idea that, by engaging in litigation, the parties transform themselves into 'objects of legal interest'[19] who cannot be allowed freedom to dispose of their own rights, which creates the dilemma. As the socialists saw, maintenance of

---

[13] Principles of Civil Procedure of the Soviet Union and the Union Republics, art. 16.
[14] N.c.p.c. arts. 10, 143 and 144.
[15] *Ibid.*, art. 147.   [16] *Ibid.*, art. 12.
[17] For the common law move to judicial case management, see chap. 2, pp. 49 and 57.
[18] *Air Canada* v. *Secretary of State for Trade* [1983] 2 A.C. 394.
[19] A. Engelmann, *Der Civilprozess: Allgemeiner Teil*, p. 159, cited in R. Millar, 'The Formative Principles of Civil Procedure' in *History*, p. 3 at p. 13.

the parties' dispositive power is ultimately inconsistent with the demand for correct decisions in the only sense that phrase can bear. Some steps may be taken in some countries, not in others, and in some the movement towards the active court has gone further than in others, but even if the dispositive power of the parties is reduced, as it has been in France, it is still unthinkable that the court, rather than the parties, should determine what allegations of fact shall be considered. If it were to do so it would not just provide the solutions but would also provide the questions, leaving the parties as little more than ciphers.

In France, even the provision of the new code of civil procedure, which requires the judge to decide what is the applicable rule of law,[20] was, in its original codified form, struck down by the Conseil d'Etat as contrary to 'general principles of law'.[21] This was, principally, because the code allowed the judge to invoke a rule of law of his own motion, without giving the parties an opportunity to argue the point. As it was put by Commissaire du Gouvernement Franc, 'in the state of law attained in Western society, the principle of contradiction is one of the most perfect manifestations of the right of self-protection in litigation and one of the golden rules of legal procedure'.[22]

Temporise and qualify as we may, such a statement is in substance and in spirit inconsistent with the view that the court must seek, through its own efforts, to discover the material truth. Though the demand for correct decisions exists and is both a healthy and a natural product of the received idea that substantive law *exists*, it creates a dilemma. The demand can be met only by restricting the freedom of the parties to manage the litigation as they please, and such restriction conflicts with the dispositive principle. To a different extent in different countries that freedom has been reduced by increasing the power of the court over the litigation, but the dilemma remains.

The demand for legality

It is one of the characteristics of a court that it cannot set its own machinery in motion, and, for so long as action and right are seen as one, it is a necessary corollary that only the person who is possessed of the right – or the action – may initiate proceedings. To the extent that a public official such as the Attorney-General in England or the ministère public in France can take proceedings in the public interest, this is

---

[20] N.c.p.c., art. 12.
[21] Conseil d'Etat, 12 October 1979, J.C.P. 1980, 19288. The subject is dealt with more fully below, chap. 10, p. 192.
[22] J.C.P. 1980, 19288, *ibid.*

explained by saying that there is a public right which may be protected by the court at the suit of, and only at the suit of, a public official. Where no public right is involved, then, if the private owner of the right does not, for whatever reason, institute proceedings, the matter will not come before the court. I may break my contract with you with impunity unless you choose to act.

This approach is appropriate, indeed essential, in innumerable different situations. It is, for example, obviously important in ordinary private life that people should be entitled and encouraged to settle their differences without recourse to the courts, even if this means that a person's disregard of his legal obligations will be condoned. Nevertheless, growth of the idea that substantive law *exists* has created a climate of opinion in which a demand for law enforcement for its own sake has developed. In other words, it is increasingly becoming the view that the non-criminal as well as the criminal law should be upheld and vindicated in the courts regardless of the wishes of those who are immediately affected by its breach.[23] This amounts, though in a muted form, to a demand for a kind of *actio popularis*: in some circumstances, at least, a person should not be allowed to 'get away' with a breach of the law simply because those actually possessed of a right do not or cannot institute proceedings.

This way of thinking seems to lie behind some of the developments in the United States of the class action,[24] which may do more than just secure redress for large numbers of small claimants; it may succeed in depriving the defendant of what are seen and described as his 'ill-gotten gains' and in deterring people from similar conduct in the future. One American author has described the class action as 'a tool for the deterrence of unlawful conduct through civil suits',[25] and an English author has dismissed as 'obviously unacceptable' the assumption that 'the law-breaker should be entitled to his *unjust* enrichment where individuals do not assert their rights by way of litigation'.[26]

Many people today probably share that opinion, and the view that gains made by, say, a seller through disregard of his obligations to his buyer are ill-gotten, has a certain plausibility even if no breach of the criminal law is involved and the buyer does not seek to be reimbursed. It is, however, essential to appreciate that this view denies the relativity of

[23] The idea that a person who has a right also has a duty to assert it in the interest of society goes back at least to R. Ihering, *Der Kampf ums Recht* (1873).

[24] See chap. 6, below, p. 111.

[25] J. B. Weinstein, 'Some Reflections on the "Abusiveness" of Class Actions' (1973) 58 F.R.D. 299.

[26] R. H. S. Tur, 'Litigation and the Consumer Interest' (1982) 2 L.S. 135, emphasis added. Note the assumption behind the word 'unjust'.

private law and private right. Only if it is accepted that the law *exists*, and that it exists independently of the individuals to whom it apparently relates, does it make sense to describe gains as ill-gotten when the individuals at whose expense those gains are made are content to leave them in the hands of those who made them.

If it is allowed to develop, the class action is capable of converting civil litigation into a process of law enforcement and thus of making of it a public as well as a private form of process, but a class action is at least begun on the initiative of a representative plaintiff who has an action in the sense already mentioned.[27] The demand for legality does not, however, stop there; it is now widely held that the mere fact that there is no one, save, perhaps, a representative of the public, who has an action should not necessarily prevent proceedings from being brought in respect of an actual or threatened disregard of the law.

This leads to the much-discussed question of the protection of diffuse interests,[28] a product of what has been called the 'massification' of society: individual actions may have adverse effects on large numbers of people belonging to some group or class, however identified, though not necessarily in respect of their traditional private rights.[29] The massification phenomenon has both led to and been encouraged by modern legislation relating to such diverse matters as employment rights, racial or sexual discrimination, the protection of the environment, and so on.

The enforcement of some of this legislation is entrusted to special agencies of one kind or another, and in some fields there is a positive desire to avoid involving the courts so far as possible. Nevertheless, growth of this kind of law, most of which is neither criminal in form nor private in the traditional sense, has brought a demand that individuals or groups – especially groups formed specifically for the purpose – should in proper cases be enabled to set the machinery of the courts in motion to ensure the maintenance of legality. As Lawton L.J. once said: 'Under the changing conditions of the modern world, in which there are powerful . . . bodies . . . whose activities affect the public generally, the time has come to look at the procedural rules of law which hitherto seem to have restricted the right of the ordinary citizen to complain about their activities.'[30]

In the United States, where the Constitution creates the possibility that even Congressional legislation may be unlawful and so enlarges the

---

[27] Above, p. 84.

[28] The subject is considered more fully in chaps. 5, 6 and 7.

[29] See, e.g. M. Cappelletti, 'Vindicating the Public Interest through the Courts: a Comparativist's Contribution' in Cappelletti and Garth, Vol. III, p. 513.

[30] *Attorney-General, ex. rel. McWhirter* v. *Independent Broadcasting Authority* [1973] Q.B. 629, 636. See further below, chap. 7, pp. 140–2 and contrast pp. 142–5.

competence of the courts, the idea of the public interest action has expanded;[31] one author has actually gone so far as to suggest that it is a waste of scarce resources to use the courts for the mere settlement of private disputes.[32] This extreme view is unlikely to represent majority opinion in the United States and certainly does not prevail in England, but we blind ourselves to reality if we believe that all that the civil courts do is to dispose of private disputes. The now received idea that law exists – and its accompanying demand that the courts should be available to those whose concern is, through the process of litigation, to uphold the law – is a healthy one and indeed a necessary one for the maintenance of a society ruled by law. It would be wrong, however, to deny the dilemma that this demand creates.

In its simplest form, the dilemma arises from the conflict between two policies or principles which, at least when stated generally, are of more or less equal value. On the one hand there is the policy represented by the demand for legality, which may be expressed shortly as the policy that no person or body should be permitted to act or continue to act unlawfully merely because no one possessed of a private right or *locus standi* decides to intervene. On the other hand, not only is it necessary to have some kind of filter or screening device to prevent the waste of time and money which absurd or frivolous allegations of unlawful conduct cannot fail to produce, it is also necessary to recognise that it is not always in the interests of society that the law should be rigorously enforced. This is true not only for genuinely private relationships which may be better handled otherwise than through strict adherence to the law, but also in many other spheres of societal activity for which a system of judicial review and scrutiny is inappropriate. Certain types of governmental activity, for example, at the lowest as well as the highest level, must as a practical matter be protected against the possibility of challenge on the ground of illegality: it is not necessarily enough to say that the law itself can be so formulated as to ensure that a challenge will fail.

In different countries, different devices are being tried to meet this dilemma. In France, for example, legislation specifically empowers certain organisations such as societies formed to combat racism or prostitution or for the protection of consumers to bring certain kinds of litigation,[33] and in Germany incentives in the form of reduced costs are

---

[31] See, e.g. A. Chayes, 'The Role of the Judge in Public Law Litigation' (1976) 89 Harv.L.R. 1281.

[32] O. M. Fiss, 'The Forms of Justice' (1979) 93 Harv.L.R. 1, 30.

[33] See below, chap. 6, p. 116.

offered to encourage certain kinds of action.[34] In the United States, where the public interest action is most highly developed, criteria of *locus standi* may be emerging from the decisions of the Supreme Court but there seem to be no clear principles,[35] while in England, although some progress may now have been made in relation to proceedings against public bodies, so far as other categories of potential defendant are concerned, the general attitude can only be described as a wish that the problem would go away. It will not. The dilemma exists and must be faced.

Conclusion

In a most valuable article on the nature of judicial process the Uruguayan jurist, Edouardo Couture, spoke of the action as civilisation's substitute for vengeance and said that in its modern form it consists in a 'legal power to resort to the court praying for something against the defendant'; as such it is a right of petition in the constitutional sense of that phrase.[36] This is an important statement, but it is incomplete, because we no longer accept the view that, the criminal law apart, the law does nothing in society but regulate relationships between individuals. Acceptance of the idea that action and right are distinct has brought with it a conception of the law as something existing and operating of its own force independently of the courts. Even if the metaphor of a legal environment is too far-fetched for some tastes, few people would be willing to assert today that there are no rights, no duties, until a court has by its judgment brought them into being; and few people would insist that no conduct which is not contrary to a penal law can be said to be unlawful unless and until a court has pronounced it to be so, and then only in relation to a specific individual.

It is not suggested that the changed perception of the law that has come about during the last 100 years or so as a consequence of the separation of action from right is alone responsible for the new demands that are now made on civil litigation in the courts. The vast changes in the nature of society, with its concentration of power in the hands of a variety of institutions, private as well as public, and the law explosion of modern times could not fail to bring in their train a demand that somehow or other the courts of law should do more than provide a forum for the settlement of private disputes on the terms in which the parties choose to put them. It is suggested, however, that our perception of the law as being *there*, all around us and capable of producing legal

[34] H. Kötz, 'Civil Litigation and the Public Interest' (1982) 1 C.J.Q. 237.
[35] See below, chap. 6, pp. 109–11.   [36] Couture, 'Judicial Process'.

consequences, is at least one of the explanations for the new demands that are being made, and for the demand for correctness and the demand for legality in particular.

These demands do not fit happily into the mould of civil litigation as traditionally conceived, and they undoubtedly create difficulties and dilemmas. Nevertheless, these new demands are good demands. They reveal an attitude to law which, though not free of fiction, is a healthy one that should be fostered; it should not be killed by the rejection of actions as inadmissible when the court's pronouncement on a question of public importance is required, and it should not be killed by excessive emphasis on the adversary character of civil litigation. The way ahead may not be easy, but the demand for correct decisions and the demand for legality must not be rejected out of hand.

Part II

Protection of diffuse, fragmented and collective interests

5   Introduction[1]

Intermediate rights

It has always been true that the activities of some members of society will produce harmful consequences for others, individually or as members of the public or of a section of the public; it has also always been true that the law and the courts have played an important role in the control of behaviour and the regulation of such redress as may be available to those harmed or threatened with harm. Until comparatively recently, however, it has been sufficient to allow access to the courts only to a representative of the public – Attorney-General, ministère public or other official body – where the right affected is 'public', and only to the affected individual, as 'owner' of the right, where it is 'private'. Now, however, changes in society itself and the law explosion of modern times have combined to create situations in which there is need to allow access to the courts on a wider basis. It is no longer sufficient to hold that only the official representative of the public, if anyone, may institute litigation where there is no private owner of a right able and willing to do so.

[1] Based on a commentary on a discussion at an International Congress on Procedural Law held in Würzburg, 12–17 September 1983, published in W. J. Habscheid (ed.), *Effektiver Rechtsschutz und verfassungsmässige Ordnung*, Vol. II (1984), p. 53. The discussion followed presentation of the General Report by Cappelletti and Garth and published in Habscheid, *Effektiver Rechtsschutz*, Vol. I (1983), p. 117 (reprinted in a revised form as 'Finding an Appropriate Compromise' in (1983) 2 C.J.Q. 111). On the subject generally, see, from the extensive literature, M. Cappelletti, 'Vindicating the Public Interest through the Courts' in his *The Judicial Process in Comparative Perspective* (1989), p. 268; W. B. Fisch, 'European Analogues to Class Actions' (1980) 27 Am.Jo.Comp. Law 51; H. Kötz, 'Public Interest Litigation: A Comparative Survey' in M. Cappelletti (ed.), *Access to Justice and the Welfare State* (1981), p. 85; H. Kötz, 'Civil Litigation and the Public Interest' (1982) 1 C.J.Q. 237. For a convenient discussion of some of the constitutional aspects of the matter, see D. Feldman, 'Public Interest Litigation and Constitutional Theory in Comparative Perspective' (1992) 55 M.L.R. 44. For a broad and simple comparative account, see V. Langer, 'Public Interest in Civil Law, Socialist Law, and Common Law Systems: the Role of the Public Prosecutor' (1988) 36 Am.Jo.Comp. Law 279.

The division between public and private rights has not yet reached the end of its useful life as an instrument of procedural law. On the contrary, even in a country such as England where the division has had much less practical effect in the past than on the continent of Europe or in countries whose law is of continental origin, it has become part of the language of practitioners as well as of academics. At the same time, however, it is coming increasingly to be appreciated that the division, however useful, can no longer be held to be all-inclusive: it is necessary to recognise the existence of rights which are neither public nor private but 'intermediate'.

So much is probably uncontroversial: there are few who would challenge the need for a concept of intermediate rights but, if there is consensus on what those rights are, it is only a consensus in broad and general terms. Perhaps most people agree that rights such as those created by environmental legislation should be included, and reference can be made to labour rights, civil rights and so on as rights of large categories, groups or classes of people. On the other hand, reference can also be made to the occasional use of the *actio popularis* as, for example, in Brazil where any citizen is qualified to bring a 'popular suit' for the annulment of acts which are detrimental to public assets.[2] It would be difficult to classify as intermediate the right protected by such proceedings.

It is, of course, possible, and it is today even common, to speak of interests or rights which are not recognised by the positive law of any jurisdiction, and certainly it is possible to speak of a right which is not recognised by the positive law of a particular jurisdiction. It is tempting, and it may even be admirable, to use the emotive language of rights with the object of encouraging their recognition by positive law, and in a comparative discussion it is almost inevitable that the word 'right' is used somewhat loosely; a right recognised in one jurisdiction may not be so in another. Nevertheless, it is imperative for present purposes that the temptation be resisted and that the procedural and the substantive be kept, so far as possible apart. It must be stressed that the subject for consideration is the protection, not the creation, of 'diffuse, fragmented and collective interests'.

It may be, especially in countries which formally recognise the rule *stare decisis*, that the distinction cannot always be maintained, for in protecting a court may simultaneously create. This does not detract, however, from the distinction's importance; if it is lost sight of, not only is discussion inevitably confused, but those who seek procedural change

---

[2] Cappelletti and Garth, 'General Report', p. 157, n. 165.

in order to improve the judicial protection of existing rights will meet opposition on the ground that their proposals are no more than proposals for political change in disguise.

The solution, it is believed, is to be found in recognition of the inadequacy in contemporary conditions of the distinction between public and private. Developments in modern society, the massification phenomenon,[3] the concern for the welfare of the weaker members of society, the desire to protect the environment in which we live, and so on, have led to the enactment of legislation which, by seeking to control conduct of certain kinds, creates correlative rights, but these rights are often rights without an owner. A Clean Air Act, for example, may create a right to breathe air that is not polluted beyond a given maximum, but to whom does the right belong?

The traditional answer is, probably, that such a right, if it exists, is public for the very reason that it has no obvious private owner. On this basis it is enforceable, if at all, only at the suit of a public authority in the civil or the criminal court as the case may be. It is, indeed, a feature of the legal life of many countries that a variety of state organs – not only the Attorney-General or his analogue – have been given by specific legislation the right to bring proceedings in the courts in certain categories of case if they consider it to be in the public interest that they should do so. It has become clear, however, that the proliferation of public authorities equipped with a power to institute proceedings is by itself insufficient to meet the need. This is due, in part, to the deficiencies inherent in a more or less bureaucratised organ of the state as an initiator of litigation – especially, but not only, when the prospective defendant is the state itself, a department of government, or a substantial organisation whose activities, even if of doubtful legality, government would prefer not to be inhibited.[4] It is due also to the fact that by no means all those rights seeking recognition as intermediate are capable even theoretically of classification as public.

The right to clean air may be public, but the right to be protected against, say, the sale of goods which are unfit for their purpose (if such a right exists), or against activities on neighbouring land which interfere unreasonably with the normal amenities of life, are not. Whether a seller sells one article or thousands, whether the offending neighbour is a private householder or a major chemical manufacturer, each and every affected individual has his private right for which, in case of infringement, he may seek judicial protection if he so chooses. Nevertheless,

---

[3] The phrase is Cappelletti's. See, e.g. his 'Vindicating the Public Interest through the Courts'.

[4] Cappelletti and Garth, 'General Report', p. 126.

though the right to redress from the court may be clear, the damage may be too small to warrant proceedings by an individual even if, as will not always be the case, he knows of his right at all. If, then, it is possible to speak of, for example, the rights of consumers, of householders or residents, even of television licence holders as in one English case,[5] such rights fall into the intermediate category because they have spilled over from the category of private rights, not from that of public rights: the category of intermediate rights has grown from both the traditional categories, not from one alone.

However widespread the dissatisfaction with the performance of official public representatives, it is not to be suggested that they achieve nothing by way of securing judicial protection of the rights and interests of groups and classes in society. Nor is it suggested that private litigation in the traditional form never achieves more than protection of the private right of the individual plaintiff which is, ostensibly, the court's sole concern. It is true, of course, that the judgment in such litigation operates as *res judicata* only with respect to the parties, but its practical consequences may be much more far-reaching. So, for example, the remedy granted may be future-oriented, as in the case of the issue of an injunction, and where this is so it is likely to benefit directly those who find themselves in the same situation as the plaintiff; again, in some cases punitive damages having effect as both a special and a general deterrent may be awarded. Most importantly of all, perhaps, once a decision has been given on the substantial question at issue, the defendant and others similarly placed are likely to respect the decision in their dealings with others even if they are not, strictly speaking, legally bound to do so.

It follows that there is overlap between the public and the private in their respective contributions to judicial protection of the interests of groups and classes within society, an overlap which is emphasised in countries in which the official representative of the public may intervene in private litigation if he considers it in the public interest for him to do so.

The principal theoretical weakness of litigation in the form of a private action as a means for protecting the rights of persons other than the nominal plaintiff is that the substance of the real question at issue can be considered by the court only at the suit of an individual who has interest – that is, generally, at the suit of one who can convincingly present himself as the owner of a private right. If the nominal plaintiff cannot do this, his action will be pronounced inadmissible or will be

---

[5] *Congreve* v. *Home Office* [1976] Q.B. 629. See below, chap. 7, p. 123.

summarily dismissed, which, for practical purposes, comes to the same thing.

Here, then, is one compelling reason for recognition of rights falling within the intermediate category. Under modern legislation it is by no means uncommon that a situation arises in which unlawful conduct causes or threatens to cause harm to the interests of many: those interests the legislation is intended to protect, and yet no single individual can claim sufficient private right to enable him to raise the matter before the court. If the official public representative does not accept that a public right is affected or if, for any reason, he fails to institute proceedings, the law can be disregarded with impunity.

In addition to this theoretical weakness, there are also various practical disadvantages to exclusive reliance on the traditional private action to supplement the activities of the official public representative, some of which may be briefly mentioned:

(1) It will not invariably be true that a defendant abides by the terms of a judgment that has been obtained against him by one individual when he comes to deal with others;

(2) The individual may often lack the resources necessary to make an effective case and to pursue the litigation vigorously against a powerful opponent. It is true that, sometimes, he may be supported by an association; he may even occasionally be no more than the puppet of an association. Nevertheless, where the interests of many are directly involved, their adequate representation should not be thus left to chance.

(3) In some cases, especially those in which the individual's personal claim is only for a small amount of money, the defendant may offer to meet his personal claim in full. It will be difficult, if not actually impossible, for the nominal plaintiff to refuse the offer, but, if he does accept it, the litigation will come to an immediate end and the principal question that it was intended to raise will not come before the court for judgment.

Other reasons could also be given in support of the view that it is no longer sufficient to allow access to the court only to official representatives of the public interest and to such individuals as can present themselves as owners of a private right, but enough has been said on this aspect for present purposes. It can, therefore, now be suggested that from the procedural point of view the characteristic of a right which falls into the intermediate category is, quite simply, that it is a right recognised by the positive law of the jurisdiction in question – at least as the correlative of a prohibition or requirement contained in that law – but is one of which judicial protection cannot be adequately secured if litigation is possible only in one of the two traditional forms. There is no need to go further, and proceduralists as such should not seek to go further. They should not attempt to specify the content of those rights: that is for the legislatures and other law-making authorities of the jurisdiction in question. In what follows, therefore, the phrase 'intermediate rights' will be used to refer to those diffuse, fragmented and collective interests which, in one way or another, are recognised by positive law as rights.

Procedural modes

If intermediate rights are given the meaning proposed, it follows that, for their judicial protection, access to the courts must be available to persons (including groups and associations) even though they can claim to be neither official representatives of the public nor owners of a private right. In some countries, but only for highly specific purposes, this is achieved occasionally by the creation of an *actio popularis* so that anyone, regardless of qualification or interest, may initiate litigation: one instance has already been mentioned, and others can be found.[6]

No one has suggested, however, that the *actio popularis* might be appropriate in all circumstances, and it probably has a limited future, if any. The relator action of some common law countries does, it is true, create the possibility that an individual who has no personal interest in the subject matter of the litigation may initiate proceedings, for a relator action is brought on the initiative of an individual but in the name of the Attorney-General whose standing is not realistically open to challenge. On the other hand, obviously, the relator can only act in the name of the Attorney-General if he has the Attorney-General's consent to do so, and it is for the Attorney-General alone to decide in each case whether to allow his name to be used and the litigation to be instituted. The relator action is thus not an *actio popularis* in the sense usually ascribed to that term, namely, an action exercisable as of right by *quivis de populo*.

In theory, at least, the relator action appears well adapted for the protection of intermediate rights for it is itself a mixture of public and private elements. It suffers, however, from the inherent defect that the exercise of his discretion by the Attorney-General is open to review only in Parliament and, save in answer to a parliamentary question, he need give no reasons for his decision to allow or refuse to allow proceedings to be brought. Another method, much used in continental Europe and

[6] See, e.g. M. Cappelletti, 'Governmental and Private Advocates for the Public Interest in Civil Litigation: a Comparative Study' in Cappelletti and Garth, Vol. II, p. 767 at p. 822, n. 26, and pp. 857–60; Kötz, 'Public Interest Litigation', at pp. 110–11.

elsewhere, that also combines public and private elements is the so-called 'Verbandsklage' – proceedings brought by an association which was formed for the purpose of protecting interests of a given character and to which the legislature has given authority to take proceedings. Here the public element does not impinge upon the decision whether proceedings should be brought or not on a particular occasion, but only those associations which qualify under the legislation may bring proceedings at all; and, since the legislation normally requires that an approved association shall have been in existence for not less than a certain minimum period of time, the *Verbandsklage*, unlike the relator action, cannot respond if the interests under attack or threat are not already covered by the statutes of an established and approved association.

One of the advantages of the *Verbandsklage* over the relator action is that under the former procedure the association which appears as plaintiff is likely to be better endowed with the expertise and resources necessary for what may be complex and lengthy litigation, than an individual relator who may or may not have an association behind him. If, however, a specialised agency of government charged with the administration of certain legislation is given explicit power to bring proceedings, both expertise and resources should be assured. It is not surprising, therefore, that such agencies should now be common in many countries or that they should contribute significantly to the protection of certain kinds of intermediate right such as the right of minority groups not to be subjected to unlawful discriminatory practices. Experience suggests, however, that such governmental agencies tend sometimes to lose motivation, to become bureaucratised, to be subjected to the will of government itself although theoretically independent, or even to be captured by those whose activities it is their business to control. The remark of the eighteenth-century writer, Pietro Verri, that *'les derniers qui voyent clair les intérêts de la société sont pour l'ordinaire ceux qui sont payés pour les voir'*[7] applies as much to specialised as to non-specialised agencies of government.

The mode of proceeding by a specialised government agency has no private element in its composition. The exact converse is true of the final mode of proceeding to be mentioned here, namely, the class action, especially the class action for damages as developed in the United States under rule 23 of the Federal Rules of Civil Procedure. This mode of proceeding is not dependent on the initiative or consent of a public authority, nor is it dependent upon the existence of any established and interested association; unlike the other modes of proceeding mentioned

[7] *Pensées détachées*, cited in Cappelletti and Jolowicz, p. 93.

here, it is capable of obtaining monetary compensation for all those who have suffered damage in consequence of the defendant's unlawful conduct. Indeed, it is even capable of imposing upon the defendant a liability in excess of the aggregate of the losses proved to have been suffered by individuals. This happens if the damages are assessed, as they may be, not by reference to those losses but by reference to the total damage caused by the defendant or to the total of the 'illicit' profit he has made.

If the class action does no more than bring into a single action a number of individual claims in such manner that the representative plaintiff represents a number of individuals, each of whom is the owner of a private right, then it may be regarded as no more than a mode of proceeding within the traditional private sphere: more efficiently and more economically than a series of actions, each brought by the individual owner of a right, it secures for each owner what is his due. Even so, it may be thought also to contribute to the protection of the interests of the class of injured persons as a whole; the availability of the class action procedure, by providing the economies of scale, makes the institution of proceedings more likely when the defendant's conduct has caused damage to numerous individuals but the loss suffered by each of them is small. Where the damages awarded against the defendant exceed the losses suffered by identified individuals, on the other hand – when it is known that a balance of the fund of damages will remain after all known losses have been compensated – then the class action becomes more than a procedural device of traditional private law: it contains an element of punishment or deterrence.

It is true that traditional private litigation may also contain an element of deterrence, and it has been argued that the class action should not be regarded as penal even when the damages awarded are greater than the sum of the proved losses: the defendant, it is said, is not punished by being compelled to give up his unlawful gains but is only restored to the position in which he would have been had he not acted unlawfully. The fact remains, however, that the class action for damages, more than the other modes of proceeding which have been mentioned, risks crossing the line between the protection and the creation of intermediate rights: if the law provides that a person who has suffered damage is entitled to compensation from the person who has caused it, it may follow, but it does not necessarily follow, that the law's intention is to prevent that conduct so far as possible and thereby to create a right that such conduct shall not occur.

The question, in essence, is whether the law under consideration does more than create a remedial right. The concept of a law which does no more than provide redress in the event of breach is more readily accepted in the common law than in other systems, but it is not unique to the common law: it would be, at best, a strained interpretation of, say, article 1644 of the French civil code, to conclude from the fact that the buyer of goods which have a concealed defect is given a remedy against the seller that there is thereby created an intermediate right that goods suffering from concealed defects shall not be put on the market. If in a class action against the seller of such goods the seller were to be required to do more than compensate those buyers whose individual cases against him had been proved, an intermediate right would have been created, not protected. It is a truism that few wise men would want all laws enforced in all circumstances, and this applies with particular force to laws that are not even intended to be enforced but only to create private rights to compensation if damage should occur.

Legitimation, due process and informed decisions

It is a corollary of recognition of intermediate rights that if proceedings are to be brought for their protection, those proceedings must be brought by a representative. This leads some to question the legitimacy of the representative, whether individual or association: but that is to miss the point. The representative's role is not to decide but only to raise a question for decision: the decision is for the court. It is, no doubt, possible to challenge the legitimacy of the courts themselves, for judges are rarely elected democratically, but that challenge goes to the entire judicial system and proves too much.

It does not follow from this, however, that whosoever presents himself as representative must necessarily be heard by the court and judgment given to the effect that his allegations of unlawful conduct on the defendant's part are well- or ill-founded. Such a decision, once given, may have far-reaching effect as *res judicata*, and if it does not it is still likely to have extensive consequences as a precedent. Even if provision is made for intervention in the litigation by other interested parties, by the Attorney-General or other public representative, or by an amicus curiae, therefore, the plaintiff, or would-be plaintiff, must still satisfy the court that certain minimum requirements can be fulfilled. These requirements, it may be suggested, include the following:

(1) That the question to be raised is justiciable.
(2) That the would-be plaintiff himself is qualified adequately to represent the interests of all those (other than the proposed defendant) who will be bound by the decision as *res judicata* and

that such steps can and will be taken as are reasonable to bring the existence of the proceedings to their attention. It may be inevitable that some of the traditional rules of due process are modified if intermediate rights are to be protected in the courts, but they must not be destroyed; if a person is to be bound by a decision as *res judicata*, he should at least have notice of the proceedings unless it is virtually impossible to reach him.

(3) That the would-be plaintiff himself, whether individual or association, has sufficient interest in the subject matter and the outcome of the proposed litigation to ensure adequate argument of the issues.[8]

As a practical matter it will almost certainly be necessary that the court, in preliminary proceedings, shall satisfy itself that these and other necessary conditions are met, much as, now, it is for the courts in the United States to decide whether an action may be maintained as a class action under rule 23 of the Federal Rules of Civil Procedure. This amounts, in general terms, to a requirement that the would-be plaintiff first apply to the court for leave to proceed but, while care must of course be taken not to restrict access to the court unnecessarily, there is nothing objectionable or novel in such a requirement. In any event, it is logically inevitable that, in the last resort, only the court itself can decide whether it should or should not accept jurisdiction in a given case, and there is no reason why that should not be put to use.

If this is right, it follows that in litigation intended to protect an intermediate right the court must be directly involved at the outset and since, by definition, more is at stake in the litigation than the private interests of the nominal plaintiff and defendant, litigation to protect intermediate rights cannot fail to place additional burdens on the court, at least as compared with private litigation conducted in accordance with the adversarial procedure of the common law. If litigation of that kind can still be regarded as little more than a contest between the parties, the same is certainly not true when intermediate rights are in issue: at the very least it must be the duty of the court to see that it has the information it considers necessary to the proper consideration and decision of the questions raised, for its role is more than the mere resolution of a dispute between the parties.

---

[8] *Baker* v. *Carr* 369 U.S. 186, 204 (1963), *per* Brennan J., cited in chap. 6, below, p. 110.

Conclusion

It has been stressed above that what is under consideration is the protection, not the creation, of intermediate rights and that for present purposes 'right' must be given a restricted meaning: it must be understood as, at the least, the correlative of a prohibition or control imposed by positive law. Even so, questions of policy cannot be wholly excluded from consideration by the courts, if only because the positive law will sometimes leave questions of policy unanswered. It has been suggested, therefore, that one of the matters for consideration should be the relationship between the protection of certain diffuse or fragmented interests, such as the interests of ecologists or consumers, through the judicial process, on the one hand, and their protection through the political process on the other. That, however, seems to be in itself a political rather than a legal question and so not one with which procedural lawyers, in their capacity as such, should be concerned, however much it may concern them personally or professionally in other capacities.

'The working assumption of a paper on the representation of diffuse interests in the courts, needless to say, must be that the courts have an appropriate role to play in enforcing the kind of rights involved with such representation';[9] it must also be the working assumption that the word 'rights' is used as a lawyer, not as a politician or, still less, a demagogue, would use it. It may be that the judges of a particular nation will develop as well as protect the diffuse, fragmented and collective interests that call for recognition as intermediate rights in contemporary society, but if and in so far as they do so, it will be under the circumstances and conditions which prevail in the legal and political systems of the nation whose judges they are; comparative law must play a part if such development is to occur, but it will be to the substantive, not to the procedural, law of other nations that the judges will turn.

The comparatively restricted and, it is hoped, apolitical, approach that is here preferred does not carry with it the implication that there is need for only limited procedural reform. The fact is that in every developed country, and in the international community, the positive law of today has created numerous rights which cannot be classified realistically as either private or public and which now go by default for lack of protection in the courts. No court can initiate proceedings of its own accord, new sources of initiative must be found and tested, and no single solution is likely, alone, to meet the need. Caution is necessary, as the

---

[9] Cappelletti and Garth, 'General Report', p. 153.

values inherent in the traditional division between the public and the private must not be wantonly discarded. It is, however, now time that the demand for the judicial protection of intermediate rights should be met with a positive response and that such evolution and adaptation of procedural law as has so far taken place should be studied, systematised and developed.

6   Aspects of U.S. and French law

The United States

'Public interest actions'

Though the Attorney-General may bring proceedings himself, the 'relator action' as known in England[1] and a number of other common law countries has not developed in the United States. For the ordinary plaintiff the basic rule used to be that only a person who could allege the infringement of a legal right of his own had the necessary 'standing' to bring civil proceedings.[2] This meant, for all practical purposes, that he must allege damage to himself and that, on the face of things, left little room for 'unselfish' litigation. In 1940, however, a licensed radio station challenged the legality of the grant of a licence to a rival station. The plaintiff's motivation is unlikely to have been unselfish and the legislation was not intended to protect radio stations from competition. Nevertheless, the action was entertained because, in the Supreme Court's opinion, judicial scrutiny of the action of the licensing authority was in the public interest, and yet only persons likely to be injured financially would have an incentive to bring errors on the part of the authority to the attention of the courts.[3]

The idea of harnessing a person's desire to obtain a personal benefit which would, at best, be no more than an unintended byproduct of the law, in order to have matters of public interest brought before the courts, led to the theory that 'injury in fact' – which does not require the infringement of a legal right – will suffice where there is thought to be need for the intervention, in the public interest, of a 'private attorney-

---

[1] Chap. 7, p. 135.

[2] *Tennessee Electric Power Co.* v. *TVA*, 306 U.S. 118 (1939).

[3] *Federal Communications Commission* v. *Sanders Brothers Radio Station* 309 U.S. 470 (1940). The legislation allowed for judicial review at the suit of a person 'aggrieved or whose interests are adversely affected'.

general'.[4] Such an approach to 'standing' does meet the requirement, itself based on the constitutional restriction of the judicial power to the determination of 'cases and controversies',[5] that the person claiming relief must have 'such a personal stake in the outcome as to assure that concrete adverseness which sharpens the presentation of issues upon which the court so largely depends for illumination of difficult . . . questions'.[6]

Even so, 'injury in fact' leads to a generous, perhaps an overgenerous, approach to standing,[7] and some courts have felt the need to impose restrictions. For example, it has been said to be necessary that the interest to be protected must be 'arguably within the zone of interest protected or regulated by the statute or constitutional guarantee in question'.[8] It has even been said that a federal court's jurisdiction can be invoked only by a person who has himself suffered 'some threatened or actual injury resulting from the putatively illegal action',[9] which seems to hark back to the earlier law and, if taken at face value, to mean that 'unselfish' litigation can be instituted only by those who would be in a position to litigate 'selfishly' if they so wished.

The fact is that clear principles are difficult if not impossible to find in the decisions and that standing falls to be determined on a case-by-case basis. This means that the matter actually rests in the discretion of the court, a position which has not gone uncriticised.[10] As suggested below in relation to English law, however, for so long as the criterion of standing rests formally on injury or damage suffered by the plaintiff, it is impossible to deprive the court of the power to decide in each case whether the damage alleged by the plaintiff is sufficient to give him

[4] The phrase 'private attorney-general' was coined by Jerome Frank J. in *Associated Industries* v. *Ickes* 320 U.S. 707 (1943). See B. Garth, H. H. Nagel and S. J. Plager, 'The Institution of the Private Attorney-General: Perspectives from an Empirical Study of Class Action Litigation' (1988) 61 Southern Calif.L.R. 353.
[5] Constitution of the United States, Art. III.
[6] *Baker* v. *Carr* 369 U.S. 186, 204 (1963), *per* Brennan J.
[7] E.g. *Flast* v. *Cohen* 392 U.S. 83 (1968); *Trafficante* v. *Metropolitan Life Insurance Co.* 409 U.S. 205 (1972); *U.S.* v. *Students Challenging Regulatory Agency Procedures* 412 U.S. 669 (1973).
[8] *Association of Data Processing Organisations* v. *Camp* 397 U.S. 150 (1970); *Sierra Club* v. *Morton* 405 U.S. 722 (1972).
[9] *Linda R.S.* v. *Richard D.* 410 U.S. 614 (1973), *per* Marshall J., cited in *Worth* v. *Seldin* 422 U.S. 490 (1975). See also, amongst later cases, *Air Courier Conference of America* v. *American Postal Workers Union, AFL-CIO* 498 U.S. 517 (1991); *Lujan* v. *Defenders of Wildlife* 119 L.Ed 2d 351 (1992).
[10] E.g. Brennan J., dissenting, in *Simon* v. *Eastern Kentucky Welfare Rights Organisation* 426 U.S. 26 (1976) and in *Allen* v. *Wright* 468 U.S. 737 (1984). The lack of clear criteria of standing may result in disagreement between the judges at different levels, with the unfortunate result that a plaintiff may, after years of litigation, finally be told that he cannot maintain his action: *Allen* v. *Wright, ibid.*

standing and thereby to assume or decline jurisdiction. The result, where the plaintiff's standing as a litigant is open to serious question, is in reality that the court is likely to be influenced by its determination that the question of law raised in the action should, or, as the case may be, should not, be dealt with in those proceedings.[11]

Class actions[12]

From beginnings little more suggestive of potential for expansion than those in England,[13] the class action in the United States has developed into a form of procedure which is capable not only of dealing collectively with large numbers of individual claims, but also of penalising or deterring unlawful conduct that directly affects the diffuse and fragmented interests of groups (including the interests, or supposed interests, of the public at large).

Originally available only in Equity (and therefore not in actions for damages), representative litigation was authorised by a Supreme Court Equity Rule of 1842 for use where the parties were very numerous, but it was also provided that 'absent parties' should not be bound by the outcome of the litigation.[14] The Federal Rules of Civil Procedure, introduced in 1938, replaced the old rule with a less restrictive, but extremely complex, rule for class actions, and that rule was completely

---

[11] See, e.g. *Trafficante* v. *Metropolitan Life Insurance Co.*, 409 U.S. 205 (1972) and *Duke Power Co.* v. *Carolina Environment Study Group* 438 U.S. 59 (1978), in both of which cases the formal justifications for allowing the actions to proceed are unconvincing but the matters at issue were important. The same may be said for the English case of *Gillick* v. *W. Norfolk AHA* [1986] A.C. 112. The proposition in the text is supported by the use and uncertain status of the subsidiary criterion of 'ripeness': G. R. Nichol, 'Ripeness and the Constitution' (1987) 54 U. of Chi.L.R. 153. A. Homburger, 'Private Suits in the Public Interest in the United States of America' (1974) 23 Buffalo L.R. 343, has proposed that a 'functional' approach concentrating on the issue rather than on the person raising it should be adopted, an idea echoed in Woolf Final, p. 255 so far as applications for judicial review are concerned.

[12] Yeazell provides an excellent account of the history and modern law. For a critique of this work, sustaining different views on certain aspects, see R. G. Bone, 'Personal and Impersonal Litigative Forms: Reconceiving the History of Adjudicative Representation' (1990) 70 Boston L.R. 213. See also the Report on Class Actions of the Ontario Law Commission (1982).

[13] Below, chap. 7, p. 130. A class action was available only in cases involving a 'common or general interest of many persons': New York 'Field' code of 1848 as amended 1849, cited in H. P. Glenn 'The Dilemma of Class Action Reform' (1986) 6 O.J.L.S. 262.

[14] Rule 48, cited in Yeazell, p. 221, n. 20. In *Smith* v. *Swormstedt* 57 U.S. (16 How.) 288 (1853) (cited Yeazell, *ibid.*) the Supreme Court seems nevertheless to have held that its decision bound absentees, a result ultimately approved in a revised rule (rule 38) of 1912. The problem of the *res judicata* effect of class actions on 'absentees' has bedevilled their history but is not directly relevant to the subject matter of this chapter.

rewritten in 1966.[15] As it now stands, the rule contemplates that a class action may be authorised where the class is too numerous for all its members to be joined, where there are questions of law or fact common to the class, where the claims or defences of the representative parties are typical of those of the class members, and where the representative parties will fairly protect the interests of the class.

If these conditions are met, the court may certify a case for class action procedure under its control in three sets of circumstances: where separate actions by or against members of the class might lead to inconsistency of decision;[16] where the claim is primarily for injunctive or declaratory relief affecting all class members;[17] where the claims of class members have questions of fact or law in common which 'predominate over any question affecting only individual members'. In the third of these cases it is a further requirement that a class action is 'superior to available methods of fair and efficient adjudication of the controversy'.[18]

Although the second, if not also the first, of these categories is certainly capable of use, and has not infrequently been used, in attempts to promote the interests of a group rather than of a number of individuals,[19] it is the third which allows for class actions for damages, the category that is probably the most controversial.[20] Though there are advantages to a plaintiff seeking injunctive or declaratory relief if he can act as a class representative rather than as an individual, if the relief is granted it will benefit all those affected by the defendant's unlawful conduct whether they are formally represented or not.[21] Damages, on the other hand, can only be recovered under a judgment by those who are parties to it.

Difficult though a large class action for damages may be to manage, if and in so far as the procedure does no more than bring together a number of individual claims which would otherwise be brought separately, it does not directly impinge on the subject matter of this chapter.

---

[15] Fed.R.Civ.P. 23. A similar rule has been adopted in many states. The literature is vast, and only a tiny proportion of it can be referred to in what follows.

[16] Fed.R.Civ.P. 23(b)(1).   [17] *Ibid.*, 23(b)(2).   [18] *Ibid.*, 23(b)(3).

[19] *Allen* v. *Wright*, 468 U.S. 737 (1984), for example, was brought as a 'nationwide class action suit', on behalf of parents of black children at public schools undergoing desegregation, against the Federal Government and the Internal Revenue Service. It was alleged that the latter had not adopted appropriate standards and procedures in the performance of its obligation to deny tax-exempt status to racially discriminatory private schools.

[20] In contemporary conditions it may also be the most important since it is one of the procedural methods for handling cases of 'mass torts'. See J. B. Weinstein, *Individual Justice in Mass Tort Litigation: The Effect of Class Actions, Consolidation and other Multiparty Devices* (1995).

[21] Non-parties cannot rely on or be bound by the judgment as *res judicata*, but this will not necessarily detract from the practical effectiveness of the judgment.

A class action for damages does, however, have the potential of doing more than simply compensate the victims of the defendant's unlawful conduct: it may impose a monetary sanction on the defendant that he would not otherwise suffer. In the first place, by bringing numerous claims together in a single set of proceedings, the class action for damages makes it possible to litigate claims none of which, individually, is of sufficient value to justify proceedings on its own: from a purely legal point of view the defendant is compelled to pay only what he ought to pay, but were a class action not available he would not in fact be compelled to pay anything. In the second place, and most obviously where the plaintiff class includes unidentified as well as identified members, as it may,[22] the result is so to increase the potential liability of the defendant as to give the proceedings a punitive or deterrent as well as a compensatory function. In one famous case, for example, where the representative plaintiff was personally entitled to recover as damages no more than a few hundred dollars, he claimed to represent some 6 million people, of whom 3.75 million were unidentified, and all of whom had suffered similar losses from the defendants' unlawful conduct. If the action had succeeded as a class action,[23] the defendants' liability would have been for more than 35 million dollars. Nothing like that amount could have been distributed as damages, but the defendants would have been deprived of their 'ill-gotten' gains[24] and the money recovered allocated to other purposes.[25]

The years following introduction of the 1966 rule saw a great increase in the number of class actions. They also saw the emergence of a lively controversy between those who welcomed a procedural device which is capable of use as a civil law enforcement measure for the 'punishment'

---

[22] This is implicit in the provisions for notice of the proceedings in Fed.R.Civ.P. 23(c)(2).

[23] It ultimately foundered on the rock of the requirement under Fed.R.Civ.P. 23(c)(2) that the plaintiff serve individual notice on the 2.25 million class members who could be identified, and that he could not afford to do.

[24] Chap. 4, p. 89.

[25] *Eisen* v. *Carlisle and Jacquelin* 417 U.S. 156 (1974). See also, e.g. *Daar* v. *Yellow Cab Co.* 67 Cal. 2d 695 (1967) where the class consisted of people who had been overcharged for cab fares over a period of three years. The action was settled on the basis that the company would reduce cab fares for a fixed period in the future. They were deprived of their illegal profits, but the advantage accrued to future customers, not to those who had overpaid in the past. Only six years after introduction of the 1966 rule, complaint was made of the excessive pressure on the defendant to settle which is created by the mere authorisation of a class action (W. Simon, 'Class Actions – Useful Tool or Engine of Destruction' 55 F.R.D. 375, 389 (1973)) and support for this view has now come from the courts. In *Re Rhone-Poulenc Rorer Inc.* 51 F. 3d 1293 (7th Cir.), cert. denied, 116 S.Ct. 184 (1995), it was actually held that, in the circumstances of that case and considering the difficulties of the plaintiffs' case, the pressure on the defendants to settle would be so great that authorisation of class proceedings was inappropriate. Cf. Note (1996) 109 Harv.L.R. 870.

and deterrence of wrongdoers, and those who insisted that the class action should not 'serve the purpose of policing business misconduct or punishing wrongdoers'; it should be used only as a procedural device for the achievement of economy.[26] For some time, the former view was in the ascendant,[27] but more recently it seems that the tide has turned and the popularity of class actions has declined.

The shift of opinion, if it has, indeed, occurred, is probably due in part to the procedural complexities of massive class actions and to the contradictions between individual and collective interests inherent in them.[28] It may be due also, however, to the fact that the class action has proved incapable of achieving the ends sought by its most enthusiastic supporters. It has even been said by some that while defendants tend to resist authorisation of class actions on behalf of large numbers of small claimants because without authorisation no claims would be brought at all, where individual damages are sufficiently large to make claims by individuals realistic, defendants welcome class actions as likely to lead to more favourable settlements overall.[29] One commentator on the American (and the Canadian) law has concluded that 'Effective class action reform, like other forms of Utopian social engineering, is impossible' and that it is time to move on to other tasks.[30]

France[31]

It was noticed earlier that in France there are two distinct jurisdictions – the 'ordre judiciaire', which deals with civil and criminal matters, and the 'ordre administratif', which deals with public law matters.[32] Their respective attitudes to 'unselfish' litigation call for separate consideration.

---

[26] Compare, for example, the view expressed by J. B. Weinstein, 'Some Reflections on the "Abusiveness" of Class Actions' 58 F.R.D. 299 (1973) and that expressed by E. S. Labowitz, 'Class Actions in the Federal System and in California: Shattering the Impossible Dream' (1974) 23 Buffalo L.R. 601.

[27] E.g. Note, 'Developments – Class Actions' (1976) 89 Harv.L.R. 1318. It may still be so for class actions in respect of breaches of securities or anti-trust legislation: J. C. Coffee, 'Class Wars: The Dilemma of the Mass Tort Class Action' (1995) 95 Colum.L.R. 1343.

[28] E.g. Coffee, 'Class Wars'; Glenn, 'The Dilemma of Class Action Reform'. Cf. Weinstein, 'Some Reflections'.

[29] Coffee, 'Class Wars', at p. 1351. See also *ibid.* at p. 1355 where the suggestion is made that, in mass tort cases, neither the goal of deterrence nor that of corrective justice is realised.

[30] Glenn, 'The Dilemma of Class Action Reform'.

[31] For Germany, see H. Kötz, 'Civil Litigation and the Public Interest' (1982) 1 C.J.Q. 237; H. Koch, 'Class and Public Interest Actions in German Law' (1986) C.J.Q. 66.

[32] Chap. 1, p. 18.

The ordre judiciaire[33]

Given the separate existence of the *ordre administratif*, it is a matter of general principle as well as of practice that the business of the civil courts is to deal with ('selfish') litigation between private persons pursuing their own interests, and the same is broadly true for the 'action civile' – the civil action based on a criminal offence:[34] *pas d'intérêt, pas d'action.* So, for ordinary civil proceedings, a party must have an existing and legitimate interest in the success or defeat of a claim or defence,[35] while the *action civile* is open only to the victim of an offence who has personally suffered damage directly caused by the offence.[36]

As an obstacle to the development of unselfish litigation, the requirement of interest is reinforced by two other rules, first that of the 'relativity' of *res judicata*, according to which only the parties to a judgment are bound by it,[37] and, secondly, the rule *nul ne plaide par procureur.*[38] Even the legislative recognition that the ministère public,[39] whose main role is the prosecution of crime, has power to bring civil proceedings in the public interest in certain circumstances, is criticised as inappropriate.[40] On the other hand, the existence of that power tends to reinforce the idea that it is for public authority, not for private persons or associations, to act in the public interest – usually called 'intérêt général' rather than 'intérêt public'.

Trade unions and professional associations
Despite this unpromising background, and despite a leading decision of 1913 denying the right of an association to institute an *action civile* in

---

[33] See S. Guinchard, 'L'action de groupe' (1990) Rev.int.dr.comp. 599; J. Pradel, *Procédure pénale*, 7th edn (1993) nos. 219 *et seq.*

[34] Chap. 1, p. 15.   [35] N.c.p.c., art. 31.

[36] C.p.c. art. 2.   [37] Code civil, art. 1351.

[38] For a hostile account of this maxim and arguments in favour of introducing the class action into French law, see F. Caballero, 'Plaidons par procureur! De l'archaïsme procédural à l'action de groupe' (1985) Rev.trim.dr.civ. 247. Cf. Glenn, 'A propos de la maxime "Nul ne plaide par procureur"' (1988) Rev.trim.dr.civ. 59.

[39] The origins of the ministère public bear a certain resemblance to those of the English law officers of the Crown, but its modern form is very different. It is a large organisation, headed by the minister of justice, and its officers are *magistrats*, as also are the judges. For brief descriptions see A. West *et al.*, *The French Legal System* (1992), pp. 223–8; R. Perrot, *Institutions Judiciaires*, 5th edn (1993), nos. 301–16.

[40] E.g. Perrot, *Institutions Judiciaires*, no. 312. The rule now in force (n.c.p.c., arts. 422–3) states that, over and above cases specifically provided for by statute, the ministère public may initiate civil proceedings for the protection of 'ordre public' on the occurrence of events which put it at risk. The earlier formula dated from a law of 1810 and was more restrictive. For the leading case, see civ. 17 December 1913, S. 1914, 1, 153.

respect of an offence against public decency,[41] the same year also saw a decision admitting the right of a professional association – an association for the defence of French wine-making – to bring such an action against a defendant accused of selling watered wine. It was held that the action was not to protect the individual interests of the wine-grower members of the association – which would have offended the rule *nul ne plaide par procureur*[42] – but to protect the collective interests of wine growers as a whole, as represented by the association.[43] In 1920 the effect of this decision was adopted by statute and is now enshrined in the code of labour law. 'Syndicats professionnels', that is, trade unions and professional associations, can exercise the rights of a *partie civile* in respect of conduct harmful to the collective interest of the trade or profession they represent.[44]

Use of the concept of collective interest, vague though it may be, implies that the *syndicat* cannot act if the interest affected is either individual to its members – in which case they must act individually – or is 'general' – in which case only the ministère public can act. Subject to what is said below about non-professional associations, the exclusive right of the ministère public to act is preserved where only the *intérêt général* is affected. It has been recognised, however, that there may be overlap between the *intérêt général* and the *intérêt collectif*; where this occurs, both ministère public and *syndicat* may act.[45] In addition, in certain specific situations, a *syndicat* is given power, by statute, to act so as to protect the collective interests of its members[46] or even, exceptionally, of persons not its members.[47]

Other associations

Associations formed with the specific object of protecting their members from certain kinds of damage may be able to take collective action in the civil courts,[48] but even that is not possible in the criminal courts where

[41] Crim. 25 July 1913, D. 1915, 1, 150.
[42] An objection which seems not to have troubled a different Chamber of the Cour de cassation a few years later: below, n. 48.
[43] Ch. réunies, 5 April 1913, D.P. 1914, 1, 65.
[44] C. trav., art. L. 411–11.
[45] E.g. Crim. 22 January 1970, D. 1970, 166.
[46] E.g. to protect the equal rights of men and women in employment: C. trav., art. L. 123–6.
[47] A trade union of workshop employees may act on behalf of home workers: C. trav., art. L. 721–19.
[48] Civ. 23 July 1918, D.P. 1918, 1, 52. This was not a class action for damages as known in the United States. Subject to one exception (below, p. 118) such an action is unknown in France. See, e.g. J. Héron, *Droit judiciaire privé* 1991, nos. 76–82; R. Martin and J. Martin, 'L'action collective' J.C.P. 1984, I, 3162. Rather, the association does collectively that which its members could do in their own right. For a

the *action civile* is open only to persons directly injured by the offence.[49] As might be expected, therefore, actions by associations formed to pursue what are sometimes called 'grandes causes'[50] – that is, in effect, matters of general public concern – are, in principle, inadmissible. Not only does an association formed, for example, to combat racism, not have the 'interest' necessary to bring proceedings in its own name for unlawful discrimination against members of a minority group, but, at least where a criminal offence is involved, that is exactly the kind of case which falls to the ministère public.[51] Even where no criminal offence is involved and the matter is therefore entirely civil, the absence of 'interest' stands in the way of proceedings by an association, and this has been held by the Cour de cassation to be fatal.[52]

The general principle denying the right of action of associations can, of course, be overturned by legislation. This has been done for a wide variety of associations by a series of distinct acts of legislation, some now incorporated into the code of criminal procedure.[53] To benefit from such legislation an association must, normally, have been in existence for a number of years and must, by its statutes, exist to pursue a particular approved objective. So, for example, an association of at least five years' standing whose statutory objective is to combat racism enjoys the rights of a *partie civile* in relation to offences of unlawful racial discrimination.[54] Similarly, an association for the protection or assistance of the disabled can act as *partie civile* in cases of discrimination against them or in cases of infringement of provisions of the building code concerning access to certain types of building.[55]

It is difficult to find a connecting link between the many types of

suggestion for the adaptation of the class action to French conditions, see Martin, 'Le recours collectif au Québec et prospective pour la France' J.C.P. 1986, I, 3255. For an account of the American class action in juxtaposition with the possibilities of its introduction in Italy, see R. B. Cappalli and C. Consolo, 'Class Actions for Continental Europe? A Preliminary Inquiry' (1993) 6 *Temple International and Comparative Law Journal* 217.

[49] Crim. 16 December 1954, D. 1955, 287. As is usually, but not invariably, the case where there is a partie civile, damages were claimed in this case.

[50] E.g. Guinchard, 'L'action de groupe', no. 35; L. Cadiet, *Droit Judiciaire Privé* (1992) no. 732. These associations are also known as 'associations à but désintéressé'.

[51] Guinchard, 'L'action de groupe', no. 43, see n. 33.

[52] Civ. 1re 16 January 1985, D. 1985, 317. Statute allowed the association in question to exercise the *action civile*. This, the court held, was insufficient to permit an action by the association for breach of contractual obligations by the defendant, and, there being no statutory authorisation, the action was inadmissible for lack of interest. See also Ch. réunies, 15 June 1923, *Cardinal Luçon*, D.P. 1924, 1, 153, Héron, *Droit judiciaire privé*, no. 74. Even so, some courts have admitted civil actions by associations for the protection of a *grande cause*: Guinchard, 'L'action de groupe', nos. 36, 46–55.

[53] C.p.p., arts. 2–1 to 2–15.

[54] *Ibid.*, art. 2–1.   [55] *Ibid.*, art. 2–8.

association to which the rights of a *partie civile* have been given, and they cannot be listed here. Their objectives range from the pursuit of crimes against humanity,[56] through protection of the environment[57] to defence of the French language;[58] they include associations having such diverse purposes as the protection of fishing[59] and the fight against proxenitism.[60] Mention must, however, be made of consumer associations whose right to act for the protection of consumer interests was introduced by the 'Loi Royer' in 1973. The scope of this right was enlarged in 1988 and the law is now codified.[61]

Under this law, an accredited consumer association can act as *partie civile* where an offence causes direct or indirect damage to collective consumer interests. It can also take action in the civil courts for damages where damage is caused to consumers as a group by breaches of contract, or, subject to certain quite restrictive conditions, as representative of identified injured consumers.[62] More importantly, perhaps, and either by intervention in an ongoing action brought by a consumer or on its own initiative, an association may seek an order that continuing unlawful conduct on the part of the defendant should cease, or that an unlawful or 'abusive' exclusion clause should no longer be included in a standard form contract.

This comes as close as anything in France to a class action, for it operates to the advantage of the entire class of consumers, but even so it lacks the characteristics of a true class action. The association, as plaintiff, does not represent consumers as parties to the litigation, and their protection does not come because they are in a position to rely on a favourable judgment as *res judicata*: it comes because the unlawful conduct stops or the unlawful clause ceases to appear in consumer contracts.

Equivalent to the class action or not, the action available to consumer associations, like all the others mentioned under this heading, is the creature of special legislation; from a procedural point of view, it differs significantly from those others only in that it may be available even where no criminal offence has been committed or alleged. In sum, though there is, apparently, a tendency in the lower courts to admit an association as *partie civile* even in the absence of specific

---

[56] *Ibid.*, art. 2–4.   [57] Code rural, art. L. 252–1.
[58] C.p.p., art. 2–14.   [59] Code rural, art. L. 238–9.
[60] Law no. 75–229 of 9 April 1975.
[61] Law no. 88–14 of 5 January 1988; law no. 93–949 of 26 July 1993, as amended by law no. 95–96 of 1 February 1995.
[62] This is not a true class action. See L. Boré, 'L'action en représentation conjointe: *class action* française ou action mort-née?', D.S. 1995, Chron. 267.

statutory provision, this is contrary to the jurisprudence of the Cour de cassation.[63]

It is clear, therefore, that the French technique for dealing with 'unselfish' litigation is still to avoid both the statement of any general principle and the adoption of a generally available form of procedure under the control of the courts. Instead, legislation is introduced on an ad hoc basis as occasion demands. In that way the conditions that an association must meet if it is to be entitled to act, and the nature of the cases in which it may act, can be closely defined by the legislature on a case-by-case basis. In general, proceedings before the courts of the *ordre judiciaire* retain their traditional character as 'subjective'. Unselfish or 'objective' litigation remains exceptional and continues to require the specific approval of the legislature.[64]

The ordre administratif

Of the two most important forms of proceeding in the *ordre administratif*, the *recours de pleine juridiction* is used principally to obtain redress for damage suffered by individuals in consequence of administrative wrong-doing.[65] The *recours pour excès de pouvoir*, on the other hand, leads to the annulment of an act of the administration on the ground of its illegality. Such an act may, no doubt, affect only one or a few identifiable individuals – a 'non-regulatory' act – but it may also be in the form of a regulation affecting large numbers of people and perhaps the public as a whole.[66] By its nature, therefore, the latter is more likely than the former to be invoked for the protection of diffuse interests; the annulment of an illegal regulation is obviously of benefit to all those adversely affected by it.

In principle, whatever the form of the proceedings, the claimant must have *intérêt* if his claim is to be admissible, but for the *recours de pleine juridiction* the claimant must, normally, be able to allege the infringement of a legal right of his own. There is no equivalent to a 'class action'

---

[63] Guinchard, 'L'action de groupe', no. 68.

[64] R. Morel, *Traité de procédure civile*, 2nd edn (1949), no. 32, speaks of 'contentieux objectif' and draws an analogy with the 'recours pour excès de pouvoir' of administrative procedure (below, p. 120). J. Vincent and S. Guinchard, *Procédure civile*, 22nd edn (1991), no. 33 describe the action brought by an association as 'mixed, midway between the civil action properly so-called and the public action'.

[65] It may be used also in some other kinds of case such as disputes about an individual's tax liability.

[66] Only parliamentary acts are exempt from the possibility of attack in the *ordre administratif*. Regulations made by the administration under the direct authority of art. 37 of the Constitution are not so exempt: C.E. 12 February 1960, *Société Eky*, Rec. 101.

for damages and an association cannot act on behalf of its members in the pursuit of their individual rights.[67] For the *recours pour excès de pouvoir*, on the other hand, the application of the principle is more relaxed.

The underlying explanation of this lies in the nature of the *recours* itself and the recognition of its essentially public character. It is not, and in practice could not be, an *actio popularis*; a certain 'subjective' element is essential.[68] Nevertheless, it was said as long ago as 1899 that the *recours pour excès de pouvoir* is an 'objective' procedure for the annulment of illegal acts and one which exists for the sake of good administration. 'While its conduct is left to interested parties, this is in order to make use of them to watch over the administration; certainly they have interests of their own, but at the same time they act in the interest of the authority of the State. They are not parties acting in defence of their own rights; their position approximates to that of the ministère public in the prosecution of an offence.'[69]

This is, perhaps, something of an overstatement since one of the aspects of the *intérêt* required of an individual claimant is that the act complained of should have an actual or potential adverse effect on him personally. He cannot found on an act which is harmful or potentially harmful only to others,[70] but must have a reasonably close link to the act complained of.[71] On the other hand, so long as he belongs to a class or group consisting of people affected by the act complained of, and so long as the class or group is not so widely defined as to include the entire nation, his interest is sufficient.[72] A national taxpayer may not complain against a decision which would have the effect of increasing his liability to tax,[73] but a municipal taxpayer may do so.[74] It has actually been held

---

[67] E.g. C.E. 4 January 1977, *S.N.J. O.R.T.F.*, A.J., 111; Debbasch, no. 303.

[68] J. M. Auby and R. Drago, *Traité des recours en matière administrative* (1992), no. 110.

[69] Hauriou, sub C.E. 8 and 15 December 1899, S. 1900, III, 73, cited Auby and Drago, *Traité des recours*, no. 110. Note the parallel with the United States and the notion of the 'private attorney-general': p. 109, above.

[70] So, for example, a trader who, at the time, had no employees, could not seek the annulment of an act requiring traders going out of business to pay three months' salary to their employees: C.E. 7 July 1948, *Demoiselle Bertrand*, Rec. 550. Similarly, ministerial advice or replies to questions cannot be challenged since they have no legal consequences: C.E. 5 December 1947, *Fédération nationale des syndicats de conservateurs de légumes et de fruits*, Rec. 456.

[71] So, for example, a municipal regulation controlling parking in a particular street may be challenged by the residents of that street but not by the residents of a different street: C.E. 14 May 1954, *Feuger*, Rec. 274, cited Perrot, *Institutions judiciaires*, no. 530.

[72] C.E. 10 February 1950, *Gicquel*, Rec. 99, concl. Chenot.

[73] C.E. 13 February 1930, *Dufour*, Rec. 176. Debbasch, no. 294.

[74] C.E. 29 March 1901, *Casanova*, Rec. 333. (M. Long *et al.*, *Les grands arrêts de la jurisprudence administrative*, 10th edn (1993), p. 47.) The same is true for a departmental taxpayer (C.E., 27 January 1911, *Richemond*, Rec. 105).

that a camper might challenge a municipal regulation controlling camping, even though it had not at the time affected him in any way; he might at some time in the future wish to pitch his tent within that municipality.[75]

It seems, therefore, that for individuals the requirement of *intérêt* does little more than filter out far-fetched or frivolous cases, and the position of associations is certainly no worse. In the first place, the right of a trade union or professional association to act in the collective interest of its members was recognised in the *ordre administratif* earlier than in the *ordre judiciaire*,[76] and, in the second place and in contrast with the *ordre judiciaire*, that right was extended without difficulty and without the need for legislation, to other associations. An association may not act where only the individual interests of its members are affected, but, subject to that, it may attack any regulatory act of the administration that affects the collective interests which, by its statutes, it exists to defend. It has even been said that ordinary people have been given the means of protection for any interest of their choice. 'It is enough for them to form an association (two people will suffice) and give it the objective of protecting the interest they have at heart.'[77]

Even if this may be thought exaggerated, there is no doubt that the possibilities for associations to bring proceedings in the *ordre administratif* are extensive. So, to give just three examples out of the many that might be given, the National League against Alcoholism could challenge a relaxation of the control over home distilleries,[78] an association for the protection of regional languages could challenge a regulation dealing with the teaching of those languages,[79] and the Central Consistory of French Jews could challenge a decree that apparently required Jewish children to attend school on the Jewish Sabbath.[80]

---

[75] C.E. 14 February 1958, Rec. 98. See also C.E. 19 December 1979, Rec. 475, where the claimant's *intérêt* came from the fact that he made use of public telephones. Apparently, where a public service is affected, it is enough to be a user of such services: C.E. 21 December 1906, *Syndicat des propriétaires and contribuables du quartier Croix de Seguey-Tivoli*, Rec. 961, cited Debbasch, no. 294.

[76] C.E. 29 June 1900, *Syndicat agricole d'Herbloy*, S. 1905, 3, 1; C.E. 28 December 1906, *Syndicat des patrons coiffeurs de Limoges*, Rec. 977. It is said that the formulation of Commissaire du Gouvernement Romieu in the second case was that adopted by the Cour de cassation in its decision of 5 April 1913, above, n. 43.

[77] R. Chapus, *Droit de contentieux administratif*, 4th edn (1993), no. 431.

[78] C.E. 27 April 1934, *Ligue nationale*, Rec. 493.

[79] C.E. 1 June 1979, *Défense et promotion des langues de France*, Rec. 252.

[80] C.E. 14 April 1995, *Consistoire central des israélites français*, Rec. 171.

7 English law[1]

Part I

If a pebble is dropped into a pool of water, ripples will spread on the surface of the water; how far the ripples will spread and with what strength depends on a variety of factors, but there will always be a ripple of some kind. The same is true of a decision of a court of law. Notwithstanding what Professor Chayes has accurately described as the bipolar character of traditional civil litigation,[2] it is almost inconceivable that the outcome of a civil action will affect no one but the parties to it: unless an exception can be found to John Donne's famous axiom that 'No man is an Island, entire of itself'[3] – and such a man, if he exists, is unlikely to bring an action in the first place – the ripple effect even of, say, a simple decision that an individual defendant must pay a sum of money by way of damages to an individual plaintiff will extend to their respective families and beyond. It is not wholly absurd to say of such a case that, for example, the retail traders, the banks, and so on with whom the parties have dealt or may deal in the future have an 'interest' that an action by an injured individual may protect; and, if they do, that interest is certainly diffuse and fragmented, even if it is not collective.

In a country such as England, where the formal principle of *stare decisis* continues to play a major role in the development of the law so that, apart from anything else, past decisions may come to have a controlling influence on future litigation, the ripple effect of even the simplest traditional private litigation may extend much further than those with whom the parties have or may form social or economic relations. In a significant sense, therefore, the entire population may be said to have an interest – certainly diffuse – in litigation of any kind: though many decisions at first instance have no measurable significance

---

[1] Based on a Report to the VIIth International Congress on Procedural Law, Würzburg, 1983, published, in a revised version, [1983] C.L.J. 222.

[2] 'The Role of the Judge in Public Law Litigation' (1976) 89 Harv.L.R. 1281.

[3] Devotions XVII.

for the continuing process whereby the common law is formed and reformed, it can never be said with certainty that a case will not reach an appellate court. Who, for example, would have predicted that a hopeless action, started by a convicted prisoner who acted without legal assistance, against the barrister who had conducted his defence before a criminal court, would terminate with a major review and restatement in the House of Lords of the professional liabilities of the Bar?[4]

It is the main purpose of this chapter to consider litigation which is actually brought for the purpose of protecting diffuse interests, rather than with traditional private litigation whose incidental result is to protect – or to damage – such interests, but the distinction is not an easy one to draw. It depends ultimately on the motives with which the proceedings are begun, and litigation which conforms in all respects to the traditional bipolar pattern may be used with the ulterior, or even the primary, purpose of securing judicial protection for the diffuse and fragmented interests of a substantial and ill-defined group of people. A simple illustration is afforded by an action for nuisance brought by a householder in a residential neighbourhood against the owners of a nearby industrial undertaking. If an injunction is issued at the suit of that householder requiring, for example, that noisy operations be restricted to normal working hours, the benefits flowing from the injunction will accrue as much to his neighbours as to himself.[5]

In a case such as that, though the interest actually protected by the injunction – the interest in having peace at night – is diffuse, the persons affected are within a relatively restricted geographical area and the benefit they receive may be no more than an incidental byproduct of litigation that was instituted by a plaintiff whose motives for doing so were entirely selfish. The court will not, however, investigate the motives of the plaintiff unless, perhaps, the defendant seeks to strike out the action at an early stage as an abuse of the process of the court.[6] Even where it is clear that the plaintiff's motives are public- rather than private-spirited, if the plaintiff can point to a private right of his own the case will be heard on its merits.

A great deal of the litigation actually instituted for the protection of diffuse or fragmented interests is of this kind, and it will be necessary to return to the subject later in this chapter. For the present, however, one example will suffice. In *Congreve* v. *Home Office*[7] the plaintiff, who had

---

[4] *Rondel* v. *Worsley* [1969] 1 A.C. 191.

[5] See, e.g. *Halsey* v. *Esso Petroleum Co. Ltd* [1961] 1 W.L.R. 683. Although only one householder brought the action, many of his neighbours had complained of the nuisance, and twenty-four of them actually gave evidence.

[6] R.S.C., Ord. 18, r. 19(1)(d); C.P.R., r. 3.4(2)(b).

[7] [1976] Q.B. 629. An action for a declaration in these circumstances might no longer be

purchased for £12, the fee then in force, a television receiving licence valid for twelve months, received a demand for a further £6 because of a later increase in the licence fee. This demand was coupled with a threat that if the £6 was not paid the licence would be revoked. He thereupon brought an ordinary civil action claiming a declaration that the revocation of his licence in these circumstances would be unlawful and invalid and, in the result, he succeeded. Ostensibly the action was the plaintiff's alone and concerned only his own television licence. In reality, however, and as was openly acknowledged in the Court of Appeal, the plaintiff was no more than the leader of a very large number of people throughout the country who had nothing in common save that each of them had received demands and threats similar to those received by the plaintiff; the action was brought to protect the fragmented interests of them all. In this it succeeded although, of course, the decision had *res judicata* effect only in relation to the plaintiff. Whether the real significance of the decision, of which everyone was at all times aware, is to be explained in terms of *stare decisis* or not is of little more than technical interest: once the court had settled the question for one it had settled it for all.

The importance of the ostensibly private action to the protection of rights and interests other than those of the parties to the action and their privies must not be underestimated, but if attention is directed to the very broadly stated rights that form part of contemporary polemics such as the rights of consumers, environmentalists or victims of discrimination, the problem takes on a different dimension. Indeed, if taken at face value, it might seem to embrace every kind of right or interest that could claim consideration in any process of decision making. This chapter is, however, restricted to civil – that is, non-criminal – litigation before a court of law in England, and such a court, if it accepts jurisdiction, must come to a final, judicial, decision on the issues raised unless the case is settled before the proceedings come to an end. It is necessary, therefore, before turning to matters of a more obviously procedural character, to attempt to relate the diffuse and fragmented rights and interests in question to the English idea of law as it is administered by the courts.

It is not intended to suggest that law and policy can always be clearly distinguished from one another, and it is certainly not intended to suggest that the courts themselves do not make law. On the other hand, unlike the legislature, courts cannot make law out of whole cloth and, though it may sometimes be possible to derive from a sequence of decisions the proposition that the law recognises a new and broadly

possible, but a similar result could be achieved by way of an application for judicial review. See chap. 8, p. 160.

stated right or legally protected interest, such propositions are almost invariably tautologous. It is a familiar feature of English legal history that 'remedies precede rights'. Although a wrong may be no more than a correlative of a right, although, today, the language of rights is regularly used within as well as outside the courts, it is still broadly true that, so far as the processes of the law itself are concerned, a right is co-extensive with its protection through the actions of the law, that is with the availability of a legal remedy from the courts.

Scepticism about rights is associated with the affection that continues to be felt in judicial circles for the idea that England 'is not a country where everything is forbidden except what is expressly permitted: it is a country where everything is permitted except what is expressly forbidden' – a proposition which, as quoted, was applied to telephone tapping by the police![8] Even where the interests of millions of people are directly involved in litigation, therefore, the approach of the courts is essentially to try to avoid the broader issues of policy by concentrating on the conduct, actual or prospective, of the defendant in order to see whether it offends against some rule or principle of law.

The politically controversial decision of the House of Lords in *Bromley London Borough Council* v. *Greater London Council*,[9] which held that a scheme that had been introduced by the Greater London Council was unlawful, provides an example. What was proposed was a major reduction in the fares charged to users of London's transport system, the reduction to be funded by an increase in the subsidy to the London Transport Executive. That, in its turn, would be financed by an increase in the rates payable by the occupiers of premises in the London area. Here, a variety of diffuse interests were involved, of which the two most obvious were the interests of travellers in paying lower fares and the interests of rate payers in not having to pay excessive rates. So far as the approach of the courts to the problem was concerned, however, the matter fell to be decided in the light of, in particular, two elements of the substantive law, namely, first, certain sections of the Transport (London) Act 1969 and, secondly, the established principle that a local authority owes duties of a fiduciary character to its rate payers.

On one analysis the *Bromley* case concerned the balance to be maintained between the interests of two distinct but overlapping groups or classes of person – rate payers in London and users of London Transport – each of which one of the parties to the action may be said to have been seeking to protect. The case may, therefore, provide an example of

[8] *Malone* v. *Metropolitan Police Commissioner* [1979] Ch. 344.
[9] [1983] 1 A.C. 768. Cf. *R.* v. *London Transport Executive, ex parte Greater London Council* [1983] Q.B. 484.

the use of civil proceedings for the protection of diffuse interests. As the case itself shows, however, litigation involving diffuse or fragmented interests of this kind is likely to arise out of conflicts of interest for the judicial resolution of which a framework of law is essential. Where no directly applicable legal framework exists, such conflicts of interest can be resolved only at the political level if, indeed, they can be resolved at all: if no available criteria for the determination of an issue can be found in the law, the issue is not justiciable. It follows that if the procedural aspects of the use of civil litigation for the protection of diffuse and fragmented interests are to be sensibly considered, the assumption has to be made that the interests in question are at least potentially capable of protection by some kind of legal process.

The point can be illustrated by comparison between the interest of members of the public in the uninterrupted availability of public services such as transport, on the one hand, and of the postal services on the other. So far as the latter are concerned, there are provisions in the penal law dealing with interference with the mails, and in the important case of *Gouriet* v. *Union of Post Office Workers*[10] the action threatened by the defendant would almost certainly have involved violation of those provisions. There was, therefore, some legal basis on which an argument could be founded that a legally recognised interest was involved, and the case is properly seen as an attempt, albeit ultimately an unsuccessful one, to invoke the civil jurisdiction of the courts for the protection of that interest. Where, however, public transport services, for example, are interrupted by strike action, the law, in England, has, for all practical purposes, nothing whatever to say; the diffuse interest of travellers in being able to use the railway is simply unrecognised by any provision contained in the law, and so the question of its protection by way of civil or any other type of proceedings before a court does not arise at all.[11]

One final point of a general character must be mentioned at this stage. Although an interest may in a certain sense be recognised by the law, it does not necessarily follow that it is recognised at other than a remedial level, and where this is so it is difficult to see that a diffuse or fragmented interest exists at all. So, for example, the Unfair Contract Terms Act 1977 provides in section 6(2) that, as against a person dealing as a consumer, liability for breach of the seller's obligations as to the quality or fitness for their purpose of goods sold 'cannot be excluded or

[10] [1978] A.C. 435, below, p. 137.
[11] In France the position may in some circumstances be different, since recognition of the right to strike does not, in that country, necessarily deprive those adversely affected of all right to redress: Conseil Constitutionnel, 22 October 1982, D. 1983, 189. J. Bell, *French Constitutional Law* (1992), pp. 162–3 and 324–5. See also, e.g. Soc. 9 November 1982, D. 1982, 621.

restricted by reference to any contract term'. This provision operates to deprive a seller of a defence that might otherwise be available to him in an action brought by the buyer of defective goods, but it does nothing else. In particular, it does not render illegal the inclusion of terms in a contract of sale which purport to limit the seller's liabilities, and it has effect only on the hypothesis that defective goods have been sold to a consumer, that the consumer makes a claim against the seller and that the seller pleads an exclusion clause in his defence.

It is, no doubt, possible that a large number of consumers have purchased similar defective goods under similar contracts from the same supplier so that, if a class action were available, damages might be recovered for all of them in one set of proceedings. As the law now stands, however, the courts would arrogate to themselves the role of the legislator to an unacceptable degree if they used such proceedings to punish the seller or, in the interest of consumers as a whole, to deter or forbid the use of similar exclusion clauses in future consumer contracts: for better or worse, Parliament in 1977 sought to do no more than deprive the seller of what would otherwise have been an effective defence. Full implementation of the E.C. Directive on unfair terms in consumer contracts[12] might bring about a change through its requirement that means should be provided to prevent the continued use of unfair terms in consumer contracts; in particular, both individuals and organisations with a legitimate interest in consumer protection should be empowered to take proceedings to achieve this end,[13] but this requirement is not at present met by English law. Only the Director General of Fair Trading, on receipt of a complaint, has standing to seek an injunction restraining the future use of terms found to be unfair.[14] In England, the legislation on unfair contract terms continues to create only remedial rights.

In the following description of the procedural possibilities for the protection of diffuse, fragmented and collective rights or interests, therefore, it is presumed throughout that the right or interest in question can be shown to have some kind of recognition from the substantive law or, rather, to adopt the more familiar approach of English law, that the conduct of the defendant which is said to infringe that right or interest can somehow or other be shown to attract the opprobrium of the law. Evidently, in some cases, and especially where the court is entitled to

---

[12] Council Directive 93/13 of 5 April 1993 ([1993] 36.5 O.J. L95/29).

[13] Directive, art. 7. For France, see chap. 6, p. 118.

[14] Unfair Contracts Regulations 1994, SI 1994 No. 3159, reg. 8. Subject to this, the Regulations incorporate the Directive into English law more or less as originally written. See, e.g. J. Beatson, 'European Law and Unfair Terms in Consumer Contracts' [1995] C.L.J. 235.

exercise a broad discretion in coming to a conclusion and determining the remedy to be awarded, the conduct in question may be connected only loosely with some pre-existing prescription of the law. Nevertheless it must, at least, always be true that, in the opinion of the court, the alleged conduct of the defendant, even if not eventually proved, is such that the court's discretionary powers may properly be invoked. Otherwise the discussion is not of procedure but of substance and falls outside the purview of this chapter.

Part II

Civil and administrative proceedings

England has never known a distinct administrative jurisdiction equivalent to that of France nor yet a body of administrative law equivalent to the French *droit administratif*. Public authorities, including, since 1947,[15] the Crown itself, are, with certain necessary qualifications, subject to the ordinary law; proceedings may be brought against them in accordance with the ordinary rules of procedure. For a time this was even true for cases in which the court was asked to examine the legality of an act or decision of a public authority: the complication and technicality of the prerogative remedies of prohibition, certiorari and mandamus were such that ordinary actions for a declaration or an injunction were commonly used in their stead.

In 1977 prohibition, certiorari and mandamus were brought together under the general heading of 'application for judicial review'; a modernised procedure was introduced and, in *O'Reilly* v. *Mackman*,[16] the House of Lords held, as a matter of general principle, that only that modernised procedure may be used where a person seeks to establish that a decision of a public authority infringes rights to which he is entitled under public law.[17] The principle of procedural exclusivity was established.

This principle is considered later in the general context of civil and administrative procedure.[18] It does, however, have obvious implications for the subject matter of this chapter, and it is necessary to deal separately with civil proceedings strictly so-called and the application for judicial review.

---

[15] Crown Proceedings Act 1947.
[16] [1983] 2 A.C. 237. J. A. Jolowicz, 'Abuse of the Process of the Court' (1990) 43 *Current Legal Problems* 77.
[17] [1983] 2 A.C. 237, 285, *per* Lord Diplock.
[18] Chap. 8, p. 155.

Civil proceedings

Discussion of civil proceedings in the present context means, essentially, discussion of procedures which are the modern descendants of those developed in the courts of common law and of equity for the determination of private rights and obligations. The ancient connection between public and private right evidenced, for example, by the requirement that the plaintiff in an action of trespass allege the invasion of his right *vi et armis, contra pacem domini regis*, disappeared long ago and, notwithstanding the importance of much civil litigation to the development of constitutional law, such litigation was, at least in form, concerned exclusively with the rights of the individual plaintiff in each case. As Dicey put it, 'We may say that the constitution is pervaded by the rule of law on the ground that the general principles of the constitution (as for example the right to personal liberty, or the right of public meeting) are with us the result of judicial decisions determining the right of private persons in particular cases before the courts.'[19]

It is principally through *stare decisis* that the decisions to which Dicey refers provide protection for rights such as the right of public meeting, but, as indicated earlier, litigation that is in form and in substance concerned exclusively with the rights of an individual plaintiff may have the direct result of protecting also the rights and interests of others. For present purposes little interest attaches to cases in which this is purely accidental.[20] This section of the chapter is concerned with the purposive use of civil proceedings to secure protection for diffuse or fragmented rights and interests: it is thus, in a significant sense, concerned with the use of civil proceedings for a purpose for which they were not, at least originally, developed, and it is this, as much as anything else, which accounts for the uncertain and often hesitant approach of the judges.

In some circumstances, it is true, there is less uncertainty than in others. The judges are, generally, willing to make the civil remedies of injunction and declaration available to the Attorney-General, and where Parliament has seen fit to confer a right of civil action on public bodies or governmental agencies as a means of enforcing the law for whose

---

[19] *Introduction to the Study of the Law of the Constitution*, 9th edn (1945), p. 195. The enactment into law of the European Convention on Human Rights and Fundamental Freedoms affects this as a statement of current law but does not falsify the history.

[20] The protection of the interests of retail traders that is achieved by the award of damages to an individual (above, p. 122) is, in the sense intended, accidental. The protection of the interests of groups such as the shareholders and employees of a company that is achieved when the company succeeds in recovering damages for the loss of, say, a profitable contract may or may not be so. For the consequences for group litigation of increase in the use of incorporation, see Yeazell, chaps. 4 and 5.

administration they are responsible, the courts have not, of course, hesitated to comply with Parliament's intentions. When they are confronted with a case in which it is manifestly the intention of the non-governmental plaintiff, whether individual or association, to secure if he can the protection of the interests of an amorphous group or class of persons, however, the judges seem to vacillate between, on the one hand, a readiness to investigate alleged infringements of the law and, on the other, an unwillingness to allow private individuals or groups, whose interest in a particular matter is no greater than that of others, to intermeddle. It is hoped to demonstrate if not to explain the differing judicial attitudes in the brief discussions of particular forms of proceedings which follow.

The class or representative action

This form of proceedings is best treated first, both because the action brought by a representative of a group or class of persons would appear on its face to provide the most obvious procedural technique for the protection of the rights or interests of the group or class, and because it is through the development of the class action, if allowed to occur, that the kind of usurpation of the role of the legislature already mentioned may come about.[21]

In contrast with the common law, whose procedure was intended to isolate and decide a single issue between the parties to litigation and which contained complex and elaborate rules about joinder of parties, it was the aim of equity as administered in the Court of Chancery to decide upon and settle 'the rights of all persons interested in the subject-matter of the suit'; it was therefore generally necessary that all such persons should be made parties either as plaintiffs or defendants.[22] This rule was, however, relaxed where the interested persons were so numerous that joinder of all of them was impossible, and in such cases their representation as plaintiffs or defendants was permitted.[23]

Following the reforms of 1873–5, the representative action became available in the court of combined jurisdiction in both law and equity, but the applicable rule then brought into operation, which has received little significant amendment since that date, is very restrictively drawn: it allows representative status to an action only where numerous persons

---

[21] Above, p. 127.

[22] Daniell's *Chancery Practice*, 8th edn (1914), p. 147.

[23] E.g. *Anon.* (1675) 1 Ch.Ca. 269 (representation of the inhabitants of a parish); *Womersley* v. *Merritt* (1867) 4 Eq. 695 (representation of the large number of partners in an unincorporated business). Those represented were bound by the judgment unless they proved that it had been obtained by fraud or collusion: *Commissioners of Sewers of the City of London* v. *Gellatly* (1871) 3 Ch.D. 610.

have the same interest in any proceedings.[24] This probably matters little where the relief sought is injunctive or declaratory, for the distinction between a representative action and an action brought by one person in his individual capacity affects little more than the binding force of the judgment as *res judicata*.[25] As was pointed out in one case, where an attempt was made to challenge a local authority's differential rent scheme which was to be operated in relation to some 13,000 houses, it made little practical difference that representative status was refused when the plaintiff's personal action was allowed to proceed; if the scheme were pronounced unlawful at the suit of even one individual it would not be implemented.[26] Where there is a claim for damages, on the other hand, it obviously makes a great deal of difference whether the plaintiff claims for himself alone or whether he claims on behalf of all the members of a class.

The limited place allowed to punitive damages in English law[27] and acceptance of the general principle that an award of damages should compensate the plaintiff rather than punish the defendant do not in themselves rule out a representative action for damages, for such an action may be no more than a convenient method of obtaining compensation for substantial numbers of persons who have suffered similar damage in similar circumstances at the hands of the proposed defendant.[28] If, however, the representative or class action seeks to do more than that, if it seeks to recover damages for members of the class who do not, to put it at its lowest, voluntarily accept representation and, a fortiori, if it seeks to recover damages in respect of losses presumed to have been suffered by unidentified members of the class, then the character of the action is transformed: it becomes a means whereby the defendant is deprived of his 'ill-gotten gains' and acquires a punitive or deterrent function.

Such an outcome may be thought to be objectionable on two distinct grounds. In the first place, as indicated earlier, it may often be true of a

---

[24] R.S.C., Ord. 15, r. 12. The rule remains in force for the time being, unchanged in substance, but according to an early draft of the C.P.R. (not yet brought into force in this respect) a representative action would be available where persons have 'the same or a similar interest' in the proceedings. It is apparently not envisaged that the form of a representative action should be used for multi-party actions, below, p. 133.

[25] A representative action may be allowed, however, even if the members of the class have independent claims, and an injunction issued in favour of them all: *Duke of Bedford* v. *Ellis* [1901] A.C. 1.

[26] *Smith* v. *Cardiff Corporation* [1954] 1 Q.B. 210. In the event the plaintiff's action failed: *ibid.* *(No. 2)* [1955] Ch. 159. It is not denied that in particular circumstances there may be advantages to a representative action even though only declaratory or injunctive relief is claimed. See, e.g. *John* v. *Rees* [1970] Ch. 345.

[27] *A.B.* v. *South West Water Services Ltd* [1993] Q.B. 507.

[28] But see below, p. 133.

rule or principle of civil law that it is intended to operate only at the remedial level, and this is particularly true of much of the law of obligations, which is the principal source of the remedial right to damages. Holmes's famous observation that the only universal consequence of a legally binding promise is that the law makes the promissor pay damages if the promised act does not come to pass[29] should not be forgotten; it should also not be misinterpreted so as to suggest that the liability to pay damages can be invoked by anyone other than the affected contracting party who remains free to choose whether he will do so or not. In the second place, if and to the extent that the class or representative action becomes an instrument of punishment and deterrence, the interests protected are, *pro tanto*, not those of the persons affected by the presumptively unlawful conduct of the defendant – that is the members of the class – but are the inchoate interests of a different and wholly indeterminate class, namely those who might be affected in the future by similar conduct on the part of the defendant or anybody else.

Whether considerations such as these provide the explanation or not, it is certain that there has been no tendency in England to transform the representative action into an instrument of deterrence. Indeed, insistence on the requirement that the persons represented must have the *same* interest has even led to the exclusion of a representative action on behalf of the owners of cargo on a ship that was lost at sea[30] and, so far as is known, damages have not been awarded in a representative action except in one case where all the members of the class had consented to the damages being paid to an association to which they belonged and which was, in effect, conducting the litigation on their behalf through a representative plaintiff.[31] Otherwise, the furthest any judge has been prepared to go was to make a declaration that each member of the class was entitled to recover from the defendant such damages as he could prove in separate proceedings in which the issue of the defendant's liability, and that alone, would be *res judicata*.[32] This, though a useful innovation, is not promising material for those who look for a development in England which might parallel that which took place in the

---

[29] *The Common Law* (1881), p. 301.

[30] *Markt and Co. Ltd* v. *Knight Steamship Co. Ltd* [1910] 2 K.B. 1021. Consolidation of independent actions arising out of the same facts so as to avoid repetition of evidence is, of course, possible: R.S.C., Ord. 4, r. 9, Ord. 15, r. 4; C.P.R., r. 3.1(2)(g).

[31] *EMI Records Ltd* v. *Riley* [1982] 1 W.L.R. 923. *Moon* v. *Atherton* [1972] 2 Q.B. 435 recognised the possibility of a representative action for damages where all the members of the class – tenants of a building – had incurred equal expenses in repairing the roof of the building. See also *Irish Shipping Ltd* v. *Commercial Union* [1991] 2 Q.B. 206, 227, *per* Staughton L.J.

[32] *Prudential Assurance Co. Ltd* v. *Newman Industries Ltd* [1981] Ch. 229.

United States following amendment to rule 23 of the Federal Rules of Civil Procedure in 1966.[33]

It is not easy to predict how far, if at all, this will change if Lord Woolf's proposals for multi-party actions[34] are adopted. These are intended to provide a procedure specifically designed for actions for damages involving numerous parties such as those arising out of mass torts, and the recommendations have no overt ulterior objective. There is nothing to suggest an intention that the new procedure should be capable of use for deterrent or punitive purposes. There are, however, at least two points of relative detail which suggest that this might nevertheless come about.

In the first place, one of the stated objectives is to provide access to justice 'where large numbers of people have been affected by another's conduct, but individual loss is so small that it makes an individual action economically unviable':[35] realisation of this objective would give effect in such cases at least to the 'punishment' inherent in the making of an order to pay damages which would not otherwise have been made.[36] Secondly, while the general tenor of the recommendations seems to contemplate that at the end of the day damages should be awarded only in respect of the losses suffered by identified persons, there are references to safeguarding the interests of unidentified and even unborn potential claimants,[37] and it is specifically envisaged that the court should have power to conduct the action on an opt-out or an opt-in basis according to the circumstances.[38] If operation of the proposed procedure has the practical consequence that a defendant is mulcted in damages which cannot then be distributed to individual recipients, the effect is punitive, whatever the intention.[39]

Proceedings by the Attorney-General

The conferment on public authorities and governmental agencies of a power to take certain forms of civil proceeding in the exercise of their public functions is commonplace.[40] No catalogue of the use of civil

---

[33] Chap. 6, p. 112.

[34] Woolf Final, chap. 17. See K. Uff, 'Recent Developments in Multi-party Actions' (1992) 11 C.J.Q. 345. On complex litigation generally, see P. H. Lindblom and G. D. Watson, 'Complex Litigation – A Comparative Perspective' (1993) 12 C.J.Q. 33.

[35] Woolf Final, chap. 17, para. 2(a).   [36] Chap. 6, p. 113.

[37] E.g. Woolf Final, chap. 17, paras. 76, 80 and recommendation 226. Paragraph 80, dealing with court approval of multi-party settlements, specifically mentions the need 'in cases where there may be unidentified or unborn potential claimants' that the judge should satisfy himself that proper arrangements have been made.

[38] Woolf Final, chap. 17, recommendation 220.   [39] Chap. 6, p. 112.

[40] In certain circumstances, for example, the Minister may petition the court for an order that a company be wound up if he considers 'that it is expedient in the public interest

proceedings by other public authorities can be given here,[41] but the common law power of the Attorney-General to do so is both ancient and general. It lies behind the relator action and other methods whereby civil proceedings for the protection of diffuse or fragmented interests can be instituted on the initiative of private individuals or groups.

It is likely that the earliest form of civil proceedings in which the Attorney-General appeared as plaintiff were those in which he acted on behalf of the Crown as *parens patriae* to seek an injunction in a court of equity to prevent the misapplication of funds subject to a charitable trust,[42] but he has for long also been entitled to seek an injunction to restrain a public nuisance.[43] Today it is probably true that he may take proceedings to protect the public interest whenever he considers it necessary to do so;[44] in particular, he may seek an injunction to restrain continuing or persistent breaches of the criminal law on the general ground that it is in the public interest that the law should be obeyed.[45]

In modern times the injunction issued at the suit of the Attorney-General to reinforce the sanctions of the criminal law is widely used in connection with minor regulatory offences but, while it may undoubtedly be useful in some cases,[46] it is not without its dangers and difficulties.

In the first place, the very effectiveness of the procedure lies in the conversion it achieves in the sanction that may be imposed for further breaches of the law by the person subject to the injunction: the law itself may, and in the kind of case in which an injunction is sought almost invariably does, impose only a minor penalty for breach such as a fine of a few pounds. Once the injunction has been issued, however, a further breach of the law will constitute contempt of court and so will attract penalties up to and including imprisonment.[47] This, it may well be

---

that he should do so': Insolvency Act 1986, s. 124A, as substituted by the Companies Act 1989, s. 60. See *Re a Company* [1994] Ch. 198.

[41] See I. H. Jacob, 'Safeguarding the Public Interest in English Civil Proceedings' [1982] 1 C.J.Q. 312.

[42] Wade, pp. 601–2. An early example is *Attorney-General* v. *Hart* (1703) Prec.Ch. 225.

[43] *Attorney-General* v. *PYA Quarries Ltd* [1957] 2 Q.B. 169.

[44] De Smith, pp. 146 *et seq.*

[45] The court will not entertain an argument to the effect that it would be more to the advantage of the public that the law should be disregarded than that it should be obeyed: *Attorney-General* v. *London and North Western Railway* [1900] 1 Q.B. 78, where the statutory rule in question required that railway trains should not exceed a speed of four miles per hour when travelling over a level-crossing.

[46] E.g. *Attorney-General* v. *Chaudry* [1971] 1 W.L.R. 1614, where the speed with which the civil jurisdiction could be invoked, as compared with the criminal, may actually have been important to the preservation of life.

[47] Contempt of Court Act 1981, s. 14; R.S.C., Ord. 52.

thought, is to go much further than Parliament can be supposed to have intended.

In the second place, although the grant of the injunction is an equitable and thus a discretionary remedy, and although the judges maintain that they are not bound to accede to the Attorney-General's request for an injunction even if persistent breaches of the law by the defendant have been established, they also insist that if the Attorney-General, having considered the case, reaches the conclusion that the issue of an injunction is called for, then his application should be refused only in exceptional cases. The fact that it is the Attorney-General who appears as plaintiff thus carries weight when the court comes to consider how it should exercise its discretion.[48] Unfortunately, however, on at least one occasion, when the Attorney-General was challenged in Parliament to explain why he had decided to proceed in a particular case, he relied on the fact that the Court of Appeal had granted an injunction to demonstrate that his action had been justified.[49]

In these circumstances it is not altogether surprising that the House of Lords should have said that the issue of injunctions at the suit of the Attorney-General to restrain breaches of the criminal law may have to be reconsidered at some time in the future.[50] For the present, however, the position is relatively clear, and, so long as it can be maintained that some public interest is involved, there seems to be practically no limit to the Attorney-General's power to invoke the civil jurisdiction of the court. Nevertheless, according to Lord Denning M.R., he has never been known to do so against a government department.[51]

Relator actions[52]

The Attorney-General can, of course, take action himself before the court, but the majority of actions brought in his name are in fact brought on the initiative of a relator who has successfully applied to the Attorney-General to be allowed to sue in his name; where this is the case, the Attorney-General retains a measure of control over the

---

[48] *Attorney-General* v. *Bastow* [1957] 1 Q.B. 514; *Attorney-General* v. *Harris* [1961] 1 Q.B. 74 where the trial judge's refusal of an injunction on the ground that the defendants' repeated breaches of the law had caused no damage to the public ([1960] 1 Q.B. 31) was reversed.

[49] H.C. Deb., Vol. 631, cols. 684–95 (1 December 1960).

[50] *Gouriet* v. *Union of Post Office Workers* [1978] A.C. 435, 481, *per* Lord Wilberforce.

[51] *R.* v. *Inland Revenue Commissioners* [1980] Q.B. 407, 419. See Wade, p. 607 and de Smith, p. 149.

[52] J. Ll. J. Edwards, *The Law Officers of the Crown* (1964), pp. 286–95; de Smith, pp. 150–4; Wade, pp. 601–10.

action,[53] but it is for most practical purposes the relator who is the *dominus litis*, and it is the relator who is responsible for the costs. Once permission for the use of the name of the Attorney-General has been obtained, no objection can be raised to the *locus standi* of the plaintiff: it is not necessary that the relator have any legally recognised interest in the subject matter of the action,[54] and the propriety of the Attorney-General's conduct in giving his consent cannot be challenged before the court.[55]

The procedural requirements for obtaining the Attorney-General's consent are relatively simple, though not without cost: a copy of the proposed writ and statement of claim, which will show the nature of the proposed action, duly certified by counsel as fit for the allowance of the Attorney-General, must be submitted, together with a statement by the solicitor in the action that the relator is a proper person to act as such and that he is able to take responsibility for the costs.[56] The relator action thus provides a convenient method whereby a person or corporation[57] may challenge the legality of something done or proposed to be done by another when no private right or interest is involved. It does, however, suffer from two inherent limitations.

In the first place, in contrast with ordinary litigation, the relator cannot act in person – both solicitor and counsel are necessary even for the original application to the Attorney-General – and he is responsible for the costs. Without financial resources, therefore, a relator action is practically impossible and for a relator action no legal aid is available.[58] In the second place, it is a matter for the Attorney-General's unfettered discretion whether he will or will not allow his name to be used in any given case.

The Attorney-General is the first Law Officer of the Crown, a Member of Parliament and a member of the Government of the day. In exercising some of his functions, including that of deciding whether legal proceedings should or should not be taken in a given case,

---

[53] The Attorney-General must be consulted before the original statement of claim is amended, his consent must be renewed if the relator wishes to appeal, and, no doubt, as nominal plaintiff the Attorney-General can terminate the proceedings against the wishes of the relator: *Supreme Court Practice 1999*, para. 15/11/3, 4; *Gouriet* v. *Union of Post Office Workers* [1978] A.C. 435, 478, *per* Lord Wilberforce.

[54] *Attorney-General* v. *Vivian* (1825) 1 Russ. 226.

[55] *London County Council* v. *Attorney-General* [1902] A.C. 165, 167–8, *per* Lord Halsbury L.C.

[56] R.S.C., Ord. 15, r. 11.

[57] Formerly the relator action was much used by local government authorities. Since 1972, however, they have been generally able to bring proceedings in their own name where they consider it expedient for the protection of the interests of the inhabitants of their areas: Local Government Act 1972, s. 222.

[58] Legal Aid Act 1988, Sched. 2, Pt 11, para. 3.

however, he is supposed to act without regard to considerations of party politics, and it is said that although he may consult, he is certainly not obliged to follow the opinion of his Cabinet colleagues.[59] On the other hand, though party-political considerations are excluded, the Attorney-General is not limited to considering only whether the proposed action is likely to succeed; he may also have regard to such matters as the balance of public interest and whether the bringing of proceedings might increase rather than reduce the risk of widespread breaches of the law.[60] The distinction thus drawn may, however, be a fine one and it has been said by a former Attorney-General that it is naive to hold that the Attorney-General may have regard to political considerations but must not act for party political reasons: it is, of course, exactly the present appearance and future possibility that he might so act which endangers both existing respect for and the future effectiveness of the rule of law.[61]

In *Gouriet v. Union of Post Office Workers*,[62] the Secretary-General of the defendant trade union had announced on television that, in support of an international week of action against the policy of the South African Government, the union intended to instruct its members not to handle mail or maintain communications with South Africa for a period of one week. Despite his somewhat cavalier treatment of a question as to the legality of the proposed action,[63] it would almost certainly have involved the members of the union, and probably the union itself, in the commission of offences against the criminal law. The following day, a private citizen, Mr Gouriet,[64] sought the consent of the Attorney-General to a relator action against the union seeking a variety of declarations and injunctions aimed at preventing the boycott of communication with South Africa. After a period for reflection the Attorney-General refused his consent, saying, 'having considered all the circumstances, including

[59] Edwards, *Law Officers*, citing Sir Hartley Shawcross, Attorney-General, in H.C. Deb., Vol. 483, cols. 679–90 (29 January 1951). See also, e.g. *Gouriet v. Union of Post Office Workers* [1977] Q.B. 729, 741–6, *per* Silkin, Attorney-General, *arguendo* and *Gouriet* [1978] A.C. 435, 442–4, *per* Silkin, Attorney-General, *arguendo*; at 489–90, *per* Viscount Dilhorne, himself a former Attorney-General.

[60] Mr Sam Silkin, Attorney-General, in H.C. Deb., Vol. 924, cols. 1699 *et seq.* (27 January 1977).

[61] Lord Shawcross in a letter to *The Times*, 2 August 1977, cited in P. P. Mercer, 'Public Interest Litigation in Britain and Canada' [1979] P.L. 214, 222.

[62] [1977] Q.B. 729; [1978] A.C. 435.

[63] In reply to an interviewer's question about the legality of the proposed action, he replied that the matter had never been tested in the courts, and that the relevant laws dated from Queen Anne and were more appropriate for dealing with highwaymen and footpads. In fact the applicable provisions were contained in the Post Office Act 1953 and the Post Office Act 1969.

[64] Though the secretary of, and probably supported by, an organisation known as the National Association for Freedom, Mr Gouriet's position was simply that of a member of the public.

the public interest . . . I have come to the conclusion that in relation to this application I should not give my consent'.

Following this refusal, Mr Gouriet began proceedings in his own name, and the fate of his action is considered later. The question was, however, also raised whether the court might review the exercise by the Attorney-General of his discretion in refusing his consent. In the Court of Appeal the Attorney-General himself appeared, in order to insist that his discretion was absolute and that he could not be called upon to disclose his reasons except in Parliament.

To Lord Denning M.R. this was a direct challenge to the rule of law,[65] for it would mean that the Attorney-General became the final arbiter as to whether the law should be enforced or not.[66] His brethren were, however, not prepared to go so far, and the majority held that there was no power in the court to consider a direct challenge to the Attorney-General's decision; when the case came before the House of Lords, this point was not further pursued.[67] It must be accepted, therefore, that while a person who has obtained the Attorney-General's consent is able to take action before the court without regard to his personal *locus standi*, there can be no legal safeguard where the Attorney-General's consent is refused. The only remedy is in Parliament. Though the relator action continues to play a most important role, therefore, interest must focus on the existing possibilities of legal action by individuals or groups for which no prior authorisation outside the courts is required.

Private litigation

With limited exceptions, the issue of a writ or other originating process is a matter of right; English law does not distinguish, as does French law, between 'claim' and 'action'.[68] Where proceedings are summarily dismissed for lack of a reasonable cause of action the court is, at least theoretically, concerned with the substance of the claim, not with a procedural point. Nevertheless, if, as is normal, damage to the plaintiff is an essential ingredient of his cause of action and no such damage is alleged, then the action should be summarily dismissed for that reason alone.[69]

It is convenient, therefore, to consider under this head, first, the case where the plaintiff alleges no damage to himself other than that suffered by the public or a section of the public as a whole and, secondly, that in which the plaintiff does allege some damage to himself, even if not

---

[65] [1977] Q.B. 729, 758.   [66] *Ibid.*, at 761.
[67] [1978] A.C. 435, 475, *per* Lord Wilberforce.
[68] Chap. 3, p. 62.   [69] *Ibid.*, p. 64.

damage such as would ordinarily be complained of in normal private litigation.

(i) Where an intending plaintiff seeking to protect a diffuse or fragmented interest has suffered no damage personal to himself, his proper course is to seek the Attorney-General's consent to a relator action. So far as is known, the question whether any action is possible without that consent was not raised until 1973. In that year the Court of Appeal indicated that if the Attorney-General refused his consent for no good reason, or if the matter was extremely urgent, then the court might, in its discretion, admit the claim of an individual at least for a declaration.[70] In the event, the court did not then have to come to a final conclusion as the Attorney-General did, belatedly, allow the action to proceed in his name.

In *Gouriet* v. *Union of Post Office Workers*,[71] the Attorney-General formally refused his consent to a relator action and in the Court of Appeal, which was evidently suspicious of the Attorney-General's reasons for his refusal,[72] it was held not only that the individual plaintiff might bring proceedings in his own name but also that an injunction should issue. In the House of Lords, however, this decision was reversed and, although there are differences between the five speeches that were delivered, the principal reason seems to have been that, so far as public rights are concerned, only the Attorney-General may take civil proceedings for their enforcement. His discretion is absolute; its exercise can be challenged, if at all, only in Parliament, and if the Attorney-General declines to take action himself or to allow his name to be used in a relator action, no citizen without a private right or who has not suffered special damage – that is, damage in excess of that suffered by the public at large – can bring a civil action.

Strictly speaking, the question decided was one of substance rather than procedure and the decision was, in form, that the plaintiff's action should be dismissed because his statement of claim disclosed no reasonable cause of action. In reality, however, it was equivalent to a decision that the plaintiff had no *locus standi* and, indeed, the language of standing was used in both Court of Appeal and House of Lords. In this respect, as well as in the importance attached by the House of Lords to the distinction between public and private rights,[73] the decision is

[70] *Attorney-General* v. *Independent Broadcasting Authority* [1973] Q.B. 629.
[71] [1977] Q.B. 729; [1978] A.C. 435.
[72] See [1977] Q.B. 729, 738, *per* Lord Denning M.R.; at 739, *per* Lawton L.J.; at 761, *per* Lord Denning M.R.; at 771, *per* Lawton L.J.
[73] See especially [1978] A.C. 435, 477, *per* Lord Wilberforce; at 496, *per* Lord Diplock. See text above, p. 128, and J. A. Jolowicz, 'The Judicial Protection of Fundamental

innovative in English law notwithstanding the weight placed in the speeches on legal history. This does not, however, detract from its authority as a precedent: it lays down the law for those cases in which the plaintiff avowedly acts unselfishly and does not claim personally to have suffered damage.

(ii) *Gouriet* v. *Union of Post Office Workers* raised the problem in an acute form because, for technical reasons, the plaintiff himself disclaimed any interest other than that of a member of the public.[74] Ordinarily, however, the ingenuity of the plaintiff or his counsel will be sufficient to formulate some kind of an allegation of damage personal to the plaintiff, and even though the sufficiency of such an allegation may be called in question, it will be for the court, and for the court alone, to decide the point.[75]

So much is, for all practical purposes, admitted by the House of Lords, for it was accepted that an action will lie at the suit of an individual with a private right or, if a public right is in issue, at the suit of an individual who has suffered special damage.[76] What is more, the individual's right of action is unaffected by the fact that numerous others have suffered or will suffer damage precisely similar in kind and in extent to that relied on by the plaintiff. In the words of Lord Wilberforce, 'a right is nonetheless a right, or a wrong any the less a wrong, because millions of people have a similar right or may suffer a similar wrong'.[77]

However much the House of Lords may have wished, as a matter of policy, to preserve the Attorney-General's monopoly control over litigation whose purpose is the protection of diffuse or fragmented interests, some such admission was inevitable both on grounds of logic and on grounds of authority. In particular the House had to accommodate, and distinguish, a famous decision of the Court of Appeal some sixty years previously, the correctness of which no one denies. In that case, *Dyson* v. *Attorney-General*,[78] the plaintiff had received a form from the Inland Revenue authorities demanding certain information and threatening that a penalty would be imposed if the information was not supplied

Rights under English Law', Part III, in *Cambridge-Tilburg Law Lectures*, second series 1979 (1980).

[74] Had he alleged damage to himself his action would have been in tort and no action in tort lay against a trade union: Trade Union and Labour Relations Act 1974, s. 14. See now, Trade Union and Labour Relations (Consolidation) Act 1992, s. 15.

[75] Chap. 6, p. 110.

[76] [1978] A.C. 435, 483–4, *per* Lord Wilberforce; at 492–3, *per* Viscount Dilhorne; at 499–500, *per* Lord Diplock; at 506, 513, *per* Lord Edmund-Davies; at 518, *per* Lord Fraser.

[77] *Ibid.*, at 483.   [78] [1911] 1 K.B. 410.

within a certain time. The plaintiff sought a declaration that the issue of the form went beyond the power of the revenue authorities, and the Attorney-General, on behalf of the Crown, objected to the proceedings on the ground, amongst others, that if they were allowed, there would be innumerable actions for declarations as to the meaning of numerous Acts of Parliament; in other words, that the matter was one of public rather than private interest, a point which was reinforced by the fact that some 8 million people had received the same form. The latter fact was, however, taken by the Court of Appeal as an argument in favour of their accepting jurisdiction:

It is obviously a question of the greatest importance; more than eight millions of Form IV have been sent out in England, and the questions asked entail much trouble and in many cases considerable expense in answering; it would be a blot on our system of law and procedure if there is no way by which a decision on the true limit of the power of inquisition vested in the Commissioners can be obtained by any member of the public aggrieved, without putting himself in the invidious position of being sued for a penalty.[79]

It is, no doubt, true that the plaintiff in *Dyson* v. *Attorney-General* was personally affected by the issue of the form, and it was on this ground that the case was distinguished by the House of Lords. At any but the most technical level, however, the distinction has little to commend it: what real difference is there between a public interest, on the one hand, and the identical private interest of eight million individuals on the other? The important point is, however, that by accepting the distinction instead of seeking to develop rules for the judicial control of actions brought by plaintiffs intent on the protection of interests other than their own, the House of Lords has, in effect, compelled the courts to reach their decisions on an artificial basis: it is claimed that the plaintiff has suffered or will suffer some damage personal to himself, and the court must then say whether that damage suffices to sustain the action. The answer is more likely to turn on the court's desire to extend or to restrict the scope of judicial intervention than on aseptic analysis of the damage alleged, and the outcome in any given case becomes more than ordinarily difficult to predict.

That this is so seems, unfortunately, to be borne out by such relevant cases as have come before the courts since *Gouriet* v. *Union of Post Office Workers* was decided and, even more unfortunately, different views on legal policy seem to be adopted by the Court of Appeal and the House of Lords. The former, it appears, is willing to accept as sufficient,

[79] *Ibid.*, at 421, *per* Farwell L.J. The plaintiff could have raised the illegality of the form as a defence if he had refused to supply the information and proceedings had then been taken against him.

damage of the most tenuous kind if this is necessary to enable it to pronounce on the legality or otherwise of action affecting large numbers of people;[80] the latter, on the other hand, appears on the whole to be anxious so far as possible to confine private litigation to its traditional role of determining only the truly private rights of the parties before the court.[81] Paradoxically, its attitude to the application for judicial review is different.

Application for judicial review[82]

The application for judicial review is commonly used to protect the rights of an individual against an act of the administration. It may, however, also be used for the protection of diffuse interests and that aspect of its use, alone, falls for consideration here. The distinction taken cannot always be rigidly drawn,[83] but it is similar to that adopted by the Law Commission between applications made by persons 'who have been personally adversely affected by the decision which is the subject of the complaint', on the one hand, and applications where 'it can be demonstrated that there is a sufficient public interest in the matter being litigated',[84] on the other.

It is a feature of the application for judicial review, as it was for the prerogative remedies, that an applicant must obtain leave to apply before the proceedings proper can be begun, and leave can be granted only to a person who has 'sufficient interest in the matter to which the application relates'.[85] This, however, does not in itself create a serious obstacle to proceedings for the protection of diverse interests. As Lord Diplock observed in the *Inland Revenue* case, where the legality of a practice of the Inland Revenue was challenged, it would be a 'grave lacuna in our system of public law if a pressure group, like the

---

[80] E.g. *Ex parte Island Records* [1978] Ch. 122 (subsequently overruled by the House of Lords in *Lonrho Ltd* v. *Shell Petroleum Co. Ltd* [1982] A.C. 173); *RCA Corp.* v. *Pollard* [1983] Ch. 135); *Meade* v. *Haringey London Borough Council* [1979] 1 W.L.R. 637. Cf. *Barrs* v. *Bethell* [1982] Ch. 294, a decision at first instance.

[81] See, e.g. *Allen* v. *Gulf Oil Ltd* [1981] A.C. 1001 and comment by J. A. Jolowicz [1981] C.L.J. 226. The point emerges most clearly in *Gouriet* v. *Union of Post Office Workers* itself. *Gillick* v. *West Norfolk Area Health Authority* [1986] A.C. 112 (below, p. 146) is an exception.

[82] Above, p. 128 and chap. 8, p. 154.

[83] The prerogative remedies and, now, the application for judicial review are nominally granted at the suit of the Crown. They have a 'public' character and there is a pervading public interest in ensuring the legality of all acts of the administration.

[84] *Administrative Law: Judicial Review and Statutory Appeals* (1994), Law Com. No. 226, paras. 5.16–5.22. The Commission recommends that a different approach to standing should be adopted for each category of case. See also Woolf Final, p. 255.

[85] Supreme Court Act 1981, s. 31(3); R.S.C., Ord. 53, r. 3(7).

federation, or even a single public-spirited taxpayer, were prevented by outdated technical rules of *locus standi* from bringing the matter to the attention of the court to vindicate the rule of law and get the unlawful conduct stopped'.[86]

Even before the introduction of the application for judicial review, there was no absolute bar to an application for the grant of one of the prerogative remedies, at least of prohibition or certiorari, by a person who had not been personally adversely affected but who acted for the public benefit.[87] Now, the *Inland Revenue* case itself, and references such as Lord Diplock's to vindication of the rule of law, show that the application for judicial review can be used for the protection of diffuse interests, interests which are, perhaps, more happily described in this context as public. So, to take a striking example, it was held in *R. v. H.M. Treasury, ex parte Smedley*[88] that a taxpayer had sufficient interest to challenge a draft Order in Council, proposed to be laid before Parliament, which provided for the payment of a large sum of public money to the European Community.

In *R. v. Secretary of State for the Environment, ex parte Rose Theatre Trust Co.*,[89] preliminary work on a building development in London, for which planning permission had been granted, revealed the remains of an Elizabethan theatre. A group of people, including archaeologists, campaigned for the preservation of the theatre and formed a company to do so. The company asked the Secretary of State to include the site of the theatre in a statutory schedule maintained by him of monuments of public importance. The effect of such inclusion would have been to prevent any work on the site without special permission. Though he accepted that the site was of national importance, the Secretary of State declined to include it in the schedule, giving full reasons for his decision. The company applied for judicial review and Schiemann J., at first instance, dismissed the application, partly as a matter of substance but also because, in his view, the company had no *locus standi*: it was not argued that the company could have sufficient interest if no individual did so, and the decision not to schedule was 'one of those governmental decisions in respect of which the ordinary citizen does not have a

---

[86] *Inland Revenue Commissioners* v. *National Federation of Self Employed and Small Businesses Ltd* [1982] A.C. 617, 644. The application for leave and the question of *locus standi* is considered more fully, below chap. 8, p. 167.

[87] See, e.g. *R.* v. *Greater London Council, ex parte Blackburn* [1976] 1 W.L.R. 550. In so far as a 'particular grievance' was required, the phrase came to acquire a very wide meaning not unlike the American 'injury in fact' (chap. 6, p. 109). For the old law on standing, see Wade, pp. 696–708.

[88] [1985] Q.B. 657.

[89] [1990] 1 Q.B. 504. See also *R.* v. *Secretary of State for Social Services, ex parte Child Poverty Action Group* [1990] 2 Q.B. 540.

sufficient interest to entitle him to obtain leave to move for judicial review'.[90]

Schiemann J. did not, of course, go so far as to insist that only a person who had a direct financial or legal interest had a sufficient interest for leave to be granted, but his decision nevertheless led the Law Commission to recommend that in addition to cases in which the applicant has been or would be personally adversely affected by the decision complained of, leave to apply for judicial review should also be granted if the court 'considers that it is in the public interest for an applicant to make the application'.[91] The decision in the *Rose Theatre* case was, however, not followed by Otton J. in *R. v. Inspectorate of Pollution, ex parte Greenpeace Ltd (No. 2)*,[92] where the judge, who treated the question as one for the exercise of his discretion, recognised that Greenpeace was a responsible and respected body with a genuine concern for the environment, that the issues raised were serious and worthy of determination by the court, and that, if leave were not granted, those represented by Greenpeace might have no effective way of bringing those issues before the court.[93]

Though a decision at first instance only, the *Greenpeace* case is of particular interest as determining that a private organisation or association, set up to protect a diffuse interest such as the interest in the environment, may, in an appropriate case, be given leave to apply for judicial review.[94] Though distinguishable, and perhaps for that reason not cited to Otton J., his decision is supported by *R. v. Secretary of State for Employment, ex parte Equal Opportunities Commission*,[95] in which the House of Lords, by a majority, held that the Equal Opportunities Commission had *locus standi* to challenge the Secretary of State's refusal to accept that the United Kingdom was in breach, in certain respects, of relevant employment law of the European Community, and also to challenge his refusal to introduce legislation claimed by the Commission to be necessary under European law. Lord Keith, with whom the majority agreed, held that it would be a 'very retrograde step now to hold that the EOC has no *locus standi* to agitate in judicial review

---

[90] [1990] Q.B. 504, 521.
[91] *Administrative Law: Judicial Review and Statutory Appeals* (1994), Law Com. No. 226, para. 5.22; also Woolf Final, p. 253.
[92] [1994] 4 All E.R. 329.
[93] *Ibid.*, at 350–1. The judge also saw positive advantages in having the case presented by a body such as Greenpeace rather than an individual who might be able to show an adverse effect on himself. See also, *R. v. Foreign Secretary, ex parte World Movement Ltd* [1995] 1 W.L.R. 386.
[94] Compare the French approach to actions by associations, chap. 6, pp. 115 and 121.
[95] [1995] 1 A.C. 1.

proceedings questions related to sex discrimination which are of public importance and affect a large section of the population'.[96]

Conclusion

The importance for present purposes of the *Inland Revenue* case is not that the applicant was ultimately held to lack sufficient interest but that the decision was reached on the basis of evidence given by the respondent, evidence which would never have been produced if leave to apply had been refused at the outset. In *Gouriet's* case, on the other hand, the single fact that the plaintiff could allege no damage personal to himself meant that his action was struck out before the defendants were called upon to justify their actions.

The contrasting positions in the two cases is explained by Lord Diplock, in *Inland Revenue*, on the basis that a private citizen, except as a relator in an action brought in the name of the Attorney-General, 'has no *locus standi* in private law as a plaintiff in a civil action to obtain either an injunction to restrain another private citizen (*in casu* a trade union) from committing a public wrong by breaking the criminal law, or a declaration that his conduct is unlawful, unless the plaintiff can show that some legal or equitable right of his own has been infringed or that he will sustain some special damage over and above that suffered by the general public'. *Gouriet's* case was, in his opinion, irrelevant in proceedings against a public authority brought by way of an application for judicial review.[97]

It is true that the application for judicial review is subject to two important procedural restrictions: first, the applicant must obtain leave to apply and, secondly, the application must be made 'promptly' and in any event within three months from the date when grounds for the application arose.[98] Subject to this, however, it emerges that the legality of the actions of public authorities is more readily susceptible to challenge at the suit of those concerned to protect diffuse or collective interests (including organisations such as the Equal Opportunities Commission and Greenpeace) than is the legality of what is done by anybody else (including powerful corporations and trade unions).

---

[96] [1995] 1 A.C. 1, 26.
[97] [1982] A.C. 617, 638–9. See also *ibid.*, at 649, *per* Lord Scarman. In *Gouriet's* case itself, Lord Wilberforce said that 'The distinction between public rights, which the Attorney-General can and the individual (absent special interest) cannot seek to enforce, and private rights is fundamental in our law': [1978] A.C. 435, 482.
[98] Supreme Court Act 1981, s. 31(6); R.S.C., Ord. 53, r. 4. The period can be extended for good reason. No period of limitation applicable to proceedings by way of action is less than three years: Limitation Act 1980. See further chap. 8, p. 158.

A private challenge to the legality of another's action can, of course, be mounted for the protection of diffuse or collective interests if the consent of the Attorney-General is obtained for the use of relator proceedings, and it may be said that the Attorney-General's grant of consent for proceedings by way of action is equivalent to the grant of leave for proceedings by way of application for judicial review. There are, however, important differences. The Attorney-General's discretion is unfettered, it does not fall within the category of judicial discretion and it is subject to no appeal. The application for leave to apply for judicial review, on the other hand, is made to a judge of the High Court who, though required to exercise his discretion, is bound to do so judicially; and, if he refuses the application without a hearing, it may be renewed before a judge in open court.[99]

It requires no demonstration that, in modern society, there are some public authorities whose power to affect adversely the diffuse interests of individuals and of groups of individuals is much less than that of many private corporations, trade unions and regulatory bodies for certain trades and professions.[100] There may be reasons of history, and perhaps even of constitutional theory, why different procedures should exist for the exercise of judicial control of the legality of their activities, but the distinction between public and private bodies for this purpose can no longer be justified in practical terms.

It was noticed earlier in this chapter that many actions which are brought in the guise of actions by individuals complaining of damage personal to themselves are, in reality, actions to protect the diffuse or fragmented interests of a group. It was also observed that where there is an allegation of such damage it is for the court, and for the court alone, to decide whether the damage alleged is sufficient to sustain the action. Often the court has no effective choice and must allow the action to proceed. This was the position in *Congreve* v. *Home Office*, where the action was manifestly brought in the interests of large numbers of licence holders; only the trivial sum of £6 of the plaintiff's own money was in cause, but this was sufficient to give him standing.[101]

It may be, however, that no similar damage of a conventional kind can be claimed, and yet some kind of damage personal to the plaintiff is alleged and is accepted by the court as sufficient. *Gillick* v. *West Norfolk*

---

[99] R.S.C., Ord. 53, r. 3(4). Despite the wording of the proviso to this paragraph, it appears that after a refusal of leave the application can be renewed again in the Court of Appeal: R.S.C., Ord. 59, r. 14(3). See, e.g. *R.* v. *Special Commissioner, ex parte Stipplechoice Ltd* [1985] 2 All E.R. 465.

[100] See G. Borrie, 'The Regulation of Public and Private Power' [1989] P.L. 552, 554.

[101] Above, p. 123.

Area Health Authority is an important example.[102] There, the plaintiff was able to challenge the legality of advice given by the Department of Health and Social Security concerning the prescription of contraceptives to girls under the age of sixteen, and to do so by way of ordinary action in her own name. The plaintiff had daughters of her own under the age of sixteen and that, in the opinion at least of Lords Fraser and Scarman,[103] was enough to give her a sufficient private right for her action to go ahead. It can hardly be supposed, however, that possession of that right set Mrs Gillick apart: there must have been many thousands of other women equally possessed of it. The true explanation for the willingness of the House of Lords to deal with the substance of the case was, as Lord Templeman accepted, that 'the legal issues raised in these proceedings cannot be allowed to remain unanswered'.[104]

The subject of the exclusivity of the application for judicial review is considered below,[105] but however that is resolved, the conditions for challenges to the legality of the actions of those who exercise power in society should be the same whether they are public or private. The judges can if they wish, and to some extent do, arrive at such a result by accepting as sufficient an allegation of what is in truth no more than fictitious damage to the plaintiff, but, as is true of every legal fiction, however benevolent, the truth must eventually be admitted. It is now time for rationalisation of the law as it applies to litigation intended to protect diffuse, fragmented and collective interests. It has been recommended that an application for judicial review should be competent where the High Court considers that it is in the public interest for the applicant to make the application.[106] Why should a similar approach not be applied to ordinary actions in which, at present, the allegation of damage, if any, to the plaintiff himself is no more than a device to prevent the proceedings from being struck out *in limine*?[107]

---

[102] [1986] A.C. 112. See the Notes on the procedural aspects of this case at (1986) 102 L.Q.R. 173; [1986] C.L.J. 1.

[103] [1986] A.C. 112, 163 and 178.

[104] *Ibid.*, 207, 437. See also the American decision in *Trafficante v. Metropolitan Life Insurance Co.* 409 U.S. 205 (1972), chap. 6, p. 111.

[105] Chap. 8.   [106] Above, p. 142.

[107] For (different) alternative solutions, see J. A. Jolowicz, 'Civil Proceedings in the Public Interest' (1982) 13 Cambrian L.R. 32, 46–8; H. Woolf, 'Public Law – Private Law' [1986] P.L. 220, 236. See also Justice, *A Matter of Public Interest: Reforming the Law and Practice on Interventions in Public Interest Cases* (1996) (J. H. Schiemann, Comment [1996] P.L. 240).

Part III

Procedural modes

8 Civil and administrative procedure[1]

A single jurisdiction: a divided procedure

The civil procedure introduced into the unified Supreme Court as a result of the nineteenth-century reforms, whose principal characteristics have survived for so long, allowed for two principal modes for the conduct of civil litigation. In the procedure by writ, written pleadings and the disclosure of relevant documents were required, and the evidence – generally oral evidence – was given at the trial. In the procedure by originating summons, on the other hand, formal pleadings were not required, a judicial order was necessary if discovery was to be made, and the evidence was mainly given in written form by affidavit. Originating summons procedure was not to be used where serious issues of fact between the parties were anticipated, but where it emerged that the choice of this procedure had been wrongly made, the proceedings could simply be ordered to be continued as if begun by writ. There was no impenetrable barrier between the two modes.[2] Each was a variant of a single procedure – 'procedure by action' or simply 'action'.

Under the C.P.R., there is only one form of originating process – the 'claim form' – and the older terminology has been abandoned, but the distinction between the two modes of procedure is preserved. What is now known as 'Part 8 procedure' is broadly equivalent to the originating summons. Like its predecessor it should not be used where a substantial dispute of fact is likely, evidence is normally given in writing, and the court may at any stage order the claim to continue as if the claimant had

---

[1] Based on a report to the XIIIth International Congress of Comparative Law held in Montreal in 1990 and published in J. P. Gardner (ed.), *United Kingdom Law in the 1990s* (1990), p. 160. Its title, dictated by the Congress organisers, reflects the French rather than the English usage of the words 'civil' and 'administrative'. See chap. 1, pp. 13–15 and 17–19.

[2] R.S.C., Ord. 28, r. 8.

not used the Part 8 procedure.[3] The developments with which this chapter is concerned did, however, mainly occur before introduction of the C.P.R. and it is therefore convenient to continue generally to use the older terminology.

The remedies that may be granted to a successful plaintiff in an action, depending on the nature of his claim, consist, principally, of an award of damages and of the grant of a prohibitory or, occasionally, a mandatory injunction. Even allowing for the fact that no injunction can be awarded against the Crown,[4] therefore, the procedure by way of action seems sufficient to meet the needs of the litigant who claims that his legal right has been infringed or threatened by the act of anyone, including a public authority. Except against the Crown, it also seems generally sufficient in cases in which a public authority makes a decision to act or to refrain from acting in a certain way: an injunction can issue to restrain it from acting if the decision to act is vitiated by illegality[5] and a mandatory injunction can issue to compel it to act where it fails to comply with a legally imposed positive duty to do so.

The one lacuna in this scheme is that none of the remedies so far mentioned is appropriate where it is sought actually to quash the decision or order of a public authority, but the lacuna can effectively be filled by the additional remedy which has been available for more than a century: the declaration. Although a mere declaration that a decision or order is unlawful does not lead to its nullity, in reality it comes close to doing so. A declaration can be granted even if no other form of remedy is or could be claimed.[6]

Over a considerable number of years it was common for litigants to use the procedure by action to obtain injunctions and declarations against public authorities, and proceedings in this form have in the past

---

[3] C.P.R., r. 8.1(2)(a) and (3). 'Standard disclosure' (chap. 2, p. 57) is, however, required in both modes.

[4] An order declaratory of the rights of the parties may be made *in lieu* (Crown Proceedings Act 1947, s. 21), but an interlocutory declaration cannot be made *in lieu* of an interlocutory injunction: *Underhill* v. *Ministry of Food* [1950] 1 All E.R. 591. An injunction may be awarded against the Crown where this is necessary to secure compliance with European Community Law (*R.* v. *Secretary of State, ex parte Factortame Ltd (No. 2)* [1991] 1 A.C. 603). An injunction may also be issued against a Minister of the Crown (*M.* v. *Home Office* [1994] 1 A.C. 377), provided that the effect is not equivalent to the grant of a remedy against the Crown which could not have been obtained in proceedings actually brought against the Crown: Crown Proceedings Act 1947, s. 21(2).

[5] Damages can be awarded if the (illegal) decision is relied on to justify what would otherwise be a tort. See the classic case of *Cooper* v. *Wandsworth Board of Works* (1863) 14 C.B. (N.S.) 180.

[6] R.S.C., Ord. 15, r. 16.

proved of great importance to the development of administrative law.[7] What is more, no procedural gulf was created between proceedings challenging the legality of decisions made by public authorities and proceedings challenging the legality of decisions made by private bodies capable of affecting the rights of individuals. To take but two examples out of many, a demand by the Inland Revenue for certain information from taxpayers has been declared unlawful,[8] and so also has a proposed change in the rules of a trade union.[9] From a procedural point of view the two cases were the same.

Important though the procedure by action has been in cases brought against public authorities, it was not through its use that the courts originally exercised control over the legality of the acts of the administration. Alongside the modern action and its predecessors, there have for long existed special procedures whereby the citizen can invoke the 'supervisory' jurisdiction of the court and apply for one of the prerogative remedies against a public authority.[10] So far as here relevant, three such remedies existed – certiorari, whereby a decision could be brought before the court to be examined and, if found to be legally defective, quashed; prohibition, whereby a proposed course of action in excess of jurisdiction could be prevented; and mandamus, whereby the performance of a legal duty could be compelled.[11]

The scope of these remedies, especially prohibition and certiorari, was at one time restricted by the idea that they are available only against bodies called upon to make judicial or quasi-judicial decisions ('inferior jurisdictions'), but it is now clear that they lie in respect of any decision that determines questions affecting the rights of subjects.[12] They are, in theory, remedies of the Crown, which can be made available, in appropriate cases, at the request of a subject. When applied for, therefore, the court's intervention is always discretionary and never obtainable as of right.[13] It was, however, not the discretionary character of the prerogative remedies which led to the use, against public authorities, of the procedure by action for injunctions or declarations, which are in any case discretionary remedies themselves. It was, rather, the complexity

[7] Zamir and Woolf, para. 2.38.
[8] *Dyson* v. *Attorney-General* [1911] 1 K.B. 410; [1912] 1 Ch. 158.
[9] *Clarke* v. *Chadburn* [1985] 1 W.L.R. 78.
[10] See de Smith, chap. 14; Wade, chap. 17.
[11] Habeas corpus is also a 'prerogative' remedy, but its subject matter falls outside the scope of this chapter. For its relation to the modern application for judicial review, see H. W. R. Wade, 'Habeas Corpus and Judicial Review' (1997) 113 L.Q.R. 55.
[12] See the classic statement of Atkin L.J. in *R.* v. *Electricity Commissioners, ex parte London Electricity Joint Committee* [1924] 1 K.B. 171, 205 as explained by Lord Reid in *Ridge* v. *Baldwin* [1964] A.C. 40, 74–9.
[13] Wade, pp. 614–15.

and technicality of the procedure by which the supervisory jurisdiction of the court could be invoked.

The prerogative remedies escaped the reforms of the nineteenth century,[14] but in 1977, by amendment to the Rules of the Supreme Court, they were substantially revised and brought together as the 'application for judicial review', with its own specialised procedure. An application for certiorari, prohibition or mandamus may be accompanied by a claim for damages, an injunction or a declaration,[15] but this does not mean that the application for judicial review is just another variant of the action. If, for example, a litigant desires that an administrative decision be quashed and is not content with a simple declaration of the decision's invalidity, he must apply for judicial review; certiorari cannot be granted in an action and there is at present no provision for proceedings begun by action to be continued as if begun by application for judicial review. The only possibility of transfer between the two forms of procedure arises where, on an application for judicial review that includes a claim for damages, an injunction or a declaration, the court considers that that remedy should not be granted on the application but might have been granted had the proceedings been begun by writ. In that case, but only in that case, the proceedings may be ordered to continue as if begun by writ.[16] The application for judicial review, like its predecessors, is properly seen not just as distinct from the action but as an independent administrative procedure in its own right, albeit one to be engaged in the same unified jurisdiction as is the action.

If, as was intended when the application for judicial review was introduced, the action for a declaration had remained as an alternative,[17] this procedural dichotomy would not have been of great practical significance. Though a court might dismiss an application for judicial review on the sole ground that the intended respondent was not subject to the prerogative but only to the general jurisdiction of the court, the action would have remained open and could have been used whatever the quality of the defendant. In its landmark decision in *O'Reilly* v.

---

[14] They were subject to relatively minor reforms as, for example, by the Administration of Justice (Miscellaneous Provisions) Act 1933.

[15] R.S.C., Ord. 53 (continued in force under the C.P.R., with only minor variations); Supreme Court Act 1981, s. 31. Since judicial review procedure may be invoked against the decisions of inferior jurisdictions, which includes the magistrates' courts, it may be employed in relation to a decision in a criminal matter. In what follows, such special rules as apply when it is so employed will not be mentioned. See R.S.C., Ord. 53, rr. 3(4)(a), 4(2), 5(1), 9(2).

[16] R.S.C., Ord. 53, r. 9(5).

[17] See Law Commission, Remedies in Administrative Law, Cmnd 6407 (1976); Wade, pp. 680–1. Cf. below, p. 173.

Mackman[18] in 1982, however, and after a period of uncertainty,[19] the House of Lords laid down as a general rule that the action, even for a declaration, is incompetent, and should be struck out as an abuse of the process of the court, where a person seeks to establish 'that a decision of a public authority infringed rights to which he was entitled under public law'.[20]

O'Reilly v. *Mackman* gave rise to what has become known as the principle of 'exclusivity', according to which the two procedures – the action and the application for judicial review – are mutually exclusive one of the other: the action is for private and the application for judicial review is for public law cases:[21] as happened in *O'Reilly* v. *Mackman* itself, a plaintiff who chooses the wrong form of procedure will fail to obtain redress to which he would otherwise have been entitled if and when the facts alleged by him had been found to be true.[22]

Procedure by action and judicial review procedure

In the past, an applicant for one of the prerogative remedies was subject to a number of procedural disadvantages as compared with the plaintiff in an action. Of these, one of the most important was the absence of any provision for discovery of documents, which was in itself one reason for the popularity of the action for a declaration,[23] and another was the almost invariable refusal of leave to cross-examine a deponent on his affidavit.[24]

---

[18] [1983] 2 A.C. 237.

[19] See, e.g. *Heywood* v. *Hull Prison Visitors* [1980] 1 W.L.R. 1386 and contrast *Steeples* v. *Derbyshire County Council* [1985] 1 W.L.R. 256.

[20] [1983] 2 A.C. 237, 285, *per* Lord Diplock. See J. A. Jolowicz, 'Abuse of the Process of the Court: Handle with Care' (1990) 43 *Current Legal Problems* 77, 90.

[21] The distinction between public and private law, however ill defined, has thus come to play a practical role in English law. Previously, it could be said that, in England, the distinction 'has exclusively academic and educational significance': O. Kahn-Freund *et al.*, *A Source-book on French Law*, 2nd edn (1979), p. 204. See, e.g. H. Woolf, 'Public Law – Private Law: Why the Divide' [1986] P.L. 220; J. Beatson, '"Public" and "Private" in Administrative Law' (1987) 103 L.Q.R. 34; H. Woolf, 'Droit Public – English Style' [1995] P.L. 57. For a comparative account see C. Szladits, 'Structure and the Divisions of the Law: the Civil Law System' in *International Encyclopaedia of Comparative Law*, Vol. II (ed. R. David) (1969), chap. 2, no. 15.

[22] 'All that is at issue in the instant appeal is the procedure by which . . . relief ought to be sought': [1983] 2 A.C. 237, 274, *per* Lord Diplock.

[23] *Barnard* v. *National Dock Labour Board* [1953] 2 Q.B. 18. So much is agreed by Lord Diplock himself: *O'Reilly* v. *Mackman* [1983] 2 A.C. 237, 280.

[24] *R.* v. *Stokesley JJ., ex parte Bartram* [1956] 1 W.L.R. 254. Cross-examination was allowed in that case, but Lord Goddard C.J. indicated the extreme rarity even of applications to cross-examine. He indicated that the case was of a very remarkable character and that he did not wish it to be thought to be an 'easy precedent'.

Judicial review procedure has now been brought more or less into line with originating summons procedure. In particular, in both procedures, the evidence is given by affidavit, not orally at a trial, and provision is made to ensure that each party has the other's affidavits in advance of the hearing.[25] Amendments to the claim as originally formulated and also additional affidavits are permitted, but only with the leave of the court.[26] Under both forms of procedure there may be discovery of documents and deponents may be cross-examined.[27] There are, however, two important differences between the two procedures, namely, first, that an application for judicial review can never be made unless the court has first granted leave to apply and, secondly, that the time limit within which proceedings must be begun is much shorter in judicial review procedure than on an originating summons. There are also certain differences relating to the joinder of parties and a few other matters.[28]

The application for leave[29]

As a general rule there are no restrictions on a person's right to start an action and to carry it at least to the point at which the defendant must make some response if he wishes to avoid judgment in default.[30] No similar freedom ever attached to the commencement of proceedings to obtain one of the prerogative remedies, and it does not attach to the

---

[25] R.S.C., Ord. 28, r. 1A; C.P.R., r. 8.5; R.S.C., Ord. 53, r. 6. Curiously, while affidavits produced by one party must be supplied to the others free of charge in the originating summons procedure (R.S.C., Ord. 28, r. 1A(7)) and by implication from C.P.R., r. 8.5, this is not the case in judicial review procedure: R.S.C., Ord. 53, r. 6(5).

[26] R.S.C., Ord. 28, r. 1A(6); C.P.R., r. 8.6; R.S.C., Ord. 53, r. 6(2), (3).

[27] 'Standard disclosure' is automatic under Part 8 procedure, but an order from the court is necessary in judicial review: R.S.C., Ord. 53, r. 8. Cross-examination of a deponent in judicial review procedure should be allowed on the same basis as on an originating summons: *O'Reilly* v. *Mackman* [1983] 2 A.C. 237, 282–3, *per* Lord Diplock. But see below, n. 131.

[28] R.S.C., Ord. 53, r. 9(4) provides that if a decision is quashed on certiorari, the court may remit the matter whence it came with a direction that it be decided in accordance with the court's findings. No similar power exists following a declaration, but a decision-making body, whether public authority or not, will know what must be done after a declaration that its decision is unlawful. See J. McBride, 'The Doctrine of Exclusivity and Judicial Review' (1983) 2 C.J.Q. 268, 276–7.

[29] A. P. Le Sueur and M. Sunkin, 'Applications for Judicial Review: The Requirement of Leave' [1992] P.L. 102.

[30] *Clarke* v. *Bradlaugh* (1881) 8 Q.B.D. 63, 69, *per* Brett L.J.; Jacob, *Fabric*, p. 183. There are a few specialised exceptions, e.g. where the intending plaintiff has been declared a vexatious litigant (Supreme Court Act 1981, s. 42) or, subject to the Civil Jurisdiction and Judgments Act 1982, where the writ is intended to be served outside the jurisdiction: R.S.C., Ord. 6, r. 7 (now, R.S.C., Ord. 11, r. 4).

application for judicial review. A person seeking to apply for judicial review must first obtain the leave of the court.[31]

The application for leave is made, *ex parte*, by filing a notice in prescribed form, which must include a statement of the relief claimed and of the grounds on which it is claimed, verified by affidavit;[32] unless a hearing is requested, the application can be dealt with by the judge without a hearing.[33] If leave is refused by the judge without a hearing the application can be renewed before a judge sitting in open court.[34] No appeal from a refusal of leave on the *ex parte* application is possible,[35] but the application can be renewed before the Court of Appeal.[36]

The grant of leave is discretionary, but leave may be granted only if the court considers that the applicant has sufficient interest in the matter to which the application relates.[37] That leave is granted on the *ex parte* application does not, however, dispose finally of the question whether the applicant does have such sufficient interest. The question remains open at the hearing of the substantive application for judicial review,[38] and the *ex parte* application has become, in effect, a procedure for the exclusion at an early stage of applications which are hopeless, frivolous or irresponsible.[39]

---

[31] The Law Commission has recommended that the application for leave should become the 'preliminary consideration': *Administrative Law: Judicial Review and Statutory Appeals*, Law Com. No. 226 (1994) (hereafter 'Law Com. 226'), paras. 5.6–5.8. Lord Woolf agrees, but as he points out, acceptance of his proposals for ordinary litigation would bring the two forms of procedure closer together: Woolf Final, pp. 252–3. This has happened. As with other forms of proceeding, an application for judicial review is now made by the issue of a claim form: R.S.C., Ord. 53, r. 5(2A).

[32] R.S.C., Ord. 53, r. 3(2).

[33] R.S.C., Ord. 53, r. 3(3). The application may be adjourned for the person against whom relief is claimed to be represented: *Inland Revenue* case [1982] A.C. 617, 642, *per* Lord Diplock. Conversely, if leave is granted the court may, at the same time, grant interim relief and, in a case of great urgency, may even do so *ex parte*: R.S.C., Ord. 53, r. 3(10); *R. v. Kensington RLBC, ex parte Hammell* [1989] Q.B. 518.

[34] R.S.C., Ord. 53, r. 3(4). If so ordered, the hearing can be before a Divisional Court of the Queen's Bench Division.

[35] *Lane v. Esdaile* [1891] A.C. 210.

[36] R.S.C., Ord. 59, r. 14(3); *R. v. Special Commissioners, ex parte Stipplechoice Ltd* [1985] 2 All E.R. 465. This must be done within seven days of the refusal. No appeal to or further renewal before the House of Lords is available: *Re Poh* [1983] 1 W.L.R. 2. Cf. *Kemper Reinsurance v. Minister of Finance* [1998] 3 W.L.R. 630 (P.C.).

[37] R.S.C., Ord. 53, r. 3(7); Supreme Court Act 1981, s. 31(3).

[38] See below, p. 168.

[39] *Inland Revenue* case at 644, *per* Lord Diplock; *R. v. Special Commissioners, ex parte Stipplechoice Ltd* [1985] 2 All E.R. 465, 469.

Time limits

The periods of limitation applicable to ordinary actions are now contained in the Limitation Act 1980, as amended.[40] Generally speaking, the shortest of the various periods within which an action must be commenced is three years from the accrual of the cause of action; in cases not involving personal injury it is six years.[41] The position with regard to the application for judicial review is quite different. There are two relevant statutory provisions:

(a) R.S.C., Order 53, rule 4(1) requires that the application for leave must be made 'promptly', and in any event within three months from the date when grounds for the application first arose, unless the court considers that there is good reason for extending the period.

(b) Section 31(6) of the Supreme Court Act 1981 provides that where the court considers that there has been 'undue delay' in making an application for judicial review and also that the granting of relief would be likely to cause substantial hardship to, or substantially prejudice the rights of, any person or would be detrimental to good administration, it may refuse to grant leave for the making of the application or it may refuse any relief sought on the application.[42]

It is clear from these provisions that the court has a discretion, and it may actually allow an application to go ahead notwithstanding even an inadequately justified delay if it considers that the matters raised are of general importance.[43] On the other hand, it is also clear that failure on the part of the applicant to act within a very short period of time[44] places his application at risk at more than one stage of the proceedings. First, the application for leave may be rejected on the ground of delay or it may be granted subject to the respondent's right to apply for it to be set

---

[40] In particular by the Administration of Justice Act 1985, s. 57 and the Latent Damage Act 1986.

[41] Limitation Act 1980, ss. 2, 5 and 11. For defamation and malicious falsehood, the period was reduced to one year by the Defamation Act 1996, s. 5.

[42] The co-existence of these two provisions has been described by Lloyd L.J. as a 'muddle': *R. v. Dairy Tribunal, ex parte Caswell* [1989] 1 W.L.R. 1089, 1094. In the House of Lords, however, Lord Goff explained the cause of the 'muddle' and found a way of making sense: [1990] 2 A.C. 738, 744–8.

[43] *R. v. Home Secretary, ex parte Ruddock* [1987] 1 W.L.R. 1482. The substantive application failed.

[44] An application for leave may not have been made promptly even if made within the period of three months: *R. v. Stratford-on-Avon D.C., ex parte Jackson* [1985] 1 W.L.R. 1319, 1322–3, *per* Ackner L.J.

aside.[45] Secondly, even if leave is granted unconditionally, undue delay may still have occurred – and will have occurred if the three-month period has been exceeded – so that the court hearing the substantive application may refuse relief on the grounds set out in section 31(6).[46]

Parties

Although the plaintiff in an action is normally entitled to decide who shall be defendants to it,[47] the court is endowed with a wide discretionary power to order a person to be added as a party, usually on application but also of its own motion.[48] Any person who ought to have been joined, or whose presence before the court is necessary for the full determination of the matters in dispute, can be joined, and so too can a person between whom and an existing party there is an issue connected with the relief claimed in the action, provided that the court considers it to be just and convenient to determine that issue along with the issue between the original parties. In addition, the Attorney-General has a right to intervene in proceedings if the prerogative of the Crown may be affected and also, at the invitation or with the permission of the court, where the proceedings raise a question of public policy on which the executive may wish its view to be brought to the attention of the court.[49]

This discretionary power of the court extends, it would appear, to applications for judicial review, but the applicant has less freedom in the choice of his defendant: notice of the application must be served on all persons directly affected.[50] It is, moreover, explicitly provided that if, on the hearing of the application, the court is of the opinion that any person who has not been served with notice of it should have been served, it may adjourn the hearing for service on him to be effected.[51] As a practical matter, if not in theory, this gives the court greater power to ensure that all proper parties are before the court. In addition, at the hearing itself under judicial review procedure, but not in an action, the court may allow any person to be heard who appears to it to be a proper person to be heard if that person, though not served with notice of the application, desires to be heard in opposition to it.[52] No parallel

---

[45] As was done by Glidewell J. in *R. v. Stratford-on-Avon D.C., ex parte Jackson* [1985] 1 W.L.R. 1319, 1322.

[46] *Ibid.* at 1326, *per* Ackner L.J.; *R. v. Dairy Tribunal, ex parte Caswell* [1989] 1 W.L.R. 1089.

[47] *Dollfus Mieg et Compagnie* v. *Bank of England* [1951] Ch. 33; *Maxfield* v. *Llewellyn* [1961] 1 W.L.R. 1119.

[48] R.S.C., Ord. 15, r. 6(2); C.P.R., r. 19.1(2) and (3).

[49] See, e.g. *Re Westinghouse Uranium Contract* [1978] A.C. 547, 589–95.

[50] R.S.C., Ord. 53, r. 5(3). See A. Lidbetter, Note (1997) 113 L.Q.R. 40.

[51] R.S.C., Ord. 53, r. 5(7).

provision covers persons who desire to be heard in support of the application.[53]

The procedural dichotomy

It was an essential element of the reasoning in *O'Reilly* v. *Mackman* that the reform of 1977 effectively placed the applicant for judicial review, once he had obtained leave, in no less favourable a position from the procedural point of view than the plaintiff in an action begun by originating summons. There was thus no reason to continue to allow the procedure by action to be used by a person seeking to establish that a decision of a public authority infringed rights to which he was entitled to protection under public law;[54] the protection provided to administrative decisions by the requirements that an applicant for judicial review first obtain leave to apply and that he do so within a very short period of time could therefore be preserved in the interests of good administration and in the interests of third parties who may be affected by the decision.[55]

The decision in *O'Reilly* v. *Mackman* was applied by the House of Lords in another case on the same day as it was given,[56] but Lord Diplock himself recognised that the general rule of exclusivity[57] admitted certain exceptions. He instanced, in particular, cases in which the public law question was collateral to a claim for infringement of a right 'arising under private law' and cases in which neither party objected to use of an action.[58] Stronger warnings than this against too ready a use of the distinction between public and private law, from the judiciary as well as from academic writers, were, however, not long in coming, and some softening of the rigour of the rule in *O'Reilly* v. *Mackman* followed.[59] Now, it seems, if a case fulfils any one of three

---

[52] *Ibid.*, r. 9(1).

[53] It has been proposed that such a provision should be introduced: Justice, *A Matter of Public Interest: Reforming the Law and Practice on Interventions in Public Interest Cases* (1996), pp. 20–1 and appendix. K. H. J. Schiemann, Note [1996] P.L. 240.

[54] [1983] 2 A.C. 237, 285, *per* Lord Diplock.

[55] *Ibid.* at 284, *per* Lord Diplock.

[56] *Cocks* v. *Thanet District Council* [1983] 2 A.C. 286. For the difficulties of this case, see Wade, pp. 686–7.

[57] Above, p. 155.

[58] [1983] 2 A.C. 237, 285. As Lord Scarman later pointed out, however, if there is an abuse of process, it cannot be overlooked by the court even if the parties are prepared to do so: *Gillick* v. *West Norfolk AHA* [1986] A.C. 112, 178.

[59] See, e.g. *Davy* v. *Spelthorne B.C.* [1984] A.C. 262, 276, *per* Lord Wilberforce. In *Wandsworth LBC* v. *Winder* [1985] A.C. 461, proceedings were brought by a local authority against a tenant who had refused to pay an increased rent. The House of Lords had no doubt that the tenant could raise, by way of defence, the argument that the increase in rent was itself unlawful (in 'public law'). For early academic criticism see the articles cited below in n. 76 and, e.g. H. W. R. Wade, 'Procedure and

linked but different criteria, proceedings by action against a public
authority will not be struck out.

(1) Where the plaintiff claims in respect of the breach of a private law
duty, it may, of course, be the case that the claim should be
struck out for reasons unconnected with the exclusivity principle;
if so, it matters not that the defendant is subjected to duties in
public law.[60] On the other hand, the fact that, in propounding his
claim in private law, the plaintiff is bound to challenge a public
law decision, does not in itself have the consequence that he may
proceed only by way of judicial review. In *Roy* v. *Kensington and
Chelsea Family Practitioner Committee*,[61] the defendant Committee, having determined that the plaintiff doctor had failed to
devote sufficient time to practice under the National Health
Service as required by applicable regulations, withheld part of his
remuneration. A challenge to that determination formed an
integral part of the plaintiff's claim for full remuneration, but the
House of Lords declined to strike the action out. Whether the
plaintiff had a contractual (and therefore private) relationship
with the Committee or not, he had a private law right to be
remunerated in accordance with his statutory terms of service:
that right he was entitled to pursue by action even though a
challenge to a public law decision formed an integral part of his
case.[62]

(2) Despite the procedural similarities between the application for
judicial review and the action,[63] substantial questions of fact
seldom arise in judicial review, and there is a consensus that,
where such questions do arise, the procedure by action is the
more suitable. So, in *Dennis Rye Pension Fund* v. *Sheffield C.C.*,[64]
where the plaintiff claimed to be entitled under the Housing Act
1985 to a grant from the defendant housing authority, the Court
of Appeal refused to strike out his action even though the Act
conferred a public law discretion on the defendant. It may be

Prerogative in Public Law' (1985) 101 L.Q.R. 180; P. Cane, 'Public Law and Private
Law' [1983] P.L. 202; McBride, 'The Doctrine of Exclusivity and Judicial Review'.
[60] *O'Rourke* v. *Camden LBC* [1998] A.C. 188; *Andreou* v. *Institute of Accountants* [1998] 1
All E.R. 14.
[61] [1992] 1 A.C. 624; *Lonrho plc* v. *Tebbit* [1992] 4 All E.R. 280; *Dennis Rye Pension Fund*
v. *Sheffield C.C.* [1998] 1 W.L.R. 840. See P. Cane, 'Private Rights and Public
Procedure' [1992] P.L. 193; A. Alder, 'Hunting the Chimera – The End of *O'Reilly* v.
Mackman?' (1993) 13 L.S. 183.
[62] See Law Com. 226, para. 3.11. This leaves the difficult distinction between 'public'
and 'private' as the controlling factor with potentially unfortunate results, as in *Avon
County Council* v. *Buscott* [1988] Q.B. 656.
[63] Above, p. 156.   [64] [1998] 1 W.L.R. 840.

that, following *Roy's* case, the plaintiff had a private law right, but, in the view of Lord Woolf M.R., the more important point was that a decision on the claim depended on 'an examination of issues largely of fact which are more appropriately examined in the course of ordinary proceedings than on an application for judicial review'.[65]

(3) The formal ground adduced by Lord Diplock for striking out the action in *O'Reilly* v. *Mackman* was that it constituted an abuse of the process of the court.[66] In *Mercury Ltd* v. *Telecommunications Director*,[67] the plaintiffs began proceedings by action, in which they contended that the defendant had misinterpreted a clause in a telecommunications licence issued under the Telecommunications Act 1984, with resulting disadvantages to them in their contractual relations with British Telecommunications plc, the second defendants. On an application to strike out, Lord Slynn, with whose speech the other Law Lords present agreed, emphasised the importance of retaining flexibility in the limits of 'what is called "public law" and what is called "private law"', and said that it must be borne in mind 'that the overriding question is whether the proceedings constitute an abuse of the process of the court'.[68] His Lordship considered that, in the circumstances, an originating summons in the commercial court was at least as well suited to the dispute as the procedure for judicial review, that it did not constitute an abuse of process, and so that the action should be allowed to continue.

These developments, though useful, do not mean that the principle of exclusivity has effectively been abolished, and the Law Commission, while recommending that transfer from the procedure by action into the procedure of judicial review should be made possible, states plainly that it does not favour a unified procedure.[69] Implementation of Lord Woolf's proposals would, it is true, bring the two procedures closer together; there is now a single form of claim for all proceedings, and it is

---

[65] *Ibid.* at 847.   [66] Above, p. 155.

[67] [1996] 1 W.L.R. 48. P. P. Craig, Note (1966) 112 L.Q.R. 531.

[68] [1996] 1 W.L.R. 48, 57. See also the judgment of Lord Woolf M.R. in *Dennis Rye Pension Fund* v. *Sheffield C.C.*, [1998] 1 W.L.R. 840, 848–9.

[69] Law Com. 226, paras. 3.5–3.15. See also, e.g. H. Woolf, 'Public Law – Private Law: Why the Divide?' [1986] P.L. 220; also his 'Judicial Review: A Possible Programme for Reform' [1992] P.L. 221; C. T. Emery, 'Public Law or Private Law? The Limits of Procedural Reform' [1995] P.L. 450. For the Commission's proposals for transfer, see Law Com. 226, paras. 3.16–3.23 (below, p. 165) and C. T. Emery, 'Transfer of Cases between Public and Private Law Procedures: the English Law Commission's Proposals' (1995) 14 C.J.Q. 163.

envisaged that what is intended to be called the 'preliminary consideration stage' for judicial review should be similar to the initial stages of
private law proceedings.[70] Nevertheless, the Woolf proposals fall short
of a recommendation for removal of the procedural dichotomy and
there will undoubtedly continue to be cases for which only the application for judicial review is permissible. An evaluation of the dichotomy
is, therefore, still necessary.

An evaluation

As noticed earlier,[71] there is not, in England, as there is in France, a
distinct hierarchy of administrative courts, separate from those of the
judicial order and manned by judges whose lives have been spent in the
administration rather than in the ordinary courts. There is not, in
England, as, again, there is in France, any suggestion that litigation that
concerns the public administration calls for a different and more
inquisitorial procedure than would be appropriate in litigation between
private persons.[72] Evaluation of the procedural dichotomy as it exists in
England and Wales means, therefore, evaluation of the advantages and
disadvantages of maintaining mutually exclusive procedures for public
and private law cases on the basis that the dichotomy does little more
than preserve, for the former, the requirement that leave to apply be
obtained, and that within a very short period of time.

Such an enquiry has two aspects that merit separate consideration.
The first is whether the dichotomy is, in itself, appropriate or necessary:
is it right, not simply that special rules should apply to protect certain
administrative decisions of particular importance or urgency against too
ready a challenge or too delayed a finding of invalidity, but to go further
and provide a separate procedure for all challenges to administrative
decisions of whatever kind and at whatever level in the administrative
hierarchy they may have been made? The second is whether the
dichotomy brings advantages which go beyond the merely procedural.

---

[70] Woolf Final, chap. 18. The Report recognises that the exclusivity principle does lead to
'wholly undesirable procedural wrangles': *ibid.*, p. 250.

[71] Chap. 1, pp. 18–19

[72] See, e.g. Debbasch, nos. 19–24; J. M. Auby and R. Drago, *Traité de contentieux
administratif*, 3rd edn (1984), no. 702; de Laubadère, *Traité de droit administratif*, 13th
edn, by J. C. Venezia and Y. Gaudemet (1994), nos. 632–6. See, however, Law Com.
226 para. 3.13. In France, even the substantive law of what may be called contract and
tort, as applied by the administrative courts, is, theoretically, distinct from that applied
by the ordinary courts: *Blanco*, T.C. 30 July 1873, D.P. 1874, 3.5; *Feutry*, T.C. 29
February 1908, D. 1908, 3.49.

Is the dichotomy appropriate or necessary?

The distinction between public and private law is a newcomer to English law that must be used with caution,[73] but it is not a purpose of this chapter to consider the value of the distinction as such. There may be good reasons why some principle or rule of law should not apply, or should only apply, where the conduct of a public authority is called in question. One example of such a rule existed in the past by virtue of the Public Authorities Protection Act 1893, which imposed a special, short, period of limitation within which actions against public authorities must be begun,[74] and similar rules are to be found today in statutes such as the Acquisition of Land Act 1981, which fixes a time limit of six weeks for a challenge to a compulsory purchase order.[75] Rules such as these, whether in themselves good or bad, relate to particular bodies or to particular categories of administrative decision. They are susceptible to individual fine-tuning and can be changed without the need to take account of the impact of change on other bodies or other categories of decision.

The technique of the procedural dichotomy is different for at least two reasons:

> (a) It restores, even if on a limited basis, the system of forms of action, with the result that a litigant may fail purely and simply because he chose the wrong form of initiating process.[76] The problem seems to be particularly acute in employment cases, for a public employee may be employed either under a contract of service, in which case judicial review procedure is inapplicable,[77] or he may hold an office the terms and conditions of which are governed, not by contract, but by public law, in which case it is mandatory.[78]

---

[73] Above, p. 160.

[74] The Act was repealed in 1954 without, it seems, causing difficulties: Wade, p. 685.

[75] Section 23(4). See *Smith* v. *East Elloes RDC* [1956] A.C. 736.

[76] H. W. R. Wade, 'Public Law, Private Law and Judicial Review' (1983) 99 L.Q.R. 166 ('It would be deplorable if the law were to take a step backwards towards the old days of the forms of action'); M. Sunkin, 'Judicial Review' (1983) 46 M.L.R. 645; J. A. Jolowicz, 'The Forms of Action Disinterred' [1983] C.L.J. 15. See also J. McBride, 'Choice of Procedure in Judicial Review' (1982) 1 C.J.Q. 296 (written before *O'Reilly* v. *Mackman*); McBride, 'The Doctrine of Exclusivity and Judicial Review'; Wade, pp. 684–6; P. Neill (Chairman), Justice-All Souls, *Administrative Justice – Some Necessary Reforms*, paras. 6–18.

[77] *R.* v. *East Berks. Health Authority, ex parte Walsh* [1985] Q.B. 152.

[78] *R.* v. *Home Secretary, ex parte Benwell* [1985] Q.B. 554; see B. A. Walsh, 'Judicial Review of Dismissal from Employment' [1989] P.L. 131. Cf. H. Woolf, 'Public Law – Private Law' [1986] P.L. 220, 233–5. See further *West Glamorgan C.C.* v. *Rafferty* [1987] 1 W.L.R. 457; *Waverley Council* v. *Hilden* [1988] 1 W.L.R. 246; *Avon Council* v.

This problem will be eased if the Law Commission's proposals on this matter are adopted. The Commission recommends, first, that the power to transfer cases from judicial review to the procedure by action should be more generously exercisable,[79] but without going so far as to recommend that the power should always be available.[80] Secondly, it is recommended that there should be a power to transfer from the procedure by action into judicial review where the circumstances are such that an application for leave would have been granted if originally sought.[81] No recommendation is made, however, for an extension of the three-month time limit in such cases.[82]

(b) It treats all administrative decisions in the same way, whether they are decisions of wide-ranging importance taken by central government or decisions taken locally and affecting only one or a few individuals.[83] It also, by implication, holds that decisions which are not administrative – that is, which are not decisions of public authorities – have little or nothing in common with administrative decisions, however important and however far-reaching their consequences may be.

That might have been satisfactory in the past, on the hypothesis that society consists of the State, on the one hand, and of individuals on the other, with all power centred in the State. That this simplistic view bears little relation to contemporary society, however, needs no demon-

---

Burcott [1988] Q.B. 656. Perhaps the variety of reasons given by different members of the House of Lords for allowing the plaintiff's action to proceed in *Gillick* v. *West Norfolk AHA* [1986] A.C. 112 indicates reluctance to follow the logic of *O'Reilly* v. *Mackman*: Wade, p. 689. See further M. J. Beloff, 'The Boundaries of Judicial Review' in J. Jowell and D. Oliver (eds.), *New Directions in Judicial Review* (1988), p. 5.

[79] Law Com. 226, paras. 3.17–3.19.

[80] The Commission considered that *R.* v. *East Berkshire Area Health Authority, ex parte Walsh* [1985] Q.B. 152, where a transfer was refused, was unduly restrictive but agreed with the refusal of a transfer in *R.* v. *Home Secretary, ex parte Dew* [1987] 1 W.L.R. 881 where a prisoner complained of allegedly inadequate medical treatment while in custody: it was held that his claim was for alleged negligence and was a claim purely in private law so that his application for judicial review should be struck out without more. Cf. *Olotu* v. *Home Office* [1997] 1 W.L.R. 328.

[81] Law Com. 226, paras. 3.20–3.21. The Commission also recommended the introduction of a 'reference' procedure, which would enable judges to transfer cases so as to ensure that they are heard by a specialist judge if they raise significant public law points even though not required to proceed by judicial review: *ibid.*, paras. 3.22–3.23.

[82] Reliance is placed on the view of the nominated judges who doubted that, in practice, a case with merits would be turned down merely for reasons of delay: Law Com. 226, para. 3.21.

[83] As in *O'Reilly* v. *Mackman* itself. Lord Woolf, though willing to avoid use of the concept of abuse of process sees it as important that the 'safeguards' of the short time limit and of standing, necessary in judicial review, should not be bypassed: Woolf Final, p. 256.

stration,[84] and in any case the distinction between the exercise of a power conferred by law and the exercise of a power conferred by contract is one which is likely to appeal only to lawyers. So much is, indeed, recognised by the courts which have, for example, applied the substantive principles for the review of decisions made by statutory bodies to the review of those made by powerful associations such as trade unions.[85] In *Cocks* v. *Thanet District Council*[86] Lord Bridge saw, as one reason for the exclusivity of judicial review procedure, that it avoided the temptation for the court to substitute its own decision of fact for that of the (public) authority. However, the temptation is not necessarily avoided by use of judicial review procedure,[87] and in any case it is equally to be resisted when the decision of a private body is in question.[88]

If this is right, then the price, in terms of the complications and difficulties to which the procedural dichotomy gives rise, is too high. If really necessary, the short time limit could be enforced by special legislation on the lines of, but more selective than, the Public Authorities Protection Act 1893,[89] and, if such legislation were introduced, a respondent public authority could apply for the proceedings to be dismissed at an early stage.[90] As to the requirement of leave to apply, no such requirement exists in Scotland[91] and a number of authorities consider that it should be removed from English law.[92] If it is so

---

[84] See, e.g. M. Cappelletti, 'Vindicating the Public Interest through the Courts' in Cappelletti and Garth, Vol. III, pp. 513, 520–1; *Breen* v. *AEU* [1971] 2 Q.B. 175, 190, *per* Lord Denning M.R.; Woolf 'Public Law – Private Law', pp. 224–5.

[85] *Breen* v. *AEU* [1971] 2 Q.B. 175; *Edwards* v. *SOGAT* [1971] Ch. 354, 382, *per* Sachs L.J. Even in *Cheall* v. *APEX* [1983] A.C. 180, where the plaintiff could prove no breach of the rules of natural justice, there is no suggestion that those rules were irrelevant. For cases not involving trade unions see, e.g. *Nagle* v. *Feilden* [1966] 2 Q.B. 633; *McInnes* v. *Onslow-Fane* [1978] 1 W.L.R. 1520 (in neither of which was there even a contract between the parties); *Endersby Town Football Club* v. *F.A.* [1971] Ch. 591. For a discussion of the common values of public and private law, see Dawn Oliver, 'Common Values in Public and Private Law and the Public/Private Divide' [1997] P.L. 630.

[86] [1983] 2 A.C. 286, 294.

[87] *R.* v. *Trade and Industry Secretary, ex parte Lonrho plc* [1989] 1 W.L.R. 525, 535, *per* Lord Keith. See also *R.* v. *Hillingdon LBC, ex parte Pulhoffer* [1986] A.C. 484, 518, *per* Lord Brightman.

[88] *Hamlet* v. *GMBATU* [1987] 1 W.L.R. 449, 452, *per* Harman J.

[89] See Oliver, 'Common Values', at p. 633.

[90] R.S.C., Ord. 18, r. 19 applied in an action begun by originating summons as it did in one begun by writ: *ibid.*, r. 3. See now C.P.R., r. 3.4.

[91] See Wade, p. 677.

[92] E.g. Justice-All Souls, *Administrative Justice*, para. 6.23; Jacob, *Fabric*, p. 183. See also H. W. R. Wade, 'Procedure and Prerogative in Public Law' (1985) 101 L.Q.R. 180; Beloff, 'Boundaries of Judicial Review', p. 16. Cf. D. P. Pannick, 'What is a Public Authority?' in Jowell and Oliver, *New Directions*, pp. 23, 24. For Lord Woolf's proposals, see above, pp. 163 and 165.

removed it will still be possible for a respondent public authority to apply for the proceedings to be struck out for want on the part of the applicant of a sufficient interest or, as would be preferable, lack of a reasonable cause of action as in any other kind of proceedings. The ordinary rules of court contain adequate provisions to cut short frivolous or vexatious proceedings, and public authorities should be expected to make use of those rules as must any other defendant. If taken at face value, the dichotomy is unjustified and should be removed from English law. It may be, however, that it has, or has had, more than merely face value.

Is the dichotomy beneficial to the law?

The jurisdictional and procedural dichotomy of French law grew out of a political and legal dogma. It is not too inaccurate a summary of a complex piece of history to say that the exclusion of the judges from matters affecting the administration[93] derived from a conviction that pre-Revolutionary judges had hindered if not prevented reform, a conviction which was linked with apparent logic to a literal approach to the doctrine of the separation of powers. The jurisdiction of the Conseil d'Etat, formally recognised as such in 1872,[94] after a period in which its role was purely advisory, developed to fill the gap.

No similar dogma has ever been accepted in England. On the contrary, the dogma, if any, has been that administrators are subject to the same law, administered in accordance with the same procedure, as are private citizens. Nevertheless, substantive administrative law and the scope of judicial review of administrative action expanded greatly in the years precedng *O'Reilly* v. *Mackman*,[95] and it is possible that concretisation of the dichotomy by that decision assisted and accelerated the expansion. Substantive law falls outside the limits of this chapter, but three points merit attention.

Locus standi

Since there are no formal restrictions to a person's right to begin an action, the concept of *locus standi*, properly speaking, has no place.[96] On the other hand, it is always open to a defendant to apply at an early stage for the plaintiff's pleading to be struck out as disclosing no reasonable

[93] Law of 16–24 August 1790, art. 13. See above, chap. 1, p. 18.
[94] Law of 24 May 1872, above, chap. 1, p. 19.
[95] See especially *Ridge* v. *Baldwin* [1964] A.C. 40; *Padfield* v. *Minister of Agriculture* [1968] A.C. 997; *Anisminic Ltd* v. *Foreign Compensation Commission* [1969] 2 A.C. 147.
[96] Above, p. 156. Cf. H. Woolf, 'Locus Standi in Practice' in I. R. Scott (ed.), *International Perspectives of Justice* (1990), p. 247.

cause of action;[97] such an application will normally succeed if the plaintiff cannot claim that a legal right of his own has been infringed.[98] In judicial review procedure, by contrast, the applicant must always obtain leave to apply, such leave not to be granted unless the applicant has a 'sufficient interest in the matter to which the application relates'.[99]

It might be supposed that an applicant to whom leave is refused can properly be said to lack *locus standi*.[100] In the *Inland Revenue* case,[101] however, the House of Lords held that the question whether the applicant has sufficient interest can be finally decided only at the hearing *inter partes*, and in the light of the evidence then available. Although the language used by their Lordships suggests that they thought otherwise, a question that can only be so decided is not one directed to the applicant's *locus standi*: once leave to apply has been granted, the preliminary question of *locus standi* has necessarily been settled.[102]

Whatever the logic of the decision in the *Inland Revenue* case, it has advantages in practice. In the first place, it makes of the original application for leave an occasion on which the court can prevent irresponsible or frivolous or vexatious applications from proceeding, but little more.[103] As Lord Diplock put it, leave should be granted on the *ex parte* application if, 'on a quick perusal of the material then available, the court thinks that it discloses what might on further consideration turn out to be an arguable case in favour of granting the applicant the relief claimed'.[104] It follows that only if the application is frivolous or irresponsible can the proposed respondent refuse to offer an answer of any kind.[105] At the same time the *Inland Revenue* case provides a convenient summary procedure for bringing the proceedings to an end on the merits if and when the respondent has made a sufficient answer to establish that the application cannot succeed. An initial grant of leave does not necessarily mean that the proceedings must run their full course.

---

[97] R.S.C., Ord. 18, r. 19; C.P.R., r. 3.4.

[98] For the relator action, see above, chap. 7, pp. 135–8.

[99] R.S.C., Ord. 53, r. 3(7); Supreme Court Act 1981, s. 31(3).

[100] This was true for the prerogative remedies under the old law. See Wade, pp. 696–708.

[101] *Inland Revenue Commissioners* v. *National Federation of Self Employed and Small Businesses Ltd* [1982] A.C. 617; *R.* v. *Monopolies Commission, ex parte Argyll plc* [1986] 1 W.L.R. 763, 773–4, *per* Donaldson M.R.

[102] It could, perhaps, be said that the question of *locus standi* has only been settled provisionally, but logically a litigant without *locus standi* cannot call upon his proposed opponent to answer his allegations in any way.

[103] [1982] A.C. 617, 630, *per* Lord Wilberforce; at 636, 643, *per* Lord Diplock.

[104] *Ibid.* at 644, per Lord Diplock; *R.* v. *Special Commissioners, ex parte Stipplechoice Ltd* [1985] 2 All E.R. 465.

[105] For the consequences of this for the protection of diffuse interests, see chap. 7, p. 142.

Decisions subject to judicial review

Because of their remote origins, the remedies of certiorari and prohibition were commonly said to be restricted to acts of a judicial character even if actually performed by administrative rather than judicial authorities.[106] That limitation was lifted finally by the House of Lords in 1964,[107] and, in *O'Reilly v. Mackman*, Lord Diplock expressed the view that the lawfulness of a determination of a statutory tribunal, or any other body of persons having legal authority to determine questions affecting the common law or statutory rights or obligations of other persons as individuals, was amenable to judicial review.[108]

Neither the reform of 1977 nor *O'Reilly v. Mackman* purported to expand the category of authorities whose decisions are subject to judicial review, and one notable extension was made as early as 1967: the decisions of the Criminal Injuries Compensation Board were held to be subject to judicial review notwithstanding that the Board's powers at that time depended on nothing more substantial than a scheme which, though considered by Parliament, had been produced by Government and set out in a written answer to a Parliamentary question.[109] Nevertheless, while any relation of cause and effect is a matter of speculation,[110] the period since *O'Reilly v. Mackman* has seen a significant increase in the willingness of the courts to subject to judicial review the decisions of bodies whose powers are not derived from statute. So, in 1984, it was held that the exercise by the Crown of its power to dismiss civil servants at pleasure, a power based on the prerogative, is amenable to judicial review except where considerations of national security otherwise dictate,[111] and in 1986 it was held that the decisions of the Panel on Takeovers and Mergers are also subject to review.[112] The latter was a particularly strong case since the Panel was an unincorporated association without legal personality and it had no statutory, prerogative,

---

[106] This is enshrined in the famous statement of Lord Atkin in *R. v. Electricity Commissioners* [1924] 1 K.B. 171, 205, above, n. 12.

[107] *Ridge v. Baldwin* [1964] A.C. 40.

[108] [1983] 2 A.C. 237, 279.

[109] *R. v. Criminal Injuries Compensation Board, ex parte Lain* [1967] 2 Q.B. 864. The claim failed in substance, but others succeeded, e.g. *R. v. Criminal Injuries Compensation Board, ex parte Lawton* [1972] 1 W.L.R. 1589. A statutory version of the scheme was enacted in the Criminal Justice Act 1988 but never brought into force; see *R. v. Home Secretary* [1995] 2 A.C. 513. Subsequently the framework of a scheme to be arranged by the Home Secretary, subject to parliamentary approval, was introduced by the Criminal Injuries Compensation Act 1995.

[110] But see *R. v. Takeover Panel, ex parte Datafin plc* [1987] Q.B. 815, 846, *per* Lloyd L.J.

[111] *Council of Civil Service Unions v. Minister for the Civil Service* [1985] A.C. 374. For other examples concerning the prerogative, see *R. v. Foreign Secretary, ex parte Everett* [1989] Q.B. 811; *R. v. Home Secretary, ex parte Bentley* [1994] Q.B. 349.

[112] *R. v. Takeover Panel, ex parte Datafin plc* [1987] Q.B. 815.

common law or even contractual powers. Lacking authority *de jure* it nevertheless exercised immense power *de facto* and performed an important public function.[113]

Since then judicial review has been held to be available against decisions such as those of prison governors in disciplinary matters,[114] of the Parliamentary Commissioner for Administration,[115] of the Advertising Standards Authority,[116] and of the 'self-regulating organisations' under the Financial Services Act 1986.[117] It appears, therefore, that, whatever may have been the position in the past,[118] the source of the power exercised is no longer decisive as to the availability of judicial review. The nature of the power must also be taken into account, and Lloyd L.J. has said that if the body in question exercises public law functions, or if the exercise of its functions may have public law consequences, that may be sufficient to bring it within the reach of judicial review.[119] This makes public law the criterion, which, given the absence of a definition of public law, means that the scope of judicial review remains uncertain, but Lloyd L.J. also observed that the essential distinction is between a 'domestic or private' tribunal, on the one hand, and a body of persons who are under some public duty on the other.[120] Though still loose, the distinction so expressed is in general capable of application, and its very looseness may be advantageous to development of the law.

Subject to the exclusion of private bodies whose power is derived purely from contract,[121] of religious organisations,[122] and of those decisions even of public bodies which are of an essentially commercial character,[123] therefore, it seems that the reach of judicial review is restricted only by the limits to which the court is willing to carry its understanding of the word 'public'. It may even be the case that the

---

[113] *Ibid.* at 826, 838, *per* Donaldson M.R. See also *R. v. Takeover Panel, ex parte Guinness* [1990] 1 Q.B. 146.

[114] *Leech v. Governor of Parkhurst* [1988] A.C. 533.

[115] *R. v. Parliamentary Commissioner, ex parte Dyer* [1994] 1 W.L.R. 621. Cf. *R. v. Parliamentary Commissioner for Standards, ex parte Al Fayed* [1998] 1 W.L.R. 669, and N. C. Bamforth, Note [1998] C.L.J. 6.

[116] *R. v. ASS Ltd, ex parte Vernons Ltd* [1992] 1 W.L.R. 1289.

[117] *R. v. Lautro, ex parte Ross* [1993] Q.B. 17. For other examples, see Wade, pp. 659–66.

[118] *R. v. National Joint Council for Dental Technicians, ex parte Neale* [1953] 1 Q.B. 704, 707, *per* Lord Goddard C.J.

[119] *R. v. Takeover Panel, ex parte Datafin plc* [1987] Q.B. 815, 847.

[120] *Ibid.*

[121] *R. v. National Joint Council for Dental Technicians, ex parte Neale* [1953] 1 Q.B. 704; *Law v. National Greyhound Racing Club Ltd* [1983] 1 W.L.R. 1302; *R. v. Jockey Club, ex parte Aga Khan* [1993] 1 W.L.R. 909.

[122] *R. v. Chief Rabbi, ex parte Wachmann* [1992] 1 W.L.R. 1036.

[123] *R. v. National Coal Board, ex parte NUM* [1986] I.C.R. 791, cited Pannick, 'What is Public Authority?', pp. 23, 33.

non-existence of a private law remedy can itself be regarded as a reason for making judicial review available.[124]

Bearing in mind that the grant of a remedy in judicial review proceedings is always discretionary and that the court is concerned only with the legality of the decision reached, not its merits, this cannot but be a welcome development.[125]

A specialist administrative jurisdiction?

Specialised courts such as the Commercial Court exist within the High Court,[126] but there is no Administrative Court. Formerly, applications for a prerogative remedy came before a Divisional Court of the Queen's Bench Division consisting normally of three judges and frequently presided over by the Lord Chief Justice. Now, however, both the application for leave to apply for judicial review and the substantive application itself are dealt with by a single judge of the High Court.[127] This has made it possible for the Lord Chief Justice, acting on and within his own authority, to create what amounts to a specialised administrative jurisdiction.[128] First, by Practice Direction, all applications for judicial review are listed in the Crown Office List.[129] Secondly, judges are assigned to deal continuously with cases in the Crown Office List for a period of time. The 'nominated judges', as they are known, thus gain experience and become expert in the field of judicial review and other cases of administrative law.[130]

---

[124] *R. v. Takeover Panel, ex parte Datafin plc* [1987] Q.B. 815, 839, *per* Sir John Donaldson M.R.; *R. v. Local Comr, ex parte Eastleigh B.C.* [1988] 1 Q.B. 855, 866, *per* Lord Donaldson M.R.

[125] Save in so far as it leads to excessive case-loads in the courts and consequent delay. The expansion of judicial review has given rise to some controversy concerning judicial interference with Government. See, e.g. M. Sunkin and M. P. Le Sueur, 'Can Government control Judicial Review?' (1991) *Current Legal Problems* 161; G. Richardson and M. Sunkin, 'Judicial Review: Questions of Impact' [1996] P.L. 79 and works there cited; H. Woolf, 'Judicial Review – The Tensions between the Executive and the Judiciary' (1998) 114 L.Q.R. 579.

[126] Supreme Court Act 1981, s. 6; chap. 1, n. 6, above.

[127] R.S.C., Ord. 53, rr. 3(2), 5(2), as amended in 1980. Also, by R.S.C., Ord. 53, r. 3(2), the documents required on an application for leave must be filed in the Crown Office, a special department of the Central Office of the Supreme Court. See R. J. F. Gordon, *Judicial Review: Law and Procedure*, 2nd edn (1996), para. 1–018.

[128] See L. Blom-Cooper, 'The New Face of Judicial Review' [1982] P.L. 250; A. Grubb, 'Two Steps towards a Unified Administrative Law Procedure' [1983] P.L. 190.

[129] *Practice Direction* [1983] 1 W.L.R. 1296. Though the Direction nominally applies only to applications in London, there is provision to see that all applications for judicial review are actually dealt with in London save in cases of great urgency: *Practice Direction (Crown Office List: Criminal Proceedings)* [1983] 1 W.L.R. 925, para. 2.

[130] By 1982 nine judges had been nominated: Blom-Cooper, 'The New Face of Judicial Review', at n. 16. Now, about one half of the Queen's Bench Division Judges have been nominated: R. J. F. Gordon, *Crown Office Proceedings* (1995), para. A1–1004.

Even without the creation of an Administrative Court, therefore, it has been possible for judicial review procedure to develop independently and it is not, in practice, quite the same as procedure in an action on an originating summons which it so closely resembles in form.[131] There may even be some reason to fear that the courts are overprotective of public authorities, but the procedural dichotomy did lead, in practice, to the existence of a specialised administrative jurisdiction, and it has been that jurisdiction which has been responsible for much of the extension in the scope of judicial review described above, most importantly, perhaps, in relation to the protection of diffuse interests.[132] It is essentially for this reason that it was suggested above that the procedural dichotomy may have produced beneficial as well as harmful consequences.

Conclusion

The reform of 1977 made it possible, for the first time, for a claim for a declaration, an injunction or damages to be joined to a claim for one of the prerogative remedies. It thus gave rise to the anomaly that the same remedy could be obtained by either of two procedures, the one requiring an initial grant of leave and subject to a short time limit, the other free of such restrictions. The existence of such an anomaly, even if of limited practical importance, made some such decision as *O'Reilly* v. *Mackman* virtually inevitable,[133] and it would not be appropriate simply to reverse it by legislation. That is not to say, however, that matters can be left as they are. It may be that the existence of the procedural dichotomy helped the expansion of judicial review, and thus the extension of judicial control of the legality of the decisions of some bodies that would otherwise have been free of such control. On the other hand, what the Law Commission has called the 'procedural trap'[134] must be removed.

So much seems to be generally agreed, and adoption of the Law Commission's recommendations[135] would help to solve some of the most pressing problems. It would not, however, remove the particular

---

This demonstrates the growth in the number of cases of judicial review, but it indicates also that administrative law may have become more a part of the ordinary work of the Queen's Bench Division than once it was.

[131] E.g. it is said that, in practice, orders for discovery or the cross-examination of a deponent are more rarely made, notwithstanding Lord Diplock's observations (above, n. 27): Justice-All Souls, *Administrative Justice*, para. 6.32. The Law Commission recommends that a more liberal approach to discovery should be introduced, but by Practice Direction rather than by amendment to the rule: Law Com. 226, paras. 7.4–7.12.

[132] Chap. 7, p. 142.   [133] Wade, p. 681.

[134] Law Com. 226, para. 3.20.   [135] Above, p. 165.

disadvantage of the procedural dichotomy that all decisions of public authorities enjoy the same procedural advantage. However important or unimportant, whether their implementation is urgent or not, and whether they affect one individual alone or the public at large, such decisions are privileged by the short time limit and the requirement of leave; great institutions which cannot, even on a generous view, be regarded as exercising a public function but whose decisions may be of similar far-reaching effect as those of local, and perhaps even of national government, enjoy no such protection.[136]

It seems to be the intention of the Law Commission, with the support of the majority of the respondents to its Consultation Paper,[137] that this should continue to be the case. The contrary view has, however, been expressed by the highest academic authority,[138] and now the recommendations in Lord Woolf's Final Report come close to, though they do not quite reach, a recommendation for procedural unity.[139] Lord Woolf even suggests that the Law Commission's recommendation for judicial review should be of general application, namely that a case should be allowed to proceed if the applicant has been or will be adversely affected, or if it is in the public interest that it should do so: 'in appropriate private law cases, such as claims for a declaration, the courts should on occasion be able to allow proceedings to continue if it is in the interests of justice or in the public interest that they should do so'.[140]

Lord Woolf's proposals for judicial review form part of his overall proposals for close judicial involvement in case management. It may be suggested, however, that a similar unity of procedure could be achieved if the procedure for striking out in ordinary proceedings and that of applying for leave were brought into juxtaposition.[141] There would be but one form of action whatever the remedy sought,[142] and there would be no fetters on a person's right to initiate proceedings. Every plaintiff who exercised that right would, as now, face the risk that his claim might be struck out.[143] On the other hand, an intending plaintiff could apply for leave in any case, and it would be important for him to do so if he made no claim of infringement of a legal right of his own. Then, if leave were granted on the ground that it was in the interests of justice or in the public interest that the proceedings should continue, no subsequent application to strike out could succeed, but the half-way house of the

---

[136] Above, p. 165.   [137] Law Com. 226, paras. 3.4, 3.13.
[138] Wade, pp. 684–6.
[139] Woolf Final, chap. 18; see above, p. 163.   [140] At p. 255.
[141] See J. A. Jolowicz, 'Civil Proceedings in the Public Interest' (1982) 13 Cambrian L.R. 32, 46–8.
[142] Woolf Final, p. 252.   [143] Above, p. 167.

Inland Revenue case[144] would remain available.[145] If necessary, special periods of limitation could be provided for particular classes of case.[146]

If a reform on these lines were introduced, the unfettered right of a person to bring proceedings when he claims the infringement of a legal right would be preserved, and so too would be the court's control of proceedings in which no such claim is maintained, whether against a public authority or not. In addition, control of the right to bring proceedings to challenge the decisions of powerful corporations and associations would belong, as it should belong, to the courts rather than the Attorney-General. The need for an artificial distinction between a private right possessed by millions and a public right,[147] as well as the need for relator proceedings,[148] would disappear.

[144] Above, p. 168.
[145] Leave might also be sought and granted by way of response to an application to strike out.
[146] Above, p. 164.
[147] Chap. 7, p. 141.   [148] Chap. 7, p. 135.

9   Adversarial and inquisitorial approaches to civil litigation[1]

It is almost an article of faith on the part of common lawyers that because their civil procedure is 'adversarial' it is therefore superior to the 'inquisitorial' procedure which they believe to be used elsewhere. The word 'inquisitorial' conjures up visions of the Inquisition, and they do not care for the methods that common lawyers have been led to believe are used by inquisitors.

It seems desirable to stress at the outset, therefore, that no system of civil procedure can in the nature of things be wholly adversarial or wholly inquisitorial. It cannot be wholly inquisitorial because there is nothing to which a civil inquisitor can direct his enquiry unless and until one person has propounded a claim against another in more or less specific terms. It cannot be wholly adversarial because, even if we speak of the winner of a contest between the litigating parties, the winner of contested litigation cannot be determined objectively as can the winner of a race. Indeed, we neither expect nor require that the judge shall act as a human photo-electric device whose only function is to declare which of the litigants was in front when the contest ended. On the contrary, even in common law countries, we expect and require that the judge make use of his own knowledge and experience on matters of fact as well as of law[2] – which means that he must enquire of himself – and we also expect, if we do not require, that he will enquire of others, as when he directs a question to a witness or engages in dialogue with counsel.

The most that could in any event be said, therefore, is that common law procedure is predominantly adversarial while some other systems of procedure are predominantly inquisitorial, and it is certainly true that some claim to be so.[3] Even the most cursory comparative study reveals,

[1] Based on a lecture delivered in 1983 to the Canadian Institute for Advanced Legal Studies, published in E. G. Baldwin (ed.), *The Cambridge Lectures 1983* (1983), p. 237.
[2] See chap. 13.
[3] E.g. the procedure of the French administrative jurisdiction: A. De Laubadère, J. C. Venezia and Y. Gaudemet, *Traité de droit administratif*, 13th edn (1994), nos. 632–3. Nevertheless, French authors cannot avoid the language of the adversarial approach.

175

however, that different procedures consist of different combinations of adversarial and inquisitorial elements, no matter to which 'family' they belong. The particular combination found in a particular procedure at a particular time is the product of gradual development and change over a long period of history, but the character of the combination provides a guide to the objectives of a given system of procedure. In particular it indicates the extent to which civil litigation is seen as a process for the settlement of disputes *inter partes* and nothing more. This, it is suggested, is the nub of the matter, but before turning to it a few preliminary observations are called for.

(a) As with the question whether a procedure is adversarial or inquisitorial, there are no absolute answers about the objectives of a legal system. There is no developed system of civil procedure whose sole and exclusive objective is the non-violent settlement of disputes, and there is no developed system of civil procedure in which the settlement of disputes plays no part.

(b) Bearing in mind that, in general, civil litigation will only take place if the parties to it are unable to come to an amicable settlement, there is some reason to believe that, from the dispute settlement point of view, an adversarial process before a judge whose role is understood to be that of choosing between the rival contentions of the parties, is more likely to leave even the defeated party satisfied with the outcome, than is a process in which the judge enquires into aspects of the case which neither party has chosen to draw to his attention.[4]

(c) The term 'adversarial procedure' is sometimes translated into French as a procedure 'fondé sur le principe du contradictoire',[5] but the translation is inexact and the distinction between the adversary principle and the 'principle of contradiction' must be noticed. There are two central notions of the adversary principle. First, it is for the parties, and for the parties alone, to fix the scope of their litigation by their allegations of fact.[6] Secondly – and it is this which is distinctive of the adversary system – the

Thus, in speaking of the *requête* in administrative procedure, one author writes that notice of it must be given to all persons 'qui sont indiquées par le demandeur comme étant ses adversaires': H. Lenoan, *La procédure devant le Conseil d'Etat* (1954), p. 109.

[4] For an empirical verification, see J. Thibaut and L. Walker, *Procedural Justice, A Psychological Analysis* (1975).

[5] Centre de traduction et de terminologie juridiques, Université de Moncton, *Vocabulaire de la 'common law'*, Vol. III (1983), p. 17. The principle is often also called *principe de la contradiction*.

[6] This is as much part of, for example, French law as it is of English law. Solus and Perrot, nos. 68, 87 and below, chap. 10, p. 189.

judge must find the facts, taking account exclusively of such
evidence as the parties choose to put forward: the parties are
adversaries, not just in the sense that they are opposed to one
another, but in the sense that the judge's role is simply to
pronounce who, in his judgment, is the winner at the end of a
forensic duel fought between the parties with the weapons of
their choice.[7] The *principe du contradictoire*, on the other hand,
does not of its own force prevent the judge from introducing
additional elements into the discussion. It ordains that the judge
shall not make use in his decision of any element of law or fact,
whether introduced by a party or by himself, unless all parties
have had the opportunity to discuss it before him. It has been
described by high French authority as 'one of the golden rules of
legal procedure',[8] but even so is not dignified in English law by
having its own independent description: *audi alteram partem*
comes close but is not quite the same.

It is true that in a system of procedure that is wholly adversarial, as the
English system is popularly supposed to be, the demands of the *principe
du contradictoire* are automatically met, and that, perhaps, explains why
English law does not recognise it as an independent principle. Be that as
it may, however, the principle can and does live as happily in a system
recognised as inquisitorial as in one claimed to be adversarial.[9]

One consequence of the common law's failure to recognise the *principe
du contradictoire* as an independent principle is the confusion that exists,
at least in England, about the use that the judge may make of legal
reasoning, or even of specific authorities, which have not been relied on
in argument before him. No one questions the propriety of the conduct
of a judge who makes a suggestion to counsel in the course of argument
– though that in itself constitutes a theoretical infringement of the
adversarial principle – but there is no consensus about the propriety of
the conduct of a judge who does his own legal research in preparing a
reserved judgment.[10]

Failure to distinguish between the adversarial principle and the
principe du contradictoire does, however, have a more important consequence than merely to produce uncertainty about the propriety of

---

[7] Seen in this light, the adversary procedure precisely reflects Couture's concept of the
civil action as 'civilisation's substitute for vengeance': E. J. Couture, 'The Nature of
Judicial Process' (1950) 25 Tulane L.R. 1, 7.

[8] Conseil d'Etat, 12 October 1979, J.C.P. 1980, 19288, concl. Franc, para. 10a; below,
chap. 10, p. 193.

[9] Debbasch, nos. 484–8.

[10] See the disagreement between Lord Denning M.R. and Bridge L.J. in *Goldsmith* v.
Sperrings Ltd [1977] 1 W.L.R. 478 and below, chap. 10, p. 192.

judges doing their own research. It leads us to believe that only retention of the adversary principle can preserve the right of the parties to know and to debate all the elements of the judge's decision; it therefore blinds us to the possibility of modifying the adversary principle without infringing the principle of contradiction. It is true that the processes of discovery can, subject to the rules about privilege, normally ensure that evidence which one party wishes to have produced will be produced, even if the other party controls it and would prefer to keep it to himself, but that applies only to evidence that can be shown by the party seeking its production to be favourable to his case. As the House of Lords has insisted,[11] 'In an adversarial system such as exists in the United Kingdom, a party is free to withhold information that would help his case if he wishes – perhaps for reasons of delicacy or personal privacy. He cannot be compelled to disclose it against his will.'

If it is taken for granted that we look to our courts for no more than the settlement of the disputes between the parties who come before them, and if it is also taken for granted that the decisions of the courts have no significance for those who are not parties to the decisions, then, probably, the nearer that our procedure can approach the ideal adversarial system, the better. The point was made by Lord Wilberforce in the *Air Canada* case already cited, when he denied the existence of any judicial duty to ascertain 'some independent truth' and insisted that, 'in a contest purely between one litigant and another', justice will have been fairly done if the decision has been in accordance with the available evidence and the law: this is so even if the decision is known not to be the whole truth of the matter by reason of the imperfection or the withholding of evidence.[12] It is, in fact, possible to go even further than Lord Wilberforce. No one – however grievous, and however obviously reparable through litigation, the wrong done to him – is obliged to bring proceedings. It may, therefore, be an important freedom that, if he so wishes, a man can abandon his legal rights against another.[13] And if he can do so in full by refraining from suit or by conceding a claim made against him, must he not also be free to do so in part by not putting forward the strongest available case? It would be an interference with his freedom if the court brought into the litigation even material that operated in a party's favour, but which he would himself have preferred to have left out of account.

[11] *Air Canada* v. *Secretary of State for Trade* [1983] 2 A.C. 394, 434, *per* Lord Fraser.
[12] *Ibid.* at 438.
[13] It is also possible, however, that the maxim *nemo agere cogatur* is no more than recognition of the inevitable (and unfortunate?) truth that normally a man cannot be compelled to bring or to refrain from bringing proceedings against his will: Cappelletti and Jolowicz, pp. 169–71.

The trouble with this, of course, is that we look to our courts for more than the bare answer to the question whether the plaintiff should get from the defendant what he has claimed,[14] and an important reason for this is that it is seldom true that the outcome of a case litigated in the superior courts affects only the parties to the litigation.[15] Even if the potential importance of almost any such litigation to the development of the law itself is ignored, account must still be taken of the following points, amongst others:

(a) Whenever the parties to litigation are or include corporate bodies, whether private or public,[16] the corporate party represents the interests of all those who are affected by the position in which the corporation finds itself – shareholders, employees, taxpayers, beneficiaries of public services and so on. The legal personality of corporations is an invaluable device, but it is a device none the less: the premise adopted by Lord Wilberforce, that litigation brought by a number of international airlines against the Secretary of State and the British Airports Authority in order to challenge the legality of increases in the charges levied for the use of London Airport (Heathrow) was a 'contest purely between one litigant and another', is unrealistic.

(b) The overwhelming majority of civil cases are settled, often before proceedings are even started, let alone brought to trial. Subject to the point just made, this is unobjectionable; indeed, it is generally acknowledged to be desirable, and not only because of the disastrous consequences which would follow even a small increase in the number of cases that proceed to trial. In negotiations for settlement and, perhaps, before an arbitrator, concessions made by one party are, again, unobjectionable, and it may also be unobjectionable that during the interlocutory stages of an action the court seeks to secure concessions or

---

[14] That the courts are sometimes reluctant to give more is unfortunate but irrelevant. See, e.g. *Allen* v. *Gulf Oil Refining Ltd* [1981] A.C. 1001 and J. A. Jolowicz, 'Should Courts Answer Questions?' [1981] C.L.J. 226.

[15] Paradoxically, in the procedure before Tribunals, whose decisions rarely have 'extended impact' and which handle far more 'civil' litigation than the courts (Royal Commission on Legal Services, Final Report, Cmnd 7648 (1979), Vol. I, para. 15.1), the adversarial element is much less pronounced.

[16] That insurance companies are the 'real', though not the nominal, defendants in many cases should not be overlooked. The decisions of the courts in, for example, personal injury cases and cases involving the loss of or damage to property are not without effect on the level of insurance premiums generally, as was recognised explicitly by Diplock L.J. (dissenting) as long ago as 1961: *Wise* v. *Kaye* [1962] 1 Q.B. 638, 670.

admissions from the parties.[17] Is it not different, however, if the case actually comes to public trial before the established courts of justice whose duty it is to apply the law to the situation as it actually exists or, at least, to use their best endeavours to do so? There is something almost indecent about the court pronouncing judgment on suppositions of fact which are known to be unreal or untrue, and the judges themselves are, rightly, unhappy if and when it seems to them that they are called upon to do so.[18]

(c) Closely associated with this is society's contemporary attitude to the law itself, an attitude which, though it is based in part on fiction, is both a healthy and a necessary one. In short, it is accepted that law *exists*; there is, or it is widely supposed that there is, a legally correct solution to every case, and it is the court's function to *declare* what that solution is whenever it is in doubt. The abolition of the forms of action more than a century ago was an essential step in the separation of procedure from substantive law, and it made possible the present understanding that it is for the court to apply the law – not just some part of the law but the law in its entirety – to the facts of each and every case that comes to trial. And this, in turn, leads to a demand that the court shall pronounce, or shall do its best to pronounce, the correct solution. If a judge is debarred from raising such enquiries about the facts presented to him as seem to him to be necessary, he is debarred from even trying to reach the correct solution.[19]

Considerations of this kind demonstrate the existence of a difficult and delicate question of balance. It is for the parties to allege in their pleadings the facts on which they rely, and this must continue to be the general rule: no one wants the judge to have a completely uncontrolled roving commission of enquiry. It is, however, also for the parties to control the evidence that is presented, and here there may be room for change. The common law idea of the single session trial, at which the presiding judge learns about the case he must decide only as the trial proceeds, leaves little opportunity for him to intervene and call for

[17] The suggestion has been made that the emphasis of the rules of procedure should be on methods of disposal of proceedings without trial rather than on preparation for trial: I. H. Jacob, 'Accelerating the Process of Law' in M. Storme and H. Casman (eds.), *Towards a Justice with a Human Face*, p. 317 (reprinted in Jacob, *Reform*, p. 100). If this suggestion were adopted the distinction taken in the text between the interlocutory stages and the trial would be strengthened.

[18] See, e.g. *Avon C.C. v. Howlett* [1983] 1 W.L.R. 605, 608, *per* Cumming-Bruce L.J. and chap. 19, p. 391,

[19] For fuller discussion of this point, see above, chap. 4, p. 85.

further evidence; any such intervention would lead to an adjournment, with all the inconvenience and expense that that entails.[20] This does not mean, however, that common lawyers should continue to set their faces against such intervention, if and when it becomes practicable, simply in order to preserve the purity of the adversarial principle itself.

The idea that civil litigation is the private affair of the parties, and nothing else, has not yet come to be as inappropriate in England as it is in countries where civil litigation may lead to the annulment of legislation for unconstitutionality. Even so, it is only when we speak of procedure that we continue to pretend that all that courts do is to settle the disputes that have arisen between the parties. We may still be reluctant to acknowledge openly the law-making function of the courts, but we know perfectly well that many decisions have direct consequences for people who are not parties to them. Far-reaching reform of civil procedure has taken place in recent years, and more is on the way; it would be unfortunate if the assumption that the courts are no more than non-violent substitutes for the duelling ground were left unchallenged.[21] We should, at least, deny to the proposition 'adversarial is best' the status of a religious dogma that no loyal common lawyer dares to challenge.[22]

The balance of adversarial and inquisitorial elements that was set for English civil procedure by the Judicature Acts 1873–5 is now under scrutiny. Reform is under way because of the costs and the delays that this balance has brought. If substantial reform rather than 'petty tinkering'[23] is to come, however, it must be a principled rather than merely an expedient change and it must be based on reassessment of what the process of civil litigation is intended to achieve.

On such a subject there is, obviously, room for disagreement and debate. It is at least clear, however, that we must abandon the myth that civil litigation deals with disputes between neighbours in a predominantly rural society – a myth which, though known to have lost the basis

[20] Unless the judge is informed in advance what evidence the parties will present, he must hear all the evidence offered by the parties before he can appreciate what additional evidence, if any, might be useful. In any case, as the law stands at present, the judge is precluded from calling a witness of his own save with the agreement of the parties: *Re Enoch and Zaretzky, Bock & Co.'s Arbitration* [1910] 1 K.B. 327.

[21] An assumption the validity of which is still further undermined by the encouragement now given to use of alternative dispute resolution. See, e.g. *Practice Statement (Commercial Cases: Alternative Dispute Resolution)* [1994] 1 W.L.R. 14; *Practice Direction (Civil Litigation: Case Management)* [1995] 1 W.L.R. 508; Woolf Interim, chap. 18, Woolf Final, p. 64; C.P.R., r. 1.4(2)(e); below, chap. 19, p. 392.

[22] The challenge in Woolf Interim, chap. 3, is a challenge to its efficiency not, in intent, to its underlying values. See further, below, chap. 19, p. 391.

[23] The phrase is Pound's: 'The Causes of Popular Dissatisfaction with the Administration of Justice' (1906) 40 Am.L.R. 729, 736.

in fact it may once have had, still seems to underlie discussion of procedural reform. If that leads us into the heresy that challenges the true faith of unquestioning belief in the adversary process, we should not be disconcerted. The adversarial principle has its virtues and it will not, for it cannot, disappear. But it is not an absolute and it does not justify itself. A balance between adversarial and inquisitorial elements in any system of civil procedure is inevitable, and that balance is reflected in the division of labour between the parties and the judge. If it comes to be thought appropriate at some time to give greater powers to the judge at the expense of the parties, we should not be inhibited from making such a change for fear that by so doing we should make our procedure less adversarial.

Part IV

The parties and the judge

10 *Da mihi factum dabo tibi jus*: a problem of demarcation in English and French law[1]

Acts performed in the 'real' world affect people in their 'real' lives, and it is one of the functions of the law to specify when and under what conditions one person is entitled to have another do or refrain from doing something in that world. In complex modern societies it is not, of course, always possible to describe the real world without recourse to the law and legal concepts, and this is most obviously the case when one person invokes the assistance of the legal process in the pursuit of his demand that another person, or the State itself, confer upon him some advantage. It would, for example, be difficult for an author to demand monetary compensation from the publisher of a pirated version of his book without reference to the legal concept of copyright, and it is impossible to reify divorce without reference to the legal structure of society: at the secular level neither marriage, which is different from cohabitation, nor divorce, the principal characteristic of which is conferment of the right to remarry, is comprehensible unless seen against the background of the law. Nevertheless, it has to be recognised that civil litigation takes place when one person demands some advantage for himself[2] – usually, but not always, at the expense of another – and that advantage proves in the event to be one that he cannot obtain without the intervention of the court.

If this is right, then the role of the law itself in relation to demands which are not, or cannot be, conceded voluntarily by the person to whom they are addressed, is to guide and control the judge in the formulation of his decision as to the legal rights and obligations of the parties, a decision which will, if necessary, be enforced by the machinery of the State itself. The starting point lies in the real world and so, at the end of the day, does the judgment.[3] A railway passenger falls and is

---

[1] Based on an article in P. Feuerstein and C. Parry (eds.), *Multum non Multa: Festschrift für Kurt Lipstein aus Anlass seines 70. Geburtstages* (1980), p. 79.

[2] The possibility of 'altruism' is not ruled out, as where proceedings are brought for the protection of diffuse, fragmented or collective interests: above, chaps. 5, 6 and 7.

[3] A judgment is, of course, 'real' only because the law itself makes it so, but the law does just that. If a student at the end of an exercise declares that A must pay B £1,000, this

injured as he descends some steps at a railway station; he demands monetary compensation from the station authority and, following a judgment in his favour, they pay him. What happens in between is the concern of the law and, save for its outcome and its possible implications for similar cases in the future, is of no direct concern to the parties: it is a matter of indifference to the injured traveller who receives £10,000, and to the station authority, whether the judgment was founded on the Occupiers' Liability Act, on *Donoghue* v. *Stevenson*, or on an implied term in a contract.[4] In other words, what matters to the parties to litigation is the actual result that is dictated by the law in the concrete circumstances in which they find themselves, not the particular legal classifications, legal rules and legal reasoning by which that result is achieved.

It is not intended to suggest that the only role of the law is to control the decisions of judges on questions raised by civil litigation. If, however, it is the function of civil litigation to decide what are the legal rights and obligations of the parties in the circumstances that have arisen, then, as a general rule and to the extent that human frailty allows, the decision should be based on the dictates of the law as a whole, not merely upon those of that particular part of the law or 'rule of law'[5] that the parties or their legal advisers may have invoked. Translated into practical terms, this means that the ultimate choice of applicable legal rule should be for the judge, not the parties: *da mihi factum dabo tibi jus*.[6]

During the formalistic period in the development of a legal system, practice does not even aspire to the realisation of this goal. In England, for so long as the forms of action survived, a plaintiff was compelled to

will make no difference to the lives of A and B even though they are actual persons and the facts put to the student have actually occurred. But if a judge makes a similar declaration at the end of properly constituted litigation between A and B, his judgment is sufficiently 'real' for it to have concrete consequences for the parties.

[4] For a French treatment of this example, see Henri Motulsky, 'La cause de la demande dans la délimitation de l'office du juge': D. 1964, 235 and *Ecrits*, pp. 101, 106.

[5] For present purposes, as for the major premise of the judicial syllogism, a 'rule of law' means a proposition recognised as authoritative by the person invoking it and stating that once facts qualified in a particular way have been established, certain legal consequences follow. This is the meaning of 'règle de droit' as that phrase is used in the 'new' French code of civil procedure of 1975 (art. 12, al. 1) and it found its way there through the writings of Motulsky from the analysis of Stammler (see, e.g. Stammler's *Lehrbuch der Rechtsphilosophie* (1922), para. 124). According to Stammler, a *Rechtssatz* has two elements: the *Voraussetzung* and the *Rechtsfolge*. See Motulsky, *Principes d'une réalisation méthodique du droit privé* (1948), pp. 18, 29; Raymond Martin, 'Le fait et le droit ou les parties et le juge', J.C.P. 1974, I, 2625, no. 25 and 'La règle de droit adéquate dans le procès civil', D. 1990, Chron. 163.

[6] The maxim is said to be one of mediaeval Roman law: Millar in *History*, p. 12, and works there cited.

choose not only a particular set of procedural rules but also, to all
intents and purposes, the unique legal rule on which, in his contention,
judgment in his favour could properly be based.[7] Since 1875 at the
latest, however, the parties to civil litigation in England have been
relieved of any formal obligation to link their claims or defences to
particular legal rules or principles. Through their counsel they may and,
exceptional cases apart, should present legal argument to the judge, but
so far as the formal constitution of the action is concerned, all that is
required of them is that they plead facts.[8] It is this which justifies
statements such as that of Diplock L.J. that 'a cause of action is simply a
factual situation the existence of which entitles one person to obtain
from the court a remedy against another person'.[9] It is also this which
justifies both the rule that if a party does plead a particular legal result[10]
he is not bound by what he has pleaded,[11] and its corollary that the
court should 'consider and deal with the legal result of pleaded fact,
though the particular legal result alleged is not stated in the pleadings'.[12]
So long as the facts are before the court, the court may and should draw
upon any rule of law that appears to it to be applicable, whether either
party has formally placed reliance on that rule or not.

In France the late Professor Henri Motulsky was probably the most
ardent, and certainly the most successful, of those who argued that it is
for the judge to find and apply the appropriate legal rule to the facts

---

[7] It may be that the expansion in scope of the action on the case during the late
eighteenth and early nineteenth centuries, and decisions such as that in *Williams* v.
Holland (1833) 2 L.J.C.P. (N.S.) 190, which extended the action on the case to a direct
injury negligently caused, reflect a desire on the part of the judges responsible to move
away from the idea that a plaintiff's choice of originating process determines the legal
principles that may be invoked in support of his claim. See M. J. Prichard, 'Trespass,
Case and the Rule in *Williams* v. *Holland*' [1964] C.L.J. 234.

[8] Under R.S.C., Ord. 18, r. 7 the rule was that a pleading must contain '*and contain only*,
a statement in a summary form of the material facts on which the party pleading relies'.
C.P.R., rr. 16.4 and 16.5 require 'a concise statement of the facts' for both claim and
defence.

[9] *Letang* v. *Cooper* [1965] 1 Q.B. 232, 242–3: 'It is essential to realise that when, since
1873, the name of a form of action is used to identify a cause of action, it is used as a
convenient and succinct description of a particular category of factual situation which
entitles one person to obtain from the court a remedy against another person. To forget
this will indeed encourage the old forms of action to rule us from their graves.' See also
Motulsky, *Principes*, p. 30.

[10] R.S.C., Ord. 18, r. 11 permitted the pleading of a 'point of law', as does a Practice
Direction appended to C.P.R., r. 16 (para. 11.3). The latter also allows the claimant to
give the names of proposed witnesses and to supply a copy of any document he
considers necessary to his claim.

[11] E.g. *Re Vandervell's Trusts (No. 2)* [1974] Ch. 269, 321–2, *per* Lord Denning M.R. See
also *Middlesex County Council* v. *Nathan* [1937] 2 K.B. 272.

[12] *Lever Bros Ltd* v. *Bell* [1931] 1 K.B. 557, 583, *per* Scrutton L.J. See also *Shaw* v. *Shaw*
[1954] 2 Q.B. 429. *Drane* v. *Evangelou* [1978] 1 W.L.R. 455 provides a neat example.

before him, whatever rules the parties may have invoked and whatever qualifications of the facts they may have proposed, and his ideas are now enshrined in the new French code of civil procedure.[13]

Most of the discussion in France revolved around the notion of the 'cause de la demande', and three main theories emerged.[14] According to the first, the *cause de la demande* is constituted by, or at least characterised by, the rule of law or the legal category that is invoked; the second, less extreme, finds the *cause* in the facts which support the claim *as placed in their legal category*; the third declares that the *cause* is constituted by the 'circonstances de fait invoquées en vue d'établir le droit subjectif par lequel se traduit juridiquement la prétention soumise au juge'.

It is this third view for which Motulsky is said to be responsible[15] and which, he maintains, is to be distinguished from the others in that it sees in the *cause de la demande* 'un complexe de faits et refuse, par suite, d'inclure dans la notion, la qualification juridique de ces faits'. On this view it is permissible for a claim to be put forward in language that avoids the use of legal concepts altogether, and to the extent that a party does use such concepts he does so 'par simple commodité de langage'.[16] Even the remedy sought by a plaintiff need not be described in legal language: 'ce n'est pas, en realité, d'une "demande en divorce", "en revendication", "en recherche de paternité" que la partie saisit le juge, mais uniquement d'une requête tendant vers le résultat social ou économique et qui ne *doit* être traduit en langage conceptuel que par le seul juge'.[17]

Not the least important of the ideas behind this analysis is Motulsky's conviction that the judge must be master of the law applicable to the case before him, and he insists, for example, that a wrong legal classification adopted by a party must not prevent the judge from awarding him what is his right under another head: 'le fait qu'en demandant la condamnation de son adversaire au paiement d'une somme d'argent, la partie indique que c'est à titre de dommages-intérêts, ne peut donc empêcher le juge de lui adjuger l'objet de sa prétention quand bien même il déduirait des circonstances à lui soumises la conclusion qu'en réalité cette prétention se définit, juridiquement, comme tendant vers l'exécution de l'obligation contractée et non pas vers la sanction d'une inexécution.'[18]

[13] See especially art. 12, set out in part, below, p. 189.
[14] Motulsky, *Ecrits*, p. 103. See Solus and Perrot, nos. 70 and 71.
[15] Motulsky himself cedes the honour to Glasson and Tissier: 'La cause de la demande', n. 4, above.
[16] *Ibid.*, p. 107.
[17] Motulsky, 'Le role respectif du juge et des parties dans l'allégation des faits', *Etudes de droit contemporain* (1959), p. 257, and *Ecrits*, pp. 38, 44.
[18] *Ecrits*, p. 45.

It may be open to question whether Motulsky's opinion was in accord with the positive law of France as it stood before the reforms of the 1970s,[19] but it seems certain that one of the objects of those reforms was to adopt it in the new legislation on civil procedure.[20] Nowhere is this clearer than in article 12 of the new code of civil procedure, the first three paragraphs of which read as follows: 'Le juge tranche le litige conformément aux règles de droit qui lui sont applicables. Il doit donner ou restituer leur exacte qualification aux faits et actes litigieux sans s'arrêter à la dénomination que les parties en auraient proposée. Il peut relever d'office les moyens de pur droit quel que soit le fondement juridique invoqué par les parties.'[21]

English law does not, of course, contain anywhere so concise and elegant a statement of the judge's role in civil litigation. Nevertheless, and given that the 'objet du litige' is determined in France by the 'prétentions respectives des parties' and that the *prétentions* are fixed by the 'acte introductif d'instance et par les conclusion en défense'[22] – these, in approximate terms, are the equivalent of English pleadings – the law as it is now stated for France would seem to be an accurate enough statement of the position in England as well: the parties plead facts and the judge should attach to the facts pleaded – or to such of them as are proved – the legal result that seems to him to be correct.

It has been said that in the English-speaking world the responsibility for the law to be applied is the parties' rather than the judge's, and even that 'the rule *curia novit legem* has never been and is not part of English law'.[23] On the continent, by contrast, 'the ultimate responsibility for the law is the court's', which means that it is for the court to carry out its own research.[24] It is no doubt true that the English style of civil proceedings and the tradition of the *ex tempore* judgment delivered immediately after the conclusion of counsel's speeches lends greater practical importance to the parties' legal submissions than does the mainly written procedure and secret *délibéré* of the judges on the

---

[19] He had some distinguished opponents. See the authorities cited in *Ecrits*, p. 103, nn. 6, 7 and 8.

[20] See Martin, 'Le fait et le droit', no. 19; 'Le juge devant la Prétention' D. 1987, Chron. 35, no. 2; Vincent, no. 372.

[21] The third paragraph was annulled by the decision of the Conseil d'Etat of 12 October 1979, D. 1979, 606; J.C.P. 1980, II, 19288 (see below, p. 193), but there is no doubt that the principle there stated survives, if only as a necessary implication of the first: Solus and Perrot, no. 100; A. Bénabent, Note, D. 1979, 606; J. Viatte, 'Les moyens de droit relevés d'office et le principe de la contradiction' 1980 Gaz. Pal. Doctr. 21.

[22] N.c.p.c., art. 4. The 'objet du litige' may be modified by 'demandes incidentes': *ibid.*, arts. 4, al. 2, and arts. 63–70.

[23] F. A. Mann, 'Fusion of the Legal Professions' (1977) 93 L.Q.R. 367, 369.

[24] *Ibid.*, at p. 375.

continent. Even so, however, two different situations that may call for different solutions are involved. In both it is supposed that a party does not invoke in his submissions a legal rule that operates in his favour, but in the first it is further supposed that this is a result of an informed choice on his part while in the second it is supposed instead that it is the result of oversight or inadvertence.[25] It is believed that few people today would favour, or maintain that it is, a rule of English practice that a judge must give judgment in a sense contrary to that which he believes to be legally correct merely because counsel for one party failed through incompetence or inadvertence to rely in argument on the applicable rule of law, and it is suggested that nothing in English law requires that the judge should do any such thing.[26]

The case where a party chooses deliberately not to invoke a particular rule of law is more difficult: on the one hand, it may be said that on such a matter the party's wishes should be respected, but, on the other hand, it may be considered objectionable that a judge should deliver a judgment which he believes to be wrong in law merely because that is what the parties have asked him to do.

In practice, that aspect of the dispositive principle that insists that, in general, the parties may dispose freely of their rights is not so attenuated, either in England or in France, as to deprive them altogether of their power to require the judge to disregard some legal principle that would otherwise apply. In England, actions brought against the Motor Insurers' Bureau provide a clear example: the defendant in these cases deliberately and regularly refrains from raising the defence that the plaintiff's claim is based upon a contract to which he is not himself a party and which binds the Bureau only to the Department of the Environment.[27] The principal exception, outside cases involving

---

[25] A similar distinction is taken by Martin, 'Le juge devant la prétention', no. 9, *in fine*.

[26] No doubt a judge to whom it appears that counsel has failed to take a particular point of law will normally invite argument on it, but that raises the distinct question of maintaining the *principe du contradictoire*, which is discussed below. Dr Mann seems to admit this when he says that 'points or authorities that occur to the judge ought (and are expected) to be put to counsel to prevent surprise'. He also says, however, that though the court may suggest new lines of argument and draw attention to authorities overlooked by counsel, it is not its duty to do so: 'Fusion of the Legal Professions', at p. 369. For discussion of a similar problem in France, see, e.g. J. Héron, Observations on Cass. civ. 2ᵉ 14 February 1985, J.C.P. 1988, II, 21030; Raymond Martin, 'La règle de droit adéquate dans le procès civil', D. 1990, Chron. 163; J. Normand, 1992 Rev.trim.dr.civ. 176; 1993 *ibid*. 413; Raymond Martin, 'Le juge a-t-il l'obligation de qualifier ou requalifier?' D.S. 1994, Chron. 308; Solus and Perrot, no. 103.

[27] See, e.g. *Albert* v. *Motor Insurers' Bureau* [1972] A.C. 301, 329, *per* Viscount Dilhorne. In *Persson* v. *London Country Buses* [1974] 1 W.L.R. 569, 572, James L.J. said, 'One point taken, inadvertently we think, before the judge, but not taken before this court, on behalf of the bureau was that the plaintiff was not a party to the contract on which he sought to rely. It is in accordance with the publicly declared policy of the bureau that

personal status, seems to lie in the rule that the court must take for itself the point that a contract sued on is illegal if the illegality appears on the face of the contract or from the evidence laid before the court – an exception obviously founded on public policy.[28]

In France, the fourth paragraph of article 12 of the n.c.p.c. forbids the judge from changing 'la dénomination ou le fondement juridique lorsque les parties, en vertu d'un accord exprès et pour les droits dont elles ont la libre disposition, l'ont lié par les qualifications et points de droit auxquels elles entendent limiter le débat'. This provision is of limited scope[29] and the English and French rules on this matter are not identical, but neither system goes so far as to require the judge to take a point of law which, as they have expressly indicated, the parties wish him not to take, public policy or *ordre public*[30] apart.

The *principe du contradictoire*

Subject to this, it seems that in both England and France it is today the policy of the law that the judge should endeavour to give the correct decision according to law on the facts before him, without being restricted to the legal reasoning submitted by the parties or their counsel. This is more easily stated than achieved, for the attempt to realise the policy in practice has called for the recognition of a reasonably clear line between matters of fact and matters of law; but before turning to that, there is a less intractable but no less important question to which attention should be drawn, namely the conflict that may arise between the judge's freedom to take points of law of his own motion and maintenance of the *principe du contradictoire*.[31] In the nature of things this conflict is less likely to arise in England than in France: in England the judge will naturally tend to put to counsel during the hearing such points of law as occur to him, while in France the judge will frequently postpone serious consideration of the law governing the case until after

the bureau does not rely on the absence of privity of contract and that policy has been fully adhered to before us.' See also *Coward* v. *Motor Insurers' Bureau* [1963] 1 Q.B. 259, 265, *per* Upjohn L.J. For a case in which the decision of the House of Lords rests on the assumption, agreed by counsel, that certain damages, if awarded, would not be subject to tax in the hands of the recipient – a point on which no authority existed – see *British Transport Commission* v. *Gourley* [1956] A.C. 185.

[28] *Holman* v. *Johnson* (1775) 1 Cowp. 341; *North-western Salt Co. Ltd* v. *Electrolytic Alkali Co. Ltd* [1914] A.C. 461; *Edler* v. *Auerbach* [1950] 1 K.B. 359; *Snell* v. *Unity Finance Ltd.* [1964] 2 Q.B. 203. Cf. *Lipton* v. *Powell* [1921] 2 K.B. 51.

[29] R. Martin, 'Retour sur la distinction du fait et du droit', D. 1987, Chron. 272, no. 7; G. Bolard, 'Les principes directeurs du procès civil: Le droit positif depuis Henri Motulsky', J.C.P. 1993, I, 3693, no. 7.

[30] Solus and Perrot, no. 105.   [31] Above, chap. 9, p. 177.

the *clôture des débats*. Even in England, however, the problem may arise if judgment is reserved and, by an interesting coincidence, it gave rise to controversy in both countries at much the same time.

In a case in 1923, Scrutton L.J. indicated his regret that 'counsel who argued this case would probably not recognise any part of the judgments as having any relation to the arguments they addressed to us',[32] but this seems to have passed unnoticed. In *Goldsmith* v. *Sperrings Ltd*,[33] however, an acute difference of opinion emerged in the Court of Appeal. In that case the defendants in a number of libel actions, who were distributors of magazines, applied for the actions against them to be stayed or dismissed on the ground that they were an abuse of the process of the court. In the Court of Appeal the case was argued by both sides on the assumption that a particular proposition of law, as stated in a well-known text book,[34] was correct. Judgment was reserved, and in his judgment Lord Denning M.R., having, as he said, read every case cited in the books on the subject, stated his conclusion that the law was not as both counsel had assumed it to be. Conscious of having been rebuked on an earlier occasion for doing his own legal research,[35] he insisted that 'an erroneous proposition should not be accepted as good law simply because counsel have passed it by in silence and have not sought to challenge it. By that means it gains currency and is never remedied.'[36] Bridge L.J. expressed his emphatic disagreement, his 'most important' reason being that 'this part of the Master of the Rolls' judgment decides against the plaintiff on a ground on which Mr Hawser, for the plaintiff, has not been heard. This is because Mr Comyn, for the defendant, never took the point, and the court did not put the point to Mr Hawser during the argument. Hence there is a breach of the rule *audi alteram partem* which applies alike to issues of law as to issues of fact.'[37]

In France, events took a curious turn. The decrees that preceded the bringing into operation of the new code contained an article similar to article 12 of the code,[38] but great care was taken to ensure that any legal reasoning that the judge was disposed to adopt of his own motion

---

[32] *Smith* v. *Smith* [1923] P. 191, 202. It appears from the report of this case that the proceedings were actually adjourned in order that Scrutton L.J. might personally make enquiries of the Registrar who had made the order appealed from. Did the learned Lord Justice thereby adopt an inquisitorial approach, and, if so, was he justified in doing so only because the case was matrimonial and the origins of the procedure used for matrimonial proceedings are found in the canon rather than the common law?

[33] [1977] 1 W.L.R. 478.

[34] J. C. C. Gatley, *Libel and Slander*, 7th edn (1974), p. 241.

[35] *Rahimtoola* v. *Nizam of Hyderabad* [1958] A.C. 379, 398, *per* Viscount Simonds.

[36] [1977] 1 W.L.R. 478, 486.   [37] *Ibid.* at 508.

[38] Decree no. 71–740 of 9 September 1971, art. 12.

should be put to the parties for their observations.[39] The position was summarised by the provision that 'le juge doit, en toutes circonstances, faire observer *et observer lui-même* le principe de la contradiction'.[40]

Notwithstanding the clarity of the texts, many judges failed to adhere to them: in 1976, Professor Perrot wrote of the 'incroyable florilège d'arrêts [of the Cour de cassation] qui durent censurer des décisions fondées sur des moyens relevés d'office à l'insu des parties'.[41] In his view the cases illustrated the tendency of some courts too easily to forget an elementary rule but they also emphasised the importance of that rule: while most judges are sufficiently conscientious to invite the observations of the parties on points that occur to them without being required by law to do so, 'ce qui va sans dire, va encore mieux en le disant . . . et certainement plus mal en cessant de le dire'. Yet the new code, as eventually brought into operation by a decree of 1975,[42] dropped all the provisions of the decrees covering the point. The revised version of the first paragraph of article 16 no longer required that the judge must himself observe the *principe de la contradiction*.[43]

The reaction of the commentators was almost universally hostile[44] and if, as had been suggested, the motive behind the change was to reduce the possible grounds of complaint to the Cour de cassation,[45] the answer given was that the remedy 'fait davantage penser à la méthode du Dr Coué qu'à une veritable réforme en profondeur'.[46] Eventually, the protests culminated in an attack on article 12, alinéa 3 and article 16, alinéa 1 by way of proceedings brought by members of the legal profession before the Conseil d'Etat.[47] In the course of his conclusions,

---

[39] See *ibid.*, art. 16, al. 2, as amended by decree no. 72–684 of 20 July 1972 and arts. 90, al. 2, 92, al. 1 of the latter decree.

[40] Decree no. 71–740 of 9 September 1971, art. 16, al. 1 (emphasis added).

[41] 1976, Rev.trim.dr.civ. 827. The article cites nine such cases decided by the Cour de cassation between January and July 1976 alone. But see Civ., 15 March 1976, J.C.P. 1976, IV, 6625, discussed by Perrot, *ibid.*

[42] Decree no. 75–1123 of 5 December 1975.

[43] An amendment of 1976 (decree no. 76–714 of 29 July 1976) did little to improve the situation. It is described by Solus and Perrot (no. 118, II) as a 'correctif en trompe-l'oeil'.

[44] Perrot, n. 41, above; J. Normand, 1977 Rev.trim.dr.civ. 180; also his 1978 Rev.trim.-dr.civ; 186, 712–13; A. Bénabent, 'Les moyens relevés en secret par le juge' J.C.P. 1977, I, 2849; D. 1977, I.R. 411, obs. P. Julien: D. 1978, I.R. 87, note P. Julien; Wiederkehr, 'Droit de la défense et procédure civile' D. 1978, Chron. 36; Colmar, 6 June 1977, D. 1978, 106, note D. Huet-Weiller; R. Martin, 'La crise du contradictoire entre juge et avocat' Gaz. Pal. 1978, Doctr. 418.

[45] It is arguable that if the 'moyen de pur droit' relied on by the court below appeals to the Cour de cassation as having been correctly applied to the facts, no purpose is served in censuring the judge for not having invited the parties' observations on it.

[46] Perrot, n. 41, above; see also Bénabent, 'Les moyens relevés'.

[47] 12 October 1979, D. 1979, 606, note Bénabent. J.C.P. 1980, II, 19288, concl. Franc, Note Boré; Normand, 1980 Rev.trim.dr.civ. 145. In his conclusions, M. Franc records

the Commissaire du Gouvernement accepted that there could be derogations from the *principe dispositif* in the interests of efficiency, but insisted that they must not be such as to impinge on the *principe du contradictoire*, a principle which, in his words was of a '*valeur supérieure*'. The Conseil d'Etat itself, while agreeing that the powers of the judge could be enhanced to achieve procedural economy, struck down articles 12, al. 3 and 16, al. 1 on the ground that they were inconsistent with the *principe du contradictoire*, which, in its opinion, formed part of the *principes généraux du droit*.[48]

The immediate effect of this decision was to restore force to the relevant parts of the decrees as they stood before introduction of the code, but the position nevertheless remained obscure until clarification came in a decree of 1981.[49] As a result, the code now makes it perfectly clear once more that the judge must himself observe the *principe du contradictoire* and that he may not base his decision on legal reasoning he has raised for himself without having first invited the parties to express their views.[50]

In England, perhaps because of the lack of recognition of the *principe du contradictoire* as an independent principle,[51] there has been little discussion of the division of opinion between Lord Denning M.R. and Bridge L.J.[52] and no attempt formally to resolve it. Probably, however, the view of Bridge L.J. represents majority opinion, and this is confirmed by a unanimous judgment of the Privy Council in 1995. Though he made no reference to the earlier controversy, Lord Mustill then said:

> It does, of course, happen from time to time that a court comes to learn of a statute or authority bearing importantly on an issue canvassed in argument but, through an oversight, not then brought forward. The court may wish to take the new matter into account. Before doing so it should always ensure that the parties have an opportunity to deal with it, either by restoring the appeal for further oral argument, or at least drawing attention to the materials which have come to light and inviting written submissions upon them.[53]

that some members of the legal profession actually demonstrated in the streets in January 1976.

[48] The Conseil d'Etat had power to act in this way because the relevant provisions were brought into law by way of decree, not parliamentary legislation. See P. Delvové, 'Le nouveau code de procédure civile devant le Conseil d'Etat', D. 1979, Chron. 281.

[49] Decree no. 81–500 of 12 May 1981. For the fate of art. 12, al. 3, see above, n. 21.

[50] Art. 16, al. 1, as amended. It has been said that the rule must not be too rigidly enforced lest the judges be dissuaded from adhering to it: A. Bénabent, 'L'article 16 du nouveau code de procédure civile version 1981', D. 1982, Chron. 55.

[51] Above, chap. 9, p. 177.

[52] Above, p. 192. See Carolyn Yates, 'The Use of Judicial Knowledge' in E. K. Banakas (ed.), *United Kingdom Law in the 1980s* (1988), p. 320 at pp. 339–43.

[53] *Hoecheong Products Ltd* v. *Cargill Ltd* [1995] 1 W.L.R. 404, 409.

Party control of the facts

It is one thing to say that, subject to observance of the *principe du contradictoire*, the judge may take points of law of his own motion. It is another thing to say that this makes him the effective master of the law of the case. What is the law of the case depends upon what are the facts of the case and the allegation of facts belongs to the parties, not the judge.

Following a trend which had begun a good deal earlier,[54] the new French code gives wide-ranging powers to the judge in the investigation of fact: he may order, *ex officio*, any *mesure d'instruction* legally admissible;[55] he may invite the parties to give him such explanations of the facts as he considers necessary;[56] he may require the parties, or one of them, to appear personally before him for examination.[57] On the other hand, and most importantly, the code makes it clear that the *objet du litige* is determined by the *prétentions* of the parties;[58] that it is for the parties to allege the facts necessary to sustain their *prétentions*;[59] that the parties carry the burden of proving those facts;[60] and that, though the judge may take into consideration facts that are 'parmi les éléments du débat' even if neither party has specifically relied on them, he may not base his decision on facts that are not 'dans le débat'.[61]

The various concepts contained in this series of provisions are complex and not easily analysed, but an English lawyer would probably not be wholly wrong if he saw running through them a distinction similar to that drawn by English law between the material facts, on the one hand, and 'the evidence by which those facts are to be proved', on the other.[62] The French judge of today has greater powers than his English brother in relation to evidence,[63] but in both countries it is for the parties alone, by their respective allegations, counter-allegations and admissions, to set the limits beyond which the judge may not go in

---

[54] The change in French thinking on these matters originated with the introduction, by a decree-law of 30 October 1935, of the 'juge chargé de suivre la procédure'. See J. A. Jolowicz, 'The Woolf Report and the Adversary Process' (1996) 15 C.J.Q. 198, 201–9.

[55] N.c.p.c., arts. 10, 143, 144, 148 and 149.

[56] *Ibid.*, art. 8. By art. 13 the judge may call for similar explanations of the law.

[57] *Ibid.*, art. 184. For the detailed regulation of this power, see arts. 185–98.

[58] *Ibid.*, art. 4. See above, p. 189.   [59] *Ibid.*, art. 6.

[60] *Ibid.*, art. 9. The judge should not order a 'mesure d'instruction' simply in order to cure a party's failure to fulfil his duty under article 9: art. 146, al. 2.

[61] *Ibid.*, art. 7.

[62] The former but not the latter must be pleaded: R.S.C., Ord. 18, r. 7; C.P.R., rr. 16.4, 16.5.

[63] See further below, chap. 11, p. 221. As the law stands, the English judge may neither call a witness nor even appoint an expert, limited exceptions apart, without the agreement of the parties. But see C.P.R., r. 32.

finding the facts on which his judgment will be based. In this way both English and French law express their continued allegiance to the general principle that it is the *parties'* dispute with which the court must deal, not the dispute which the court might have preferred to have before it: the law may be for the judge, but he is bound by the parties' choice of material facts.

The distinction between fact and law has given a good deal of trouble in the past and will, no doubt, continue to do so. Almost certainly, no universal criterion of distinction will ever be found. It is no disrespect to a number of distinguished writers[64] to suggest that much depends on the context in which the application of the distinction falls to be made and even that the particular solutions of positive law are often reached on grounds that are more teleological than analytical.[65] In the context of the respective roles of parties and judge in civil litigation, it seems that the distinction between fact and law has excited little or no discussion in England and that the position was much the same in France until Motulsky sought to remove all elements of law from the concept of the *cause de la demande*. In 1974, however, the subject was taken up and impressively argued by M. Raymond Martin against the background of the French law as contained in the decrees that preceded the code of 1975.[66]

The essence of Motulsky's position is that the parties bring the facts before the court and that it is for the judge to identify or qualify those facts in accordance with a rule of law so as to apply that rule and arrive at the legal solution. This presupposes – as do the opening paragraphs of this chapter – that facts exist independently of legal classification or qualification. At least for the purposes of this discussion, Martin does not deny the existence of an objective reality independent of all conceptualisation, but he observes that such a reality can only enter into human discourse through the use of language, and that inevitably involves a degree of conceptualisation of some kind.

Referring specifically to litigation, Martin points out that a case does not begin with the first formal step in an action; it begins with the client who tells his story to his lawyer,[67] and the lawyer immediately begins to

---

[64] The leading work is still G. Marty, *La distinction du fait et du droit* (1929). For present purposes, see in particular, R. Martin, 'Le fait et le droit ou les parties et le juge', J.C.P. 1974, I 2625; 'Retour sur la distinction du fait et du droit', D.S. 1987, Chron. 272.

[65] See below, chap. 15, p. 301.

[66] R. Martin, 'Le fait et le droit ou les parties et le juge', J.C.P. 1974, I, 2625. See also the same author's 'Retour sur la distinction du fait et du droit', D.S. 1987, Chron. 272.

[67] Some, including, probably, Motulsky and, certainly, the present writer, would prefer to say that the case begins with the actual events which created the client's need to consult his lawyer, but this makes no practical difference. Note that Martin attaches importance for the purposes of his argument to the fact that legal representation is

translate that story into the language of the law with, at the back of his mind, the result that his client wishes to achieve. This he does by trying out various possible rules of law, a process which leads him to reject as irrelevant some of the facts told to him by his client, and to see whether certain additional statements of fact not originally mentioned by or, perhaps, not actually known to, the client personally, can be made. The claim as formulated by the lawyer is the outcome of this first application of law in the progress of the case, and the claim does not consist, as Motulsky would have it, of a *complexe de faits*, but of a 'proposition de qualification (ou de plusieurs qualifications possibles)'.

Once the claim has reached the defendant, he and his lawyer go through a similar process, but by reference to the claim as formulated, and this results in the defendant's answer. Martin argues, essentially, that the claims and defences thus produced do not so much represent allegations of fact as proposals for judgment. Moreover, even if it is theoretically possible for a case to be put before a judge without the use of legal language, this is of only marginal importance in practice: 'la justice de paix paternaliste a disparu. De plus en plus les avocats abandonnent la rhétorique pour la démonstration juridique.'

Martin's position cannot be discussed further here,[68] but one point which he makes – an important one for the purposes of this chapter – is that where the parties, through their lawyers, have expressed themselves in legal terminology, the judge will normally do no more than choose between the rival classifications of the facts which are proposed: he will not search for a third possible solution. 'A plus forte raison, si les parties sont d'accord sur une qualification, semble-t-il déraisonnable que le juge lui même en substitue une autre.' Translated into English terminology and reduced to a simple example, this means that if the defendant has admitted a paragraph in his opponent's pleading which reads 'By a contract between the plaintiff and the defendant . . .', no judge is going to enquire whether the transaction between the parties is correctly classified as a contract within the legal meaning of that word. The parties, by their pleadings, have deprived the judge of the possibility of

---

normally obligatory in France. For him the term 'party' always indicates client and lawyer together. See also his 'La crise du contradictoire', see n. 44.

[68] His own suggestion is, in short, that the parties must propose 'moyens' sufficient to motivate the decision and that the judgment must itself be motivated only 'par une combinaison de moyens qui ont été proposés par les avocats dans leurs conclusions, à l'exclusion de tout autre moyen élaboré *proprio motu* par le juge, quand bien même celui-ci le soumettrait préalablement au débat contradictoire'. For Martin's understanding of 'moyen' see, in addition to the articles cited, his 'Sur la notion de moyen', J.C.P. 1976, I, 2768; 'Le juge devant la prétention', D.S. 1987, Chron. 35.

bringing under consideration for the purposes of his decision that part of the law which defines the legal concept of contract.[69]

Motulsky might have replied to this that the parties in this example have used the word 'contract' 'par simple commodité de langage' – and so, strictly speaking, they have. Rather than set out, as facts, the actual exchanges between the parties, the pleader uses the word 'contract' to convey the allegation that the parties together went through a sequence of actions of a pattern that he describes generically as contracting: if the defendant admits 'contract' in his pleading, he too is dealing only with facts, and if he denies the allegation he will be entitled in England to further and better particulars of the exchanges between the parties as alleged by the plaintiff. The point is, however, that at this stage the distinction between fact and law disappears. If 'contract' is admitted, the question of law is foreclosed. Only a judge with the most sweeping powers of investigation *proprio motu* such as no Western system of procedure has so far admitted could go behind the admission (of fact) and demand to be given detailed information about the actual exchanges between the parties.[70]

Here, then, is one way in which the parties by their allegations and admissions of fact can deprive the judge of the power to introduce points of law of his own motion. Even more significant than the use of legal terms of art as collective nouns, however, is the choice that the parties have severally to make of the facts that they will allege. The former English rule actually stated the obvious proposition that only material facts should be pleaded, and the criteria of what is material for the purposes of litigation can be found only in the law itself. In reducing to a series of allegations the story as he has had it from his client, therefore, the pleader is guided by the content of the rule (or rules) of law that he regards as applicable to the case; he will not include allegations which would be material only on the dismissed hypothesis that some other rule is also or alternatively applicable. The omission of such allegations will effectively prevent the judge from invoking a rule of law that the pleader has discarded as inapplicable, whatever the judge himself might have thought of its applicability if the relevant facts had been included in the pleading.

[69] In England, a defendant who does not, in his pleading, deny an allegation pleaded by the plaintiff may be taken to admit the truth of the allegation: R.S.C., Ord. 18, r. 3; C.P.R., rr. 16.5 (3), (4) and (5). In France, by contrast, the judge is not necessarily bound in all cases to accept as true an allegation made by one party and not contested by the other: J. Normand, 1992 Rev.trim.dr.civ. 447. Cf. G. Bolard, 'Les principes directeurs du procès civil: Le droit positif depuis Henri Motulsky', J.C.P. 1993, I, 3693, no. 12.

[70] But see Cappelletti and Jolowicz, pp. 257–8.

If this is right, then there is no possibility that the judge can rethink the law applicable to the case *de novo* and unfettered by what the parties may have said or done. The only rules of law which he can invoke, other than those which have guided the lawyers in drawing up the pleadings, are those which can be applied to facts that they have actually alleged with something else in mind. In other words, the extent of the judge's power to search independently for the law of the case depends on accident; the only facts which the judge may take into account in invoking a rule not previously regarded as applicable by the parties, or one or other of them, are those which the parties happen to have alleged for a different purpose or in error.[71]

In practice the judge's power of initiative in relation to the law of the case is not as restricted as this analysis would imply[72] but, it is suggested, it does come close to describing the position so far as the 'moyens de pur droit' of article 12, alinéa 3 of the French code are concerned.[73] This phrase, though not used in connection with the powers of the judge until introduction of the original version of article 12 in 1971,[74] has for long been part of the terminology of the Cour de cassation: since a 'moyen' commonly involves elements of fact as well as law, new *moyens* may not be taken for the first time before that court for it is a court exclusively of law. The exclusionary rule does not, however, apply to *moyens de pur droit*[75] and, for this purpose, *moyens* are *de pur droit* if, and only if, they 'ne donnent à examiner aucun fait qui n'ait été constaté et apprécié, qui n'ait pu être envisagé dans ses rapports avec le chef considéré'.[76] *Moyens de pur droit* are admitted before the Cour de cassation because 'le juge de cassation, comme les autres juges, mieux que les autres juges, détient la plénitude du droit. Il doit pouvoir introduire dans le débat, même d'office, la règle "applicable" négligée par les parties et par les juges du fond. Les parties elles mêmes doivent pouvoir proposer au Tribunal de Cassation la règle de droit oubliée jusque-là.'[77]

Given that it was the intention of the code to give the judge maximum control over the law of the case, it is both logical and natural that the

---

[71] The 'error' lies in the pleader's supposition that a fact is material for the purposes of the rule of law he has in mind when in truth it is not.

[72] See below, p. 200.

[73] Though struck down by the Conseil d'Etat, the principle of this paragraph survives: above, n. 21. It may be, however, that the principle is no longer rigidly restricted to 'moyens de *pur* droit': Solus and Perrot, no. 103.

[74] Decree no. 71–740 of 9 September 1971, art. 12.

[75] Vincent, no. 1045 and authorities cited at p. 698, n. 2. See also *ibid.*, no. 373.

[76] Normand, see n. 44, above; E. Faye, *La Cour de cassation* (1906) nos. 125 *et seq.*; J. Voulet, 'L'irrecevabilité des moyens nouveaux devant la Cour de cassation' J.C.P. 1973, I, 2544, nos. 19 *et seq.*

[77] Martin, 'Le fait et le droit', no. 9.

commentators should have turned to this rule of the Cour de cassation in their analysis of the phrase 'moyen de pur droit' as used in article 12, especially when it appeared that the judge was not obliged to observe the *principe du contradictoire* in relation to a *moyen* that he proposed to introduce *ex officio*. The judge may only base his decision on facts 'qui sont dans le débat',[78] and it was argued that this must not be taken to extend beyond 'les faits que les parties ont mis dans le débat parce qu'ils constituent, à leurs yeux, la justification de leurs prétentions';[79] if that is right, then only *moyens* based on such facts, as distinct from facts that appear in the dossier but to which the parties in presenting their respective cases have not attached particular importance, would qualify as *moyens de pur droit*.[80]

French 'pleadings' are not restricted, as are the English, to material facts.[81] If, however, the meaning just attributed to 'faits qui sonts dans le débat' is correct, then the English lawyer may conclude that French law does indeed make use of a distinction close to the English distinction between material facts, on the one hand, and 'the evidence by which those facts are to be proved', on the other: facts which are in the dossier but are not put there because, in their eyes, they form the 'justification de leurs prétentions', must have been put there because, in their eyes, they amount to no more than mere evidence supporting the facts on which they actually rely.[82] And, just as the English judge may not base his judgment on facts that have not been pleaded (as material facts), so the French judge may not base his judgment on facts that are in the dossier only as evidence rather than as material facts in their own right.[83]

---

[78] N.c.p.c., art. 7, al. 1.

[79] Normand, 1974 Rev.trim.dr.civ. 450.

[80] Normand, 1977 Rev.trim.dr.civ. 180. It is there suggested that the removal of the judge's obligation to observe the *principe du contradictoire* might have so have restricted the judge's powers of initiative as to produce a result directly opposed to that which was intended.

[81] On the contrary, the 'assignation' must include both a statement of the 'objet de la demande' and an 'exposée de moyens' (n.c.p.c., art. 56), and the judge may invite the *avocats* of the parties to respond to 'moyens' they have hitherto left unanswered (*ibid.*, art. 765).

[82] Motulsky coined the phrase 'éléments adventices': 'La cause de la demande dans la délimitation de l'office du juge', *Ecrits*, pp. 101, 110. Bolard, 'Les principes directeurs', no. 12.

[83] For English law this is so self-evident that authority is hard to find, but the proposition is inherent in the decision of the House of Lords in *Esso Petroleum Co. Ltd* v. *Southport Corporation* [1956] A.C. 218. See also *Fookes* v. *Slaytor* [1978] 1 W.L.R. 1293; *Beacon Carpets Ltd* v. *Kirby* [1988] Q.B. 755, 766–7, *per* Lawton L.J. For French law, in addition to the provisions of n.c.p.c., art. 7, it is noteworthy that by art. 26 the judge may, '*en matière gracieuse*', found his decision on all the facts that are before him, 'y compris ceux qui n'auraient pas été allégués'. This does not apply to contentious

The distinction between a material fact and evidence is no more precise than that between fact and law, but it is of particular importance here because what is no more than evidence of a material fact for the purposes of one rule of law, may itself be a material fact for the purposes of another. That the defendant acted without reasonable care is a material fact for the purpose of establishing his liability in England for negligence at common law and if, for example, a workman sues his employer after a fall from a ladder in the course of his work, it may be evidence of lack of reasonable care on the part of the employer that the ladder had a missing rung. For the purposes of the statutory rule that 'no ladder shall be used which has a missing or defective rung',[84] however, it is a material fact that the ladder used by the plaintiff lacked a rung. If, therefore, a judge who has heard the evidence or studied the dossier, as the case may be, invokes a rule of law which treats as a material fact something which is before him only as evidence of a different material fact, he is actually restructuring the litigation and altering the nature of the dispute as it was presented to him by the parties.

In England, if evidence presented at the trial comes to appear suitable for treatment as a material fact in its own right and as the basis for the application of a rule of law not hitherto relied on, an amendment of the pleadings will be required. Under the Rules of the Supreme Court the judge did have the power to order an amendment of the pleadings *ex officio*,[85] but the power was very rarely used, there is no equivalent in the Civil Procedure Rules, and the general principle is that it is not the court's duty to thrust upon the parties amendments for which they do not ask.[86] The judge may, of course, suggest to one of the parties that he should apply for leave to amend and such a suggestion will normally be followed; but if the judge's suggestion is not accepted by the party to whom it is addressed, then the judge will leave the pleadings as they stand and decide the case accordingly.[87] In other words, the English judge does not restructure the litigation against the expressed wishes of the parties.

In France there is no equivalent to the formal amendment of the

proceedings. Note further art. 5: 'Le juge doit se prononcer sur tout ce qui est demandé *et seulement sur ce qui est demandé*' (emphasis added). It is, however, possible that the French judge may bring facts into the 'débat' through the use of his power to invite the parties to supply such explanations of fact or law as he considers necessary: n.c.p.c., arts. 8, 13.

[84] Building (Safety, Health and Welfare) Regulations 1948, reg. 29(7), now superseded.

[85] R.S.C., Ord. 20, r. 8. See chap. 17, n. 37.

[86] *Cropper* v. *Smith* (1884) 26 Ch.D. 700, 715, *per* Fry L.J.

[87] See the description by Lord Asquith of an experience of his own when a trial judge: (1953) 69 L.Q.R. 317.

free

pleadings, and this may make it appear that the French judge can restructure the litigation without the consent of the parties,[88] but he should not do so without giving the parties an opportunity to present their observations on the new material facts which the judge has found in the evidence. Apart from preservation of the *principe du contradictoire*, if this were not done, the risk of actual error in the finding of facts would be unacceptably high.[89] In any case, as has already been mentioned, the parties are normally at liberty, if they so choose, to limit the judge to consideration only of those possible qualifications of the facts and of those points of law that they wish to have discussed.[90] In practice it may be easier in France than in England for the judge to restructure the litigation without reference to the parties, but in both countries, if they so wish, the parties are generally entitled to prevent him from doing so and to demand a decision on the material facts that they have chosen to allege.

Conclusion

It has been the main purpose of this chapter to consider how English and French law seek to reconcile the modern legal policy of securing, so far as possible, that judges decide their cases in accordance with the applicable rules of law as they see them, on the one hand, and the more ancient principle that it is for the parties, not for the judge, to determine the ambit of the dispute, on the other. In both countries the main technique for achieving this reconciliation is to insist that the allegation of facts is for the parties, while the ultimate determination of their legal consequences is for the judge. It is not surprising that in neither country is the slippery distinction between fact and law proving adequate for its task. What is, perhaps, surprising is the similarity of the subsidiary questions to which the weakness of the distinction has given rise and of the solutions to them that have been attempted; even the question whether the parties must be allowed the opportunity to present their

[88] See Normand, 1978 Rev.tr.dr.civ. 186–7. Cf. Martin, 'Le juge devant la prétention'.
[89] 'On ne peut raisonnablement tolérer que le juge procède a une telle substitution sans que les parties soient invitées à débattre de faits, qui, pour la plupart sont jusque là restés dans l'ombre, sous la nouvelle coloration juridique qu'il est envisagé de leur donner. Sinon l'on s'expose inéluctablement à de graves erreurs de fait, et par voie de conséquence, à l'application inexacte de la loi. Pour huit espèces dans lesquelles les faits seront tellement constants que le risque sera négligeable, il s'en trouvera deux dans lesquelles les parties auraient pu, si elles avaient été informées, dévoiler au juge un contexte qui en aurait infléchi la portée, mais qu'elles n'avaient aucune raison de révéler auparavant, puisque ce n'était pas là la question': Normand, see n. 44, above. See also Huet-Weiller, n. 44, above.
[90] Above, p. 191.

observations on a point that the judge is minded to take for himself became a matter of controversy in both countries at much the same time and both, in the end, gave the same answer.[91]

It may now be suggested that the clue to a satisfactory pragmatic solution to the overall problem lies in that answer. More is involved than mere ritual adherence to the *principe du contradictoire*; it is only by putting his point to the parties that the judge can discover whether, in the context of the litigation that is actually before him, it comes within his province or theirs.

For some purposes, such as those of the Cour de cassation in France, it may be necessary to find a workable definition of a *moyen de pur droit*, and it is unobjectionable, if the judge is to be master of the law, that he may apply such a *moyen* regardless of the wishes of the parties. Any definition will, however, be narrow and uncertain in its application, and it is important that a case should not be decided wrongly on the sole ground that neither party has taken a point that appears to the judge after examination of the evidence to be a decisive one, whether it be a point of law or a point of mixed law and fact. It is, however, also important that any power that the judge may have to impose upon the parties a solution to a dispute which they have chosen not to put before him should be carefully controlled.[92]

The only way in which a judge can be sure that he is not trespassing on the preserve of the parties when he is minded to found his decision on a point not expressly relied on by either of them, is for him to put his point to the parties before finalising his decision, if necessary by reopening the case for further argument. He should not hesitate to do this whenever he thinks that his intervention will assist the realisation of justice according to law, but he should never adopt reasoning as the foundation of his judgment if the parties have not, at the very least, had the opportunity to present their observations on it.[93]

If the judges adhere invariably to this rule, then it will be unnecessary for the higher courts to undertake the often impossible task of deciding whether the judge's new point was one of pure law or not. If, to adhere by way of example to English terminology and procedure, the judge's point calls for an amendment to the pleadings and the parties decline to apply for leave to amend, the judge may still decide the case in accordance with his own opinion by ordering an amendment *ex officio*.[94] But if he does so and there is an appeal, the appellate court will have to decide whether the circumstances were such that the judge was justified

[91] Above, pp. 191–4.   [92] Note the distinction taken above, p. 190.
[93] Cf. the proposal of Normand, 1978 Rev.trim.dr.civ. 712–13.
[94] Above, p. 201.

in ordering the amendment and thus, in effect, in restructuring the parties' dispute against their expressed wishes on the matter. That is an important question of substance which will focus attention on the point that is ultimately at issue, namely, the extent to which, if at all, the legislation actually in force empowers the judge to override the wishes of the parties and impose a solution for which neither of them has asked. Both English and French judges apparently have power to do this under existing legislation, at least in some circumstances, and it may be right for them occasionally to use their power even when public policy or *ordre public* is not obviously at stake. But when they do so they must do so openly and in a manner which makes their decisions susceptible to the control of an appellate court or a court of cassation, as the case may be.

11 Fact-finding[1]

Introduction

It has been rightly said that lawyers must learn to appreciate some of the more basic assumptions that are made by their counterparts in other countries and of the consequences of them.[2] Common lawyers must not, of course, fall into the trap of supposing that all continental systems are the same, but Western European countries do have a common heritage in the Romano-canonical procedure of Byzantium.[3] This makes it possible to differentiate on a broad scale between common law and continental systems and to suggest that, in terms of assumptions, the fundamental difference is that the common law system assumes that there will be a trial while the continental assumes no such thing. In other words – and it really is 'in other words' – the fundamental division between the two principal families of procedural law of the Western world is that between those legal systems which do – or did in the past – make use of the civil jury and those to which the civil jury has always been unknown.

The significance of this to the fact-finding process as such lies in the fact that the members of a jury can be brought together only for a single session; once it came to be settled that the jury must decide on the basis of materials presented to it in court – largely, if not entirely, by word of

---

[1] Based principally on a report delivered to the Colloquium of the United Kingdom National Committee of Comparative Law on 'The Option of Litigating in Europe' in 1991, published as chapter 10 of Carey Miller. The chapter also draws on an article published under the title 'The Parties, the Judge and the Facts of the Case' in M. Taruffo *et al.* (eds.), *Studi in Onore di Vittorio Denti* (1994), Vol. II, p. 233.

[2] D. Edward, 'Different Assumptions – Different Methods', SSC Biennial Lecture 1990, published by the Society of Solicitors in the Supreme Court of Scotland. See also Edward, 'Fact-finding – A British Perspective', in Carey Miller, p. 43.

[3] The Romano-canonical influence can be detected in the procedure of the old Court of Chancery, but it played no part in the formation of the procedure of the common law. Scottish civil procedure may be classified as a common law procedure for present purposes since civil jury trial was introduced into Scotland in 1815. See Edward, 'Fact-finding', p. 46.

mouth – the essential characteristic of the trial was established. 'Trial' means a single uninterrupted session of the court at which all the evidence furnished by the parties is presented once and for all.

On the continent of Europe the civil jury never emerged, and there is no compelling need for a single session trial where professional judges deal with all aspects of a case. Continental procedure has nothing that corresponds to the common law trial and the word 'trial' itself is untranslatable. When continental lawyers write in English they tend to use the word 'trial' to refer to the proceedings as a whole.[4]

More is involved here than a mere matter of language. There is a divide – perhaps no longer unbridgeable given recent developments on both sides of the Channel, but a divide none the less. The basic assumption of the common law is – or was until recently – that the information on which the judgment will be founded is supplied to the court only at the trial. On the continent, no such assumption is, or could be, made: on the contrary, provision is made for the information on which the decision will be founded to come in piecemeal. Both types of system see the legal process as consisting of two principal stages, the first of which is preparatory. However, common lawyers see the business of the preparatory stage as preparation for trial; the others see it as preparation for decision. What is more, once the decision stage has been reached, it is, virtually by definition, too late for additional information about the facts to be offered to the court. It is during the preparatory stage – the 'instruction', as it is known in France – that the court acquires the information on which its decision will be based.

This being so, it is almost inevitable that the process of 'fact-finding' should be differently conducted in the two systems, but before turning to that it is necessary, first, to say a word about the constitution of the action and, secondly, about the concept of fact-finding as such.

The constitution of the action and the parties' documents

Whether it is seen as a matter of principle, as it usually is, or as no more than an unavoidable necessity, as it might be in an avowedly inquisitorial system of procedure, it is undoubted that it is for the parties, at least in the first instance, to allege the facts that form the basis of their claims and defences. An account of the process of fact-finding must, therefore, refer at the outset to the procedures whereby an action is constituted and to the mode in which the parties' allegations are presented to the

---

[4] For the dangers of this, see P. Gottwald, 'Fact-finding: A German Perspective', in Carey Miller, p. 67 at p. 69.

court. For this purpose the English, French and Italian systems are briefly compared.

The constitution of the action

In France and Italy the initial act of the plaintiff, by which proceedings are started, is to serve on the defendant, through an official process-server, a full statement of his claim – in France, usually, an 'assignation', in Italy, usually, a 'citazione'.[5] The machinery of the court is engaged when the plaintiff deposits a copy of this document; the court is thus informed of the particulars of the plaintiff's claim as soon as the action is on foot. In Italy the defendant is also required, in order to constitute himself a party, to deposit with the court his full answer to the claim – his 'comparsa di risposta'.[6] In France, on the other hand, the defendant joins the proceedings simply by the appointment of his *avocat*, giving notice of the appointment to both the plaintiff and the court. The judge to whom the case is assigned from its inception – the 'juge de la mise en état' – will, however, fix a time within which the defendant must produce his 'conclusions en défense', a copy of which is supplied to the court at the same time as it is communicated to the plaintiff.[7] In both countries, therefore, the court is informed of the parties' contentions at an early stage of the proceedings.

This is not the case in England. There, in the normal procedure in the High Court, the action is started – the machinery of the court is engaged – when the plaintiff 'issues' his 'writ' or other originating document. The writ is prepared by the plaintiff, is addressed to the defendant and, in its modern form, calls on the defendant either to satisfy the plaintiff's claim or to acknowledge service and indicate whether he proposes to contest the proceedings or not.[8] To issue his writ the plaintiff must have it sealed in the office of the court – but this is, exceptional cases apart, a mere administrative act – and it is then for him to serve it on the defendant. It is true that a copy of the writ is kept in the office of the court and it is true also that the defendant makes his acknowledgment of service to the court, but there is no requirement that the writ must contain more than an abbreviated statement of the plaintiff's claim,[9]

---

[5] N.c.p.c., arts. 54, 750; c.p.c., art. 163.   [6] C.p.c., art. 167.

[7] N.c.p.c., arts. 755, 756, 763 and 764.

[8] Formerly the writ contained a command in the name of the sovereign that the defendant 'appear' in the action at the suit of the plaintiff, and, although the sovereign's name no longer appears, the document still bears the royal arms. For changes under the C.P.R. to this and the following topic, see chap. 2, p. 54.

[9] The plaintiff's full statement of his claim – the first 'pleading' in the action – often accompanies the writ, but this is not mandatory: R.S.C., Ord. 6, r. 2; R.S.C., Ord. 18, r. 1; C.P.R., r. 7.4.

while the acknowledgment of service states only whether the defendant does or does not intend to contest the claim. At this stage, therefore, the court is informed of little more than the identity of the parties to the action. Subsequently, there must be an exchange of pleadings between the parties, but this does not require the formal involvement of the judge and, unless problems arise, the court will not even receive copies of the pleadings until the action is 'set down for trial' – that is, until the parties are ready for the trial at the end of which the final decision will be made.

The contents of the parties' documents[10]

In the modern English rules of pleading it is required that the parties state, in summary form, the facts on which they rely for the claim or defence as the case may be[11] and that the defendant makes it clear which of the plaintiff's allegations of fact he admits and which he denies.[12] The statement of claim must disclose a cause of action, which means that the facts alleged must, on the hypothesis that they are true, be such as to entitle the plaintiff to judgment in his favour, and a parallel rule applies to the defence: if this requirement is not met, the pleading may be struck out and judgment entered accordingly.[13] On the other hand, neither the rules or principles of law relied on[14] nor the evidence to be adduced in support of the allegations of fact are mentioned in the claim or the defence. A party may not, however, adduce evidence tending to prove a fact which has not been pleaded, nor may he seek to invoke a rule or principle of law which is not capable of application to the pleaded facts. The object of the pleadings is, therefore, first to determine the questions of fact on which the parties are in controversy and, secondly, to delimit the matters on which evidence may be adduced and to which legal reasoning may be addressed.

That English pleadings are restricted to the parties' allegations of fact contrasts with the position in Italian law. There it is required that, on pain of nullity, the *citazione* must state precisely the subject matter of the claim and it must also state the facts and the rules or principles

---

[10] Matters of form, including such matters as designation of the court in which the action is brought, will not be mentioned here.

[11] R.S.C., Ord. 18, r. 7; C.P.R., rr. 16.4, 16.5.

[12] R.S.C., Ord. 18, r. 13; C.P.R., r. 16.5.

[13] R.S.C., Ord. 18, r. 19(1)(a); C.P.R., r. 3.4. See *Williams and Humbert* v. *W. and H. Trade Marks* [1986] A.C. 368, for the position where an application to strike out raises complex questions of law.

[14] A point of law can sometimes be pleaded: R.S.C., Ord. 18, rr. 8, 11; C.P.R., r. 16, Practice Direction.

(*elementi*) of law on which the plaintiff relies. In addition it must indicate the specific modes of proof and, in particular, the documents, by which the plaintiff proposes to substantiate his allegations of fact.[15] As for the defence, the defendant must put forward the whole of his defence and counterclaim, if any, must state his position with regard to the facts alleged by the plaintiff, and must indicate the specific modes of proof and the documents by which he will substantiate his answer.[16]

French law seems to stand, on this matter, between the English and the Italian. It is a general rule of the new code of civil procedure that the parties have the obligation to allege the facts necessary to support their pretentions.[17] Only the contents of the *assignation*, however – not of the *conclusions en défense* – are specified in the code and then only in fairly general terms. Formal matters apart, the plaintiff must set out the object of his claim with an exposition of the grounds on which it is based.[18] In addition he must indicate the documents on which he will rely.[19]

Variation of the parties' documents

The Italian code of 1940, in its original form, placed severe limits on the possibilities for amendment or variation by the parties of the original documents put in by them. At the first hearing of the *trattazione*, which takes place very soon after the commencement of the proceedings, the party could clarify or modify his *citazione* or *comparsa di risposta*, as the case might be, could request modes of proof not already mentioned and could put forward additional documents. Thereafter, however, modification of either document was possible only with the leave of the *giudice istruttore*, such leave to be given only for grave cause: the purpose was to settle both the *thema decidendum* and the *thema probandum* at the earliest possible moment.[20]

This regime of preclusion was radically altered by the reforms of 1950.[21] While the prohibition of new claims remained in force in order to preserve the immutability of the subject matter of the action, amendments could be made up to the time when the *giudice istruttore* remitted

---

[15] C.p.c., art. 163.   [16] *Ibid.*, art. 167.   [17] N.c.p.c., art. 6.

[18] N.c.p.c., art. 56, 2° as amended by decree no. 98–231 of 28 December 1998: 'L'objet de la demande avec un exposé des moyens en fait et en droit.' The amendment, adding the words 'en fait et en droit', confirms what was previously assumed from the fact that the *assignation* operates as the '*conclusions*' of the plaintiff. There is probably no obligation to cite specific legal texts: Solus and Perrot, no. 140.

[19] N.c.p.c., art. 56, al. 2.

[20] F. Carpi, V. Colesanti and M. Taruffo, *Commentaria breve al Codice di Procedura Civile*, 2nd edn (1988) *sub* art. 183 at point I. For the changes introduced in 1990, see the same authors' *Appendice di Aggorniamento* to the earlier work (1991).

[21] C.p.c., arts. 183 and 184 in their versions of 1950.

the case to the full court for decision.[22] Now, however, as part of a reform aimed primarily at the reduction of procedural delays,[23] the old rule of preclusion has been restored in a form that seems even more severe than the original. At the first hearing of the *trattazione*, amendment is still possible, but now only with the leave of the judge.[24] Thereafter no amendments are allowed.[25]

In France, under the new code of civil procedure, the juge de la mise en état has wide powers to control the development of the action, including the provision of time limits for the performance of the various procedural acts by the parties,[26] but the parties' conclusions themselves are communicated directly by one party to the other, copies being supplied to the office of the court.[27] There appears to be no formal limit to the number of *conclusions*, subject to the control of the judge in the individual case, and the law specifically permits the making of 'demandes incidentes' – additional claims, counterclaims and demands for intervention.[28] Every *demande incidente* must, like the original *assignation*, set out the pretentions of the party making it, together with a statement of their grounds, and must indicate any documents relied on. Furthermore, a substantial, as distinct from a purely procedural, defence, can be proposed at any stage.[29] On the other hand, an additional demand or a counterclaim is not admissible unless sufficiently connected to the original pretentions of the party making it[30] and, as a general rule, once the *instruction* is at an end no further conclusions or documents in support can be admitted.[31]

Under the modern English rules the number of pleadings is limited.

---

[22] Article 183 conferred a wide freedom to amend at the first hearing of *trattazione*; article 184 allowed for subsequent amendments. Since the coming into force of the reforms of 1990 (below, n. 23), it is only in certain specified cases that the court of first instance is collegiate. Ordinarily the judge appointed as *giudice istruttore* acts also as a single judge to decide the case: Ordinamento giudiziario, art. 48, as amended.

[23] The reform was introduced by law no. 353 of 26 November 1990, and brought into force in 1995. See, in addition to Carpi *et al.*, *Appendice di Aggiornamento*, Fazzalari, 'La Giustizia Civile in Italia' in E. Fazzalari (ed.), *La Giustizia Civile nei Paesi Communitari*, Vol. II (1996), p. 73 at p. 75 (English edition (1998), p. 239 at p. 241).

[24] C.p.c., art. 183, 4.

[25] The former c.p.c., art. 184, no longer exists and a new article 184 deals with a different subject matter. See Carpi *et al.*, *Appendice di Aggiornamento*, *sub* art. 183 at point IV. The parties can, however, clarify ('precisare') their claims or defences without leave, which raises the delicate distinction between clarification and amendment. See, e.g. G. Tarzia, *Lineamenti del nuovo Processo di Cognizione* (1991), pp. 89–91.

[26] N.c.p.c., arts. 763 and 764.

[27] *Ibid.*, art. 753.   [28] *Ibid.*, art. 63.   [29] *Ibid.*, art. 72.

[30] *Ibid.*, art. 70. It is a question for the judge in each case whether the connection is sufficient.

[31] *Ibid.*, art. 783.

The plaintiff may answer the defence with a reply,[32] but no further pleadings are possible without the leave of the court, which is rarely given. On the other hand the possibilities for the amendment of the pleadings are extensive. Until the pleadings are 'closed',[33] either party may amend his pleading once without leave. Thereafter, at any stage of the proceedings, the court may grant leave to amend.[34] Nevertheless, there can at no stage be an amendment without leave if the effect is to add or substitute a new 'cause of action'[35] – a rule that is equivalent to, but less draconian than, the prohibition in other systems of new demands. The result is, in effect, that though English law has no equivalent to the giudice istruttore or juge de la mise en état,[36] the court still has control over the amendment of pleadings, a control which it exercises primarily with a view to ensuring that the real questions in controversy between the parties will ultimately be determined.

The power of the court to allow amendments at any stage is unfettered, but the later the application for leave the more reluctant the judge will be to grant it. For this there are two principal reasons. In the first place, though consequential amendments by the other party will be allowed, a late amendment to the pleadings may create serious difficulties for him. In the second place, late amendments tend, in any case, to delay the progress of the proceedings and to add to their cost.

The concept of fact-finding

The first thing to be said under this head is that, whatever is meant by a 'fact', and whatever system of procedure is envisaged, fact-finding is the business of the judge, or of the jury if there is one. It is not the business of the parties. It may be – it is – for the parties to *allege* facts; it may be, to a greater or lesser extent, that a party must prove the facts that he alleges or lose his case because he carries the burden of proof, but this

[32] Seldom used except as a defence to a counterclaim.

[33] The pleadings are deemed to be closed fourteen days after the service of the reply or the defence, as the case may be: R.S.C., Ord. 18, r. 20. Under the C.P.R., once a statement of case has been served it may be amended only with the permission of the court unless all other parties consent: C.P.R., r. 17.1.

[34] R.S.C., Ord. 20; C.P.R., rr. 17.1, 17.3. The party seeking leave to amend must propose a specific amendment; his opponent has the opportunity to object and may make consequential amendments.

[35] A new cause of action can in any event be allowed only if it arises out of the same facts as those originally relied on: R.S.C., Ord. 20, r. 5 (5); C.P.R., r. 17.4(2).

[36] Until the introduction of the C.P.R., the judge who deals, for example, with an application for leave to amend during the preparatory stage would ordinarily play no part in the actual decision of the case. Now, with the advent of case management, it is more likely, but by no means necessary, that the 'procedural judge' will also be the trial judge.

means no more than that he must furnish the judge with the materials –
the evidence or proofs – on which the judge will base his findings of fact.
The parties do not find the facts.

What, then, are facts?

No one doubts that, at a theoretical level, distinctions exist between,
first, facts, secondly evidence or proofs and, thirdly, law. In England, for
the purposes of the pleadings, these distinctions are purportedly maintained, however difficult in practice that may be, but, as has been seen
for France and Italy, this is not necessarily the case elsewhere.[37] In
Germany, where the parties are not obliged to plead law, they nevertheless commonly do so, 'because a combination of factual and legal
argument is more likely to persuade the court as to the merits of the
case'.[38]

The significance of this for present purposes is that there is no need in
continental procedures to get unduly fussed about the distinctions. It is
certainly not the case that the parties are relieved of the obligation to
allege facts. On the contrary, the French code, for example, provides
that 'the parties must allege the facts on which their claims or defences
are founded',[39] and this, like the English insistence that the parties
plead the material facts, demonstrates what is a fact, as distinct from
evidence or proof. The point is simple in principle, if not in practice. A
rule of law – any rule of law – must take as its premise a fact or a
complex of facts. If it does not then it cannot be applied, because it has
no point of reference outside itself. The word 'fact', in the present
context, means, and means only, that which is envisaged more or less
explicitly by a rule or principle of law.[40]

Sometimes, where the rule of law in question is both simple and
simply stated, the fact to which it refers may actually be visible or
tangible, in which case it can relatively easily be found or found not to
exist in a given case. Usually, however, the existence of a fact can be
revealed only by the prior revelation of other visible or tangible
phenomena – the 'underlying' facts – followed by the application of
some kind of reasoning process and, as often as not, a value judgment.
In his reasoning, and in his formation of a value judgment, the judge
may be assisted by the arguments and submissions of counsel, but the
reasoning and the value judgment are, necessarily, for the judge alone.
To enquire about fact-finding is, therefore, to enquire about the way in

---

[37] Above, p. 208.   [38] Gottwald, 'Fact-finding', p. 68.
[39] N.c.p.c., art. 6. 'A l'appui de leurs prétentions, les parties ont la charge d'alléguer les
faits propres à les fonder.'
[40] This understanding of a 'fact' is more fully explained in chap. 10, p. 201.

which the judge performs this essential part of his function and about the role of the parties in enabling him to perform it.

The process of fact-finding

Free evaluation

It comes as something of a surprise to common lawyers of today when they discover for the first time that the law of some continental countries actually contains explicit provision to the effect that the judge must evaluate the proofs in accordance with his own appreciation of them.[41] What else can he or should he do? What sense is there in having a judge, the *raison d'être* of whose office is the exercise of judgment, if he is not to exercise that judgment in the assessment of the evidence?

It probably comes as still more of a surprise when the common lawyer finds that the rule of free evaluation is actually qualified. Yet the Italian rule reads, in approximate translation, 'the judge must evaluate the proofs in accordance with his own prudent appreciation of them *except where the law provides to the contrary*'.[42] In France, where there is no explicit provision for free evaluation, it is accepted by the authors that the system is 'mixed'.[43] It is in part a system of 'legal proof', which means that particular modes of proof have particular value or weight attached to them, and in part a system of moral or rational proof where free evaluation is the rule.

The common lawyer may have heard of ancient rules such as the rule that the evidence of one man is to be preferred to that of two women, but that kind of thing is likely to appeal to him as so far in the past that its interest is purely antiquarian. Even so, his surprise at the continental approach to free evaluation should be tempered by his recollection that, until recently, the system of legal proof remained in effect for contracts as much part of everyday life as are contracts for the sale of land,[44] and even now is not entirely eliminated.[45] He should also remember that the common law has a law of evidence – a branch of law

---

[41] E.g. Germany, ZPO §286, Gottwald, 'Fact-finding', p. 77; Italy, c.p.c., art. 116, M. Serio, 'Fact-Finding: An Italian Perspective', in Carey Miller, p. 123 at p. 126.

[42] C.p.c., art. 116 (emphasis added). See also, e.g. Netherlands, c.p.c., art. 179(2), Punt, 'Fact-finding: A Dutch Perspective', in Carey Miller, p. 109 at p. 117.

[43] E.g. J. Ghestin and G. Goubeaux, *Traité de droit civil*, 4th edn, Vol. I (1994), nos. 629–32.

[44] Law of Property Act 1925, s. 40, according to which written evidence was necessary to the enforceability of such contracts. The rule is now superseded by the Law of Property (Miscellaneous Provisions) Act 1989, s. 2, which requires an actual written agreement.

[45] The Statute of Frauds 1677, s. 4 is still part of the law.

whose nature and purpose continental lawyers have some difficulty in understanding.[46]

The law of evidence consists mainly of exclusionary rules and exceptions to them. Today the scope of the exclusionary rules is much reduced by comparison with the past so far as civil cases are concerned,[47] and this is largely, if not entirely, due to the virtual disappearance of the civil jury. Nevertheless, it is broadly true that the rationale of the exclusions is the idea that some kinds of evidence – hearsay, for example – cannot safely be left to a jury. In other words, so long as we have a law of evidence we allow the jury or, now, the judge alone, to take account only of what the law considers it safe to let them know. To complicate the situation further by attributing special weight to certain kinds of evidence would be not only unnecessary but, in general, absurd.[48]

The continental approach is different. There are no exclusionary rules such as those of the law of evidence but there is recognition of the existence of a number of different modes of proof, to some of which specific weight is attributed while others are left to the free evaluation of the judge. So, for example, any so-called 'authentic' or public act, such as a notarial act or deed, provides conclusive proof of certain matters unless it is displaced by a special procedure attacking its validity,[49] and even a private writing may be conclusive unless it is disavowed by the party whose signature it bears.[50]

Naturally, the oral testimony of witnesses is included within the recognised modes of proof,[51] but such testimony does not enjoy pride of place as it does in the common law system, nor is it taken in the common law manner by examination and cross-examination at a trial: witnesses are usually examined by the judge at a special hearing specified for the purpose. What is more, oral testimony is traditionally regarded

---

[46] It is not unimportant to note that continental rules about proof, as distinct from rules about the administration of the modes of proof, are usually found in the civil code, not in the code of civil procedure.

[47] In particular the Civil Evidence Act 1995.

[48] Even so, the law does, sometimes, attach specific weight to certain kinds of evidence, e.g. Civil Evidence Act 1968, ss. 11 and 13: the former provides for a reversal of the burden of proof in certain cases; the latter creates an irrebuttable presumption. The Civil Evidence Act 1995, s. 4 (2), indicates a number of factors to which regard may be had in estimating the weight to be given to hearsay evidence, but this is only a guide.

[49] E.g. French code civil (hereafter 'French c.c.'), art. 1319; Italian codice civile (hereafter 'Italian c.c.'), art. 2700.

[50] E.g. French c.c., arts. 1322–4; Italian c.c., art. 2702.

[51] French c.c., art. 1341–8; Italian c.c., arts. 2721–6. As a rule, a special order from the court is required before oral testimony can be taken and, even so, such testimony is not always permissible. Other 'modes of proof' include presumptions, admissions and even a 'decisory oath': French c.c., arts. 1349–69; Italian c.c., arts. 2727–39.

as untrustworthy because it comes into existence only after the dispute between the parties has arisen and, indeed, after the litigation has itself come into existence. Preference is given to modes of proof, such as deeds and other forms of writing, that existed before the dispute arose – *preuve préconstituée*.

Other modes of information

In the common law something is either admissible as evidence or else it is not; and if it is not admissible as evidence then the judge is not allowed to know about it.[52] On the continent it is generally maintained that the case is to be decided on the basis of the proofs offered by the parties. This is made explicit in the Italian code,[53] and while the French code does empower the judge to order, *ex officio*, any lawful means of proof,[54] that power is not supposed to be exercised so as to relieve a party of his obligation to provide the proofs necessary in support of his pretentions.[55] On the face of things, therefore, '*ex officio* proof-taking' is excluded. Nevertheless, the continental judge may acquire information in the course of the proceedings by methods which are not considered to involve the taking of evidence or proofs and which may, therefore, and do, depend on his own rather than on party initiative. Two important examples, and one hybrid, must be mentioned.

Examination of the parties

It is a general principle in continental countries that the parties to litigation may not give evidence: they are not competent witnesses.[56] They may, nevertheless, be interrogated by the judge on his own initiative. Originally such interrogation had as its only purpose the clarification by the party of his actual claim or defence as the case might be, but it is now common that the judge may examine the parties on the facts of the case. French law, for example, allows the judge to invite the parties to provide such explanations of fact as he considers necessary for his decision[57] and, by separate and more elaborate provision, also allows him to order the personal appearance of the parties for interrogation.[58]

---

[52] For the use by the judge of knowledge he has acquired independently of the proceedings on which he is engaged, see chap. 13.

[53] C.p.c., art. 115; Serio, 'Fact-finding', p. 126.

[54] N.c.p.c., arts. 10 and 143.   [55] *Ibid.*, arts. 9 and 146.

[56] Since 1988, in the Netherlands, the parties – if natural persons – may themselves be heard as witnesses. Even so, a party's statement concerning facts on which he has the burden of proof cannot itself constitute proof in his favour: at best it may supplement incomplete proof from other sources: Punt, 'Fact-finding', p. 117.

[57] N.c.p.c., art. 8.   [58] *Ibid.*, arts. 184–98.

Italian law provides that, at a preliminary hearing, the judge may seek necessary clarification from the parties of the facts alleged,[59] and in addition he may order their personal appearance 'in order that he may freely interrogate them about the facts of the case'.[60]

The use of these procedures does not form part of the proof-taking process: neither the answers of the parties nor their behaviour in response to the judge's interrogation amount to evidence or proof.[61] In reality, however, they are clearly capable of having an effect on the ultimate decision, if only by influencing the judge in the exercise of his power of free evaluation.[62] In France it is actually provided that the judge can draw any conclusions from the parties' answers, or their refusal to answer, and also that he may treat them as equivalent to a 'beginning of written proof'.[63] This has the potentially important consequence of allowing the use of oral testimony where such testimony would not otherwise be admitted.

Experts[64]

Where the assistance of experts in a particular art or science is required in litigation, such assistance is provided, in the common law procedure, by expert witnesses, called by the parties and examined and cross-examined by them in much the same way as are other witnesses. Continental systems, on the other hand, provide for the appointment of an expert by the judge, and the judge will himself instruct the expert on the questions on which he is to report. The status of such a court-appointed expert is not entirely clear, but there is at least agreement that the expert is not a witness, not even a witness called by the judge rather than by a party. In Germany he is considered an 'assistant' to the judge;[65] for Italy it is said that the expert's job is 'fiduciary' in the sense that he acts on the judge's instructions, answers his questions and reports directly to him;[66] for Greece it is said that the role of the expert is not a judicial one – the judge has resort on his own initiative to the expert to supplement his own understanding when that is inadequate.[67] In France the expert is 'auxiliaire de la justice'.[68]

---

[59] C.p.c., art. 183 as amended.
[60] C.p.c., art. 117. For Germany, see Gottwald, 'Fact-finding', p. 78.
[61] In Germany, it appears, they are deemed to be part of the written 'pleadings': Gottwald, 'Fact-finding', p. 78.
[62] *Ibid.*
[63] 'Commencement de preuve par écrit': n.c.p.c., art. 198.
[64] This subject is treated more fully below, chap. 12.
[65] Gottwald, 'Fact-finding', p. 78.   [66] Serio, 'Fact-finding', p. 129.
[67] C. D. Magliveras, 'Fact-finding: A Greek Perspective', in Carey Miller, p. 87 at p. 92.
[68] Solus and Perrot, nos. 898 and 908–11. The grounds on which an expert can be challenged are the same as those applicable to judges: n.c.p.c., art. 234.

As a matter of principle, the continental judge is not bound by the expert's report, however difficult in practice it may be for him to disregard it. That, however, is not the present point, which is, rather, its converse. The expert's report is not 'evidence', and the procedure by which it is obtained may not even be regarded as part of the proof-taking process. Nevertheless, the expert's report unquestionably provides material that the judge will take into account in the performance of his fact-finding function.

Witness testimony

The taking of witness testimony is, of course, included in the recognised modes of proof. The subject nevertheless calls for mention here since, on the continent, it is for the judge, not the parties, to question the witnesses[69] and, secondly, the testimony heard is not necessarily restricted to that given by witnesses whom the parties wish to be heard or to matters that the parties wish to be drawn to the attention of the court.

In Italy, the judge's right to question the witnesses does not, it is true, give him any significant power since the parties, in their request for oral testimony, must set out the facts on which they wish a given witness to testify[70] and the judge's questions may be directed only to those facts.[71] On the other hand, the judge may, at the request of a party or of his own motion, call upon a person to testify if a witness has, in the course of his testimony, indicated that that person has knowledge of the facts.[72] The judge may also call any person named by a party as a witness but not previously heard, either because the judge had previously excluded that person's testimony as superfluous or because the parties had agreed that he need not be heard. In addition, the judge may recall for further examination a witness who has already been examined, if this is necessary to clarify that witness's testimony or to correct irregularities.[73]

In France the judge's powers are more extensive. First, although it is normally for a party to request an order for the hearing of witnesses, in

---

[69] The advocates may be allowed to question a witness after the judicial interrogation has ended. In Germany they are invited to do so, but under the control of the court: Gottwald, 'Fact-finding', p. 76. In Italy and France, on the other hand, they may only propose to the judge that certain questions be put to a witness and it is then for the judge to decide whether the question should be put or not: c.p.c., art. 253; n.c.p.c., art. 214, al. 2; Solus and Perrot, no. 879.
[70] C.p.c., art. 244; Serio, 'Fact-finding', p. 126.
[71] In questioning the witness the judge may, however, refer to the claim as a whole for the purposes of clarification: c.p.c., art. 253.
[72] C.p.c., art. 257.
[73] *Ibid.* The judge's power to exclude superfluous testimony is contained in article 245.

which case it is for that party to state the facts he seeks to prove[74] and to indicate the witnesses to be heard,[75] it is open to the judge to make such an order *ex officio*.[76] If he does so, the statement of facts to be proved and the designation of the witnesses is, at least in the first instance, for him.[77] Secondly, in his examination of a witness the judge is not restricted to the facts previously admitted to proof but may question the witness in relation to any facts of which proof is legally admissible.[78] Thirdly, the judge may, at the request of a party or of his own motion, call for examination, and examine, any person whose testimony would, as it appears to him, be useful to the revelation of the truth.[79]

The role of the parties and the role of the judge

Even where a procedure openly purports to be inquisitorial, it is not the case that the judge takes his magnifying glass and looks for the facts as if he were Sherlock Holmes. To say that a procedure is inquisitorial is to say little more than that the judge's role may extend beyond the actual finding of the facts to that of playing a more or less active part in revealing the underlying facts on which the findings of fact will be based. The extent to which an inquisitorial judge actually makes enquiries may, however, vary not only from one system of procedure to another but from one kind of case to another within a single system. In French administrative law, for example, the judge will be inclined to intervene more actively in the 'recours pour excès de pouvoir' than in the 'recours de pleine juridiction'. In the former the plaintiff seeks the annulment of an administrative decision or order of which he may have had no knowledge before publication: such a plaintiff might be in an impossible position if he carried the burden of proving its illegality. In the latter, on the other hand, he claims compensation for damage that he has suffered as the result of a wrongful act for which the administration is responsible: there will have been dealings such as negotiations for a settlement

---

[74] N.c.p.c., art. 222, al. 1. It is, however, ultimately for the judge to decide what facts shall be open to proof: *ibid.*, al. 2.

[75] *Ibid.*, art. 223, al. 1. Opposing parties may bring evidence in rebuttal without further order (art. 204) and must designate the witnesses they wish to be called: art. 223, al. 2.

[76] *Ibid.*, arts. 10 and 143.

[77] *Ibid.*, art. 224, al. 2. If the judge is unaware of the exact identity of the witnesses he wishes to be heard, he may call for the assistance of the parties: Solus and Perrot, no. 861.

[78] N.c.p.c., art. 213; Solus and Perrot, no. 881.

[79] '. . . toute personne dont l'audience lui paraît utile à la manifestation de la vérité': n.c.p.c., art. 218. Solus and Perrot, no. 882.

before action brought, and accordingly there is less reason for the judge
to pursue enquiries himself.[80]

As a general rule, continental civil procedure – civil procedure as
distinct, for instance, from administrative procedure – is not considered
to be 'inquisitorial'. Though it has been described as 'accusatorial',[81]
this does not mean that it is adversarial in the common law sense.[82]
Both subscribe to the dispositive principle, and though the common law
does so implicitly rather than explicitly, the adversary system can be
explained as an exaggerated application of the principle: because the
parties choose to litigate in the first place, they must be free to decide
not only what will be the subject matter of the litigation but also the
basis on which it will be conducted and, in particular, on what evidence
the issues of fact will be resolved.[83]

It is improbable that the common law arrived at the adversary
procedure as a result of the application of this or any other principle. It
is more likely that it is, or was, the inevitable consequence of adoption of
trial by jury.[84] In continental systems, on the other hand, where there is
no trial in the common law sense, the 'evidence' is introduced at various
times during the preparatory stage,[85] and a judge is normally assigned to
the case from its inception to take charge, amongst other matters, of the
instruction.[86] Sometimes that judge, alone, will ultimately decide the
case, but even where the final decision is for a collegiate court he will be
a member of the panel.[87] One member of the court is thus in a position
to take note of the 'evidence' as it comes in, and there is no such obstacle
as exists in common law procedure to his active participation in the
preparation of the case for decision. He may, for example, appreciate
from the reading of a document that another document is also relevant,
in which case there is no practical reason why he should not call for its

---

[80] E.g. Debbasch, no. 542.

[81] E.g. R. Morel, *Traité de Procédure Civile*, 2nd edn (1949), no. 425. In France, at least, it
has become less accusatorial than it was. See, e.g. J. A. Jolowicz, 'The Woolf Report
and the Adversary System' (1996) 15 C.J.Q. 198, 201–9.

[82] Above, chap. 9, p. 176.

[83] Above, chap. 9, p. 177. For a convenient, if now somewhat dated, theoretical
discussion of the dispositive principle, see M. Millar, 'Formative Principles of Civil
Procedure' in *History*, pp. 14 *et seq*.

[84] Chap. 18, p. 373.

[85] The modern tendency in some countries is to try to 'concentrate' the taking of
'evidence'. See Gottwald, 'Fact-finding', p. 72.

[86] E.g. Italian c.p.c., art. 168 *bis*, as amended; French n.c.p.c., arts. 762 and 763. In
France, if the President of the Tribunal considers that the case can be decided on the
basis only of the materials supplied by the parties in their initial claims and defences, he
may send the case immediately for decision: n.c.p.c., arts. 760 and 761.

[87] This was not always so in the past. Under the Italian code of 1865, for example, the
judge who received the 'evidence' was not necessarily a member of the collegiate court
that would decide. This was altered by the code of 1942. See c.p.c., art. 174.

production. If there is a legal obstacle to his doing so, it will be because of adherence to the dispositive principle.[88]

The extent to which the judge actually plays an active role in relation to the facts during the preparatory stage varies from one country to another and it is not always clear, at least to an outside observer, what is the precise intention of the relevant legislation. This is the case, for example, for French law, where the code provides that the parties must prove the facts necessary to the success of their claims or defences,[89] that a 'mesure d'instruction' may not be ordered unless the party alleging a fact lacks the means of proving it and that a *mesure d'instruction* cannot be ordered to cure a party's own failure in the matter of proof.[90] But the code also provides that the judge may order, *ex officio*, any *mesure d'instruction* and may do so at any time if he lacks sufficient material for his decision.[91]

As a general rule, initiative in relation to 'evidence' remains with the parties, who proceed by way of request for an appropriate order from the judge when they wish a particular *mesure d'instruction* to be employed: the judge's role is to satisfy himself that it really is necessary that he should accede to the request.[92] It is nevertheless clear to common law eyes that the judge's role in continental procedures generally can be far more significant in the preparation for fact-finding than under the common law. It is for the judge to examine the witnesses, if any,[93] it is for the judge to decide whether to summon the parties for interrogation,[94] and it is the judge who acts to obtain the assistance of an expert when required.[95] Not all these activities are, however, regarded by continental lawyers as the taking of 'evidence',[96] and a common lawyer who is confronted by the statement of a continental lawyer that the judge's role in the taking of evidence is muted must bear this in mind.

Even in the adversary procedure of the common law it is, in reality, impossible that the judge should rely wholly and exclusively on the

---

[88] So, for example, in France, although the judge may compel a party to produce a document, he may only do so at the request of the other party: n.c.p.c., art. 11, al. 2. See J. A. Jolowicz, 'La production forcée des pièces: Droits français et anglais', in P. Théry (ed.), *Nouveaux Juges, Nouveaux Pouvoirs? Mélanges en l'honneur de Roger Perrot* (1996), p. 167. In practice the pressures of a heavy case-load may seriously inhibit the exercise by the judge of the powers with which the law endows him. See Serio, 'Fact-finding', p. 125.

[89] N.c.p.c., art. 9.

[90] *Ibid.*, art. 146.   [91] *Ibid.*, arts. 10, 143, 144.

[92] See Gottwald, 'Fact-finding', p. 73; Punt, 'Fact-finding', pp. 114–15 and Serio, 'Fact-finding', p. 124. Article 147 of the French n.c.p.c. requires that the judge should limit the *mesures d'instruction* to those necessary for the disposal of the litigation and that he should order the simplest and the least costly which are capable of meeting the need.

[93] Above, p. 217.   [94] Above, p. 215.

[95] Above, p. 216.   [96] Above, p. 215.

evidence presented by the parties for his finding of the facts. Both the reasoning and the value judgments required must be those of the judge himself, and he cannot fail to rely on his own knowledge and experience.[97] He may also, of course, take judicial notice of notorious facts, a concept which, today, seems to extend to whatever the judge himself regards as a matter of common knowledge.[98] The one thing which he cannot do is to initiate an enquiry of his own motion.[99]

In practice, no doubt, the production of the underlying facts is the business of the parties. So, though the judge examines the witnesses, there will ordinarily be no witnesses other than those nominated by the parties;[100] though, in some countries he may call for documents not produced by either party, and though the judge may order a *mesure d'instruction* of his own motion, it nevertheless appears that the judge's interventions are, as a general rule, more likely to be negative than positive. The judge will refuse a request for proof-taking submitted by a party if he considers it unnecessary but, if only by reason of pressure of work, he is unlikely in practice to take much of an initiative himself. On the other hand – and this must be stressed for the purposes of comparison with the common law – continental procedure enables the judge to take much more of an initiative than his common law counterpart: at least so far as the written law is concerned, continental procedure retains less of the original concept of civil litigation as a forensic duel between two opponents who would otherwise resort to physical violence than does the adversary procedure of the common law.

[97] Above, p. 212. See also below, chap. 13, p. 256.

[98] It is a long way from taking judicial notice of the fact that 'rain falls from time to time' to taking judicial notice of the facts that 'the life of a criminal is an unhappy one' (*Burns v. Edman* ([1970] 2 Q.B. 541, 546, *per* Crichton J.) or that 'the community charge legislation has aroused strong feelings and that political protests of one sort or another have been widespread' (*R. v. Leicester City Justices, ex parte Barrow* [1991] 2 Q.B. 260, 282–3, *per* Lord Donaldson M.R.).

[99] An English judge can, however, proceed of his own motion to a view of the *locus in quo*, even against the expressed wishes of the parties: *Tito v. Waddell* [1975] 1 W.L.R. 1303, 1306, *per* Megarry J. See also *Salsbury v. Woodland* [1970] 1 Q.B. 324. For the more generous French equivalent, see n.c.p.c., arts. 179–83. Note the French insistence on the presence of the parties or, at least, their notification.

[100] Note the restrictions on the powers of the Italian judge, above, p. 217.

12 The expert, the witness and the judge in civil litigation: French and English law[1]

There is a presumption that the judge knows the law. There is no need, in theory, for the parties to provide him with the materials and information necessary for the decision of questions of law. No similar presumption is possible in relation to questions of fact. *Jura novit curia* may be plausible; *facta novit curia* is absurd. Nevertheless, as has been pointed out in a previous chapter,[2] at the end of the day, decisions of fact are as much for the judge as are decisions on the applicable law. It is the purpose of this chapter to examine the way in which French and English law, respectively, deal with the particular problem that is raised when the judge is called upon to decide technical questions, that is, questions of fact which, because of their scientific, technical or technological character, cannot be understood or resolved by a non-specialist without the assistance of an appropriately qualified specialist.[3] Before turning to that, however, it is necessary to say something about the nature of questions of fact in general.

Questions of fact

It is a general principle as much of French as of English law that each party must prove the facts necessary to the success of his claim or defence. Since nothing is literally 'proved' in litigation, however, what is meant by the general principle is that the party carrying the burden of proof must discharge it by producing materials – evidence or proofs – which will persuade the judge to decide the issue in his favour.

---

[1] Based on a lecture delivered to the Assemblée générale of the Société de législation comparée in Paris, published in 1977 Rev.int.dr.comp. 285. The comparison in the main part of the chapter is between the French law and the English law as it was before introduction of the C.P.R. Such a comparison is a necessary preliminary to consideration of the new law, for which see the postscript to this chapter.

[2] Chap. 11, p. 211.

[3] See *L'expertise dans les principaux systèmes juridiques d'Europe*, published under the auspices of the Centre français de droit comparé with the assistance of the CNRS, Paris, 1969.

It follows that, at this stage, the mind of the judge must be engaged, for it is rare that he can be offered a mode of proof – a document, a witness, an item of real evidence – which relates directly to the legal right that is in contention. Motulsky correctly insisted that legal rights are generated by facts,[4] but the facts which generate a given right are themselves defined by law. In most cases the raw facts that gave rise to the proceedings are not those to which the law refers in terms: they must be related to those facts, they must be qualified – that is, 'translated' – by the advocates and ultimately by the judge, into the language of the law. Suppose, for example, an action for damages in which, at the end of the *instruction*, or after the evidence has been heard, as the case may be, the judge is persuaded that the defendant householder made no attempt to remove accumulated snow from his steps, and that that was the cause of the injury of which the plaintiff complains. To hold the defendant liable under a rule imposing liability for fault, the judge must qualify the defendant's omission as *faute*, within the meaning of article 1382 of the French civil code, or as a breach of the common duty of care within the meaning of the English Occupiers Liability Act.

It is of no importance for present purposes whether the question of the qualification of facts is classified as a question of law, as it is by the Cour de cassation, or as one of fact, as it is by the House of Lords;[5] what is important is that in either case it is a question which the judge must answer. But the judge also has to answer questions of pure fact, as distinct from the qualification of fact, which are capable of solution only by the application of an element of logic. Is he justified in drawing the conclusion that an otherwise unknown fact is established by the existence of other facts which are known? The judge is persuaded, for example, that a component of a washing machine broke on the first use of the machine: should he draw the conclusion that the machine suffered from a concealed defect, or was not of satisfactory quality, at the time of sale, which are the facts that generate the buyer's right against the seller in such circumstances?[6]

In both of the examples used above, the existence of certain 'raw' facts has been supposed. In other words, it has been supposed that the judge's reasoning had a certain point of departure already known to him. Otherwise the hypothesis that the judge is 'persuaded' of something would be unfounded. It is not unusual, however, for there to be

[4] 'La cause de la demande dans la délimitation de l'office du juge', in *Ecrits*, p. 101 (D. 1964, Chron. 235) and works cited at n. 4 of that work; 'Prolégomènes pour un futur Code de procédure civile', D. 1972, Chron. 91. See chap. 10, p. 187.
[5] *Qualcast (Wolverhampton) Ltd* v. *Haynes* [1959] A.C. 743.
[6] French code civil, art. 1641; Sale of Goods Act 1979, s. 14(2) as substituted by the Sale and Supply of Goods Act 1994, s. 1.

disagreement between the parties on the raw facts – one party alleges 'white', the other 'black' – and the judge must say which of them is right or, conceivably, reach an independent conclusion that both are wrong and that the truth is grey or even yellow.

Three types of question

It is implicit in what has just been said that there are three different kinds of question of fact. The first, which may be called the simple perception of fact, arises where a party alleges a relevant fact and the question is simply whether the allegation is true or false. The second, which may be called perception by presumption, arises where a party alleges that the established existence of one fact justifies a decision that another fact also exists; it involves the perception of a relevant fact by way of presumption. The third arises where facts that have been perceived or presumed must be given their legal qualification.

Whichever the category to which a question of fact belongs, it is the judge who must resolve it, but, normally, he is neither required nor allowed to decide questions of the first or second categories save on the basis of evidence or proofs put in by the parties.[7] When it comes to questions of the third category, on the other hand, evidence or proof is beside the point. The parties may, of course, present argument through their advocates, but argument is quite different from evidence, and it is the opinion that the judge forms for himself, after hearing argument, which is decisive. There is also a difference between the first category and the second: in the first, the only question at the end of the day is whether the judge, having heard the evidence, believes or disbelieves the allegation. In the second, on the other hand, the intellectual processes of the judge himself are crucial. There is no question of belief or disbelief where it is claimed that one fact is to be presumed from the existence of another: there is only the question whether the judge agrees or disagrees with the reasoning for an affirmative answer.

This, then, is the theoretical division: the parties supply the judge with the materials necessary to his decision of questions of fact, but it is the judge who qualifies them and draws from the established facts such relevant conclusions as he considers justified. Though most litigation presents questions belonging to all three categories, which means that the theoretical division cannot be rigidly maintained in practice, the division nevertheless provides a useful tool for examination of the

---

[7] For the possibility that the judge may himself bring 'evidence' into the proceedings, see chap. 11, p. 215.

different methods adopted by different systems for dealing with technical questions.

Technical questions

It is axiomatic that no judge is omniscient. We do not – and we cannot – in reality demand of a judge a universal knowledge even of the rules of law in force in his own jurisdiction. Certainly we demand of the judges a certain initiative on legal issues, but, above all, we demand that they have the ability to understand and evaluate legal reasoning put forward by others – the advocates and, for the judges of appellate courts, the reasoning of their colleagues in the courts below.[8] As regards the facts, since we cannot demand of the judges that they have knowledge of every branch of science, of every art and of the mysteries of every profession, we cannot demand either that they resolve questions of fact requiring such knowledge unless they have help from suitably qualified experts. The point is obvious, but the relevance of technical knowledge to each of the three categories of question of fact requires examination.

First category – simple perception of a relevant fact. Even if the judge may actually make his own observations, by, for example, visiting the *locus in quo*,[9] this is likely to be pointless if he lacks the technical knowledge to benefit directly from his observations. If a judge inspects a ruined building, he can see that it has collapsed, but he cannot see, or discover for himself, that the foundations had been built in accordance with, or contrary to, the architect's instructions.

Second category – perception by presumption. If it were proved, for example, that the ink used in a manuscript was of a particular chemical composition, a suitably qualified expert, but not a judge, would be able to say that the manuscript could not have been produced before a certain date.

Third category – qualification of the facts. Although French law explicitly requires the judge to give or restore to the facts their correct qualification,[10] it is only possible for a judge to do this unaided where the facts come within his own experience. He can, for example, qualify, or decline to qualify, as negligent the act or omission of a motorist, or of a pedestrian crossing the street, since he understands the norms of vehicular or pedestrian traffic. On the other hand, he can qualify, or

---

[8] For the significance of this, see below, p. 233.

[9] N.c.p.c., arts. 179–83; R.S.C., Ord. 35, r. 8; *Tito* v. *Waddell* [1975] 1 W.L.R. 1303.

[10] N.c.p.c., art. 12, al. 2.

decline to qualify, as negligent the act or omission of a surgeon in the operating theatre only if he has expert help.[11]

The classic work of Glasson and Tissier[12] states that 'the procedure of *expertise* is found in every legal system for the simple reason that omniscience cannot be demanded of the judges'. More recently, Motulsky wrote, in his comparative introduction to a volume on the *expertise* in the principal European legal systems, that 'among those consulted, there is no system which has not provided for the working of the *expertise*'.[13] Nevertheless, he found himself obliged to add, in the same paragraph, that 'the position is peculiar in England, where institutions not easily compared with the *expertise*, as understood in countries of codified law, are governed by a few texts and by case law'. In truth, as every comparative lawyer knows, the English and the French systems differ greatly from each other in practice. As it is hoped to show, they differ also in their underlying theory.

In general terms, two forms of procedure for the solution of technical questions are possible. The first leaves it to the judge to inform himself on the relevant technicalities by turning to an independent and impartial expert of his choice. The second leaves it to the parties to supply the judge with the materials and the information that he needs in order to make up his mind on all the questions in issue, no matter how technical they may be. French law has chosen the first system, English law the second.

French law

French law has never known the expert witness of the common law, but, under the old law, a judge could order a procedure, known as *expertise*, whereby expert reports on particular facts at issue in the litigation could be obtained. Unless the parties agreed on a single expert, three were required, all three to be nominated by the parties or, in the event of their failure to do so, by the judge.[14] In 1944, however, it became the general rule that only one expert, chosen by the judge, should be appointed.[15] Though less expensive and time-consuming than its predecessor, this

---

[11] For the position if the judge happens to have relevant specialist knowledge, see chap. 13, p. 257.

[12] Glasson and Tissier, no. 706.

[13] *L'expertise*, see n. 3, above, p. 14.

[14] Code de procédure civile (ancien), arts. 303–7 in their original version. Until 1961, an expert could be challenged on the same grounds as could a witness: *ibid.*, art. 310. See below, p. 230. For a convenient short account of the old law, see H. A. Hammelmann, 'Expert Evidence' (1947) 10 M.L.R. 32.

[15] Law of 15 July 1944, incorporated in the code de procédure civile as article 305.

form of *expertise* was still over-elaborate for many cases, but the only alternative was the so-called 'constat d'huissier'.

The *constat d'huissier*[16] came into French practice after the First World War and involved an order by the judge, normally at the request of a party, that a judicial officer – a *huissier de justice*[17] – should investigate and provide a purely factual statement, a *constat*, of his findings. In litigation between landlord and tenant, for example, a *constat* could state the condition of property as found by the *huissier*, but it could not go on to draw conclusions or give opinions. For obvious reasons the *constat d'huissier* could not be used where technical skills were required for an investigation.[18]

As things stood, therefore, the *expertise* might be unnecessarily complex and expensive for a given case, while the *constat d'huissier* was of limited value. In 1973 a more flexible system was introduced and is now contained in the new code of civil procedure.[19] Three different procedures are available to the court, one of which is the *expertise*, but that procedure should be used only where neither of the other, less elaborate, procedures will suffice. Where a question arises which requires elucidation by a 'technicien', as he is now known, the judge may commission a person[20] of his choice[21] to enlighten him on such a question by way of 'constatation', 'consultation' or 'expertise'. The three procedures – none of which is possible without an order from the court and all of which are conducted separately from the procedure for taking oral testimony – the 'enquête' – are collectively known as 'mesures d'instruction exécutées par un technicien'.

The *constatation* is an extension of the old *constat d'huissier*: it is still restricted to pure findings of fact, but now it may be used even where only a technically qualified *constatant* is capable of acting. The *expertise* is

---

[16] Solus and Perrot, nos. 940 and 943.

[17] See L. Cadiet, *Droit judiciaire privé* (1992), nos. 415–19; R. Perrot, *Institutions judiciaires*, 5th edn (1993), nos. 471–4.

[18] The *constat d'huissier* gained legal recognition in 1955: *Ordonnance* of 2 November 1945, art. 1, as amended by decree of 20 May 1955. In 1965 it became possible for a judge of a tribunal de grande instance to order any person of his choice to proceed to *constatations*: see now, n.c.p.c., art. 249.

[19] N.c.p.c., arts. 232–84.

[20] Natural or corporate, for example an association of architects or engineers: n.c.p.c., art. 233, al. 2. In principle only one *technicien*, who must execute his function personally, should be appointed, even for the *expertise*, unless the judge considers more to be required: n.c.p.c., arts. 264 and 265. The *technicien* in an *expertise* may, however, seek the help of another *technicien* in a speciality other than his own: n.c.p.c., art. 278.

[21] Lists of suitably qualified experts who have taken the required oath, known as 'experts agréés', are maintained on a national level by the Cour de cassation, and on a regional level by each Cour d'appel, but the judge is entitled, if he wishes, to appoint a person not on any list: law of 29 June 1971; decree of 31 December 1974.

subject to new regulation but retains its original character; it involves an investigation and report – including opinion and advice – by a *technicien*. The *consultation*, which is new, enables the judge simply to consult and obtain advice from a *technicien* in cases where no complex investigations are required.

When the experts were appointed by the parties, observation of the *principe du contradictoire*[22] was assured automatically, as it is where expert witnesses are used. Now, however, the *technicien* receives his 'mission' from the judge and is answerable to him, not to the parties. It has become necessary, therefore, to insist that the conduct of a *mesure d'instruction exécutée par un technicien*, especially the *expertise*, must conform to that principle. It is not enough that the parties have the opportunity to debate the report of the *technicien* before the judge: any observations or objections they may wish to make must be taken into consideration by the *technicien* and included in his report with an indication of the action taken in response.[23] To this end, the parties must be duly notified of, and given the opportunity to attend, with their legal advisers and even their own experts, one or more 'réunions d'expertise' – meetings at which the *technicien* and the parties can put their respective points of view on the investigations to be undertaken – and on those already carried out.[24]

English law

The original idea of the civil jury in England was that the jurors should decide the questions at issue from their own knowledge[25] and, in a sense, the jury was thus 'expert'. At a later date, Lord Mansfield and other eighteenth-century judges empanelled juries of merchants for commercial cases so as to ensure that the court – judge and jury together – had the required expertise.[26] An expert court of this kind is no longer found save in courts of limited and specialised jurisdiction,[27] but English law does have two procedures which are, according to the actual language of the law, widely available and which conform to the first of

---

[22] Chap. 9, p. 177.   [23] N.c.p.c., art. 276.

[24] Solus and Perrot, nos. 977–9. It is not always easy to know on what occasions the parties should be summoned. In practice, the expert normally summons the parties to a preliminary *réunion*, and to a second when his investigation is sufficiently advanced: *ibid.*, no. 978(b).

[25] W. S. Holdsworth, *History of English Law*, Vol. I, pp. 317–33.

[26] *Ibid.*, Vol. XII, p. 256 and n. 7; C. H. S. Fifoot, *English Law and its Background*, p. 131.

[27] The Restrictive Practices Court, for example, is composed of professional judges and of members qualified by reason of their experience in industry, commerce or public life: Restrictive Practices Court Act 1976, s. 3(1). See further below, chap. 13, p. 264.

the two forms of procedure mentioned.[28] First, the High Court and the Court of Appeal have the right to summon one or more assessors to sit with the judges and to give their advice on technical issues that arise in the course of the litigation.[29] Secondly, the judge can, usually at the request of a party, appoint an independent expert to carry out investigations and research and to present his report.[30] Neither of these procedures has proved popular.

It has for long been the practice of the Admiralty Court to use nautical assessors in cases of maritime collision or other accidents at sea, and, in the past, medical assessors were used in cases under the Workmen's Compensation Acts. Those Acts were, however, repealed and replaced after the Second World War by a system of national insurance in which assessors had no place.[31] When the Law Reform Committee published its report to the Lord Chancellor in 1970 on Evidence of Opinion and Expert Evidence,[32] it somewhat reluctantly approved the continued use of assessors in maritime cases but declined to recommend any general extension of their use elsewhere.[33]

The Committee was equally unenthusiastic about use of the independent, court-appointed expert save in two special categories of case where this was already the practice.[34] On the contrary, having looked at that procedure, the Committee saw in it only disadvantages.[35] Even in patent cases, where the law allows the court to appoint an independent scientific adviser of its own motion,[36] this is rarely done. For all practical purposes, the court-appointed expert is not used by English law.[37] As things stand, English law adheres to the principle, subject only to

---

[28] Above, p. 226.

[29] Supreme Court Act 1981, ss. 70 and 54(9). *Owners of S.S. Australia* v. *Owners of Cargo of S.S. Nautilus* [1927] A.C. 145; *Richardson* v. *Redpath Brown and Co. Ltd* [1944] A.C. 62. See A. Dickey, 'The Province and Function of Assessors in English Courts' (1970) 33 M.L.R. 494; T. Hodgkinson, *Expert Evidence: Law and Practice* (1990) p. 68.

[30] R.S.C., Ord. 40. J. Basten, 'The Court Expert in Civil Trials' (1977) 40 M.L.R. 174; Hodgkinson, *Expert Evidence*, p. 60.

[31] National Insurance (Industrial Injuries) Act 1946.

[32] Seventeenth Report, Cmnd 4489 (hereafter 'Report'). See also, Evershed, paras. 286–95.

[33] Report, paras. 11 and 12.

[34] Where a report is required on a matter concerning the welfare of a child (now Children Act 1989, s. 7) and in proceedings for nullity of marriage on the ground of incapacity to consummate: Family Proceedings Rules 1991, r. 2.22. See also Family Law Reform Act 1969, s. 20, as amended (tests for establishing paternity).

[35] Report, paras. 13 and 14. [36] R.S.C., Ord. 104, r. 15.

[37] The opinion of Lord Denning M.R. on the merits of the system in *Re Saxton* [1962] 1 W.L.R. 968, notwithstanding. The more recent decision of the Court of Appeal in *Abbey National Mortgages plc* v. *Key Surveyors Ltd* [1996] 1 W.L.R. 1534, suggesting a change in judicial attitudes has been overtaken by the C.P.R. See the postscript to this chapter.

limited exceptions, that it is for the parties to call their witnesses –
expert if necessary – on all questions of fact, including the technical, and
for the judge to decide the issues between the parties in the light of that
evidence. Indeed, in the Law Reform Committee's view, while the
expert witnesses should be encouraged to produce an agreed report,
where agreement cannot be reached it is the 'constitutional function of
the judge' to resolve the differences between them.[38]

Is the French *technicien* a witness called by the judge?

At one time, in France, the grounds on which court-appointed experts
could be challenged were the same as those for witnesses,[39] and Glasson
and Tissier accept that the roles of expert and of witness can sometimes
approximate to one another, especially if a technically qualified witness
is called to give information and advice to the court.[40] The same authors
stress that the expert does not exercise jurisdiction and that it is a
fundamental principle that the expert's opinion does not bind the
judge.[41]

There are, it is true, some formal distinctions between expert and
witness – the grounds for challenging an expert are no longer the same
as those for challenging a witness but are the same as those for challenging a judge;[42] the expert takes an oath that he will perform his task,
make his report and give his opinion on his honour and his conscience,[43]
while the witness swears to tell the truth.[44] According to Glasson and
Tissier, however, the essential difference lies elsewhere. 'The witness
called by a party testifies to what he knows about the facts subject to
proof; the expert is chosen by the judge to give his opinion, after
enquiry, on the points in the case put to him on his appointment.'[45]

The fact remains, however, as just mentioned, that the same authors
recognise that a witness can be called, on account of his technical
knowledge, to give information and an opinion to the court; such an
opinion does not bind the court, and the witness does not exercise
jurisdiction, but both statements are equally true of the expert, at least
according to the language of the law. An English lawyer might be
tempted to say, therefore, that the expert of French law is a witness as

---

[38] Report, para. 13.   [39] Above, n. 14.
[40] Glasson and Tissier, no. 708.   [41] N.c.p.c., art. 246.
[42] *Ibid.*, art. 234. Solus and Perrot, no. 909.
[43] Law no. 71–498 of 29 June 1971, art. 6.
[44] N.c.p.c., art. 211.   [45] Glasson and Tissier, no. 708.

English lawyers understand the word, albeit a witness independent of the parties and called by the judge. Would he be right to do so?

A French lawyer would deny the parallel, probably basing himself on such particularities of French law as those mentioned above and on the fact that a witness – even if called by the judge – testifies at a special hearing known as an *enquête*,[46] while an expert gives his report either in writing or at the final hearing.[47] A comparative lawyer might well reject these reasons as too technical for his purposes, but does it follow that the French expert should be regarded as equivalent to an English witness? Part of the justification for a negative answer, it is believed, lies in French insistence that the operations of the *technicien* – his investigations, in particular – must be carried out by him in accordance with the *principe du contradictoire*. No similar principle binds a witness, even a witness who is called to give evidence as an expert and who carries out an investigation in the preparation of his testimony.

However this may be, the feature that best distinguishes the witness from the expert is probably to be found in the weight that attaches to a single, non-partisan,[48] expert report. It is, of course, true that the judge is not bound by the findings or the opinion of the *technicien*.[49] It is, however, also true that, exceptional cases apart, there will be nothing to counterbalance the weight of the report: though more than one *technicien* may have been involved,[50] only one report is submitted unless there are irreconcilable differences between them.[51] It may be supposed that something out of the ordinary would be necessary to persuade the judge to disregard the opinion of the *technicien* he has appointed. A party may, for example, appoint a *technicien* of his own choosing to conduct an 'expertise officieuse', and the report of that *technicien* can be put in for consideration in the proceedings. Such a report might justify rejection of the official report, but is unlikely ordinarily to do so. In the first place, the *technicien officieux* is the adviser of just one of the parties, not of the judge; in the second place, his investigations will have been conducted

[46] N.c.p.c., arts. 204–31.   [47] *Ibid.*, art. 282.

[48] A *technicien* may not receive from a party even reimbursement of out-of-pocket expenses without the prior authorisation of the judge: n.c.p.c., art. 248.

[49] *Ibid.*, art 246. It is unclear whether the judge must give explicit reasons if he rejects a report. Cf. the views of Solus and Perrot, no. 934 2° and E. Blanc, *La preuve judiciaire* (1974), p. 88. If the judge were to reject a report without explanation, he might incur suspicion of having used his personal knowledge without disclosure, as he might if, faced with a technical question, he declined to appoint a *technicien* in the first place: H. and G. Le Foyer de Costil, 'Les connaissances personnelles du juge', 1986 Rev.int.dr.comp. 517, 525; below, chap. 13, p. 259.

[50] Above, n. 20.   [51] N.c.p.c., art. 282, al. 2.

without the safeguards of the law, especially that of observance of the *principe du contradictoire*.[52]

The weight thus carried by the report of a *technicien* is implicitly recognised in the statutory rules, which place limits on the kind of question that may be put to an expert. The law of 15 July 1944, which reduced the number of experts from three to one, that one to be chosen by the judge,[53] prescribed that an expert could be called upon to report only on questions which were 'purely technical'.[54] The new code is more liberal, but it is still the law that the report of a *technicien* can be legitimately obtained only on questions of fact for the solution of which the knowledge and skills of a technically qualified person are required. A *technicien* may not be called upon to deal with questions of fact that a judge can be expected to answer for himself; still less can he be called upon to deal with a question of law.[55]

An English lawyer might see in these restrictions not a recognition of the weight which in practice attaches to the report of a *technicien* but, rather, a parallel with the English rule which prescribes that only expert witnesses may give evidence of opinion, or as to the conclusions to be drawn from known to unknown facts: the ordinary witness may testify only to facts personally known to him.[56] It is suggested, however, that the parallel, if it exists, lends no support to the idea that the French *technicien* is in reality a witness called by the judge. The English and the French rules serve quite different ends.

It may be that the English rule that only expert witnesses may give evidence of opinion strengthens the idea that expert witnesses, like *techniciens*, should be used only where technical questions of fact are raised, but there is no more to the parallel than that: the principal reason for the English exclusion from evidence of the opinions of ordinary witnesses is simply that such opinions are useless for the purposes of the litigation.[57] Opinions which are of use are admissible, and the utility of certain opinions, including opinions on questions of law, is clear. What do advocates do if they do not give opinions – not independent and impartial opinions, it is true, but opinions – on the questions of law in the case? What is more, though the judge may take points of law of his

---

[52] Solus and Perrot, no. 958. The *technicien officieux* resembles the expert witness of the common law much more closely than does the judicially appointed *technicien*.

[53] Above, n. 15.

[54] Incorporated in the code de procédure civile, art. 302. See P. Hébraud, 'Commentaire de la loi du 15 juillet 1944 sur les rapports d'experts', 1945 D.L. 49.

[55] N.c.p.c., arts. 232 and 238. Solus and Perrot, no. 916.

[56] R. Cross and C. Tapper, *Evidence*, 8th edn (1995), pp. 543–5.

[57] *Ibid.*, pp. 545 and 549–50; *Wigmore on Evidence*, 3rd edn (1940), Vol. II, para. 557 and Vol. VII, para. 1918.

own motion, ordinarily his role in relation to questions of law is to assess the arguments of the advocates and to judge their respective merits. For English law, there is more even than that: so far as decisions of the House of Lords are concerned, importance is attached not only to the arguments of the advocates before the House, but to the judgments of the courts below, especially of the Court of Appeal.[58]

What is the value of those judgments to the House of Lords? They cannot control the decision of the House; it is not a court of cassation but a court of appeal that must give its own decision on the case as a whole. The answer is that they serve as the opinions, the advice, of expert lawyers on the questions of law before the House, and as such they make valuable contributions to the formation by the judges of the House of Lords of their own views.[59]

It is unlikely that a French judge, if asked, would deny that expressions of opinion by others can be useful, and, of course, legal argument is always admissible. There is nothing improper in the admission in evidence of the opinions, the advice, of anybody on anything. The explanation of the restrictions imposed by French law on the use of *techniciens* lies elsewhere: it lies in the basic requirement of the administration of justice that a judicial decision must be the work of the legally appointed judge who has been assigned to the case, and no one else. However free the judge may be to disregard the opinion of a *technicien*, however free he may be to substitute his own opinion, it will only be in exceptional circumstances that he is capable of doing so, and that is why French law restricts the role of the *technicien* to questions which the judge is incapable of resolving without help. The restriction exists to prevent excessive delegation of the powers and the duties of the judge.[60]

The conclusion has to be that, whatever the form of the law, and exceptional cases apart, in practice in France it is the *technicien* who makes the decision on those questions that are committed to him. The English expert is a witness, but in France the *technicien* is nothing of the kind: he is an extension of, and contributes directly to, the decision-making process of the court. He does not actually exercise jurisdiction since he acts under the control of the judge who may reject his opinion, but he shares with the judge the task of deciding questions of fact, to which end he is permitted to receive information, written or oral, from anybody and, with the support of an order from the judge, if necessary,

[58] Evershed, para. 495. Administration of Justice Act 1969, ss. 12–15, especially s. 12(3).
[59] In this respect the judgments of the courts below are comparable to the *conclusions* of the avocat général in the Cour de cassation and of the Commissaire du gouvernement in the Conseil d'Etat.
[60] Solus and Perrot, no. 916.

he can obtain the production to him of documents held by the parties or others.[61] If he is not a judge, he is much more like a judge than like a witness. It is logical that the grounds on which he may be challenged should be the same as those for a judge, and it is right that he should be included amongst the 'auxiliaires de justice' and classed as 'auxiliaire du juge' as distinct from those who are classed as 'auxiliaires des parties' such as, in particular, the *avocats*.[62]

A divergence of approach

As an *auxiliaire du juge* who is chosen by the judge, who is called upon only where a case raises a technical question of fact which the judge cannot resolve unaided, and whose mission is defined and entrusted to him by the judge, the *technicien* of French law lends his knowledge and skills to the court to supplement those of the judge. He is, for all practical purposes, best seen as an extension of the court. English expert witnesses, on the other hand, may be urged to present evidence to the court which 'should be and should be seen to be, the independent product of the expert, uninfluenced as to form or content by the exigencies of litigation',[63] but they are selected and called by the parties; and it is the parties, not the judge, who determine the subject matter of their testimony. They are, inevitably, identified with the parties, not with the court of which they cannot, on any intelligible analysis, be said to form a part.

It was indicated earlier that the powers of the French judge in relation to fact-finding procedures are greater than those of his English counterpart,[64] but it remains the basic principle in both systems that the parties must prove the facts on which they rely;[65] it is not for the court to conduct its own investigations. On the other hand, it is for the court to decide for itself what inferences should be drawn from known facts and it is for the court to decide for itself how established facts should be qualified.[66] How, then, do the English and French approaches to the solution of technical questions correspond with this general principle?

On the first category of question – simple perception of fact – it is clear that the English solution conforms more closely to principle. The French gives to the court – judge and *technicien* together – the task of producing evidence, a task which properly belongs to the party alleging

---

[61] N.c.p.c., arts. 242 and 243.
[62] Cadiet, *Droit judiciare privé*, nos. 371–5; Solus and Perrot, no. 898.
[63] *Whitehouse* v. *Jordan* [1981] 1 W.L.R. 246, 256–7, *per* Lord Wilberforce.
[64] Above, chap. 11, p. 221.
[65] Above, chap. 11, p. 220.   [66] Above, p. 223.

the fact. A party alleges, for example, that a machine suffers from a certain (specified) defect. In principle it is for him to prove the defect by the evidence he adduces, including, if necessary, evidence given by an expert after examination of the machine. It is, of course, for the judge to say whether the evidence is convincing, but it is not for him, with or without expert help, to examine the machine. Yet, in France, the examination of the machine will be entrusted to a *technicien*.

For the second category – perception by presumption – things are more complex. Where conclusions must be drawn from known facts to unknown facts, it is for the judge, not the party, to say whether a conclusion can properly be drawn. If the judge lacks the necessary knowledge or understanding to do so unaided, he should seek help from his own expert, not from experts chosen and called as witnesses by the parties. Theoretically, therefore, for this category of question a mixed procedure is required. Suppose an action in which one party alleges that the cause of an accident was the unforeseeable breakdown of a component of his car. The car was destroyed in the accident, and only an expert motor engineer is capable of carrying out a useful investigation of the remains or of drawing useful conclusions from what he finds. The general principle requires that engineers chosen by the parties should carry out the investigation and report their findings by giving evidence as witnesses; a different engineer, chosen by and working with the judge, should advise him on the conclusions that can be drawn about the cause of the accident.

For the third category – qualification of the facts – the French solution is correct; the English contravenes the general principle. Here there is no question of the perception of facts and there is no question of drawing inferences from known to unknown facts: by hypothesis the facts have already been established and the only thing left is their qualification. On that, the parties may present argument, but argument is the business of an advocate, not of a witness. The decision is for the judge, and if he lacks the knowledge to do it alone he should be assisted by an expert of his choosing. The English system is paradoxical: it allows the expert witness to testify on the qualification of facts, and so allows him to act as an advocate. There is confusion of two different functions.

Since questions of all three categories are likely to arise in any case requiring the solution of technical questions, the mixed system using both expert witnesses and court-appointed *techniciens* should, in principle, be employed. For obvious reasons of economy, if nothing else, however – and save in some specialised tribunals and in those rare instances in which an English judge sits with assessors – the mixed system is not found in either England or France. French procedure has chosen the system of the court-appointed *technicien* for all three categories of question, while English procedure has chosen the system of expert witnesses.

The divergence between the two systems is not just one of practice; they diverge in their understanding of the respective roles of the parties and the judge. When it comes to the solution of technical questions, French law departs from the general principle by giving to the court what properly belongs to the parties; English law departs by giving to the parties what properly belongs to the judge. The English system has been converted into a curious hybrid,[67] but in the years leading up to that conversion, developments in the law of both countries have accentuated rather than reduced the divergence.

Developments in the law

England

One of the incidental inconveniences of the use of expert witnesses comes from the temptation that it offers to a litigant to call as many experts as he can, in the hope of persuading the court by weight of numbers. This is avoided by the exercise by the court of its power to limit – normally to two – the number of experts allowed to each party.[68] On the point of principle, this makes no difference.

A second inconvenience comes from the general rule of English law that no party is – or, rather, was – obliged to let his opponent know in advance what his witnesses will say at the trial.[69] Until the trial, the expert of one party knew nothing of the investigations, the opinions or the conclusions of the expert on the other side. It was not uncommon, therefore, that experts were summoned to attend the trial at which it emerged, for the first time, that no technical questions were actually in dispute.

To avoid what came to be seen as useless expenditure of time and money, it has for some time been the practice for the court to order that the parties agree, if possible, on a single written expert report that can

---

[67] See the postscript to this chapter.

[68] R.S.C., Ord. 38, r. 4. The rule became statutory in 1954, but entered judicial practice in 1927: *Graigola Merthyr Co. v. Swansea Corp.* [1927] W.N. 30.

[69] Winn, paras. 368–9. In 1953, even the suggestion that the parties should be required to exchange lists of the names of the witnesses they proposed to call was rejected: Evershed, paras. 299–302. Since the introduction, in 1992, of R.S.C., Ord. 38, r. 2A (C.P.R., r. 32.4) providing for the exchange of witness statements, the general rule stated in the text has lost most of its force.

be used at the trial and the attendance of expert witnesses thereby avoided.[70] Until 1972,[71] however, the practice was unsupported by any sanction. In that year it became the law that, subject to agreement to the contrary, no expert witness may be called to give evidence at the trial unless application has first been made to the court for a decision whether a summary of the expert's report should be disclosed to the other party in advance. Such disclosure is now normal in many classes of case,[72] and the court has power to direct a meeting of experts with a view to obtaining maximum agreement between them.[73]

Desirable though these changes may have been in the interest of promoting economy, one of their byproducts has been to reinforce the idea that it is for the parties, not for the court, to find the expertise necessary to the solution of their litigation and even, if possible, to relieve the court of technical questions altogether: if the parties' experts reach agreement, the court is informed by way of an agreed expert report and nothing more is ordinarily required. Only if the experts fail to reach agreement will they be called as witnesses, and it then falls to the court to resolve the controversy between them.

France

If the English reforms enhance the role of the parties, the French enhance that of the judge. As has been noticed, since 1973 there have been added to the procedure of the *expertise* two other, less elaborate, procedures, the *constatation* and the *consultation*.[74]

Article 249 of the code empowers the judge to charge a person appointed by him to make *constatations*. The role of the *constatant* falls clearly within the scope of the first category of question – the simple perception of relevant facts: the *constatant* must not express any opinion on the conclusions of fact or of law that may flow from the facts he has established.[75] Since the *constatant* is more a judge of fact than a witness and since the *constatation* is a considerable expansion of the *constat d'huissier*,[76] its introduction increases the extent of the transfer to the

---

[70] See *Harrison* v. *Liverpool Corporation* [1943] 2 All E.R. 449. It has been pointed out that difficulties may arise if the judge has to rely on a written expert report without having the opportunity of obtaining explanations from an expert present in court: *Jones* v. *Griffith* [1949] 1 W.L.R. 795; *Mullard* v. *Ben Line Steamers* [1970] 1 W.L.R. 1414.

[71] Civil Evidence Act 1972; R.S.C., Ord. 38, rr. 35–44.

[72] Disclosure of medical reports in most cases of personal injury (R.S.C., Ord. 38, r. 37) and of the reports of motor engineers in cases of accident on land (*ibid.*, r. 40) is mandatory.

[73] R.S.C., Ord. 38, r. 38 (C.P.R., r. 35.12).   [74] Above, p. 227.

[75] N.c.p.c., art. 249, al. 2.   [76] Above, p. 227.

court of what belongs to the parties – the proof of the facts they have alleged.

The *consultation* is more difficult to assess, since the governing text seems ambiguous.[77] It may be that the *consultant* acts as a mere adviser to the judge, in which case he acts as a true auxiliary of the judge, helping him to perform his proper role. But the new code specifies that a *consultation* may be ordered when a technical question does not call for 'complex investigations': it does not say that a *consultation* may be used only where a technical question does not call for 'additional investigations'. On this basis it is possible for the *consultation* to be used as a kind of 'mini-*expertise*',[78] and if that is right, the role of the *consultant*, like that of the *expert* carrying out the full procedure of the *expertise*, includes that of finding the materials – the evidence – on which the actual findings of fact will be based.

Conclusion

It is sometimes a matter of surprise outside the common law world that the system of expert witnesses requires the judge – who is not an expert – to resolve disagreements on technical matters between witnesses who are experts, and that he must do this, a few exceptions apart, without the assistance of a technical adviser of his own. The procedure of cross-examination, to which there is no equivalent in French law, helps the judge in the performance of his task and so, probably, do the arguments of counsel, but there is nevertheless a deep underlying difference in the thinking of the two systems. French law, accepting the evident truth that the judge lacks technical competence, provides him with an auxiliary for the determination of technical questions even if that means that it is the auxiliary, more often than not, who really makes the decision. English law insists, in practice as well as in theory, that the judge alone must resolve every controversy of fact arising between the parties, whatever its nature.

If this is right, comparison of this aspect of English and French procedure provides one more indication that, while neither is 'inquisitorial' and neither is entirely self-consistent, French law comes closer than English law to the idea that the court's role is to discover where the truth lies between the rival contentions of the parties. In France, where the court – judge and *technicien* together – has transferred to it matters which, in England, are left to the parties, less attention is paid to deciding whether a party has discharged a burden of proof placed upon

[77] N.c.p.c., arts. 256–62.
[78] This seems to be the opinion of Solus and Perrot, no. 950.

him and more is paid to deciding the question of fact as such. In England, where the parties are left to deal even with matters that properly belong to the judge, and where expert witnesses are required to respond on questions that are properly the subject of argument, not evidence, concentration on the burden of proof is inevitable. The French and the English procedures for the resolution of technical questions of fact in the course of litigation differ from one another not only in their techniques, but in their underlying theory.

Postscript

Lord Woolf's Interim Report records widespread concern at the expense, delay and increased complexity caused by the parties' need to engage experts, and it attributes the problem largely to the fact that experts are usually recruited as part of the team which investigates and advances a party's contentions. This is said to make it difficult for the expert subsequently to adopt an independent attitude.[79]

That an expert is brought in by one party or another, at a time and for a purpose of that party's choosing, is inherent in a system that treats experts as *witnesses* called by the parties. If, then, the system is thought to be a source of serious difficulties, the logical solution would be to adopt the alternative system, using an expert independent of the parties, who is appointed and instructed by the court: such an expert is not a witness. To adopt that solution, however, would be to adopt the continental solution, and that seems to be sufficient to persuade most English lawyers to reject it out of hand. Lord Woolf does not advocate it, even though his criticisms of the existing system received a large measure of agreement. At the same time, however, the proposals actually made in the Interim Report met with strong opposition.[80] They were, therefore, modified for the Final Report,[81] and have since been modified yet further.[82] Nevertheless, the new law is undoubtedly intended to, and does, bring about major changes.

Lip service, at least, is paid to maintenance of the adversary system;[83] such power as the court has to appoint an expert itself is

---

[79] Woolf Interim, pp. 181 and 182. This means, according to Lord Woolf, that the expert subsequently has to change roles to provide the independent advice which the court is entitled to expect.

[80] Woolf Final, p. 137.

[81] Summarised in Woolf Final, p. 152.

[82] LCD Working Paper, *Access to Justice: The Fast Track and the Multi Track*, July 1997 (hereafter 'LCD'), para. 6, p. 38. C.P.R., r. 35.

[83] Or, rather, it is claimed that the new law is consistent with it: Woolf Final, p. 140; LCD, para. 6.7, p. 40. See chap. 19, p. 391.

restricted;[84] and even where it exercises its power to direct use of a single expert, its powers to give instructions to the expert are also restricted.[85] On the other hand, the new Civil Procedure Rules make their intention perfectly clear: before descending to detail they lay down the general principles that it is the overriding duty of an expert to help the court impartially on the matters relevant to his expertise, and that this duty overrides any obligation to the person from whom he has received instructions or by whom he is to be paid.[86] As shown by an anticipatory decision of the Court of Appeal, this carries the implication that the expert enjoys immunity from suit, even by his own client, in respect of work done in preparation for the trial.[87]

Cardinal features of the new system are, first, that no party may call an expert or put in evidence an expert's report without the court's permission;[88] secondly, that the court may direct that only one expert may be used on a given issue;[89] thirdly, that, unless the court otherwise directs, the expert is not to be called but may provide only a written report.[90] This is taken so far that provision is actually made for a kind of written interrogation of the expert.[91] The emphasis throughout is on the avoidance, to the maximum possible extent, of conflicts or contradictions in the expert reports or evidence that are put before the court. The court may direct disclosure of experts' reports,[92] and also that the experts, if more than one, shall meet,[93] and there are provisions for the use by one party of an expert's report disclosed by another.[94]

---

[84] If the court has directed that one expert only may be used, and if the parties are unable to agree who should be the expert, the court may appoint an expert from a list prepared by the parties or it may direct some other method of appointment: C.P.R., r. 35.7(3).

[85] Each party is entitled to give instructions to the expert while the court may do so only in relation to fees and expenses and to any inspection, examination or experiment the expert may wish to carry out: *ibid.*, r. 35.8. On the other hand, the expert may ask the court for directions and this he would be likely to do in the event of conflicting instructions from the parties: *ibid.*, r. 35.14.

[86] *Ibid.*, r. 35.3. The expert is required to certify, amongst other matters, that he understands and has complied with his duty to the court: *ibid.*, r. 35.10(2).

[87] *Stanton v. Callaghan* [1998] 4 All E.R. 961, where the defendant expert had met with the expert instructed by the opposing party to determine and indicate the matters not in issue between them.

[88] C.P.R., r. 35.4. The court cannot call for the assistance of an expert of its own motion, but it does retain the power to appoint an assessor (above, p. 229) who may be called upon not simply to 'assist' the court but specifically to prepare a report for the court 'on any matter at issue in the proceedings': *ibid.*, r. 35.15. This opens the possibility that the assessor will develop into a genuine court-appointed expert.

[89] *Ibid.*, r. 35.7.   [90] *Ibid.*, r. 35.5.   [91] *Ibid.*, r. 35.6.

[92] *Ibid.*, rr. 3.1, 35.11 and 35.13.

[93] *Ibid.*, r. 35.12. There is no provision for the parties to be present or represented at a meeting of experts (cf. the French *réunion d'expertise*, above, p. 228), but the content of the discussion at such a meeting may not be referred to at the trial.

[94] *Ibid.*, r. 35.11.

This part of the C.P.R. is evidently intended to provide a system that will normally ensure that the court receives a single uncontradicted expert report, and to secure the advantages of such a system, without at the same time offending the sensibilities of die-hard adherents of the traditional adversary style.[95] Only time will tell whether this objective will be achieved, but it is feared that the system envisaged will fall into, rather than bridge, the gulf between the common law system of the expert witness and the continental system of the expert appointed by the court.

At one point Lord Woolf expressed his intent to distinguish between the fact-finding and the opinion-giving roles of experts,[96] but this did not lead him to propose that each role should be performed by different people. The phrase 'expert witness', used in earlier drafts of the C.P.R., has been dropped in favour of 'expert', but this is at best cosmetic; the 'expert' of the new system still gives evidence, and that is the function of a witness and of no one else. Yet the Rules impose on the expert the overriding duty to help the court impartially on the matters relevant to his expertise. Is there not here a failure of analysis and so a failure to appreciate the incompatibility of the roles of witness, on the one hand, and of 'auxiliaire du juge',[97] on the other?

There is nothing new in attempts to increase the area of agreement between the parties on technical matters arising in their litigation, and the time may now be propitious for further such attempts, particularly with reference to what have above been called 'questions of perception':[98] there is no reason why the parties who might agree, say, that a machine suffered from a certain defect, should not instead agree that the condition of the machine will be taken to be as found by an expert after examination of it.

When it comes to perception by presumption and the qualification of the facts, however, the expert 'witness' of English law plays the role of an advocate, not that of a witness. That is anomalous, but it is not inconsistent with the adversary system as usually understood. But if, as a matter of general principle subject only to limited exceptions, the judge is to be assisted by one expert opinion only on such questions, it cannot be for the parties, even in agreement with one another, to determine from whom that opinion will be obtained. At this stage, the expert is 'auxiliaire du juge' and as such should be selected by the judge, if necessary over the objection of the parties. It may be objected that in the French and other continental systems a court-appointed expert has

---

[95] See Woolf Final, p. 138 for Lord Woolf's attempt to win over the die-hards.
[96] Woolf Interim, p. 181.
[97] Above, p. 234.   [98] Above, p. 225.

excessive influence on the ultimate decision, but is the objection any less forceful in a system in which the court orders the use of a single expert only, the parties then agree on the selection of an expert, and the expert then comes under an overriding duty to the court?

It is suggested, therefore, that the system envisaged by the C.P.R. is flawed in that it attempts to combine two incompatible systems. It may work more or less satisfactorily for a time, and while it does so it may prove cheaper in operation than its predecessor. Eventually, however, the inherent inconsistencies in its underlying structure are likely to bring serious practical difficulties in their train. There is, in the last resort, no half-way house between an expert witness and an expert 'auxiliaire du juge'.

13   The use by the judge of his own knowledge (of fact or law or both) in the formation of his decision[1]

The subject matter of this chapter lies at the heart of the judicial process, and, perhaps for that reason, is one to which the rules of positive law seldom refer in explicit terms. It is more intractable than many: in the last resort it is concerned with the mental processes of the judge himself, and those processes cannot ordinarily be known save to the extent that the judge is willing to disclose them in his exposition of the reasons for his decision or in the course of the proceedings leading up to his decision. Nor is it possible rigidly and accurately to enforce such rules as there may be which purport to restrict use by the judge of knowledge that he happens to have: only an Orwellian 'Thought Police' equipped with futuristic 'thought detection' devices could do that. For the time being, only two means of control exist – a judge possessed of knowledge of which he cannot make legitimate use in a given case can be disqualified, and a decision which is seen to be based in part on such knowledge can be set aside by a court of appeal or cassation.

The inadequacy of these controls is shown in the report for France. Following an account of a number of cases in which the French Cour de cassation quashed the decision of a lower court for improper use by the judges of their 'personal knowledge', it is observed that

la nature de ces décisions et le libellé des formules censurées révèlent, à l'évidence, de la part des juridictions de fond une franchise ingénue, de la maladresse, et une parfaite, mais peut-être excessive, bonne foi; elles eussent échappé à la cassation si ces mêmes juges, affirmant souverainement, n'avaient pas cité les sources de leur motivation.[2]

---

[1] Based on a Report to the XIIth International Congress of Comparative Law in 1986, published in E. K. Banakas (ed.), *United Kingdom Law in the 1980s* (1988), 3. The chapter draws on the national reports listed at the end of this chapter. All are held on file by the International Academy of Comparative Law and many have been independently published, as shown. For conformity, page references in the following text are to the original versions.

[2] France, p. 8.

Such frankness is refreshing,[3] as is the approach through the 'méthode de l'examen de conscience'.[4] Most other reports, while not neglectful of the central problem, tended to pay greater attention to the associated and more familiar, but different, subject of 'judicial notice' and its equivalents outside the common law. As ordinarily understood, 'judicial notice' refers to the question whether the judge can take account of a fact even though it has not been formally proved in the course of the proceedings, and that is not what is at issue here. The subject of the present chapter may be clarified by the statement of three propositions – propositions which, it is believed, are uncontroversial, even self-evident – after which working definitions can be given of 'personal knowledge' and its 'use'.

(1) The judgment of a judge sitting alone, the contribution of a judge sitting as a member of a collegiate court, even the contribution of a member of a jury to its verdict, is in each case the product of a single mind, its subconscious as well as its conscious elements: in the nature of things it can be nothing else. Whatever the 'knowledge' of which the judge makes use, subconsciously as well as consciously, in coming to his conclusion, that knowledge is necessarily 'personal' to him, no matter how he acquired it or how many other people share it. If a judge lacks a certain item of knowledge, define 'item of knowledge' how we may, that item of knowledge cannot influence his decision. If, objectively and with hindsight, it can be said that the item of knowledge in question was relevant then, no doubt, it can also be said that the judge's decision might have been different had he possessed it: but that is another matter.

(2) A very great deal of knowledge is conveyed to the judge in the course of the proceedings. It would not be inaccurate to describe much of the law of procedure and evidence as concerned primarily to regulate the supply of information to the judge, but it must be appreciated that it is not only through evidence or proof – including procedures for the obtaining of information that the judge may be empowered to initiate of his own motion[5] – that he is actually informed. Most importantly, so far as the 'facts' of the case are concerned, the judge may acquire knowledge – knowledge he will usually have to accept without question

---

[3] It is also revealing, coming as it does from the only reporters who were practising members of the judiciary – Conseiller à la Cour d'appel de Paris and Vice-Président au Tribunal de grande instance de Paris.

[4] France, p. 8. See also USSR, p. 1.

[5] See above, chap. 11, p. 215.

– from the parties' allegations and admissions, but even an unadmitted allegation of fact draws his attention, and if the fact alleged needs no proof because it is 'notorious', no more is needed: it is not necessary that the judge himself shall actually have known the fact in question before the proceedings began, as is shown, for example, by rules allowing judicial notice to be taken after 'enquiry'.[6]

Information is also given to the judge in the course of the proceedings by way of 'argument', usually by advocates acting for the parties. Typically this is considered to relate to the 'law' rather than to the 'facts', and even if that is an over-simplification of the nature of legal argument, no one can pretend that every judge really knows, independently of the proceedings on which he is engaged, 'all the law' of his jurisdiction. If a judge is informed by counsel, for example, of a precedent decision of which he was previously unaware, then, plainly, he has acquired knowledge of it in the course of the proceedings; the same is, essentially, true where the judge was aware of the precedent decision: his prior knowledge of it becomes immaterial once counsel has 'reminded' him of it in the course of the proceedings.

(3) It is both expected and required that the judge has in his possession a vast but indeterminate mass of knowledge before he enters upon his task of adjudication in any given case. Every legal system lays down the qualifications necessary for appointment to judicial office, and jurors and other lay participants in the judicial process must also be qualified even if the only qualification required is to have reached the age of majority.[7] In other words, a minimum experience of life – and in the case of professional judges very much more – is demanded of anyone upon whose intellectual processes the outcome of litigation depends, wholly or in part.

'Personal knowledge'

Given that the knowledge used by the judge in making his decision is 'personal' to him, it becomes critical to distinguish between the knowledge that he acquired in the course of the proceedings on which he is engaged (whether he already possessed it and was merely 'reminded' of

---

[6] Australia, pp. 11–16; England, p. 5; New Zealand, pp. 2–3; USA, p. 16. See also the interesting discussion of the use of 'atypical' proofs in Italy, pp. 5–6. In the FRG and in Japan it is recognised that a fact may be 'known to the court' (*gerichtskundig*) and as such require no proof: FRG, pp. 4–5; Japan, pp. 8–9.

[7] See USSR, p. 7.

it or not), on the one hand, and all other knowledge possessed by the judge, on the other. It is of the essence of litigation that he is entitled, even required, to make use of knowledge in the former category; it is only in relation to the latter that any question can arise. Henceforward, therefore, the phrase 'personal knowledge' is used only in relation to the latter.

'Use' of knowledge

It is impossible to know the extent to which a judge is unconsciously or subconsciously influenced by his personal knowledge when he comes to make his decision; even his conscious use of such knowledge can ordinarily be known only to the extent that he is willing to disclose it.[8] On the other hand, it is not only in the explicit motivation of his decision that the judge's use of his personal knowledge may be observed; he 'uses' such knowledge whenever it is he rather than any other participant in the proceedings who introduces a new element into the debate. To give just one simple illustration, if counsel refers a judge to a precedent decision on which the judge subsequently relies, then the judge does not use his personal knowledge of that decision however well he actually knew it; conversely, if in the course of counsel's argument the judge intervenes and draws attention to a decision to which counsel has not yet referred, the judge does make use of his personal knowledge of that decision. That virtually every legal system would regard such use of personal knowledge as wholly unobjectionable is relevant to the scope of any rule which purports to exclude the use by the judge of personal knowledge, but it does not change the fact that the judge is making use of knowledge that has not been conveyed to him in the course of the proceedings.

The 'rule of exclusion'

For the purposes of this chapter, the 'rule of exclusion' means a rule that forbids, or purports to forbid, the use by the judge of personal knowledge which he happens to possess. In the light of what has already

---

[8] The use of personal knowledge is thus more likely to be revealed where the judgment is discursive than when it is in the compact style typical of France. Some reporters from common law countries have thus been able to refer to the judge's use of personal knowledge in decisions which 'develop' the law – 'legislative facts' as they are called in the United States (USA, p. 2). See also Australia, pp. 7–8; USA, pp. 22–3. Whenever the law is not so 'clear' that the decision itself becomes clear once the facts are known, it is intrinsically probable that the judge uses his personal knowledge in deciding what the law 'is', whether he is formally directed by law to appeal to broadly stated principle or not. As the U.S. reporter puts it, 'the assumption of social, political and economic facts relevant to determining the content of the law plays a major role in judging': USA, p. 23. This large and important topic cannot be further considered here.

been said – in the light of the principle which, surely, is universal, that every judge must devote to his task the whole of his intellect, not excluding, as a general rule, the knowledge and experience he has acquired in the course of his life – the rule of exclusion is more of an exception to that principle than a rule in its own right. Nevertheless, restrictions on the use by the judge of his personal knowledge exist in every developed legal system.

Broadly speaking, the rule of exclusion appears in two forms. In its first and more draconian form it forbids altogether the use by the judge of certain knowledge he happens to possess; in its second form it permits such use, but only upon condition that the judge has disclosed his knowledge to the parties, giving them the opportunity to challenge its accuracy and debate its relevance to the matter in hand. The first, with which it is proposed to begin because of its drastic character and because it lays the foundation for what follows, can refer only to matters of fact: the judge is, universally, expected to have and to use personal knowledge of the law of his jurisdiction. The second, on the other hand, may apply as much to matters of law as to matters of fact, since its principal role is to ensure observation of the *principe du contradictoire*.[9]

Section I: knowledge of which use may not be made

The only effective way to ensure that a judge does not make illegitimate use of knowledge he happens to possess is to prevent him from adjudicating in litigation to which that knowledge is or might be relevant. It is true that disqualification of a judge can occur for this reason only if his possession of certain knowledge is known, or is made known, to others in advance, but even so it would seem that examination of the rules for the disqualification of judges from adjudicating in particular cases should reveal something about the rule of exclusion in its basic form.

Of the countries here considered, only the United States, the former Soviet Union and, possibly, Israel, treat the judge's possession of certain knowledge as in itself a ground of disqualification. In Israel the matter is dubious,[10] but in the United States legislation provides that a judge

[9] Above, chap. 9, p. 177.
[10] See Cr.A. 84/75 *Yadid v. State of Israel* 29(Z) P.D. 375, cited Israel, p. 3. In footnote 7 the reporter comments that, in the circumstances, it was rather that the judge had already expressed an opinion on liability, than that he had personal knowledge, that led to his disqualification.

should not sit if, amongst other reasons, he has 'personal knowledge of *disputed evidentiary facts concerning the proceeding*',[11] and in the former Soviet Union the legislative rule that 'the court shall base its judgment only on the evidence examined by it at the trial' was understood as excluding all use of personal knowledge by the judge:

a judge in possession of information related to the case and obtained by him prior to the beginning of the hearings should disqualify himself as a judge and assume the status of a witness. To put it otherwise, he does not qualify as a judge not only if he has already acted as a witness in this case, as provided for by article 18 of the C.P.C., but also if he can be called upon to act as a potential witness in it.[12]

Elsewhere the point is made less directly, but there is widespread recognition that the role of judge and the role of witness are incompatible.[13] This forms part of the technique for preserving the actuality and the appearance of judicial impartiality,[14] but it also has a more specific objective – the exclusion from use by the judge of personal knowledge of matters of which he should be informed, if at all, only by way of testimony given in the course of the proceedings.

So far as the actual rules for disqualification are concerned, a judge is disqualified in many countries only if he has actually testified in the litigation in question; the mere possession of knowledge that he might impart in the character of a witness is not alone enough.[15] Nevertheless, from the rule of disqualification of the witness-judge a consequential sub-rule can be drawn to the effect that if a judge is possessed of knowledge on which he could be called upon to testify, then, even if he is not so called upon, he still should not sit. In Mexico, for example, where the code expressly disqualifies only the judge who has acted as a witness, the prevailing opinion is that possession of knowledge of the factual situation involved in litigation is sufficient to constitute him a 'witness'.[16] For Japan it is said that the statutory basis for what is here called the rule of exclusion is to be found in a similar code provision.[17] Even for England, where relevant legislation is virtually non-existent, it is said that 'if anyone concerned with a trial in an adjudicative capacity has material facts to impart, he should be sworn as a witness. When so sworn, a judge

---

[11] The words are those of a federal statute (28 U.S.C.A. §455(b)(1)) and of the American Bar Association's Code of Judicial Conduct (Canon 3(C)(1): USA, p. 4 (emphasis added)).

[12] USSR, pp. 2–3.

[13] 'From a psychological point of view it seems to be impossible to be a witness and a judge at the same time': FRG, pp. 1–2.

[14] In addition, as is pointed out, for example, in Israel, p. 1, if a judge bases his judgment on personal knowledge the parties may be deprived of their right of contradiction.

[15] Argentina, p. 4; GDR, p. 6; FRG, p. 2, Italy, p. 6; Netherlands, pp. 11–12.

[16] Mexico, p. 40.   [17] Japan, p. 5.

must not, either when acting alone or with others, adjudicate on his own testimony or take any further judicial part in the proceedings.'[18]

The existence of these rules indicates a general opinion that the judge must not make use of his personal knowledge if and in so far as it relates to matters which should be conveyed to the court in the form of witness testimony. As an element in the rule of exclusion, however, there is no reason to limit the principle which lies behind them to testimony strictly so-called. By parity of reasoning a judge should not use his personal knowledge of any matter in respect of which it is required that the court be informed in the course of the proceedings and through use of a procedure prescribed by law.

Such a definition of the scope of the rule of exclusion, relying, as it does, on a requirement that certain matters be brought to the court's attention only by procedurally proper methods, contains an element of circularity: the judge must not make use of his personal knowledge of matters that must be independently proved, and independent proof is required of matters in respect of which the judge must not use his personal knowledge. There are, however, at least two ways in which the circle is broken. First, it sometimes happens that the law itself actually requires that the court be informed of a particular matter in a particular manner. In the second place, and more generally, it is the underlying purpose of the rule of exclusion, in its absolute form, to preserve the intrinsic character of *legal* adjudication, and the concept of *legal* adjudication contains within itself the independent principle that certain matters must be established by legally approved procedures or left out of account altogether.

Particular rules of proof

As has been noticed, general acceptance of the principle of 'free evaluation' does not mean that specified modes of proof are never required,[19] and where they are then, obviously, no judge may rely on his personal knowledge, should he happen to possess it. If not established by the particular mode of proof required, it cannot be relied on.

Legal adjudication

'Material facts'
English rules of pleading distinguish between 'material facts' and 'the evidence by which those facts are to be proved'.[20] The distinction,

---

[18] England, p. 31, n. 1.   [19] Chap. 11, p. 213.
[20] R.S.C., Ord. 18, r. 7; C.P.R., r. 16.2.

imprecise and difficult to maintain in practice, is sound in theory, and the concept of 'material facts' corresponds to what Motulsky called 'les éléments générateurs des droits subjectifs'.[21] Both, it is suggested, refer to the circumstances which are actually contemplated by a rule or complex of rules whose application is in question.

If a rule is to be invoked, then, to the degree of probability required, the court must be satisfied of the existence of the circumstances contemplated by that rule. If the rule is simple, then it will be simple to ascertain from it what are the circumstances contemplated, what are the 'material facts': a rule that a valid marriage can be contracted only by persons over the age of sixteen plainly treats as a material fact the ages of the parties to a marriage whose validity is in question. Even in a case that is simple in this sense, however, the 'material facts' may be stated only in broad generic terms, as where a rule imposes liability for 'fault', and frequently it will be difficult to discover what precisely are the 'material facts' contemplated by a complex rule. It is, however, a necessary hypothesis of the entire process of legal adjudication that certain circumstances, certain 'material facts', are contemplated by each and every legally binding rule: otherwise it would have no reference to the social, economic or political life of the society in which it purports to have effect.[22]

At the end of litigation the judge must decide whether the 'material facts' have been adequately established. In doing so he cannot fail to draw to some extent on his personal knowledge, but if by chance his personal knowledge extends to one or more of the facts which are 'material' in the case before him – if, for example, he happens to know that one of the parties to a questioned marriage is under age – then, if he acts in the case at all, which he should not, he must dismiss that knowledge from his mind. The concept of *legal* adjudication itself demands no less.

'Secondary facts'

It is improbable that the 'material' facts of a case can all be established directly. To decide whether they have actually been established, it will almost invariably be necessary for the judge to consider whether their existence can be inferred from what has been directly established, or whether the generic terms in which they are stated by the law are apt to cover the circumstances before him or, most commonly, both. The intellectual processes involved are complex, but they must include – if

[21] Motulsky, 'Le "manque de base légale", pierre de touche de la technique juridique' in *Ecrits*, p. 31 at p. 34. See also chap. 10, p. 201.
[22] See chap. 11, p. 212.

they do not consist entirely in – the selective and sometimes subconscious correlation of other facts known to the judge. Such facts, being other than the 'material' facts, are here called 'secondary', and ordinarily a great deal of information about secondary facts will have been conveyed to the judge in the course of the proceedings. To what extent, if at all, is the judge required, if he can, to dismiss from his mind relevant secondary facts of which he has personal knowledge?

An attempt to answer this question must first distinguish between two categories of secondary fact, here called 'particular' and 'general'.[23] The distinction is not precise, for the borderline between the two cannot be precisely defined, but a fact may be regarded as 'particular' if it is unique; if it relates to the nature of things – human behaviour or the laws of nature, for example – it is 'general'. So, for example, in a paternity suit, the latest date on which intercourse could have taken place between the mother and the putative father, and also the maximum period of human gestation, might be relevant 'secondary' facts: the first is 'particular', the second 'general'.

Particular facts

A particular fact that is not only unique but is uniquely related to a question in issue in the litigation is as much within the rule of exclusion as a material fact, and for the same reasons. It clearly falls within the phrase 'evidentiary fact' used in the American legislation already cited, and it is precisely the kind of fact for proof of which the testimony of an ordinary witness – not an expert – is required. For the Federal Republic of Germany it is pointed out in terms that 'the principle of fair proceedings requires that the subject of litigation should be independent of the judge's unpredictable and incalculable knowledge',[24] and similar sentiments are expressed for other countries. If the judge happens to have personal knowledge of a fact of this character he must, so far as possible, dismiss it from his mind.

It is, however, possible that a relevant secondary fact, though 'particular', is none the less known to great numbers of people, even to all reasonably educated members of a given society. If the judge made use of his personal knowledge of a fact of this character – if, for example, a French or an English judge used his personal knowledge of the fact that there is a great deal of traffic in the English Channel – there would be no danger that the outcome of the litigation might depend on the judge's 'unpredictable and incalculable knowledge'. In other words, if a fact is

---

[23] A 'material fact' as defined above is necessarily 'particular'.
[24] FRG, p. 2. See also England, p. 7.

sufficiently well known, there appears to be no reason of principle why the judge should not make use of his personal knowledge of it.

It cannot be seriously maintained that some use by the judge of his personal knowledge of such 'notorious' facts is either uncommon or illegitimate even in procedures that are avowedly 'adversary' in character: 'The assumption that triers of fact will determine disputes in accordance with "common sense" flies in the face of any such notion.'[25] On the other hand, it cannot be claimed that this is the consequence of the doctrine of judicial notice for that doctrine is, at least explicitly, concerned only with relieving a party from proof of a 'notorious' fact on which he relies, not with use by the judge of his personal knowledge.

The explanation of this is probably to be found in the emphasis that continues to be placed on the dispositive principle and on the unspoken assumptions to which it leads. The principle is inherent in the adversary process of the common law, it is widely recognised in explicit terms elsewhere, and it is the source of the principle that it is for the parties and for the parties alone to fix the ambit of their litigation. The principle thus denies to the judge the right to introduce into the debate, let alone to take into account without disclosure, any fact which no party has put forward in support of his case.

No difficulty arises, therefore, where the procedure in question endows the judge with a positive investigative role, where the *Untersuchungsmaxime* applies[26] or where, as in the former German Democratic Republic, the judges were called upon to use 'all their knowledge and experience' to obtain a 'full knowledge of the facts of the case' through a process of 'finding out', beginning on the first occasion that the litigation came before the court.[27] Elsewhere, however, a self-contradictory situation seems to be revealed about which little can be said, save that it is apparently maintained as a general principle that the judge may not use his personal knowledge of any particular fact, however notorious, and that that principle is disregarded, silently and without objection, when the 'common sense' of the judge inspires him to take account of some fact of which he would be prepared to say, in effect, 'That goes without saying.'

The problem seems to have received little attention in common law jurisdictions, but in Japan an 'obvious' fact need not be alleged if it is circumstantial or auxiliary: the judge may take account of such a fact

---

[25] Australia, p. 2.

[26] E.g. in the FRG, in proceedings concerning the nullity of marriage or the status of children: FRG, pp. 5–6. Problems may arise where the proceedings are governed partly by the *Verhandlungsmaxime* and partly by the *Untersuchungsmaxime*, as in the case of divorce.

[27] GDR, pp. 2 and 5–6.

from his personal knowledge of it, but should indicate his intention to do so and allow a challenge to its accuracy.[28] In the Federal Republic of Germany, a controversy has emerged between those writers who maintain that even notorious facts must be introduced by a party and those who maintain that the judge may take account, of his own motion, at least of circumstantial or auxiliary notorious facts the neglect of which would lead to a wrong decision.[29] The controversy has, however, lost most of its importance in light of the enhancement in 1976 of the judge's duty to call upon the parties to introduce all necessary facts into the proceedings.[30] Similarly, in France the judge can order the personal appearance of the parties before him and can invite them to provide explanations of facts that he considers necessary to the solution of the litigation thereby, in substance, bringing facts into the proceedings himself.[31] Even where the personal appearance of the parties ostensibly retains its original function of mere clarification of claims and defences, as in Mexico, it can be used by the judge to similar purpose:[32] in Japan it is specifically provided that the court can induce the parties to allege facts.[33]

General facts

Nothing need be said on this subject at this stage. A rule that purported absolutely to forbid any use by the judge of his personal knowledge of general facts would render the entire process of litigation impossible.

Section II: disclosure of personal knowledge

In this section of this chapter it is assumed that the judge is entitled to make some use of his personal knowledge. The principal question is whether, and to what extent, he must first disclose his knowledge and submit it to debate by the parties. A number of different topics call for consideration.

Law

Obviously the judge must use his own legal knowledge to evaluate the rival legal contentions of the parties, but literal adherence to the theory of the adversary process would allow no more than that. So, for

---

[28] Japan, pp. 10–11.   [29] FRG, pp. 5–6.
[30] ZPO §139, as amended in 1976: FRG, p. 6.
[31] N.c.p.c., arts. 8 and 184 *et seq.*; chap. 11, p. 215.
[32] Mexico, pp. 51–9.   [33] C.p.c., art. 127: Japan, p. 2.

example, in the Mexican procedure of *amparo* the 'suplencia de la queja' – a procedure whereby the court lends its assistance to the complainant to supply deficiencies in his formal statement of complaint – is allowed only in certain cases specified by the law, usually those in which the complainant can be considered as needing special protection.[34] So, too, for England, it is said that 'the generally accepted principle is that a court should reach a decision only on the arguments presented by counsel', because of the need, 'in a truly adversarial system, to allow counsel to produce evidence in the form of arguments, and to decide the case on the basis of those arguments which the judge believes to be correct, or the more persuasive'.[35] It is accepted, however, that too close adherence to such a principle can lead to injustice,[36] and in the dialogue between counsel and judge, which is a regular feature of the common law trial, a suggestion from the judge to counsel in the course of argument – perhaps a reference to a precedent decision not yet mentioned by counsel – is perfectly normal.

The position where counsel declines to accept a suggestion from the judge that is favourable to his client's case, is less clear, but it is not difficult to find cases which have been decided on the basis of a concession of a point of law made by one side, even where the judge himself considers the concession to have been wrongly made.[37] The position is, perhaps, similar to that envisaged by the French code, according to which the parties may by agreement, and subject to certain exceptions, limit the judge's consideration to those points of law alone which they wish to have discussed.[38]

Whatever the position where the parties decline to accept a suggestion from the judge, there seems to be no doubt that he can make one when opportunity offers – he can scarcely be prevented from doing so – and where he does, then, certainly, he discloses his personal knowledge and opens it to discussion. The critical question is whether he can do more – that is to say, whether he can ground his decision on a point of law without having first disclosed the point he has in mind and invited the parties to comment on it. On this question the answers given by different legal systems are not unanimous.

Negative

The negative view – insistence on disclosure – is most strongly asserted in France where the Conseil d'Etat actually struck down, as contrary to

[34] Ley de Amparo, art. 76: Mexico, pp. 62–7.
[35] England, pp. 23–4.   [36] *Ibid.*
[37] E.g. *Imperial Chemical Industries v. Caro* [1961] 1 W.L.R. 529, 541–2.
[38] N.c.p.c., art. 12, al. 4. Above, chap. 10, p. 191.

'general principles of law', a provision in the code that purported to allow the judge to take points of law of his own motion without submitting them to debate.[39] According to the amended form of the code, while the judge may still take points of law of his own motion, 'il ne peut fonder sa décision sur les moyens de droit qu'il a relevés d'office sans avoir au préalable invité les parties à présenter leurs observations'.[40]

Positive

The contrary view, adopted, it appears, in other non-common law countries, takes the maxim *iura novit curia* at its face value,[41] and the same is, it seems, true for Israel: there, the judge is not only authorised but required to carry out his own legal research.[42] In a slightly attenuated form, the positive solution is also adopted in the United States, where the judges are not required to rely on counsel for help in finding the law, though they usually do so; notice of their intention to rely on law not submitted to them need not be given, provided that the parties have a subsequent opportunity to seek reconsideration of the decision or to exercise a right of appeal.[43]

Although it is clear in, for example, Argentina, the Federal Republic of Germany, Italy, Japan and the Netherlands, that the judge must apply the law as he finds it to be, treating the legal submissions of the parties as mere 'suggestions' and without the duty to invite discussion on his own view of the law, an important limitation to this may follow, as it does in the Federal Republic of Germany, from the rule that it is for the parties to present the facts. The choices made by the parties in their allegations of fact depend on the legal rules to be applied, and, because the court should not take the parties by surprise, the code provides that the judge must inform the parties if he proposes to base his decision on a legal rule they have overlooked.[44]

Equivocal

Some uncertainty on the point under discussion is revealed by English law,[45] and the position is similar in Australia[46] and New Zealand.[47] According to one view, the judge may do his own research after the argument has been concluded, and if he finds that the argument has proceeded on the basis of an erroneous proposition of law he should

[39] Conseil d'Etat, 12 October 1979, J.C.P. 1980, II, 19288.
[40] N.c.p.c., art. 16, al. 3; France, pp. 13–14. See chap. 10, p. 194.
[41] Argentina, pp. 6–7; GDR, pp. 11–12; FRG, p. 14; Italy, pp. 1–2; Japan, pp. 4–5; Netherlands, pp. 3–4.
[42] Israel, pp. 20–1.   [43] USA, pp. 21–2.   [44] FRG, p. 14.
[45] England, pp. 21–6.   [46] Australia, pp. 16–18.   [47] New Zealand, p. 6.

correct it rather than let it 'continue to disturb the course of justice'. But, in the same case as that in which those words were used by one judge in the Court of Appeal, another dissented strongly from them, insisting that the rule *audi alteram partem* 'applies alike to issues of law as of fact'.[48]

The latter view is, probably, the more accurately representative of prevailing English law;[49] it has even been said that cases in which the judge has made undisclosed use of his personal knowledge of the law are 'generally recognised as contrary to principle and a flagrant departure from the principles underpinning the adversarial system'.[50] This is, probably, to put the point too forcefully; the Israeli view that, once the parties have had their day in court, it is their fault if arguments have been overlooked,[51] would not be accepted in England. On the other hand, the cost, both in time and in money, of calling the parties back to a reconvened hearing is so great that such a solution cannot always be adopted. The problem can probably be overcome by inviting counsel to put their observations to the judge in writing.[52]

General facts

There is, as might be expected, virtual unanimity of view that the judge may use his personal knowledge of the ordinary course of human affairs, his 'general knowledge', his 'common sense'. Otherwise, of course, it would be impossible for him to perform his judicial function in relation to disputed questions of fact. Only in Israel does there seem to have been some hesitation about this basic proposition, but the prevailing view now seems to be that personal knowledge may be used, provided that this is not prejudicial to the rights of the parties.[53]

That may imply that disclosure to the parties is a condition of the judge's use of all personal knowledge, and the same seems to be true for the Federal Republic of Germany, especially since the 1976 amendments to the code of civil procedure. The principle does not, however, extend to ordinary rules of experience that are self-evident and which, obviously, the judge will take into account.[54] In the Netherlands the judge has a positive duty to apply the rules of experience, the knowledge of everyday life,[55] and in the United States 'both judges and juries as

[48] *Goldsmith* v. *Sperrings Ltd* [1977] 1 W.L.R. 478, 486, *per* Lord Denning M.R. and at 508, *per* Bridge L.J. respectively.
[49] Chap. 10, pp. 192 and 194.
[50] England, pp. 25–6.   [51] Israel, p. 21.
[52] New Zealand, p. 6. See also *Hoecheong Products Ltd* v. *Cargill Ltd* [1995] 1 W.L.R. 404, 409, *per* Lord Mustill, above, chap. 10, p. 194.
[53] Israel, pp. 12–13.   [54] FRG, pp. 9–11.   [55] Netherlands, p. 8.

triers of fact utilize much non-adjudicative fact of a generalized character – most often without explicit statement simply as part of the
reasoning process, to which formalized rules of judicial notice, such as a
requirement to be heard on the propriety of using them, are inappropriate'.[56] It is intrinsically probable that, *mutatis mutandis*, a similar
statement could be made for other countries' legal systems.

If what has been said is true for the ordinary rules of experience –
matters of fact known to every adult member of society – it does not
follow that it is also true for matters of fact which, though 'general', are
not part of common knowledge but are, more or less, specialised. If the
judge happens to have personal knowledge of, say, medicine or the laws
of physics, may he make use of that knowledge or must he rely upon the
supply of information to him by experts?

Occasionally, a specific rule of law requires the supply of information
by an expert, and then the judge may not rely, or, rather, may not rely
exclusively, on his personal knowledge – he cannot be prevented from
using his knowledge in performance of his duty to consider the information that the expert has provided.[57] Subject to that, the former Soviet
Union was unusual in insisting generally on the use of an expert: there,
the use of an expert was mandatory whenever the decision called for
'special scientific, technological, art or craft knowledge'.[58] In Japan the
question is controversial,[59] but elsewhere, while the use of experts is not
mandatory, differences of attitude emerge between, on the one hand,
countries of the common law, in which experts are witnesses called by
the parties, and, on the other hand, non-common law countries, where
they are entrusted with their task by the judge himself and are regarded
not as witnesses but as assistants or auxiliaries of the judge.

Expert as witness
Such is the strength of the adversary tradition of common law procedure
that, even where the judge is entitled to call of his own motion for the
assistance of an expert, he does so in exceptional circumstances only. In
England, for example, the court may, in any case, call in aid one or more
technically qualified 'assessors', but in practice this power is used only in
cases of maritime collision.[60] In principle it is for the party upon whom
a particular burden of proof rests, to call such expert witnesses as he

---

[56] USA, p. 19.
[57] *R. v. Field Justices, ex parte White* (1895) 64 L.J.M.C. 158, 159–60, *per* Wills J.
[58] USSR, pp. 7–8.   [59] Japan, pp. 13–16.
[60] Law Reform Committee, Seventeenth Report (Evidence of Opinion and Expert
Evidence) 1970, Cmnd 4489, paras. 11 and 12. Greater use of assessors is now
recommended: Woolf Interim, p. 187; Woolf Final, p. 59; chap. 12, n. 88.

considers necessary, and his opponent can call his expert witnesses in reply. It is, then, inevitably for the judge to decide between any conflicting expert testimony there may be: it has even been said to be his 'constitutional' duty to do so.[61]

In this situation, if the judge has relevant scientific or technical knowledge of his own, he can scarcely avoid making use of it to understand and evaluate the expert evidence which has been given,[62] and it may even occur that a particular judge is assigned to a particular case because of his personal knowledge of a particular science. In one English case the critical question concerned the sex of a person who had undergone a 'sex change' operation, and a great deal of scientific evidence was given about human sexual characteristics; the judge assigned to the case – by accident or design – was himself medically as well as legally qualified.[63]

As a general rule, however, the question is dealt with in terms of burden of proof. A judge may take the view, for example, that a plaintiff has failed to prove the negligence of a surgeon because he provided no evidence of usual professional practice in like circumstances, against which the defendant surgeon's conduct could be measured, and a similar result may follow if the expert evidence in favour of a finding of negligence is balanced by equally strong expert evidence against. A judge is not justified in finding negligence simply because he preferred one body of respectable medical opinion to another.[64] It may happen, however, that the judge, having heard the plaintiff's evidence, including expert evidence, concludes on the basis of 'common sense' or general lay understanding that a *prima facie* case has been established, which *prima facie* case the defendant may be able to displace only by calling expert testimony himself.[65]

It is not surprising, therefore, that the use of expert witnesses is widespread. Indeed, in the interests of economy, efforts are made to restrict their excessive use, in England by appropriate rules of procedure[66] and in some states of the United States by reading the word 'only' into legislation that permits the use of experts where an expert

---

[61] Law Reform Committee's Report, para. 13. For the changes introduced by the C.P.R., see chap. 12, postscript, above.

[62] *R.* v. *Field Justices, ex parte White*, (1895) 64 L.J.M.C. 158.

[63] *Corbett* v. *Corbett* [1971] P. 83.

[64] See, e.g. USA, p. 21 and the English case of *Maynard* v. *West Midlands RHA* [1984] 1 W.L.R. 634. Paradoxically, but understandably, English judges are readier to exercise their own judgment where the question is whether a legal practitioner was guilty of negligence: *G. & K. Ladenbau Ltd* v. *Crawley and de Reya* [1978] 1 W.L.R. 266; *Edward Wong Ltd* v. *Johnson, Stokes* [1984] A.C. 296.

[65] As in *Brown* v. *Rolls Royce* [1960] 1 W.L.R. 210.

[66] Above, chap. 12, p. 236 and postscript.

opinion would 'assist' the judge: expert testimony is then excluded when the judge considers that 'common knowledge' is sufficient.[67] This cannot fail to increase use by the judge of his personal knowledge to the extent that he considers appropriate in the case before him.

It is doubtful whether greater precision is possible in this uncertain area. As an English judge has observed, 'All that can be said is that, within reasonable and proper limits, a judge . . . may make use of his specialist knowledge on general matters, but no formula has yet been evolved for describing those limits.'[68]

Expert as auxiliary

Even if, as in France,[69] it is specifically laid down in the code that the judge should not act so as to cure a party's default in the administration of proofs, where the expert is an auxiliary of the judge, the judge is usually free to decide whether to seek assistance from an expert or whether he can rely upon his own knowledge. It is, however, recognised that, on a technical matter, the judge should normally call upon an expert rather than rely on his personal knowledge even if he believes it to be adequate: otherwise he would be suspected or even presumed, in relying on his own knowledge, to have denied the parties their right to be heard.[70] Similarly, in the Federal Republic of Germany, if the judge does consider his own knowledge to be sufficient on a technical question, he may rely on it, but he will have to explain why he chose not to call on an expert; he will also have to disclose his use of his own knowledge in such a way as to make it clear to the parties what he has done, and thereby to open it to debate.[71]

In Italy and the Netherlands the position according to the texts seems to be different. In both countries the appointment of an expert is at the discretion of the judge, who may use his personal knowledge, if he has it, on a technical question, but in neither do the texts require disclosure to the parties. However, in Italy, though this is in accordance with the code of civil procedure, it may not be in accordance with the Constitution. In the Netherlands, a decision of the Hoge Raad in 1985 effectively requires disclosure.[72]

---

[67] USA, p. 20.

[68] *Dawson* v. *Lunn*, *The Times*, 13 December 1984, *per* Goff L.J.; cited, England, p. 31, n. 34.

[69] France, p. 16 (n.c.p.c., art. 146).

[70] France, p. 17.   [71] FRG, pp. 11–13.

[72] See Italy, pp. 9–13; Netherlands, pp. 9–10.

Foreign language

Courts will, normally, recognise only one 'official' language,[73] but this does not mean that material in another language – including the oral testimony of a witness – cannot be used. If the judge happens to have personal knowledge of that other language, can he make use of it, or is he bound to have regard only to its translation into the language of the court?

It is, of course, impossible to prevent a judge from using his knowledge of a foreign language when he hears it spoken by a witness, whether interpretation is provided or not,[74] or when he sees a document. And if in coming to his decision the judge prefers his own to the interpreter's understanding, this will usually be impossible to detect if, indeed, the judge is aware of it himself. A question of greater importance, and a real one, may, however, arise when the applicable rule is contained in a text written in a foreign language, or where it exists in more than one authentic version, as may happen in the case of international conventions that are incorporated into domestic law.[75]

For many countries it can be inferred from their acceptance of the maxim *iura novit curia*, with the gloss that the judge is called upon to research the law for himself, that he may resort to foreign language materials to the extent that he is able and considers it useful to do so. This seems inherent, for example, in the statement for Japan that the judge may, 'on his own motion investigate the law as he sees fit'[76] and in the statement for Italy that the judge can 'find the rule of law by any means'.[77] For the former German Democratic Republic it was stated explicitly that the judges could use their knowledge of foreign languages in interpreting documents, but that translations must be supplied in order to ensure openness of the proceedings.[78] In the United States, on the other hand, although the judge may use 'whatever sources are appropriate' to find the law, it is held that the meaning of words in a foreign language is not 'a proper subject for judicial notice', and that 'the judge's *personal, extra-judicial* knowledge of foreign languages is ordinarily to be excluded'.[79]

The question has received most attention in Israel, where some of the written law in force is in languages other than Hebrew; it has also

---

[73] The use of regional languages may be permitted where appropriate, as it is in Wales (Welsh Language Act 1993, s. 22).

[74] Interpretation is normally required: e.g. Argentina, p. 3; GDR, p. 8.

[75] The following observations are not specifically directed to the ascertainment of foreign law when required by a conflict of laws rule.

[76] Japan, p. 5.   [77] Italy, p. 14.   [78] GDR, p. 8.

[79] USA, pp. 21 and 16 (emphasis in original). It is not explained how this can be achieved.

received some attention in England, especially in cases involving multi-lingual conventions. In neither country is there any general ban on the use by the judge of his linguistic abilities.

In England, in 1976, Lawton L.J. justified his reference to the French text of a convention on the ground that it must be permissible for a judge to show 'a modicum of knowledge of a European language which for some centuries in its archaic form was the language of our courts and which in more modern times has been the language of diplomacy'.[80] Though some members of the House of Lords were unenthusiastic about this,[81] in a later case in which both the English and the French texts of an international convention had been incorporated into English law, the House agreed that a judge could use his own knowledge of a foreign language but should keep the parties informed so that they can supplement his resources if they so wish. No hard and fast rule can be laid down and flexibility is essential because, 'between a technical expression in Japanese and a plain word in French there must be a whole spectrum which calls for suitable and individual treatment'.[82] A judge may even use, for the purposes of his judgment, his own translation from a foreign language as was done, for example, in the case just mentioned where Lord Wilberforce cited, in his own translation, an extract from the *conclusions* of the avocat général in a case before the French Cour de cassation.[83]

In Israel, matters have been carried further. Judges have used their own linguistic knowledge to check the translations into English of the Turkish of the Mejelle, a judge has come to his decision after comparing Arabic, English and French translations of a provision in the Ottoman law of civil procedure, and Supreme Court justices, using their knowledge of French, have sought guidance to its interpretation in the Napoleonic code from which it was derived.[84]

At this point, however, a complication arises which, at least in countries that acknowledge the force of precedent, could lead to a restriction on the judge's right to use his personal knowledge of a foreign language. In an Israeli case decided in 1952 the judge of first instance had used his own knowledge of the Turkish language, and the interpretation he gave to the legislation was commended in the Supreme Court. That court nevertheless adopted a different interpretation, partly, at

---

[80] *Buchanan & Co. v. Babcock Ltd* [1977] Q.B. 208, 223. For earlier use by judges of their own knowledge of French, see *Smith v. Wheatcroft* (1878) 9 Ch.D. 223 and the other cases cited in England, p. 16.

[81] *Buchanan & Co. v. Babcock Ltd* [1978] A.C. 141, 167, *per* Lord Edmund-Davies; *ibid.* at 170, *per* Lord Fraser. Cf. *ibid.* at 152, *per* Lord Wilberforce.

[82] *Fothergill v. Monarch Airlines* [1981] A.C. 252, 274, *per* Lord Wilberforce.

[83] [1981] A.C. 252, 277.   [84] Israel, pp. 10–12.

least, because that interpretation had been followed in the past and had itself been approved by a judge of the Supreme Court.[85] It may be expected that, as the need to use foreign language material develops in countries other than Israel, a similar restriction on the use by judges of their personal knowledge of foreign languages will also develop through the force of precedent.

Direct perception

Litigation is a process which continues over a period of time, and as the proceedings develop the judge cannot fail to use his personal knowledge as a means to the understanding and appreciation of what he perceives in their course. So, for example, when oral testimony is taken at a trial in the common law manner, it is for the judge (or jury) not merely to listen to and follow what the witnesses say, but to observe their demeanour under examination in order to assess their credibility and the value of their testimony. Subject to this, however, direct perception by the judge ordinarily contributes little to the formation of his decision: the information that is conveyed to him in the course of the proceedings comes in the form of words.

This is not the case, however, when 'real evidence' – that is, a physical object – is produced and examined by the judge, and it is not the case when the judge visits and views a location with which the litigation is concerned or to which it relates. Even so, the judge's attention will commonly be directed (by words) to certain aspects of what he sees for himself, but this does not mean that the information he obtains is limited to what he is told. And what he perceives for himself can be interpreted by him only in the light of his personal knowledge.

Where the judge accedes to a party's request that he personally examine an object or proceed to a view, then, though the judge's personal knowledge is engaged, no particular problem is raised since this must be assumed to be in accord with that party's intention; but even so there may be limits to what the judge may do. So, in Israel, there has been dissent from the idea that a judge may himself compare two samples of handwriting because graphology 'is a subject which is a real science and we have no judicial notice of it', and it has also been held more generally in that country that if a professional specialisation is involved, then the judge should not rely on an experiment done by him or by the parties in his presence.[86] Similarly, in England, the conviction of a person accused of using motor tyres with insufficient tread was set

[85] C.A. 62/52 *Dayan* v. *Abuttul* 9 P.D. 1047, cited in Israel, p. 11.
[86] Israel, p. 14.

aside because the lay justices, to whom the tyres were produced, procured a gauge and measured their tread themselves. They did so, however, in private and the accused thus had no opportunity to challenge either their knowledge of the way in which such a gauge should be used or their actual use of it. Had they conducted their 'experiment' in open court the result might have been different.[87]

In most cases the judge will examine an object or proceed to a view following a request from a party that he should do so, but in many countries, including England, he may do so of his own motion and even against the expressed wishes of the parties: that, at least, has been stated by one English judge.[88] If, then, the judge decides of his own motion to proceed to a view, he also decides for himself to make use of his personal knowledge; in some countries he may even supplement it by requiring an expert to accompany him. On the other hand, it is provided in many codes of procedure that the judge must make an appropriate order giving the time and place of the view, thereby giving the parties the opportunity to be present and to make representations.[89]

Paradoxical as it may seem in light of the general adherence of English law to the adversary tradition, no such formal requirement exists there. Normally, no doubt, the parties will know and will have the opportunity to be present if the judge decides upon a view, and this is mandatory if what is intended is some kind of demonstration or reconstruction. But there is apparently no objection to the judge going informally and alone to see some public place 'where all that is involved is the presence of the judge using his eyes to see in three dimensions and true colour something which had previously been represented to him in plan and photograph'.[90] So, in one case, the Court of Appeal upheld the decision made by a judge following such an informal view, a view which, as the judge made clear in his judgment, had greatly influenced his understanding of the facts.[91]

Specialist courts and tribunals, and local courts

These three categories of adjudicative authority can be grouped together for present purposes. Their common feature is that their judges – not

[87] R. v. *Tiverton JJ., ex parte Smith* [1981] R.T.R. 280; England, pp. 7–8.
[88] *Tito* v. *Waddell* [1975] 1 W.L.R. 1303, 1306, *per* Megarry J. The English rule is different in relation to the production of articles in court, but a party's failure to make relevant production may lead to an adverse inference against him: R. Cross and C. Tapper, *Evidence*, 8th edn (1995), p. 49.
[89] E.g. Argentina, p. 5; France, pp. 15–16; FRG, p. 8; Israel, p. 5; Mexico, p. 60; Netherlands, p. 15. The position in Italy may be otherwise: Italy, pp. 2, 4 and 10–13.
[90] *Goold* v. *Evans* [1951] 2 T.L.R. 1189, 1191, *per* Denning L.J.
[91] *Salsbury* v. *Woodland* [1970] 1 Q.B. 324.

always professional members of the judiciary – have or acquire personal knowledge not only of the relevant areas of the law but also of relevant general facts or, in the case of local courts, even of particular facts.

The concept of a 'local' court may be strange in countries where the jurisdiction of all courts of first instance is limited geographically, but elsewhere, as in England, only courts whose jurisdiction is limited *ratione materiae*, such as the county courts, are also restricted geographically. In England, it is now recognised that the judges of county courts may, within certain limits, take into account their own knowledge of general conditions in the neighbourhood,[92] but a similar result is achieved in, for example, Japan, where it is accepted that a fact may be 'notorious' for the purpose of judicial notice if it is sufficiently well known in the locality in which the court sits, even if it is not well known throughout the country.[93]

In some countries there are deep-rooted objections to the creation of special 'tribunals', that is, special adjudicative bodies created by the legislature to handle particular kinds of litigation which are, usually, separate from the regular hierarchy of courts.[94] Elsewhere the number of such 'tribunals' may be very large.[95] There is also, in some countries, a general view that, in principle, ordinary judges should have the competence to try cases of every kind.[96] Nevertheless, in one way or another, specialist adjudication is by no means unusual, both in the shape of specialised divisions or chambers of the Supreme Court or at first instance. This is, of course, in addition to the kind of specialisation that is found where more than one system of law exists, as with the ordinary and the administrative jurisdictions of countries which have followed the French model or, as in Israel, where special religious courts act in certain kinds of case.[97]

Where specialisation is found at the level of the Supreme Court, especially if it is a court of cassation rather than appeal, then, no doubt,

[92] *Reynolds* v. *Llanelly Tin Plate Co.* [1948] 1 All E.R. 140; England, pp. 9–14. The limits may be difficult to define. See, e.g. the two criminal cases cited in Australia, p. 10.

[93] Japan, p. 7. In one sense, of course, all national courts are 'local', and this affects the kind of fact of which judicial notice may be taken. See, e.g. *Malone* v. *Smith* (1946) 3 W.N. (N.S.W.) 54, cited in Australia, p. 9.

[94] Italy, pp. 16–17. The Constitution forbids the setting up of special courts. Although specialised sections within the regular courts are allowed, little use has been made of the possibility.

[95] England, pp. 17–18; New Zealand, pp. 6–7.

[96] GDR, pp. 12–13, but note the interesting Italian method of achieving a measure of specialisation by channelling all cases of a particular kind to a particular district court; Italy, p. 16. The report for the former USSR, in which country there were no formally specialised courts of first instance, contains a valuable discussion of the advantages and disadvantages of specialisation: USSR, pp. 11–16.

[97] Israel, pp. 25–6.

it can be claimed that the specialist personal knowledge of the judges relates to law rather than to fact. Even leaving out of account the special tribunals, however, there are many specialist courts of first instance for which it is actually seen to be desirable that the judge should have specialist knowledge. Thus, for example, France has its Tribunal de commerce, its Conseil de Prud'hommes, and so on, with specially qualified judges; England has its Restrictive Practices Court, its Industrial Tribunals and Employment Appeal Tribunal, and so on, of which two of the three judges are not legally qualified but are selected for their relevant knowledge and experience.[98] In these cases, personal knowledge of non-legal matters is regarded as a positive advantage, and the same in reality is true of such specialist courts in England as the Admiralty Court, the Commercial Court and the Patents Court,[99] in each of which the judge, though a professional judge of the High Court sitting alone, is nominated to the court in question because of his special expertise in the relevant field. That expertise is not, and cannot be, restricted to matters of law strictly so-called: in the case of the Commercial Court, for example, it is known that the judges are expected to have, and to make use of, extensive knowledge of commercial practice in general.[100]

Conclusion

It was suggested in the opening paragraph that the subject of this chapter lies at the heart of the judicial process. On the one hand, it seems to be the antithesis of that process that litigation should be decided by the judge on the basis of his personal knowledge – knowledge he has acquired independently of the litigation on which he is engaged. On the other hand, even if it were possible, it would be altogether undesirable that a judge should enter upon his task in each case as if he were not merely a computer, but a computer that has not yet been programmed. Compromise is both inevitable and essential, and it is a proper observation for a comparative lawyer that it is for each legal system to work out and develop for itself the particular compromise that best meets the needs of the society it exists to serve.

The force of this observation is increased rather than diminished by the near non-existence of positive law explicitly directed to the subject of

[98] Many other examples could be given. See, e.g. FRG, pp. 16–18; Israel, pp. 22–5. The commonest kind of specialist court appears to be that concerned with labour cases.

[99] These 'Courts' are all parts of one division or another of the High Court. See also chap. 8, p. 171 for the Crown Office List.

[100] See 'F.D.M.', 'The Origin of the Commercial Court' (1944) 60 L.Q.R. 324.

this chapter – more depends on inference, on the unspoken assumptions of a legal system, than on its rules of procedure or law of evidence. That said, the following concluding observations may be made.

1. Leaving out of account those cases in which a judge acts to all intents and purposes as an administrator, it is an inherent characteristic of the judicial process that the judge is a third party to a dispute between the parties litigant, and that he only learns of that dispute when it is brought to his attention by a party. The law prescribes the methods whereby the court is informed, or may inform itself, of the details and surrounding circumstances of the dispute, and it is, therefore, also inherent in the judicial process that the court must acquire that information in accordance with the prescribed methods or not at all. If the judge happens to have personal knowledge relevant to the issue he has to decide, he must dismiss it from his mind or disqualify himself. That is the 'rule of exclusion' in its pure form and, though it is taken by many to be the basic rule, it is in reality more an exception than a rule. It applies only to 'material' facts and to a relatively restricted class of other 'particular' facts. It extends neither to 'general' facts nor to well-known 'particular' facts.

2. There is no general objection to use by the judge of his personal knowledge as a source of questions or suggestions which he may put to the parties in the course of the proceedings, but whether he may go further – whether he may, of his own motion, pursue, or cause to be pursued, enquiries which his personal knowledge suggests as being potentially useful – depends on the character of the procedural system in question. In the traditional common law systems, subject to certain possibly anomalous exceptions, he cannot. Elsewhere, as a general rule, and within limits, he can:

Connaissances personnelles du juge et mesures d'instruction! Encore une fois on aperçoit que le juge civil n'est pas un simple 'récepteur' et peut vouloir chercher à savoir ce que ni l'une ni l'autre partie n'auraient souhaité lui soumettre. Ainsi d'office . . . le juge peut ordonner toutes les mesures d'instruction légalement admissibles.[101]

3. With certain exceptions, exceptions that are generally subject to adverse criticism, the personal knowledge of which the judge proposes to make use, must be disclosed to the parties and their observations must be invited. Only thus can the *principe du contradictoire* be sustained. As is recognised by some commentators, however, there must be limits even to this: it is not necessary that every elementary proposition whether of fact or law, be opened to debate. The limits are probably

---

[101] France, p. 16.

impossible to define. They depend on the good sense of the judge – whether he considers the proposition in question to be reasonably susceptible to contradiction or not – and ultimately to the view of a court of appeal or cassation. It may, perhaps, be suggested that there is a concept of 'judicial knowledge' which consists, essentially, of the knowledge which a judge must possess if he is to be able to perform his task. The extent of such knowledge thus depends on the nature of the judge's task, and may extend in some countries to 'legislative facts'.[102] Nevertheless, save for matters that are not capable of reasonable controversy, whenever the judge proposes to make use of his personal knowledge then, as a general principle, he must make his intention clear to the parties and invite discussion. The limits are rather those dictated by the need for common-sense economy of time than by clear considerations of principle.

4. Reference has been made earlier to the observation that 'the principle of fair proceedings requires that the subject of litigation should be independent of the judge's unpredictable and incalculable knowledge'. This does not mean, however – it neither can nor should mean – that the personal knowledge of the judge must in all respects be excluded from the decision-making process. On the contrary, in the last resort, it is an essential of human justice that judicial decisions be informed by the personality of the judge who makes them.

Ne peut-on pas concevoir qu'un ordinateur reçoive des informations, – qui ne seraient jamais des connaissances personnelles de l'ordinateur et ne seraient pas non plus des connaissances personnelles de juges puisqu'elles émaneraient d'un vaste collège d'informateurs, – si nombreuses, si étendues, si variées et si subtiles qu'elles donneraient à cette machine une faculté de réponse supérieure à celle dont dispose un juge moyen? Certainement si! Mais il semblerait à tous que la justice rendue par un tel engin serait celle de l'un de ces mondes froids et implacables dont regorge la littérature d'imagination. Pourquoi? l'appareil pourrait bien rendre une justice exacte! Mais il n'est pas de vraie justice sans le filtre incertain, subjectif, hasardeux mais toujours humain de la conscience et de l'individualité du juge.[103]

---

[102] See note 8, above and USA, pp. 22–3; Australia, pp. 7–8.
[103] France, p. 21.

This chapter draws on the following national reports:
Argentina: Santiago Nino;
Australia: M.S. Weinberg, Australian Reports to 12 I.A.C.L. 269;
England: Yates, in Banakas, *United Kingdom Law*, see n. 1, above;
France: Huguette and Germain le Foyer de Costil, 1986 Rev.int.dr.comp. 517;
FRG: Coester Waltjen;
GDR: H. Kietz, East German Reports to 12 I.A.C.L. 55;
Israel: S. Ottolenghi, Israeli Reports to 12 I.A.C.L. 248;
Italy: M. Taruffo, Italian Reports to 12 I.A.C.L. 221;
Japan: H. Matsumoto;

Mexico: Flores García (1986) 36 *Revista de la Facultad de Derecho de México* 67;
Netherlands: R. W. Holzhauer, Netherlands Reports to 12 I.A.C.L. 233;
New Zealand: G. P. Barton;
USA: W. B. Fisch (1986) 34 (Suppl.) Am.Jo.Comp.Law 237;
USSR: V. M. Savitsky.

The following reports were also received:
Belgium: J. Krings;
Canada: C. Fabian (1987) 66 Can. Bar Rev. 433;
Philippines: M. A. Maceren.

Part V

Recourse against judgments

14   Civil appeals in England and Wales[1]

Rights of appeal

Final decisions

In certain restricted circumstances and only with leave, an appeal may be taken directly from the High Court to the House of Lords, 'leap-frogging' over the Court of Appeal.[2] Subject to this, until 1999, appeal to the Court of Appeal lay as of right from final decisions of the High Court, and, provided that the 'value of the appeal' was sufficient, also from final decisions of the county court. Now, however, leave ('permission') is required in all cases, with the exception of three special classes of case all affecting the liberty of the subject.[3] Further appeal is possible from the Court of Appeal to the House of Lords, but leave is always required.[4]

Interlocutory decisions[5]

In the High Court, interlocutory decisions are made in the first instance by a 'Master', or, in the provinces, by a district judge, not by a High

---

[1] Based on a report to the IXth World Congress on Procedural Law in Coimbra and Lisbon, 1991, published (in French) 1992 Rev.int.dr.comp. 355. For reforms proposed in Bowman, see postscript to this chapter.

[2] Administration of Justice Act 1969, ss. 12–15.

[3] R.S.C., Ord. 59, r. 1B as amended under the C.P.R. The change was brought in on 1 January 1999 by *Practice Direction (Court of Appeal: Leave to Appeal and Skeleton Arguments)* [1999] 1 W.L.R. 2.

[4] Administration of Justice (Appeals) Act 1934. Leave to appeal to the House of Lords may be granted either by the Court of Appeal, at the end of the hearing, or, on petition, by the House of Lords itself. This is in accord with the general principle that, where leave to appeal is required, it may be granted either by the court *a quo* or by the court *ad quem*. Leave may sometimes be refused by the Court of Appeal in order to allow the House of Lords to decide for itself whether the appeal should be entertained.

[5] Now that leave to appeal is required generally, the complexities of the distinction between final and interlocutory decisions under R.S.C., Ord. 59, r. 1A are no longer necessary and have disappeared, but the distinction itself survives.

Court judge. From him appeal lies as of right to such a judge.[6] Further appeal to the Court of Appeal and the House of Lords is possible, but only with leave. In the county court, interlocutory decisions are usually made by the district judge and there is an appeal to the judge.[7] Any further appeal to the Court of Appeal lies only with leave.[8]

Powers of appellate courts

Substantive

The Court of Appeal has 'all the authority and jurisdiction of the court or tribunal from which the appeal was brought'.[9] For the House of Lords the language is different and more antiquated: the House must decide 'what of right and according to the law and custom of this realm ought to be done in the subject matter of the appeal'.[10] For practical purposes, however, the two formulae produce the same result. If the court *a quo* is a tribunal of fact as well as law, so too is the appellate court. If, on the other hand, the court *a quo* has only limited power to reconsider findings of fact, as on an application for judicial review, then the appellate court's powers are similarly restricted.

The powers of an appellate court thus depend on the nature of the case at hand, but, in ordinary civil cases and subject to what is said below, it is generally true that the appeal is not restricted to a review of the decision at first instance; the court considers the decision as a whole (unless the appeal is brought against a part of the decision only) and must give its own decision even if, in the result, it does no more than dismiss the appeal.

Procedural

Like procedure at first instance, appellate procedure is divided between the preparatory stage and the hearing. Applications to and orders from the court at this stage are dealt with separately from the decision-making process itself. Traditionally, all activity during the preparatory stage is

---

[6] R.S.C., Ord. 58.

[7] Formerly 'Registrar', see Courts and Legal Services Act 1990, s. 74. The district judge also has a limited jurisdiction to decide relatively small cases, subject to appeal to the county court judge.

[8] An appeal to the Court of Appeal from an interlocutory decision in the county court is extremely rare.

[9] Supreme Court Act 1981, s. 15(3).

[10] Appellate Jurisdiction Act 1876, s. 4.

for the parties, but the Registrar of Civil Appeals[11] has for some time
exercised a power of initiative on certain matters, and now there are
'Supervising Lords Justices' who will give directions concerning the
progress and future conduct of a case either on application or of their
own motion. In addition, where leave to appeal has been granted by a
single Lord Justice, it is expected that he will give directions for the
future conduct of the case.[12]

The introduction of Supervising Lords Justices was effected by
Practice Direction, and it is accepted doctrine that any court has the
power, subject to the rules, to regulate its own procedure. In recent
years the Court of Appeal has made substantial use of that power,
sometimes by way of judicial decision but frequently by way of 'Practice
Note' or 'Practice Direction', thereby supplementing the rules of court.
Two other important aspects of the Court of Appeal's exercise of its
power may be mentioned:

(i) Time limits. The time limits within which the necessary procedural acts should be performed are specified in the rules but
there is a general power vested in the court to extend or abridge
these time limits.[13] A time limit is unlikely to be abridged unless
the case is urgent, but, in the past, extensions of time were
commonly agreed between the parties and, if not, were liberally
granted by the Court. In a decision of 1983, however, the Court
warned that its attitude to 'the previous lax practices' was hard-
ening;[14] time limits will be enforced unless there are good
grounds for granting an extension.[15] As observed by Lord
Donaldson M.R., once the time for appealing has elapsed, the
respondent is entitled to regard the judgment already given in his

[11] The Registrar has both judicial and administrative functions. His judicial decisions are
subject to appeal to a Lord Justice. Applications for leave to appeal are, however,
usually considered in the first instance by a single Lord Justice on the papers: *Practice
Note* [1995] 1 W.L.R. 1191, paras. 5–8.
[12] *Practice Direction (Court of Appeal: Skeleton Arguments and Case Management)* [1997] 1
W.L.R. 1535. Directions should, so far as possible, be dealt with on paper, and if a
hearing is necessary the Supervising Lord Justice will have read the papers so that
advocates should make their points immediately without opening or preamble. It is
stated specifically that hearings should not develop into 'satellite litigation'.
[13] Formerly explicit (R.S.C., Ord. 3, r. 5) the power is now contained in the court's
general power of case management: C.P.R., r. 1.4. It is not unknown, though
admittedly it is rare, that an appeal is heard on the same day as the judgment appealed
from was delivered. See, e.g. *Attorney-General v. IBA* [1973] Q.B. 629.
[14] *C. M. Stillevoldt BV v. E. L. Carriers Ltd* [1983] 1 W.L.R. 207, 212, *per* Griffiths L.J.
The parties may no longer vary any date set by the Order or by the court for the doing
of any act: R.S.C., Ord. 59, r. 2C, as inserted under the C.P.R.
[15] *Practice Direction (Court of Appeal: Procedure)* [1995] 1 W.L.R. 1191.

favour as final; he should only be deprived of that entitlement on the basis of a discretionary balancing exercise by the court.[16]

(ii) Skeleton arguments. There is nothing in the Rules of Court or other legislation to require written submissions in advance of the hearing of an appeal and there is nothing to restrict the time allowed for oral argument. The advent of skeleton arguments has, however, brought with it changes in practice.

In 1983, Lord Donaldson M.R. noted that, in complex cases, the voluntary submission by counsel of skeleton arguments, which could be read by the Court in advance of the hearing, was of value in reducing the time necessary for the hearing. At that time, however, he did not consider it appropriate to make the submission of skeleton arguments a matter of Direction: whether they were necessary and what they should contain depended on the peculiarities of the appeal concerned.[17] Six years later, however, by a Practice Direction issued by the Court under Lord Donaldson M.R., skeleton arguments were made compulsory in virtually all cases and were required to be lodged in the Court not less than four weeks before the hearing.[18]

In the Practice Direction of 1989 it was clearly stated that the purpose of skeleton arguments is not to present argument, only to identify the points to be argued, giving the relevant authorities, and Lord Donaldson went out of his way to stress that the introduction of compulsory skeleton arguments was not a step towards adopting the American system of full written 'appellate briefs' and severely restricted oral argument.[19] Now, however, although it continues to be stressed that skeleton arguments should do no more than identify the points to be argued, a more recent Practice Direction[20] takes the compulsory nature of skeleton arguments as a given starting point and makes elaborate provision for their preparation and for a timetable for their submission. What is more, it is now envisaged that, where possible, the Court will make its own estimate of the time that oral argument should take, basing itself on the judgment appealed from, the notice of appeal and the

---

[16] *Norwich and Peterborough Building Society* v. *Steed* [1991] 1 W.L.R. 449. Lord Donaldson's judgment contains a valuable analysis of the authorities subsequent to *C.M. Stillevoldt BV* v. *E. L. Carriers Ltd* [1983] 1 W.L.R. 207.

[17] *Practice Note (Court of Appeal: Skeleton Arguments)* [1983] 1 W.L.R. 1055.

[18] *Practice Direction (Court of Appeal: Presentation of Argument)* [1989] 1 W.L.R. 281.

[19] *Ibid.*

[20] *Practice Direction (Court of Appeal: Procedure)* [1995] 1 W.L.R. 1191. A Practice Direction of 1997 (n. 12, above) adopts additional measures to ensure timely submission of skeleton arguments. See further, *Practice Direction (Court of Appeal: Leave to Appeal and Skeleton Arguments)* [1999] 1 W.L.R. 2, which brings forward the time by which skeleton arguments must be lodged and requires the use of skeleton arguments on applications for leave to appeal.

skeleton arguments; it will then inform the parties how much time will be allowed for oral argument. In the space of about twenty years, the Court has worked a transformation in its pre-hearing procedure,[21] has engineered a potentiality for ending the unrestricted oral argument which was once its hallmark, and has done so without the aid of legislation.

The scope of the appeal

The scope of an appeal is determined by the appellant's 'notice of appeal' and, in most cases, the 'respondent's notice'. The appellant must always serve a notice of appeal specifying, amongst other matters, the grounds of the appeal and the order that he wishes the court to make.[22] A respondent's notice is required if the respondent intends to do more than support the judgment of the court below on the grounds relied on by that court.[23] Either notice may be amended by supplementary notice served before the case is listed for hearing or, thereafter, by leave of the court.[24] Leave may even be granted at the hearing, and it is not unknown for a judge to indicate to counsel that an application to amend would be sympathetically received. Subject to that, the court cannot introduce new grounds of appeal of its own motion. On the other hand, given the oral nature of the proceedings, appellate judges can and do suggest points of law to counsel in the course of argument.

In some countries, including France and Belgium, an appellate court originally seised only of a particular point may – or even, as in Belgium, must – give its own decision on outstanding questions and so conclude the entire litigation.[25] No such possibility exists in England. If, for example, it is held that the trial judge was wrong to dismiss the plaintiff's claim, the Court of Appeal cannot go on to assess the damages to which the plaintiff is entitled.[26] Equally, the court cannot decide issues of substance on an appeal on an interlocutory question. The explanation,

---

[21] The Practice Direction of 1995 actually empowers the Court, of its own motion, to invite the parties' advocates to attend a 'directions hearing' in advance of the main hearing. It also deals, in great detail and not for the first or last time, with the documentation to be lodged in advance of the hearing: *Practice Direction (Court of Appeal: Amended Procedure)* [1997] 1 W.L.R. 1013.

[22] R.S.C., Ord. 59, r. 3(2). The grounds of appeal are stated in quite general terms. Neither party may rely on a ground of appeal not specified in his notice without prior leave: R.S.C., Ord. 59, rr. 3(3) and 6(2).

[23] R.S.C., Ord. 59, r. 6(1).

[24] R.S.C., Ord. 59, r. 7.

[25] France, n.c.p.c., art. 568; Belgium, Code judiciaire, art. 1068.

[26] The case will have to be remitted for the damages to be assessed at first instance. Frequently, however, even though the trial judge decides against the plaintiff on liability, he will go on to assess the damages in case of appeal.

at least in part, is that any issue of fact outstanding between the parties must be decided at a trial at which witnesses may be heard, before any appeal is possible.

The nature of the appeal

According to the theory of English law, all appeals are 'statutory', which is to say that no right of appeal exists in the absence of explicit statutory provision.[27] This, it is true, has little direct practical significance so far as appeals from the High Court and the county courts are concerned,[28] but it does mean that the principle of double instance (*double degré de juridiction*), recognised elsewhere, is not as such accepted. It also means that the question whether, and in what circumstances, the leave of the court should be a condition of the right to appeal raises no issue of great principle. In addition, judgments at first instance are immediately enforceable unless a stay of execution is ordered:[29] it is both intended and expected that the decision at first instance will normally dispose of a case once and for all.[30]

According to the rule, appeals to the Court of Appeal are by way of 'rehearing',[31] but this cannot be taken at its face value. The appeal is not a 'second first instance' as is shown by the following points, amongst others:

(a) The witnesses who testified orally at the trial do not do so again on the appeal. The appellate court has only a written transcript of their evidence and, for this reason, will only most exceptionally disturb the trial judge's findings of fact where those findings depend on the judge's assessment of the credibility or reliability of witnesses; the trial judge, unlike the appellate judges, has the opportunity to observe the demeanour of the witnesses under examination and cross-examination. On the other hand, the appellate court does have jurisdiction to 'retry the case on the

---

[27] *Attorney-General* v. *Sillem* (1864) 10 H.L.C. 704.

[28] See, e.g. *National Telephone Co.* v. *Postmaster-General* [1913] A.C. 546, 552, *per* Viscount Haldane L.C.

[29] See, e.g. *Barker* v. *Lavery* (1885) 14 Q.B.D. 769; *The Annot Lyle* (1886) 11 P.D. 114; cf. *Linotype-Hell Finance* v. *Baker* [1993] 1 W.L.R. 321. D. M. Gordon, 'Effect of Reversal of Judgment on Acts done between Pronouncement and Reversal' (1958) 74 L.Q.R. 517; (1959) 75 L.Q.R. 85. In many 'civil law' countries the rule is to precisely the opposite effect, but in an increasing number the rule is modified. In Italy it has been abandoned: c.p.c., art. 337 as amended in 1990. See below, chap. 16, p. 347.

[30] It is 'fundamental to the due administration of justice that the substantial issues between the parties are ordinarily settled at the trial': *Coulton* v. *Holcombe* (1986) 60 A.L.J.R. 470, 473, *per* Gibbs C.J.

[31] R.S.C., Ord. 59, r. 3(1).

shorthand note';[32] this means that questions of fact that are essentially matters of inference from or the evaluation of the basic, or 'primary', facts found by the judge of first instance can be reconsidered on appeal.[33]

(b) An appellate court does have the power to admit 'further' evidence – that is, evidence which was not before the trial judge – but this power is sparingly exercised. The applicable rule[34] distinguishes between evidence which does, and evidence which does not, relate to matters which have occurred after the date of trial and provides that, except for the former, further evidence shall not be admitted 'except on special grounds'. In neither case, however, will further evidence be admitted unless it substantially alters the basis on which the original decision was made.[35] The case law on this matter has, in effect, laid down three conditions for the admission of further evidence.[36] First, it must be shown that the evidence could not have been obtained with reasonable diligence for use at the trial; secondly, the evidence must be such that, if admitted, it would have an important, though not necessarily a decisive influence on the decision; thirdly, the evidence must be apparently credible.

(c) For reasons connected with the two points just made, there are restrictions on the right of the parties to argue points of law that were not taken before the judge of first instance. In principle, a point of law cannot be taken for the first time in an appellate court unless that court is satisfied that no evidence not actually adduced at the trial would have been adduced there even if the point had then been taken.[37] Formerly, a stricter rule applied to appeals from the county court, according to which only points of

---

[32] *S.S. Hontestroom* v. *S.S. Sagaporak* [1927] A.C. 37, 47, *per* Lord Sumner. See *Practice Direction*, n. 3, above, paras. 13–15.

[33] The distinction between the finding of primary facts and the inference from or the evaluation of such facts is made explicit in *Benmax* v. *Austin Motor Co. Ltd* [1955] A.C. 370, 373, *per* Lord Simonds. See also *Watt* v. *Thomas* [1947] A.C. 484, 487–8, *per* Lord Thankerton.

[34] R.S.C., Ord. 59, r. 10 (2).

[35] So, for example, where the trial judge has made allowance for an uncertain prognosis in assessing the damages to be awarded for personal injury, further evidence of changes in the plaintiff's condition subsequent to the trial will not normally be admissible since the judge has already taken the possibility of such changes into account: *Mulholland* v. *Mitchell* [1971] A.C. 307, 312, *per* Lord Wilberforce; *Hunt* v. *Severs* [1993] Q.B. 815 (reversed, without affecting this point, [1994] 2 A.C. 350).

[36] E.g. *Ladd* v. *Marshall* [1954] 1 W.L.R. 1489; *Sutcliffe* v. *Pressdram Ltd* [1991] 1 Q.B. 153.

[37] *The Tasmania* (1890) 15 App.Cas. 223; *Ex parte Firth, Re Cowburn* (1882) 19 Ch.D. 419, 429, *per* Jessel M.R.

law raised at the trial could be used as grounds of appeal.[38] Now that an appeal on fact as well as on law may be brought from the county court, however, the rule is the same for appeals from both county court and High Court.[39]

(d) In cases in which the decision is said to depend on the 'discretion' of the judge, or where it involves the assessment by the judge of such matters as the respective shares of responsibility of two or more actors for the same damage, the appellate court exercises a high degree of self-restraint. It will not disturb the judge's assessment unless there is a demonstrable error of principle in his decision or there are conflicting decisions at first instance and the intervention of an appellate court is necessary to promote consistency of decision in the future.[40] This self-restraint is not exercised because an appellate judge is any less well placed than the trial judge to come to his own decision, as in the situations previously mentioned. Its purpose is, fundamentally, to discourage appeals on the matters in question.[41]

The hearing

For the purposes of the hearing of an appeal, the court will be supplied with a substantial volume of documentary material.[42] It will have the appellant's and the respondent's notices, together with the pleadings, the judgment or judgments of the court below, all the documents that were before that court and a transcript of the oral evidence given at the trial. Argument on the appeal is, however, oral,[43] and it is usual for dialogue to develop between counsel and the judges in the course of which points both of law and of the qualification of the facts can be put to counsel by the court.[44] In the Court of Appeal, reasoned judgments are often delivered orally by the judges there and then – before the

[38] *Smith* v. *Baker* [1891] A.C. 325.
[39] *Pittalis* v. *Grant* [1989] Q.B. 605.
[40] *The Macgregor* [1943] A.C. 197; *Birkett* v. *James* [1978] A.C. 297, 317, *per* Lord Diplock.
[41] *Brown* v. *Thompson* [1968] 1 W.L.R. 1003, 1008–11, *per* Winn L.J.; *Eagil Trust* v. *Piggott-Brown* [1985] 3 All E.R. 119, 121, *per* Griffiths L.J.
[42] In complex cases the volume has grown to such an extent that, unless the appellant is unrepresented, only 'core bundles' are required to be lodged in advance of the hearing. These must contain only those documents that members of the court will need to pre-read or to which it will be necessary to refer at the hearing. Other documents ('full trial bundles') are brought to the hearing but not lodged in advance: *Practice Note* [1997] 1 W.L.R. 2017.
[43] But see p. 275, above.
[44] In addition, the judges may test counsel's submissions by putting questions to him in the course of argument. Given the orality of the process, problems with the principle of

hearing is brought to an end. In a case of difficulty, however, the Court may prefer to 'reserve judgment' – that is, to take time for consideration and to reduce its reasons to writing. Because of the importance of its decisions to development and clarification of the law, judgment in the House of Lords is always reserved.[45]

In the past it was not always the case that judges in the Court of Appeal had read the documents in the case before the hearing of the appeal, and they had no written indication from the parties, beyond that contained in their respective notices, of the arguments that would be advanced. In the House of Lords, on the other hand, the parties have for long been required to produce in advance of the hearing a written 'case' containing, amongst other things, 'a succinct statement of their argument in the appeal'.[46] Now, however, practice in the Court of Appeal is assimilated to that in the House of Lords by the requirement of skeleton arguments.[47]

The purpose that lies behind both the House of Lords case and the skeleton argument is to render the hearing itself more efficient and to ensure that it concentrates on the real questions to be decided. As is often stated, neither the House of Lords case nor the skeleton argument is intended to replace oral argument or to provide a full statement of the argument to be presented.[48] Nevertheless, in complex cases at least, counsel seem to find it difficult to resist the temptation to elaborate their arguments in writing. This may hasten the day when time limits for oral argument are imposed.[49]

The judgments of appellate courts

The judgment

Strictly speaking, the word 'judgment' refers to the actual order of the court at the end of the proceedings, and, since an appellate court delivers its own judgment, it may affirm or reverse the judgment of the court below or it may vary it. It is also possible that a new trial is ordered if it appears that the 'primary' facts[50] found at the trial cannot be relied on – perhaps because fresh evidence is admitted and shows this to be so,

---

contradiction do not normally arise even if the judge raises a point of law of his own motion.

[45] Because the House of Lords is not a part of the Supreme Court, its orders must be made orders of the Supreme Court, but this is little more than a technicality.

[46] Directions, para. 22(i)(a).   [47] Above, p. 274.

[48] E.g. *Yorke Motors* v. *Edwards* [1982] 1 W.L.R. 444 (H.L.); *Practice Directions* [1989] 1 W.L.R. 281 and [1995] 1 W.L.R. 1188 (CA).

[49] Above, p. 275.   [50] Above, p. 277.

or because the trial judge erred in law in his treatment of the evidence before him. Because of the cost in terms of time and expense, however, an appellate court will be most reluctant to adopt this course.[51]

The obligation to give reasons

Certain administrative tribunals are obliged by statute to give reasons for their decisions[52] and a similar obligation rests on 'inferior' courts at common law.[53] No such legal obligation to motivate their decisions attaches to the superior courts, perhaps because an appellate court must come to its own conclusion in the case before it, rather than act as a court of review.[54]

In practice, and subject only to a few well-recognised exceptions,[55] the superior courts always do give their reasons, sometimes at great length, and in common parlance a judge's reasons are described as his 'judgment'.[56] Nevertheless, the absence of legal obligation has the result that every judge is free to motivate his decision as he sees fit and, while every member of a court in which more than one judge sits must come to his own independent conclusion, there may be one or more judgments as the judges themselves prefer. Sometimes all the members of the court will collaborate in a single judgment – the 'judgment of the court' – and sometimes, after one judgment has been delivered, the other judges are content to add a few comments on particular points or simply to express their agreement. Nevertheless, it is by no means uncommon for several judgments to be delivered in a single case, even if

---

[51] See, e.g. *Hunt* v. *Severs* [1993] Q.B. 815, 832, *per* Bingham M.R.

[52] Tribunals and Enquiries Act 1992, s. 10. Some administrative authorities may be required to give reasons for their decisions: see, e.g. *R.* v. *Civil Service Appeal Board, ex parte Cunningham* [1991] 4 All E.R. 310; *R.* v. *Home Secretary, ex parte Doody* [1994] 1 A.C. 531. Cf. *R.* v. *Higher Education Funding Council, ex parte Institute of Dental Surgery* [1994] 1 W.L.R. 242.

[53] *R.* v. *Thomas* [1892] 1 Q.B. 426. Even so, failure to give reasons may not be sufficient in itself to justify quashing a decision: *Crake* v. *Supplementary Benefits Commission* [1982] 1 All E.R. 498; *R.* v. *Secretary of State for Social Services* [1986] 1 W.L.R. 421. Cf. *R.* v. *Civil Service Appeal Board* [1991] 4 All E.R. 310.

[54] Where, in effect, the appellate court acts as a court of review, as it does where the judge's exercise of his discretion is called in question, it has been recognised that a judge must give his reasons sufficiently for the principles on which he acted to be understood: *Eagil Trust* v. *Pigott-Brown* [1985] 3 All E.R. 119, 122, *per* Griffiths L.J.

[55] E.g. on an application for leave to appeal. Even here, when a decision is announced, the court may give some guidance on principle: *Re Wilson* [1985] A.C. 750; *Smith* v. *Cosworth Casting Processes Ltd Practice Note* [1997] 1 W.L.R. 1538; *Practice Direction*, n. 3, above.

[56] In the House of Lords, because of the connection with the legislature, it is customary to use the word 'speech'.

all the judges agree in the result. If one or more judges dissent, a reasoned dissenting judgment will certainly be delivered.

The motivation of decisions[57]

It has already been noticed that each judge is free to formulate his judgment as he sees fit. Every judgment is the work of one or more judges individually, identified by name, and a judgment in an appellate court may vary in length from the two words 'I agree' to an elaborate exposition of the facts and the law running to many pages. In what follows it is assumed that the judgment under consideration is intended by its author to deal with all the matters involved in the case before the court.

It is often said that the role of the judge is to apply the law to the facts. This is an over-simplification, but it shows the lingering desire on the part of many judges that their decisions should appear to be no more than the product of syllogistic reasoning involving no creativity on their part. In reality, creativity on the part of the judge is an inescapable factor in the process of adjudication, and this is often as true for questions of fact as it is for questions of law: the case in which the judicial finding of the facts does not require the exercise of value judgment is a rarity.

In what follows, the attempt will be made to describe some of the principal methods used by the judges in the motivation of their decisions of both fact and law. It must, however, first be stressed that the conventional distinction between questions of fact and questions of law, even though regularly used by the judges, is often in practice a distinction without a difference. This has two aspects which must be briefly mentioned.

(a) Although an appellate court will not normally interfere with the trial judge's findings of primary facts, it can and will substitute its own view on matters of inference from, or the qualification of, those facts. In a case in which negligence is alleged against a medical practitioner, for example, the legal standard by which the conduct of the defendant is to be judged is well settled,[58] but it is, necessarily, stated in general terms. A court which is called upon to apply a test of that kind is still dealing with a question of

---

[57] See, e.g. R. Stevens, *Law and Politics, The House of Lords as a Judicial Body, 1800–1976* (1979); A. Paterson, *The Law Lords* (1982); B. S. Markesinis and S. Deakin, 'The Random Element of their Lordships' Infallible Judgment' (1992) 55 M.L.R. 619. Only judicial motivation as revealed in the judgments is considered here.

[58] The statement of McNair J. in *Bolam* v. *Friern Barnet Hospital Management Committee* [1957] 1 W.L.R. 582 has been approved on many occasions, e.g. by the House of Lords in *Sidaway* v. *Governor of Bethlehem Royal Hospital* [1985] A.C. 871.

fact, not law,[59] but in applying a legal standard in a given case, a court is necessarily refining it, is giving it a more specific meaning than can be found in its original formulation. If it can be said that the court must evaluate the facts in order to apply the law, it can equally be said, if evaluation is itself a matter of fact, that the court must interpret the law before it can be applied to the known facts. The coin has two sides, but there is only one coin.[60]

(b) Decisions which may, considered in isolation, be regarded as pure decisions of fact are not infrequently referred to in later cases, and even if they are regarded only as illustrations of the application of a known rule of law, they tend to have a direct influence on the way that rule of law is applied. They thus become, in themselves, legal precedents and, as such, sources of law. It is true that appellate judges have, from time to time, objected to the over-citation of precedent cases by counsel,[61] but it is also true that questions that were at one time regarded as pure questions of fact – questions to be answered by the jury, if there is one – have become 'judicialised' by the accretion of numerous decisions dealing with particular aspects of those questions.

An important example of this phenomenon exists in relation to the assessment of damages in cases of personal injury. In the past, when juries were regularly used, the law amounted to little more than a rule that the jury should be told to award such damages as, on a reasonable view of the case, would give what they consider under all the circumstances to be fair compensation.[62] Today, in the interest of conformity and predictability, awards are itemised by the judges, and there is a great deal of case law on many aspects of the matter, such as the balancing of losses against gains, the effect of inflation, the award of interest on damages and so on.[63] It is in the nature of a case law system that this kind of thing should happen once trial by jury ceases to be the norm.

[59] *Qualcast (Wolverhampton) Ltd* v. *Haynes* [1959] A.C. 743. McNair J.'s statement (see n. 58, above) was contained in his direction to a jury.

[60] See, e.g. *Whitehouse* v. *Jordan* [1981] 1 W.L.R. 246, where the essential facts, viewed with hindsight, were that an obstetrician had made an error of clinical judgment with disastrous results. No less than five days of argument preceded the decision of the House of Lords, given in five substantial speeches, that, in the circumstances, the obstetrician's conduct had not fallen below the required standard. Was this a decision of fact or of law?

[61] E.g. *Roberts Petroleum Ltd* v. *Kenny Ltd* [1983] 2 A.C. 192, 202, *per* Lord Diplock.

[62] *Rowley* v. *LNW Ry* (1879) L.R. 8 Ex. 221; *Phillips* v. *LSW Ry* (1879) 4 Q.B.D. 406; (1879) 5 Q.B.D. 78.

[63] See, on these and related topics, e.g. *Wise* v. *Kaye* [1962] 1 Q.B. 638; *West and Son Ltd* v. *Shephard* [1964] A.C. 326; *Fletcher* v. *Autocar and Transporters Ltd* [1968] 2 Q.B. 322; *Parry* v. *Cleaver* [1970] A.C. 1; *Cookson* v. *Knowles* [1979] A.C. 556; *Lim* v.

The facts

An appellate court will, normally, accept the primary facts as found by the judge at the trial. So far as the facts are concerned, therefore, it is concerned only with questions of inference and evaluation, questions to which evidence is rarely directly relevant. They require the application of logical reasoning or of judgment or of both; they arise, of course, at first instance as well as on appeal.

Where the primary facts fall within the knowledge or experience to be expected of a judge, questions of either type will be answered by him in the light of that knowledge or experience, influenced, it may be, by the arguments of counsel.[64] This is not to say, however, that evidence is never necessary or used at the trial in relation to such questions. Most obviously, this occurs where questions involving knowledge of science or technology arise, and one or both of the parties call expert witnesses.[65]

It is not uncommon, today, for the parties to reach an agreement on the presentation to the court of one or more written expert reports so that the need for oral expert testimony can be avoided. Where this occurs, the expert testimony comes before the appellate courts in the same form as in the court of first instance. Where, on the other hand, expert witnesses testify at the trial the appellate courts have only a transcript of their evidence, and in that case the appellate court will not ordinarily be willing to disturb the trial judge's conclusion in so far as it depends on his assessment of the relative credibility of the expert witnesses.

The fact is, however, that the demeanour of expert witnesses under examination at the trial is rarely a factor in assessing the reliability of their evidence, and appellate judges often examine minutely the transcripts of expert testimony. Where they see fit to do so they will not hesitate to disagree with the trial judge. In justifying their decisions they

---

Camden AHA [1980] A.C. 174; *Wright v. British Railways Board* [1983] 2 A.C. 773; *Hunt v. Severs* [1994] 2 A.C. 350. The questions raised have sufficient legal content for the Law Commission to have taken them under review and to have published a number of Consultation Papers and reports.

[64] Such knowledge or experience is not necessarily limited to matters within the experience of the man in the street. For example, without having evidence on the point, one judge used for the purposes of his reasoning the fact that 'every carrier by sea knows that the goods he carries are liable to be bought and sold in the course of carriage under a form of contract known universally as a c.i.f. contract': *Schiffart v. Chelsea Maritime* [1982] 1 Q.B. 481, 485, *per* Lloyd J. The decision, but not the 'fact' relied on by the judge, has since been held to be wrong: *Leigh & Sillivan Ltd v. Aliakmon Shipping Co. Ltd* [1986] A.C. 786. For a general consideration of the use by the judge of his own knowledge, see chap. 13.

[65] Chap. 12.

will frequently quote verbatim from the transcripts and they will exercise their own judgment where judgment is required, as it is, for example, in considering the quality of the conduct of a professional such as a doctor or a lawyer.[66]

It is probably not possible to isolate particular methods of reasoning in relation to the facts. Even the judges' use of the rules about burden of proof is flexible. Sometimes, no doubt, they will be content to hold simply that the party on whom the burden of proof rests has failed to discharge it, but if that approach leads to an apparently absurd result they will disregard it. So, for example, in one well-known case in which an action was brought in respect of a gaming debt incurred in Monte Carlo, the defendant pointed out that such a debt could not be recovered under English law. The law of Monaco applied, but the plaintiff produced no evidence of the law of that country. This meant, in principle, that the law of Monaco had to be assumed to be the same as English law, but the judge declined to decide on that basis. 'It is notorious', he said, 'that at Monte Carlo roulette is not an unlawful game.'[67]

The law

At one level, the process of reasoning in relation to the law can be said to be aimed at discovery of the rule of law applicable to the case before the court. As René David has said, 'Dans le droit anglais, élaborée par la jurisprudence, la *legal rule* représente autre chose que la règle de droit, systematisée par la doctrine ou énoncée par le législateur, à laquelle nous sommes habitués; elle se situe à un niveau de généralité moindre que notre règle de droit . . .'[68] In fact, the search for the applicable rule of law is the search for a formulation of a legal rule that is uniquely applicable to the facts of the case at hand. The reasoning of a judge in relation to the law is therefore tied closely to the facts before him.

In this section the attempt will be made to describe some of the forms of reasoning that are used by the judges in their handling of the cases and statutes that control their decisions. It must be observed at the outset, however, that there are no set forms of reasoning and it is not intended to suggest that there is a clear division between reasoning in relation to the law and reasoning in relation to the facts.

---

[66] Chap. 13, n. 64.
[67] *Saxby* v. *Fulton* [1909] 2 K.B. 208.
[68] David, *Grands Systèmes*, pp. 273–4.

Reasoning by example

This is sometimes said to be the typical mode of reasoning of the common law.[69] Certainly it is regarded as axiomatic that like cases should be treated alike, and the idea is inherent in the doctrine of precedent.[70] A previous case whose facts are similar to those before the court provides an example of how such a case should be decided and, in its reasoning, of why it should be so decided. Indeed, under the English system according to which every court is 'bound' by the decisions of higher courts, the mere existence of the precedent itself supplies a reason for the subsequent decision. That, however, will only be so where the two cases are on all fours, a point which leads directly to the vitally important aspect of the case law system, namely the process of distinguishing one case from another.

Although it is part of the English doctrine that even a single precedent may be binding, it is binding only in so far as it applies, and it does not apply as a precedent to a case whose material facts are not the same, whatever its persuasive value may be. A judge may, therefore, avoid the compulsive effect of a precedent by distinguishing it, that is to say by pointing to the differences of material fact. Since no two cases ever have facts that are absolutely identical, the judge's reasoning must relate, at least in part, to consideration of the question whether the actual differences of fact are such that the precedent case is or is not applicable. In other words, he must decide whether it provides an example which is appropriate to decision of the case before him.

Multiplicity of precedents

Cases of any complexity for which the reports reveal only one possible precedent are in the nature of things unusual, and where a multiplicity of precedents exists – where, that is, there are numerous decisions which deal with questions sufficiently close to those raised in the case before the court that they can reasonably be regarded as examples – the judge is confronted with what may appear to be a paradox. Subject to the rule that a higher court is not bound by the decisions of lower courts, the basic premise of the case law system is that all previous decisions are binding. From this it follows, subject to the same proviso, that all previous decisions must be assumed to have applied the law correctly: no judge can say that, or act on the basis that, the decision of a higher court was wrong. He should not, therefore, give a decision which is inconsistent with, which cannot be reconciled with, any precedent decision. Nevertheless, it may appear to a judge, confronted with a

[69] E.g. E. Levi, *Introduction to Legal Reasoning* (1949), p. 1.
[70] R. Cross and J. W. Harris, *Precedent in English Law*, 4th edn (1991), p. 26.

number of precedents, that that is exactly what some of his predecessors have done.

The paradox is more apparent than real. Indeed, the situation reveals one of the corner-stones of the English system and thus of the reasoning of the judges. Bearing in mind that the common law is 'unwritten' and that it lacks the authoritative textual formulation of a statute, it follows that the 'true rule of law' is to be found in a proposition, or a series of propositions, which will justify the decisions in all the precedent cases. The decisions must be reconciled.

The process of reconciliation, where precedent decisions appear to conflict with one another, necessarily requires analysis and exposition of the distinctions between them, and this too is to some extent a form of reasoning by example. The process also serves, however, to reveal distinctions that, however compelling they may appear a priori to the judge to be, must nevertheless be regarded as immaterial: if two cases have been decided in the same way notwithstanding a factual distinction between them, it follows that that distinction is not, as a matter of law, a material distinction. In this way principles or rules of law are continually refined: the more numerous the precedents, the narrower and more precise the rule to be extracted from them.

The language of the judges

In the course of their judgments it is usual for the judges not only to analyse the precedent decisions but to discuss them, sometimes at length, and to attempt their rationalisation and synthesis. This process sometimes results in the formulation of a rule or principle by the judge in a manner which appeals to his successors, and it is common for judges to incorporate into their judgments verbatim passages from the judgments in earlier cases.

Such passages, especially when they are succinct, to the point, and frequently repeated, may come to acquire great authority. This is in part a reflection of the absence of anonymity and the respect that one judge will display for the opinion of a distinguished predecessor. It is also in part due to the continuous search for certainty in the law, and in part it is the product of the system of precedent itself.[71]

In the theory of the doctrine of precedent it is the *ratio decidendi* of a decision which is binding, not the judge's actual words, still less words which he may use which are not strictly necessary to the reasoning that

---

[71] Every decision constitutes a precedent, and each time that a judge adopts and repeats a formulation of the law that constituted part of the *ratio decidendi* of a previous case, it comes also to constitute part of the *ratio decidendi* of the later case and its authority is reinforced.

leads him to his conclusion (*obiter dicta*).[72] This means, amongst other things, that the actual form of words used by a judge, however distinguished, can never have the force of statute. A judge's statement of the law is necessarily provisional in the sense that later judges may hold that it is too wide or too narrow, as the case may be. Nevertheless, some judicial formulations of the law do come to acquire in practice a force which is almost equivalent to the force of a statute. Certainly, it would require considerable courage on the part of a judge to hold that an oft-repeated statement of one of his eminent predecessors did not accurately state the law.

Consequential reasoning

The House of Lords is no longer bound by its own decisions,[73] but even within a quite rigid system of precedent there is room for a judge to have regard to the consequences of his adoption of one line of reasoning rather than another. Broadly speaking, the consequences to which reference may be made fall into two distinct but overlapping categories.

(i) Consequences within the law. Though it is not always easy to explain,[74] certain principles or doctrines are regarded as embedded in and fundamental to the law. So, for example, the rule of privity of contract and the doctrine of consideration are inveterate. Even if there is a contract between the plaintiff and X, a sub-contract between X and the defendant, and a breach by the defendant of the sub-contract which causes loss to the plaintiff, there is no possibility that the defendant is liable to the plaintiff for breach of the sub-contract. On this basis, although he made it clear that, in his view, a remedy must be found for the intended beneficiary under a will, where the intended gift failed because of the negligence of the testator's solicitor, Lord Goff accepted that a contractual solution could not be adopted because it could be criticised as an 'illegitimate circumvention of these long-established

---

[72] Not the least of the complications of the doctrine of precedent lies in the fact that, in the last resort, it is for the judges in subsequent cases to say what was the *ratio decidendi* of a previous decision. They must 'interpret' the precedents, and a body of precedent on the interpretation of precedents can, itself, come into existence in much the same way as a body of precedent can come into existence on the interpretation of a statute. See Cross and Harris, *Precedent in English Law*, pp. 42–3.

[73] *Practice Statement (Judicial Precedent)* [1966] 1 W.L.R. 1234. The Court of Appeal is, however, bound both by the House of Lords and, normally, by its own previous decisions: *Young* v. *Bristol Aeroplane Co.* [1944] K.B. 718; *Davis* v. *Johnson* [1979] A.C. 264.

[74] It is not always easy, for example, to say why one thing is the rule, another the exception to that rule. See, e.g. *Scruttons Ltd* v. *Midland Silicones Ltd* [1962] A.C. 446, 487–8, *per* Lord Denning. It is possible that what is regarded as the rule and what is regarded as the exception may be reversed after a period of time.

doctrines'.[75] The defendant's liability to the plaintiff, if any, must be founded independently on tort.

One consequence of this kind of reasoning was a pronounced expansion of the scope of liability in tort.[76] Subsequently, however, the expansion was halted and, indeed, the older law reinstated, partly, at least, because the expansion had the effect of subverting the rule of privity of contract.[77] In other words, if the court considers that to allow the plaintiff to recover in tort would be contrary to that rule, liability is generally denied. 'It should be no part of the general function of the law of tort to fill in contractual gaps.'[78]

(ii) Consequences outside the law. Though a suggested proposition of law may produce a result which appears acceptable on the facts before the court, and though the proposition itself does not run counter to any existing principle or precedent, it may still be seen to produce results in other – often hypothetical – cases that are regarded as self-evidently unacceptable. In one case, goods had been carried in a ship that was illegally overloaded. The owner of the goods contended that he was, therefore, not obliged to pay for the carriage of his goods, but in dialogue with counsel the judge showed that if that was right one consequence would be that a carrier of goods by road who exceeded the speed limit would lose his right to be paid. In an elegant pretence that the applicable law existed and had only to be discovered, the judge agreed that 'one must not be deterred from enunciating the correct principle of law because it may have startling or even calamitous results. But', he added, 'I confess I approach the investigation of a legal proposition which has results of this character with a prejudice in favour of the idea that there may be a flaw in the argument somewhere.'[79]

Sometimes, reasoning of this nature is used to justify a positive legal development as in cases where, without it, a claim to damages would

---

[75] *White* v. *Jones* [1995] 2 A.C. 207, 266. In *Hunt* v. *Severs* [1994] 2 A.C. 350, 363, Lord Bridge rejected an argument advanced on the plaintiff's behalf because it 'would represent a novel and radical departure in the law of a kind which only the legislature may properly effect'.

[76] *Anns* v. *Merton LBC* [1978] A.C. 728. See also *Junior Books Ltd* v. *Veitchi Co. Ltd* [1983] A.C. 520.

[77] *Murphy* v. *Brentwood District Council* [1991] 1 A.C. 398. The *Anns* case, itself a decision of the House of Lords, was actually overruled.

[78] *Banque Keyser* v. *Skandia (U.K.) Insurance* [1990] 1 Q.B. 665, 800, *per* Slade L.J. (in a 'judgment of the court'). More recent cases such as *White* v. *Jones* [1995] 2 A.C. 207 and *Henderson* v. *Merrett Syndicates Ltd* [1992] 2 A.C. 145 may mark a renewal of the willingness of appellate judges to expand tortious liability. On the other hand, the Law Commission has recommended relaxation of the doctrine of privity of contract: *Privity of Contract: Contracts for the Benefit of Third Parties*, Law Com. No. 242 (1996).

[79] *St John Shipping Corporation* v. *Joseph Rank Ltd* [1957] 1 Q.B. 267, 282, *per* Devlin J.

disappear 'into some legal black hole' and the wrongdoer escape scot-free.[80] So, in *White* v. *Jones*,[81] Lord Goff drew attention to what he called the 'extraordinary fact' that if a duty were not owed by a testator's solicitor to an intended beneficiary and the gift failed by reason of the solicitor's negligence, 'the only persons who might have a valid claim (i.e. the testator and his estate) have suffered no loss, and the only person who has suffered a loss (i.e. the intended beneficiary) has no claim',[82] and then went on to hold that a tortious duty could be 'fashioned' to avoid such a result.[83]

(iii) Policy. The previous paragraph may be said to illustrate, in a somewhat different form, further use of reasoning by example. It is, indeed, a common feature of judicial reasoning to argue by reference to examples, hypothetical or otherwise, in which the solution is taken to be self-evident. It may, however, also be said that this form of reasoning appeals to policy. That the carrier who exceeds the speed limit should not therefore forfeit his right to be paid may be self-evident, but if so this is because it is taken for granted that it is the policy of the law that he should not suffer such a civil sanction in addition to the sanction prescribed by the penal law.

Until comparatively recently judges were unwilling to admit openly that policy considerations enter into their reasoning, and one judge went so far as to say that 'policy need not be invoked where reason and good sense will at once point the way'.[84] Nevertheless, save in cases in which the only applicable rule of law is not only clear but so narrow and precise as to leave the judge no choice, and the facts are not in doubt even as to their qualification, policy considerations are bound to influence the decision, whether the judge himself is aware of this or not.

In reality, thanks to the doctrine of precedent, the result of many decisions is, in effect, to convert policy into law.[85] The so-called 'flood-

---

[80] *GUS Property Management Ltd* v. *Littlewoods Mail Order Stores Ltd* [1982] S.C. (H.L.) 157, 177, *per* Lord Keith.

[81] [1995] 2 A.C. 207.

[82] *Ibid.* at 259, where Lord Goff also advances other arguments of a non-legal nature under the general heading of 'The impulse to do practical justice'.

[83] *Ibid.* at 269. See also *Linden Gardens Trust Ltd* v. *Lenesta Sludge Disposals Ltd* [1994] 1 A.C. 85, 115, *per* Lord Browne-Wilkinson.

[84] *Dorset Yacht Co.* v. *Home Office* [1970] A.C. 1004, 1039, *per* Lord Morris. Lord Morris did not explain the distinction he had in mind.

[85] The conversion is, of course, more subtle and more restricted than the conversion of policy into law which is effected by the act of legislation. Sometimes the judges will decline to act on overt policy reasoning on the ground that the questions of policy involved can only be settled after an investigation that is neither possible or appropriate in a court of law. See, e.g. *Morgans* v. *Launchbury* [1973] A.C. 127; *Murphy* v. *Brentford D.C.* [1991] 1 A.C. 348, 482, *per* Lord Keith and at 491–2, *per* Lord Oliver.

gates' argument provides a simple and obvious illustration. It may be, and it sometimes is accepted as, an adequate reason for refusing redress in certain circumstances that to do so would be to admit innumerable similar claims.[86]

The floodgates argument is a crude argument of policy which, needless to say, is not always regarded, but not only is it the fact that certain legal principles may make consideration of policy inevitable even if not avowed as such,[87] it is also the fact that explicit reference to policy has been made on numerous occasions. Policy considerations, openly admitted, have, for example, influenced such questions as the extent of an advocate's liability to his client,[88] the extent of the liability for negligence of the police,[89] and the procedure to be used in certain types of proceedings against public authorities.[90] The courts even came close to overt admission, as a factor to be taken into account in the assessment of damages, of the risk that large awards could lead to increased insurance premiums and so affect the cost of living,[91] but this was too much for the House of Lords, which, while recognising the problem, held that any necessary reform must be by way of legislation.[92]

---

[86] For an early example, see *Cattle* v. *Stockton Waterworks* (1875) L.R. 10 Q.B. 453. For a more recent and more sophisticated example, see *Murphy* v. *Brentwood D.C.* [1991] 1 A.C. 348, 469, *per* Lord Keith.

[87] It is, for example, now accepted that the 'duty of care', on which liability for negligence depends, will exist only if, in the circumstances, the court considers it 'fair, just and reasonable that the law should impose a duty of a given scope upon the one party for the benefit of the other': *Caparo Industries plc* v. *Dickman* [1990] 2 A.C. 605, 618, *per* Lord Bridge. For a clear instance of the use of this formula to import policy considerations, see *Marc Rich and Co.* v. *Bishop Rock Marine* [1996] A.C. 211, 241–2, *per* Lord Steyn. In *Alexandrou* v. *Oxford* [1993] 4 All E.R. 328, Glidewell L.J. held that it would not be 'fair or reasonable' for a duty of care to be imposed on the police in the circumstances, giving essentially the same reasons of policy as are mentioned below, n. 89.

[88] *Rondel* v. *Worsley* [1969] 1 A.C. 191.

[89] *Hill* v. *Chief Constable of West Yorkshire* [1989] A.C. 53. In *Ancell* v. *McDermott* [1993] 4 All E.R. 355, 366, Beldam L.J. referred specifically to the unfortunate effects by way of diversion of police resources which would hamper the performance of ordinary police duties if the police were held to owe a duty of care to road users to warn of traffic hazards of which they had become aware. The law resulting from these and similar cases may have to be modified following the decision of the European Court of Human Rights in *Osman* v. *United Kingdom* (Case 87/1997/871/1083, *The Times*, 5 November 1998).

[90] *O'Reilly* v. *Mackman* [1983] 2 A.C. 237.

[91] *Wise* v. *Kaye* [1962] 1 Q.B. 638, 669–70, *per* Diplock L.J.; *Lim* v. *Camden Health Authority* [1979] Q.B. 196, 217, *per* Lord Denning.

[92] *Lim* v. *Camden Health Authority* [1980] A.C. 174, 182, *per* Lord Scarman.

The arguments of counsel

A court must, of course, hear the argument that counsel wishes to present before delivering a judgment unfavourable to his client.[93] There is, however, no rule that every argument, or even every unsuccessful argument, of counsel must be dealt with in a judgment. Nevertheless, given the orality of argument and its extent, not to mention the dialogue between judges and counsel, it would be remarkable if the arguments presented did not feature prominently in the judgment. Now that counsel are required to produce skeleton arguments in writing, a judge has these as well as his notes to which he can refer in preparing a reserved judgment.

It is not always that a judge will refer to the argument directly, but it is not uncommon for him to go through the arguments, explaining why he does or does not accept them as valid. He may refer specifically to an individual statute or precedent relied on by counsel to show why, in his view, it is irrelevant. He may also set out, in juxtaposition to each other, the competing arguments before expressing his preference for one rather than the other.

The adversary philosophy and the orality of English procedure tends to keep the judge's reasoning within the parameters of what is proposed by counsel, but it does not follow that a judge may never motivate his decision by reasoning of his own, at least if he observes the principle of contradiction.[94] Nevertheless, it cannot be doubted that in a case of any complexity it is the arguments of counsel, including argument on the facts, which provide the main foundation upon which the judge will build his reasoning. Judges rely, and are entitled to rely, to a substantial extent upon counsel to draw their attention, not only to the facts, but also to the statutes and precedents that are relevant to the solution of their cases.

The judgment as a whole

Judgments in the English style are discursive and they often play a role which can be compared to that of academic writings (*doctrine*) in other countries.[95] There is, of course, a substantial academic legal literature

---

[93] If the court is convinced, after hearing appellant's counsel, that the appeal cannot possibly succeed, the respondent's argument need not be heard.

[94] Chap. 10, p. 191.

[95] Some judges are even inclined to provide historical introductions to the judgments. See, for example, *Fowler v. Lanning* [1959] 1 Q.B. 426 and *Sutcliffe v. Pressdram Ltd* [1991] 1 Q.B. 153. In the latter case Nourse L.J. began his judgment with an account of the history of jury trial in libel actions running to nearly four pages of print, before

and, from time to time, the judges acknowledge their indebtedness to an academic writer.[96] Nevertheless, even where the words of a judge do not carry the force of precedent – where they are, in reality, no more than *doctrine* – they are generally regarded by later judges as having greater weight than academic writings.[97]

Perhaps for this reason, many appellate judgments are prepared with far more in mind than the mere justification of the decision itself. Important though motivation of judgments may be from the point of view of the litigants, in a case law system all judges, and especially appellate judges, must have in mind that their judgments become bricks in the edifice that is the common law. And, in order that his reasons may be understood in their context, it is common practice for a judge to set out at length, and in detail, the facts to which his decision relates, whether those facts have been in dispute or not. It is of great importance that the reader of a judgment has available to him the detailed facts of the case: 'Every judgment must be read as applicable to the particular facts proved, or assumed to be proved, since the generality of the expressions which may be found there are not intended to be expositions of the whole law, but governed and qualified by the particular facts of the case in which such expressions are to be found.'[98]

A further reason for full exposition of the facts is that, in litigation, the law and the facts are ultimately inseparable. What are the material facts depends on what is the applicable law, and what is the applicable law depends on what are the material facts. It is inevitable, therefore, that the judge's reasoning should reflect this interplay. A judge may, for example, hold that an issue of fact between the parties needs no resolution because, given his conclusion on the law, the result will be the same either way. Alternatively, he may find it unnecessary to resolve a difficult question of law because, given his findings of fact, its resolution will make no difference to the result. The interplay of facts and law can, however, be much more complex than that, and only if a judgment contains all that the judge himself considered relevant to his final decision can his reasons for that decision be adequately expressed and understood.

saying, 'With these general considerations in mind, I come to the particular question which we have to decide.'

[96] Judicial encouragement is now given to counsel to cite academic writings in argument.

[97] At one time only the works of certain, dead, writers could, by convention, be cited in court, but the convention is no longer regarded. One explanation of the preference for judicial observations, even when the judge goes beyond the needs of the case before him, may be that he has the facts of that case in mind, so that his words are thought by other judges to be likely to be more 'practically' orientated than those of an academic writer.

[98] *Quinn v. Leathem* [1901] A.C. 495, 506, *per* Lord Halsbury.

It is not only the interplay of facts and law that is reflected in the judgment. Any or all of the elements mentioned above, and perhaps some others, may find their place according to the nature of the case and the manner in which the judge seeks to justify and explain his decision. If the case raises a novel point of law, or if the judge seeks to take the opportunity to clarify or develop the law in a certain way, he must remember that the system is a flexible one. He can rarely compel a later judge who is reluctant to do so to follow the view he has expressed: he must persuade his successors,[99] and in the last analysis it is the reasoning of the judgment as a whole, not this or that consideration advanced in the course of its delivery, to which they will look.

Conclusion

To a lawyer who is unfamiliar with it, the English appellate system may appear anomalous. There is no formal recognition of a principle equivalent to the French *double degré de juridiction*, but, subject to certain limitations, a decision at first instance may be the subject of two appeals, one after the other. A continuing flow of decisions from the higher echelons of the judicial system is essential to the life of the common law, but there is no court of cassation: both the Court of Appeal and the House of Lords are ostensibly concerned only with the rights and obligations of the parties, not with the clarification or development of the law as such.

In reality, given the extremely small number of appeals and the requirement of leave to appeal, it can scarcely be doubted that, while the interests of the parties are not ignored, the House of Lords is primarily concerned with the questions of law involved. In most cases, after all, the case will already have been considered a second time in the Court of Appeal.[100]

It is clear, however, that the Court of Appeal must perform the dual function of correcting erroneous decisions in the interests of individual justice between the parties and of clarifying and developing the law. This produces a certain tension. It may, indeed, be in the true interest even of the losing party, to deny him the right of appeal if the chances that the decision at first instance will be disturbed are negligible, and that is one reason given for limitations on the right of appeal. No doubt a good deal

[99] J. A. Jolowicz, 'La jurisprudence en droit anglais' (1985) 30 *Archives de la philosophie du droit* 105.
[100] It is a condition of the 'leap-frog' procedure (see n. 2, above) that a point of law of general public importance must be involved. Yet, under that procedure there is no appeal before the case reaches the House of Lords.

of the Court's time is taken up simply with the correction of erroneous decisions at first instance, but its principal concern seems more and more to be its role as producer of decisions that are of value to the future of the law. It is stressed that the decision at first instance should normally be regarded as final,[101] it is stressed that the Court will normally be unwilling to reconsider the decision at first instance on certain types of question,[102] and now there are virtually no appeals without leave.[103] Though the case-load of the Court of Appeal is numerically much lower than the equivalent in other countries, the view that the time of its judges should not be 'wasted' is strongly and widely held.

None of this should be surprising. Any procedural system, but especially a procedural system such as that of the common law in which procedure and substance are so closely linked, must constantly seek the appropriate compromise between competing objectives. It is the English view that such a compromise is better maintained by gradual shifts in the balance of preference between one objective and another than by attempting to provide for it by legislation. The system is intended to be adaptable to changing circumstances. If the result is, from the theoretical point of view, anomalous, and if that is the price of maintenance of the pragmatism of the common law, such a price is not thought to be excessive.

Postscript

Lord Woolf dealt briefly with the subject of appeals in his report,[104] but a separate Review of the Civil Division of the Court of Appeal under the chairmanship of Sir Jeffery Bowman was set up in 1996 and its report appeared in September 1997.[105] The principal concern of the Review was to reduce delays in, and to ease the workload of, the Court of Appeal.[106] Implementation of the most important recommendations of the Review would, however, bring substantial change to the appellate system and for that reason three topics covered by the Review are mentioned here.

In terms of general principle, the Review follows Lord Woolf's report

---

[101] Above, n. 30.   [102] Above, p. 278.

[103] Above, p. 271; Woolf Final, p. 158. The idea that all appeals should require leave seems to have been first mooted in *Court of Appeal: Civil Division, Review of the Legal Year*, 1989.

[104] Woolf Interim, p. 51; Woolf Final, chap. 14.

[105] Lord Woolf was himself a member of the review team.

[106] Nothing in the report relates to appeals to the House of Lords: Bowman, p. 9. The problem of overload in appellate courts is addressed in chap. 16.

on two basic points. First, its recommendations are intended to reflect Lord Woolf's statement of the necessary characteristics that a legal system must possess if it is to ensure access to justice;[107] case management for appeals 'from beginning to end' is recommended.[108] Secondly, the Review agrees with Lord Woolf's observation that appeals serve two purposes – the 'private' and the 'public'.[109]

Leave to appeal

According to the Review, there should be no automatic right of appeal in any case, but, on the other hand, a litigant who has ground for dissatisfaction should always be able to have his case looked at by a higher court to see whether there appears to have been an injustice and, if so, to allow an appeal to proceed. In conformity with this, it is recommended that the requirement of leave to appeal should be extended to all categories of case except adoption and child abduction cases, and cases involving the liberty of the subject.[110]

As now, leave should be sought at first from the court below, and the criteria for the grant of leave set out in *Smith v. Cosworth Casting Processes Ltd Practice Note*[111] should continue to apply: leave should be granted unless the applicant has no realistic prospect of success on appeal, and may be granted even if no such prospect exists.[112] Three changes are, however, proposed. First, all applications for leave should be accompanied by skeleton arguments;[113] secondly, leave to appeal against an interlocutory decision should be granted only if it is appropriate that the appeal should be heard at that stage of the proceedings;[114] thirdly, the court granting or refusing leave should give brief reasons for its decision.[115]

---

[107] Bowman, p. 23, referring to Woolf Interim, p. 2.

[108] Bowman, p. 74.

[109] Bowman, p. 25, referring to Woolf Final, p. 153. On the division between the private and the public purposes of appellate systems, see below, chap. 15, p. 316; chap. 16, p. 330 and J. A. Jolowicz, 'The Role of the Supreme Court at the National and International Level' in P. Yessiou-Faltsi (ed.), *The Role of the Supreme Courts at the National and International Level* (1998), pp. 39–42.

[110] Bowman, p. 35. Acceptance of this recommendation has been anticipated with effect from January 1999: above, p. 271.

[111] [1997] 1 W.L.R. 1538. There is, of course, no suggestion that similar criteria should apply where leave is sought to appeal to the House of Lords.

[112] E.g. because it is in the public interest that the case should be considered at a higher level.

[113] Bowman, p. 85. Acceptance of this recommendation has been anticipated with effect from January 1999: *Practice Direction*, n. 3, above.

[114] Bowman, p. 39. See chap. 16, p. 336.

[115] Bowman, p. 39.

Jurisdiction of appeal

At present, all appeals from final judgments within the judicial hierarchy are to the Court of Appeal. Appeal lies to a High Court judge, or to a circuit judge in the county court, only in the case of interlocutory decisions and, to the High Court, in the case of the decisions of certain tribunals outside the judicial hierarchy. Since it is one of the purposes of the Review to relieve the Court of Appeal of cases of minor importance, advantage is taken of the intended introduction of the system of 'tracks',[116] to propose a wider spread of appellate jurisdiction and, though to an unspecified extent, to allow appeals, including appeals against final judgments, to be heard by a single judge. The 'vital consideration', according to the report, is that an appellant should feel that his appeal will be given a fair hearing by a tribunal prepared to overturn the court below; ordinarily that requires no more than that the appellate tribunal – whether single or multi-judge – should have a jurisdiction superior to that of the court of first instance.[117]

(1) Small claims. These are not mentioned in the Review, but the Civil Procedure Rules contemplate an appeal on the grounds of serious procedural irregularity or mistake of law.[118] In light of the principle just stated, it may be expected that where the decision was reached by a district judge the appeal will be to a circuit judge, and where it was reached by a circuit judge, the appeal will be to a High Court judge.

(2) Fast track. These cases will be tried by either district or circuit judges. From a district judge, appeal will lie to a circuit judge, and from a circuit judge sitting at first instance to a High Court judge sitting alone.[119]

(3) Multi-track. From final decisions in multi-track cases appeal will lie to the Court of Appeal. As for appeals from interlocutory decisions, a distinction is drawn between cases to be tried by circuit judges and cases to be tried by High Court judges. So far as the former are concerned, appeals from interlocutory decisions made by a district judge will lie to a circuit judge; so far as the latter are concerned, appeals from interlocutory decisions made

---

[116] Above, chap. 2, p. 54.
[117] Bowman, p. 27.
[118] C.P.R., rr. 27.12 and 27.13. The application to set aside is now available only to a party who, for good reason, was not present or represented at the original hearing and has a reasonable prospect of success: C.P.R., r. 27.11.
[119] Bowman, p. 47.

by a district judge, circuit judge or Master will lie to a High Court judge.[120]

Despite its view that most appeals in fast track cases (and a fortiori small claims cases) will not be of sufficient weight to merit hearing by the Court of Appeal, the Review recognises that an appeal which, ordinarily, would not reach that Court should nevertheless be dealt with at that level in three categories of case:[121]

(1) Where a case raises an important point of principle or practice, or for some other reason merits consideration by the Court of Appeal. In cases in this category, leave to appeal to the Court of Appeal might be given before or in the course of the ordinary appeal. The criterion for the grant of such leave would be more severe than the general criterion mentioned above, since the court granting leave would need to be satisfied that the case was indeed one that ought to reach the Court of Appeal.

(2) Where the Court of Appeal itself recognises the need for a point of law or practice to be settled. To deal with such cases, the Master of the Rolls should have power to direct that the appeal in one case, or in a number of cases raising similar points, should proceed directly to the Court of Appeal.

(3) Where legal or other developments render it desirable for a particular class of appeal to be heard regularly in the Court of Appeal. The power to make an appropriate Rule, subject to parliamentary approval, should be provided by legislation.

Procedure

Various relatively detailed proposals for procedural change, and for the increased use of information technology, are made in the Review, and various ideas are put forward to achieve a greater level of pre-hearing agreement between the parties; it is, for example, suggested that there should be a pilot scheme to assess the practicability of agreed statements of fact and of agreed 'appendices' to contain the full texts of those parts of the documents which the parties agree the Court will need to see.[122] Two particular matters call for specific mention:

---

[120] Bowman, p. 50. Separate recommendations are made for certain specialist appeals such as family and bankruptcy cases: *ibid.*, pp. 51–4.

[121] *Ibid.*, pp. 45–6.

[122] Bowman, p. 87. The use of such appendices would save the time of the Court and would reduce the amount of copying required.

(1) Though the oral hearing of appeals should continue to be the
norm, if both parties and the Court itself agree, an appeal might
be decided on the papers alone. Indeed, it is proposed that
consideration should be given to reducing the court fee to
encourage the parties to adopt this course.[123]

(2) The possibility that the time for oral argument may be limited
already exists,[124] and the Review, while supporting the right to
such argument and rejecting for England the very short time
limits imposed in the United States, proposes that time limits for
individual cases should be fixed by the Court, subject to the
possibility of objection by the parties.[125] The primary purpose is
said to be avoidance of the expenditure of time at the hearing on
matters where explanation and argument are not required. This
makes it clear that the assumption now generally made, which is
so different from that of the past,[126] is that appellate judges will
have familiarised themselves with all the documents in the case
before the hearing.

[123] Bowman, p. 89.   [124] Above, p. 275.
[125] Bowman, p. 88. An estimate of the time required for oral argument could usually be
made when leave to appeal is given or by a member of the court which will hear the
appeal.
[126] Above, p. 279.

15 Appeal, cassation, amparo and all that: what and why?[1]

Introduction

Generally speaking, the law governing recourse against judicial decisions recognises two categories of procedure, and the distinction between them is reflected by the use of two different words: *appel, cassation*; *appello, cassazione*; *apelación, casación* (or *amparo-casación*); *Berufung, Revision*. No such pairing exists, however, in English, which has only 'appeal'.

This does not mean that procedures which would be classified elsewhere as cassation rather than appeal did not and do not exist in the common law. On the contrary, until the major reforms of the nineteenth century,[2] an appeal properly so-called existed in England only in the courts of Equity; in the courts of 'common law' the only forms of recourse available had far more in common with the cassation than with the appeal of other countries. What is more, while England itself substituted for those forms of recourse a procedure of appeal in the nineteenth century, reserving a procedure analogous to cassation for limited classes of case including, most importantly, recourse against the decisions of administrative authorities or tribunals, in the United States of America the older English forms of recourse – including what is actually now called an 'appeal' to a 'Court of Appeals' – have been developed rather than replaced: for the purposes of this chapter, therefore, the American appeal is treated as a form of cassation rather than of appeal.

In principle, and as established in practice in the legislation of post-Revolutionary France, which provided the model for so many of the legal systems whose languages contain both appeal and cassation, the

---

[1] Based on a contribution to *Estudios en Homenaje al Doctor Héctor Fix-Zamudio en sus treinta años como Investigador de las Ciencias Jurídicas* (1988), Vol. III, 2045 and on part of a Report to the First International Congress on the Law of Civil Procedure, 1977, published in M. Storme and H. Casman (eds.), *Towards a Justice with a Human Face* (1978), p. 127.

[2] Finally achieved by the Supreme Court of Judicature Acts 1873–5.

distinction of kind between the two is clear.[3] On appeal the litigation as a whole – or so much of it as is the subject of the appeal – devolves upon the appellate jurisdiction whose function it is to consider afresh the questions at issue between the parties, whether of fact or law or both. Its business is to decide for itself, as a court of second instance, and its decision replaces the first instance decision for all purposes. An appellate jurisdiction should not, in principle, deal with questions not dealt with at first instance, for otherwise it would not act as an appellate court but as a court of first instance,[4] but it is not bound to have regard only to the legal arguments and to the evidence or proofs that were available at first instance. New demands may be excluded on appeal, but new proofs are not.

From the appeal as thus defined, cassation is usually held to differ sharply. There is no devolutive effect; the role of a jurisdiction of cassation is said to be exclusively to examine the legality of the decision under attack – and 'attack' is here an appropriate word, which it is not in relation to appeal.[5] No proofs are admissible on cassation – the facts must be taken as already found – and the court has only two options: it must either affirm or annul. In the latter event the parties are restored to the position in which they were before the defective decision was made; questions left outstanding must be resolved in another court, and that court must reach its own decision unfettered by anything that may have been said on cassation, even with regard to the correct interpretation of the law.

French procedure as it remained until 1837[6] provides an example of cassation in this sense, and so too does the old English writ of error. Under that procedure the record of the proceedings at first instance was brought before a court of error. If error was found on the record – a mainly formal document, consideration of which gave no opportunity to the court of error to reconsider questions of fact – the decision must be

---

[3] For the appeal, see Book III of the Code de procédure civile of 1806 (and, now, n.c.p.c., arts. 542–70, 899–972). The Court (originally Tribunal) of cassation was created by the law of 27 November to 1 December 1790, but its procedures were governed partly by a pre-Revolutionary decree of 1738 and partly by a number of uncodified laws and decrees of the post-Revolutionary period. See, e.g. E. Faye, *La Cour de Cassation* (1903). For the present law, see Code de l'organisation judiciaire, Livre premier and n.c.p.c., arts. 604–39, 973–1037.

[4] Adherence to this rule was formerly insisted on as a necessary aspect of the right of the parties to a 'double degré de juridiction', but in some legal systems it has now been much relaxed. See further, below, n. 62, and J. A. Jolowicz, 'Introduction' in J. A. Jolowicz and C. H. van Rhee (eds), *Recourse against Judgments in the European Union* (1999), pp. 1, 10.

[5] Cf. P. Herzog and D. Karlen, 'Attacks on Judicial Decisions' in *International Encyclopaedia of Comparative Law*, Vol. XVI (ed. M. Cappelletti) (1982), chap. 8.

[6] Law of 1 April 1837.

quashed and a new trial ordered. The powers of a court of error went no further; it could not even disregard an error which in its view could not have affected the outcome of the trial.[7]

The main purpose of this chapter is to examine how the two principal forms of recourse – cassation and appeal – have become impure, but preliminary mention must be made of two general matters, namely, first, the distinction between fact and law, which is so widely used in the regulation of methods of recourse, and, secondly, the character of the proceedings at first instance: if the methods of recourse, and in particular the appeals, of two different legal systems are to be compared, each must be considered against the background of the proceedings from which the appeal is brought.

Fact and law

The distinction between questions of fact and questions of law is widely used to define the functions of the various levels of the judicial hierarchy. Where a jury is the judge of fact, for example, an appeal on fact would deprive the jury of its sovereign right to decide questions of fact,[8] and so only the judge's decisions of law are open to challenge. Similarly, in countries that distinguish between courts of appeal and courts of cassation or review, the judges of a court of appeal are as much judges of fact as are the judges of first instance, but the judges of a court of cassation or review are judges of law alone.

That there is a real distinction between questions of fact and questions of law is undeniable. If witness A testifies that he was present at a discussion between the plaintiff and the defendant and that the defendant had replied 'Yes' to a proposal put by the plaintiff, while witness B testifies that he too was present at the discussion and that the defendant had replied 'No' to the plaintiff's proposal, no one could possibly say that the issue whether the defendant actually replied 'Yes' or 'No' was anything other than one of fact. It is, however, only at the extreme ends of the spectrum that an issue can be confidently identified as either of fact or of law. Whether the defendant actually said 'Yes' or 'No' may be a question of fact, but what of the question whether the conversation between the plaintiff and the defendant, the exact wording of which is in

---

[7] W. S. Holdsworth, *History of English Law*, Vol. I, 7th edn (1956), pp. 222–4. For a late example, see *Househill Coal & Iron Co.* v. *Neilson* (1843) 9 Cl. and Fin. 788.

[8] See, e.g. *Mechanical and General Inventions Co. and Lehness* v. *Austin and The Austin Motor Co.* [1935] A.C. 346. The quashing of a verdict as contrary to the weight of the evidence is more an apparent than a real exception: the case must be so extreme as to suggest that the jury has not performed its duty. See also the discussion of the sufficiency of the evidence as a matter of law, below, p. 302.

controversy, was such as to create contractual obligations between them?

If it is difficult to find any satisfactory criterion for distinguishing a question of law from one of fact, the difficulty is often compounded by jurisprudential developments, developments which stem less from rigorous analysis of the distinction than from considerations of judicial policy relating to the category of question which, it is felt, should, or should not, be brought within the higher court's powers of control.

A clear example of this phenomenon is found in the operation of the jury system. The transformation of the jury from a body of neighbours, expected to answer questions of fact from their personal knowledge, to a body charged with the judicial task of deciding exclusively upon the evidence put before it, enabled and, indeed, required the judges to assume a degree of control over jury verdicts. It thus became a matter for the judge to rule on the preliminary question whether an issue of fact should be put to the jury at all; this required the judge to decide whether the party carrying the burden of proof had gone far enough in discharging it for the other party to be called upon to make an answer. Two questions were made out of one: it was for the jury to decide whether the burden of proof of a particular alleged fact had been discharged, but it was for the judge to decide whether sufficient evidence had been produced for that question actually to be put to the jury in the first place. And, simply because it was a question for the judge, the latter was, by definition, a question of law and susceptible to appeal.[9]

If this curiosity of the history of the common law illustrates how the distinction between fact and law may be manipulated to enlarge (or, occasionally, to diminish)[10] the extent of an appellate court's control, the different English and French positions on the qualification of the facts illustrates how the same question may be differently classified in different legal systems. In France, as in other countries that distinguish between appeal and cassation, the qualification of the facts is treated as a question of law so as to bring it within the competence of the court of cassation: the appreciation or the evaluation of the facts as they have been found by the judge of fact, is said to be to give them their legal quality.[11] In England, on the other hand, the quality of conduct is

---

[9] See J. A. Jolowicz, 'Procedural Questions', in *International Encyclopaedia of Comparative Law*, Vol. XI (ed. A. Tunc) (1969), chap. 13, nos. 131–4.

[10] As has happened, for example where the question is mainly one of impression, such as that of the apportionment of responsibility for damage between two persons both of whom have committed a fault. See chap. 14, above, p. 278.

[11] Mazeaud, no. 2207. It has been said that this reasoning reflects a 'conception humaine de la Cour Suprème; celle ci ne peut plus constater une erreur sans être en mesure de la réparer': *ibid.*, no. 2211. See further, e.g., France, Vincent, no. 1035; Italy, Liebman,

traditionally regarded as a typical jury question and has actually been held to be a question of fact:[12] if it were classified as a question of law, a body of binding precedents would be built up on a matter which is better dealt with from case to case. That is not a relevant consideration for French law, but the House of Lords, unlike the Cour de cassation, is not restricted to questions of law, and so the qualification of facts – itself seen as a question of fact – is as much open in the House of Lords as it is – seen as a question of law – in a court of cassation.

In much of what follows, references to the distinction between fact and law is unavoidable. It must not be assumed, however, where courts in two countries are both restricted to appeals on points of law alone, that in real terms their competences are necessarily the same. For the purposes of comparative law, at least, there is little, if any, difference between the statement, 'the court may only entertain appeals on points of law' and the statement, 'a point of law is a point which may be entertained by a court which may not entertain appeals on points of fact'.

Proceedings at first instance

If the proceedings at first instance were entirely oral and unrecorded, no appeal would be possible: an appellate court would have nothing on which to act. So, in the remarkable Water Court of Valencia, the proceedings are oral and unrecorded, save for a brief written summary of the judgment, and there is no appeal;[13] in the old common law, too, and for somewhat similar reasons, there was no appeal, only proceedings for error on the record.[14] On the other hand, under the Romano-canonical procedure, to which European continental procedure owes so much, the decision at first instance was reached on the basis of a file of documents prepared in the course of the proceedings;[15] there was therefore automatically in existence a body of material capable of being passed on to an appellate court, which was thus in as good a position as

---

p. 329; Spain, Fairén Guillén, 'Los procesos europeos desde Finlandia hasta Grecia (1900–1975)' in III *LXXV años de 'evolución jurídica en el mundo* (1978) (hereafter 'Fairén') at p. 55 and authorities cited, n. 207. The position in the French Conseil d'Etat when acting as a court of cassation differs somewhat from that in the Cour de cassation itself: Debbasch, no. 716.

[12] *Qualcast (Wolverhampton) Ltd* v. *Haynes* [1959] A.C. 743.

[13] Fairén Guillén, *El Tribunal de las Aguas de Valencia y su proceso*, 2nd edn (1988), p. 552.

[14] Above, p. 300.

[15] The procedure of the unreformed Court of Chancery in England, which had roots in the canon law, was not dissimilar, but grotesque. For a graphic account see A. Birrell, 'Changes in Equity, Procedure and Principles', a lecture delivered in 1900 and published in *A Century of Law Reform* (1901), p. 177.

the court of first instance to pronounce on all questions, whether of fact or law.

The technicalities of the old writ of error have been swept away, but in the United States what is called an 'appeal' is ordinarily limited to the record of the proceedings at first instance. An appellate court can consider factual issues only to the extent of ascertaining whether the record discloses evidence sufficient to support the decisions of fact reached below. Bearing in mind that the sufficiency of evidence is treated as a question of law, this may be thought to justify the observation that a characteristic of Anglo-American procedure is the limitation of the appeal to questions of law.[16] If this were right, there would be obvious and major differences between the appeal of the civil and of the common law systems.

What may be true for the United States is, however, not true for most other common law countries. There it is not the old common law writ of error that lies behind the modern appeal but the equity concept of a rehearing. In England the relevant rule of court states, and has stated since 1875, that appeals to the Court of Appeal are 'by way of rehearing'.[17] The statutory obligation of the House of Lords, when seised of an appeal, is differently expressed,[18] but, in practice, the House of Lords has the same powers to deal with an appeal as does the Court of Appeal. Neither court is formally restricted to questions of law and it appears, therefore, that the powers of English appellate judges to consider questions of fact are the same as those possessed by their continental brethren.

The appearance is deceptive. For a good many years after the general introduction of the appeal by way of rehearing in 1875, English appellate judges disclaimed the power to substitute their own decisions on questions of fact for those of the courts of first instance, even when no jury was involved. As late as 1951 a judge of the House of Lords insisted that, on a question of fact raised before the House, the decision of the trial judge 'should have been respected as equivalent to a verdict of a jury on a question of fact'.[19] By then, however, this had become a minority opinion; other judges had stressed that appellate courts have jurisdiction to retry a case on the transcript of the shorthand note of the evidence taken at the trial,[20] and had even said in so many words that where the case had been tried by a judge alone both the Court of Appeal

[16] M. Cappelletti, *Procédure écrite et procédure orale* (1971), p. 19.
[17] R.S.C., Ord. 59, r. 3. chap. 14, above, p. 276.
[18] Appellate Jurisdiction Act 1876, s. 4. See chap. 14, p. 272.
[19] *Bolton* v. *Stone* [1951] A.C. 850, 863, *per* Lord Normand.
[20] *S.S. Hontestroom* v. *S.S. Sagaporak* [1927] A.C. 37, 47, *per* Lord Sumner.

and the House of Lords, 'have a duty to exercise their jurisdiction as tribunals of appeal on fact as well as on law'.[21]

It was once suggested that 'when the appellate judges are in agreement with the trial judge, they take the view that they are bound by his conclusions of fact, but when they disagree with his conclusions they do not hesitate to overrule them'.[22] There may be something in this, but it is now clear, which it was not before, that a distinction falls to be taken between two kinds of question of fact. On the one hand there are those questions of fact to the solution of which the opportunity to observe the demeanour of witnesses, as they give their evidence orally in court, is likely to be useful: that opportunity is given to the trial judge, but not to the judges of appeal. On the other hand, there are those questions of fact to which that opportunity is irrelevant.[23] So, for example, if it falls to be decided whether witness A or witness B is a witness of truth, then no appellate court will disturb the trial judge's finding; but if the question relates to the inferences or conclusions to be drawn from, or the quality to be attributed to, basic facts that are not in dispute, then the appellate court, equipped with a verbatim record of all the evidence given at the trial, is as well able as the trial judge himself to form an opinion. And if the appellate judges do not agree with the trial judge on such a question, they may replace the judge's decision with their own.[24]

The conclusion to be drawn for present purposes is clear. If a comparison is made between the English Court of Appeal, and, say, a French Cour d'appel, both of two apparently contradictory statements can be made. The first is that, unlike the French appellate judges, the English do not have full and complete power to decide for themselves every question raised by the litigation. The second is that the English appeal is by way of rehearing and that English appellate judges, like their French brethren, are judges of fact as well as of law.

The solution lies in the difference between the French, and other civil law, systems of procedure at first instance, on the one hand, and the English, and other common law, systems, on the other. The French judge of first instance reaches his decision on the basis of a collection of documents, not on the oral testimony of witnesses examined and cross-examined in his presence: the material before an appellate court does not, therefore, differ markedly from that available to a court of first

---

[21] *Powell* v. *Streatham Manor Nursing Home* [1935] A.C. 243, 256, *per* Lord MacMillan.

[22] A. L. Goodhart, 'Appeals on Questions of Fact' (1955) 71 L.Q.R. 402, 410.

[23] For two of the more important judicial pronouncements, see *Watt* v. *Thomas* [1947] A.C. 484; *Benmax* v. *Austin Motor Co. Ltd* [1955] A.C. 370.

[24] Cf. the different emphasis in the United States, where the federal rule provides that findings of fact shall not be set aside unless 'clearly erroneous': Fed.R.Civ.P. 52(a) and James and Hazard, no. 13.8.

instance. The English appellate judge, on the other hand, though equally charged with the decision of questions of fact as well as of law, is forced to recognise that, so far as certain types of question of fact are concerned, he is less well situated to make a decision than is the trial judge. A realistic comparison of the powers of different appellate courts must take account of the differences in procedure of the courts from which appeal is brought.

Blurring the distinction

It is often said, and even more often assumed, that the purposes which the distinct procedures of cassation and appeal exist to serve, are themselves quite different. It must not be overlooked, however, that neither can be invoked until after a decision that affects a person's legal rights has actually been made or that, subject to limited and rarely used exceptions,[25] neither is open save to persons directly affected by the decision. This being so, it is in the nature of things unlikely that either will be invoked in any case, unless a person actually affected by the decision in question considers that it would be to his own advantage to do so. Calamandrei has observed, in relation to cassation, that the State makes use of the private, self-interested initiative of the disappointed party by putting it to the service of the wider interests of society.[26] However, even if it is true that cassation in its pure form is primarily concerned with those wider interests while the appeal is concerned primarily with the private interests of the parties, it is increasingly difficult in modern conditions to find either institution in pristine condition. Pure cassation, in particular, is today something of a rarity, and if a pure appeal means a genuine *novum judicium*, few appeals are pure. Even where there are both courts of appeal and courts of cassation, it is no longer possible to distinguish sharply between their respective functions; the differences between them are blurred. Some of the changes which have led to this blurring stem from the universal need to reduce the cost and the delays of litigation. Others, perhaps, have had broader objectives. But be this as it may, it is time for fresh consideration to be given to the purposes actually served by the various forms of recourse that are available.

It is not the intention of this chapter to provide answers to questions

---

[25] In particular, the recourse 'in the interest of the law' (for France, see law of 3 July 1967, art. 17).

[26] Piero Calamandrei, *La Cassazione Civile*, Vol. II, chap. 6, no. 64, in Piero Calamandrei, *Opere Giuridiche* (a cura di Mauro Cappelletti), Vol. VII (1976), p. 133. See also Jolowicz, in Storme and Casman, see n. 1 above, p. 154.

for which different solutions are appropriate in different countries. Its intention is only to show, in general terms and through examples, how the institutions of appeal and cassation, both once internally consistent, have lost their individual character, and to offer some general observations on the subject. The particular form of the Mexican amparo, which is now generally known as 'amparo-casación', and the debate to which it has given rise, provide a convenient starting point.

The Mexican amparo

The Mexican amparo is an extraordinary constitutional remedy, which fulfils a variety of purposes connected, at least theoretically, with the protection of the individual's constitutional rights. It may, for example, serve as an equivalent to *habeas corpus* but it may also be used to attack legislation for unconstitutionality.[27] Before the coming into force of the Constitution of 1917, however, it was not used to attack judicial decisions: a form of cassation existed in the various Mexican jurisdictions.

Beginning in 1919,[28] cassation was progressively abolished in Mexico and its place taken by the *amparo-casación*. This change led to lively discussion on the relationship between the amparo itself and cassation, two aspects of which are relevant to the purposes of this chapter.[29]

(1) In seeking to distinguish the amparo from a procedure of cassation, some authors argued that the *amparo-casación* could lead to no more than the quashing of the decision attacked and the remission of the case elsewhere for decision; on a cassation for error *in judicando*, by contrast, the court of cassation could proceed to give its own decision, disposing of the litigation. As was pointed out by adherents of the other view, however, this was to confuse the institution of cassation as such with the Spanish model which had been adopted and which had previously prevailed in Mexico.[30] The Spanish, and thus the Mexican, form of cassation was not restricted to the mere annulment (or affirmation) of the decision under attack. In that characteristic, however, the cassation of Spain differed sharply from the original French

[27] A leading textbook is H. Fix-Zamudio, *El Juicio de Amparo* (1964) (hereafter 'Fix'). For a work in English, see R. D. Baker, *Judicial Review in Mexico, A Study of the Amparo Suit* (1971).

[28] Ley Orgánica de los Tribunales del Fuero Común en el Distrito y Territorios Federales, art. 9, transitorio.

[29] See, in particular, H. Fix-Zamudio, 'Presente y futuro de la casación civil a través del juicio de amparo mexicano' (1978) 9 *Memoria de El Colegio Nacional* 91.

[30] Fix, no. 49.

model and has been described, even within Spain, as impure.[31] The *amparo-casación* of modern Mexico is in fact closer to pure cassation than was its predecessor.

(2) Over and above discussion of the legal character of cassation, the Mexican debate also involved discussion of the respective purposes of cassation and of the amparo. In short, it was argued that the two must be distinguished because cassation has as its purpose the protection of the legal order, while amparo exists for the protection of individual constitutional rights. To this it has been answered that no such clear distinction of purpose can be drawn between the two institutions. Once a procedure is confined within a judicial system, as had happened with cassation in France by 1837, it ceases to be possible to set up a rigid distinction between the purposes supposedly served by the different elements of that system.[32] This is an answer whose lessons go beyond the particular controversy that arose in Mexico.

Such is the nature of the judicial process and its impact on society that, however clearly a legislator may envisage the purposes he intends his legislation to achieve, the purposes actually achieved by it can be ascertained only from its operation in practice. Of course, appreciation by the legislator that his legislation has failed to achieve the purpose he had in mind may lead to its modification, and indications by the legislator of his purpose may sometimes control the interpretation and application of the legislation by the judges. There is, nevertheless, no necessary identity between the original purpose of a legal institution and the numerous purposes that the institution actually serves at any given time.

Appreciation of this elementary fact of legal life is of particular importance when procedural institutions and their development are under consideration, and even if the initial purposes of appeal and cassation are distinct, as each institution has developed they have come much closer together. As has been indicated above, pure cassation has become something of a rarity,[33] and many appeals are more impure than pure. It may even be true that the differences between them have been reduced to differences of degree rather than of kind.

---

[31] Fairén, p. 53. See also the same author's national report to the International Congress on the Law of Civil Procedure, Ghent, 1977, on Appellate Proceedings: 'La "casación" española tiene bastante poco que ver con la francesa'.

[32] Fix, nos. 50 and 51.

[33] The *amparo-casación* itself provides one example and another, though never so described, is the English application for judicial review. See below, 'The right to decide'.

The impurity of cassation

Three main aspects of pure cassation must be considered, first in relation to countries of the civil law tradition and then to the common law.

Control of decisions of fact

Civil law

Without openly transgressing the rule that it is concerned only with questions of law, thanks to the imprecision and fluidity of the distinction between questions of fact and questions of law, a court of cassation can extend the scope of its review to decisions that are more easily seen as of fact than of law. At least three different techniques are available. First, the qualification of the facts is made a question of law.[34] Secondly, the traditional idea that the interpretation of a private document such as a contract or a will is a question of intention and thus of fact is overcome by the concept of 'distortion'.[35] Thirdly, as a jurisprudential development[36] or by actual legislation,[37] a decision may be quashed on cassation if its findings of fact are inadequately motivated: through reliance on the idea that a court of cassation cannot perform its function, especially that of considering the qualification of the facts, if the facts are not adequately stated, the door is opened for the court to consider almost any point of fact. It has, indeed, been said of France that of the elements of the dossier produced in the lower courts the court of cassation can do with them what it likes,[38] and, of Germany, that, contrary to the intention of the legislature, *Revision* before the *Bundesgerichtshof* has become a *'Tatsacheninstanz'*.[39]

Common law

In England, as already mentioned, the principal analogue of cassation, the writ of error, was replaced by an appeal more than a century ago. Most other common law jurisdictions have followed suit. In the United

---

[34] Above, p. 302.

[35] 'Distortion' ('dénaturation') appears in France as early as 1868: Civ. 20 January 1868, D.P. 1868, I, 12. See J. Boré, 'Le contrôle de la dénaturation des actes', 1972 Rev.trim.dr.civ. 249.

[36] As it still is in France. See Henri Motulsky, 'Le "manque de base légale", pierre de touche de la technique juridique', J.C.P. 1949, I, 775, reprinted, *Ecrits*, p. 31.

[37] E.g. Italy, c.p.c., art. 360(5). See also Fairén.

[38] Mazeaud, p. 473.

[39] P. Gilles, 'Die Berufung in Zivilsachen und die zivilgerichtliche Instanzordnung', in P. Gilles (ed.), *Humane Justiz* (1977), p. 147 at p. 156.

States, however, in what is there called an 'appeal', the procedure is not a rehearing of the case. Having grown out of the old writ of error, it is 'a review concerning whether prejudicial error occurred in the original determination';[40] the court is limited to errors on the record. The decision of disputed questions of fact is held to be the province of the jury and, since there is no jury in a Court of Appeals, attention is directed in principle to alleged errors of law. On the other hand, the record has been transformed from a largely formal document to a written account of the entire proceedings; it may even include a verbatim transcript of the oral testimony given at the trial as well as all documentary evidence.[41] It thus becomes possible for an appellant to argue that the jury's verdict was 'perverse' – that it was contrary to the weight of the evidence – and that is essentially an argument on the facts. The court will not intervene except in clear cases, but if it does consider a verdict to be contrary to the evidence it will order a new trial.[42]

Control of court of remand

Civil law

Where a decision is quashed and the case remanded to another court for a new decision, then, under pure cassation, the procedure is exhausted unless and until the new decision is also attacked: the court of cassation cannot control in any way the decision of the court of remand. As early as 1837, however, France found it necessary to modify this rule by providing that, following a second cassation, the rulings of the court of cassation on matters of law bind the second court of remand.[43] This remains, in its essentials, the position in France to the present time,[44] but other countries have gone further: the rulings of the court on a first cassation bind the first court of remand.[45]

---

[40] James and Hazard, no. 13.8. Space precludes discussion of procedures available in the court of first instance whereby, for example, a litigant can apply for a new trial after the jury has delivered its verdict. See *ibid.*, nos. 7.16 to 7.22.

[41] Federal Rules of Appellate Procedure (Fed.R.App.P.), rule 10.

[42] That the verdict is against the weight of the evidence is a ground for an application to the trial judge for a new trial: Fed.R.Civ.P., rule 59. Strictly speaking, the appeal is brought against the substantive judgment at first instance which will have followed the judge's refusal to order a new trial: Fed.R.Civ.P., rule 59.

[43] Law of 1 April 1837. Under this law the second cassation came before a special formation of the Court, the Chambres Réunies, not before the chamber originally seised.

[44] Law no. 79–9 of 3 January 1979 (C.org.jud., art. L. 131–4, al. 2). The Chambres Réunies is replaced by the Assemblée Plénaire. If, as may happen (*ibid.*, art. L.132–2, al. 2), the Assemblée Plénaire is seised on a first cassation, its rulings bind the court of remand. The position in Belgium is similar: Code judiciare, arts. 1119 and 1120.

[45] E.g. since 1942, Italy (c.p.c, art. 384), which requires the court of cassation to

Common law

No similar explicit provision for control by the American Court of Appeals of the court in which a new trial is held exists, but none is necessary. The common law doctrine of precedent gives to the Court's determinations of questions of law the force of law. If, therefore, the judge of first instance at the new trial were to disregard them, he would necessarily commit an error of law.

Power of decision

Two questions fall to be considered here. First, if the decision is quashed, can the court of cassation replace the defective decision with its own and dispose of the litigation? Secondly, if the legal reasoning of the decision is found to be defective but, in the opinion of the court of cassation, its actual disposition of the litigation is correct, may it affirm the decision on the basis of what it holds to be the correct legal reasoning? An affirmative answer to the first, even when limited to cases in which all the facts necessary are stated in the decision under attack, is an obvious element of impurity; it also, in substance if not in form, embraces an affirmative answer to the second. Even taken on its own, however, an affirmative answer to the second question introduces an element of impurity. It is impossible for a court to conclude that the dispositive part of a decision correctly resolves the dispute between the parties to litigation without itself giving consideration to its substance; and that, in a pure system, a court of cassation must not do.[46]

Civil law

Power to replace defective decisions
Somewhat surprisingly, the existence of this power, though not universal even today, is not an exclusively modern development. It has for long been within the powers of some courts of cassation, including that of Spain, to replace a defective decision with a decision of its own if it can do so without further investigation of facts.[47] It is true that there are still

enunciate the correct principle of law and its mode of application in the circumstances. See Liebman, p. 348; E. Fazzalari, *Istituzioni di Diritto Procesuale*, 8th edn (1996), p. 417. In Mexico the Supreme Court determines the bases on which the court of remand must proceed and which that court may not disregard: Fix, pp. 131–2.

[46] By parity of reasoning the Mexican 'suplencia de la queja' (chap. 13, p. 254), where it is allowed, is also a sign of impurity, and the reluctance of Mexican law to extend it beyond the special cases covered by art. 76 of the Ley de Amparo is understandable. Art. 79 introduces a further, but limited, element of impurity. See Fix, pp. 293–8.

[47] Ley de Enjuiciamiento Civil (L.E.C.), art. 1745; Germany, ZPO §565; H. Salger, 'La Cour Fédérale de Justice de la République Fédérale d'Allemagne', in P. Bellet and

some courts of cassation which lack the power of final decision,[48] but the law has been changed in France and, more recently, in Italy.[49] In France, the first step was taken in 1967, when it was enacted that the Assemblée pléniaire of the Court of cassation, on a second cassation, could come to a decision of substance if the second cassation was founded upon the same grounds as the first, and provided that the facts were sufficiently set out for the court to proceed wholly upon considerations of law.[50] Since 1979, the power to decide finally, on purely legal grounds, has been possessed by every chamber of the court on a first cassation.[51]

Affirmation on different legal grounds

The Belgian Constitution states that the Court of cassation 'ne connaît pas du fond des affaires'.[52] Perhaps for this reason, the Belgian court has no power to affirm a decision if it disapproves of its legal reasoning, even if the court regards the result as correct on different grounds. In Mexico, too, it appears, the Supreme Court has no such power.[53] In Italy, on the other hand, even before the court of cassation acquired power to replace a quashed decision with its own, that court could affirm the decision of a lower court if its dispositive part was in accordance with the law: if the reasons given by the court below are incorrect, the Court of cassation corrects them.[54] In France, since 1979, the court may refuse cassation where substitution of correct for incorrect legal reasoning is sufficient to cure the defect in the decision of the court below.[55]

A. Tunc (eds.), *La Cour judiciaire suprème* (1978), pp. 311, 340; Netherlands, G. J. Wiarda, 'Le Hoge Raad des Pays-Bas', *ibid.*, pp. 275, 288.

[48] E.g., Belgium, Constitution, art. 95 and A. Fettweiss, *Manuel de procédure civile*, 2nd edn (1987), no. 837; Mexico, Ley de Amparo, art. 80 and Fix, pp. 131–2.

[49] In Italy, art. 384 of the c.p.c., as amended in 1990, allows the Court of cassation to substitute its own decision after a cassation where it can do so without the need for further ascertainment of the facts. See, Fazzalari, *Istituzioni di Diritto Processuale*, p. 418; G. Tarzia, *Lineamenti del nuovo Processo di Cognizione* (1991), pp. 281–5.

[50] Law no. 67–523 of 3 July 1967, art. 16.

[51] Law no. 79–9 of 3 January 1979; C.org.jud., art. L. 131–5; n.c.p.c., art. 627. The finality and completeness of the judgment is emphasised by the explicit provision that it is enforceable and that the Court of cassation decides on the allocation of the costs between the parties.

[52] Art. 95.

[53] See Fix, no. 111 and note 138.

[54] C.p.c., art. 384, comma 2. The same position applies in the Netherlands (Wiarda, 'Le Hoge Raad', p. 288) and Germany (ZPO §563; Salger, 'La Cour Fédérale de Justice', p. 339).

[55] Now n.c.p.c., art. 620.

Common law: United States

Power of decision

Given the prevalence of jury trial in the United States, a finding of error by a Court of Appeals will normally require a new trial before a new jury.[56] Trial by judge alone is, however, no longer unusual, and where it occurs the judge is required to state separately his findings of fact and his conclusions of law.[57] If, then, a Court of Appeals is content with the judge's findings of fact but disagrees with his conclusion of law upon them, nothing prevents that court from substituting its own judgment for that at first instance. There is, however, also a possibility that a Court of Appeals will decide for itself disputed questions of fact. The trial judge's decision of fact will not be overturned unless it is 'clearly erroneous', but where nothing turns upon the credibility of the witnesses – witnesses who have given oral testimony in the presence of the judge and whose demeanour he will have observed – the possibility exists that the Court of Appeals will adopt its own view of the facts, in preference to that of the judge of first instance.[58]

Affirmation on different legal grounds

In the common law system, judgments themselves are not formally motivated. They consist only of what elsewhere would be called the dispositive part: the extensive exposition of reasoning given by common law judges – the 'opinion', as it is known in the United States[59] – is independent. There is nothing, therefore, to prevent a Court of Appeals from affirming a judgment with which it agrees, albeit for reasons different from those given by the judge of first instance. There is, furthermore, a well-established rule that even if error is found in the record, the Court of Appeals will not intervene unless the error is 'prejudicial', and this is for the appellant to establish. It is not always easy to determine whether an error is 'prejudicial' or 'harmless',[60] but if it is clear that the error did not affect the substantive rights of the parties it will be disregarded and the decision will be affirmed.[61]

---

[56] The possibility exists, in a jury trial, that a party applies to the judge of first instance for judgment in his favour *non obstante veredicto*. Such an application is unusual, but from the judge's decision upon it an appeal may be brought; the decision of the Court of Appeals then disposes of the matter finally.

[57] Fed.R.Civ.P., rule 52(a).

[58] James and Hazard, no. 13.8.

[59] In England the word 'judgment' covers both meanings.

[60] See, e.g. R. J. Traynor, *The Riddle of Harmless Error* (1970).

[61] Fed.R.Civ.P., rule 61.

The impurity of appeals

The most important matter for consideration here is the extent to which new evidence or proofs – evidence or proofs which for one reason or another were not available to the court of first instance – may be taken into account on appeal. A pure appeal calls for fresh adjudication of the questions of which the court of appeal is seised at second or subsequent instance,[62] and this, in principle, requires that the same procedures – including those for informing the court with regard to the facts – shall be used on appeal as were used at first instance. As will appear, a *novum judicium* in that sense is more easily achieved where the court of first instance reaches its decision after a distinct process of *instruction* than where, as in the common law, it does so at the end of a trial at which oral testimony is given in the presence of the judge (or judge and jury) to whom the decision is entrusted.

Civil law

In some countries the appeal remains relatively pure. The procedure, especially its most important part for present purposes – the *instruction* – follows the pattern of the *instruction* at first instance and there is no restriction on the admission of new proofs. This is the case, for example, in Belgium and France.[63] Italy, having formerly adopted a similar position, has, however, now joined those countries in which a court of appeal may admit new proofs only if certain conditions are fulfilled.[64] The conditions are not, of course, stated in identical terms everywhere, but in general they require that the omission at first instance of the proofs in question must not be attributable to any fault or lack of adequate preparation on the part of the litigant seeking their admission on appeal.[65]

---

[62] If a court seised of an appeal decides an issue in the litigation which has not previously been decided at first instance it acts, *pro tanto*, not as a court of appeal but as a court of first instance. In some countries, notably Belgium and France, the possibilities for a court of appeal to act in this way have nevertheless been expanded, mainly, it seems, in the interests of economy, and the court can dispose of the case once and for all. In Belgium the Code judiciaire (1967) requires the court of appeal, in effect, to deal with all outstanding matters: arts. 1068 and 1069 and Fettweiss, *Manuel de procédure civile*, nos. 813–15. In France the court's power to do so is discretionary: n.c.p.c. arts. 562, al. 2 and 568 and Vincent, no. 971. For critical appraisal see J. Vincent, 'Les dimensions nouvelles de l'appel en matière civile', D. 1973, Chron. 179. Though an element of impurity in the appeal, this development does not impinge directly upon the subject matter of this chapter.

[63] For Belgium see Code judiciare, art. 1042; for France see n.c.p.c., art. 910.

[64] C.p.c., art. 345, comma 3, as amended in 1990: Tarzia, *Lineamenti*, no. 62.

[65] E.g., Austria, ZPO no. 482; Mexico, Código Federal de procedimientos civiles, art.

From this point of view the Federal Republic of Germany presents something of a special case. There, traditionally, the appeal has been held to involve a complete re-examination of the whole case with all that that involves, including freedom for the parties to offer new proofs. In practice, however, it seems that this led to a widespread opinion not only that the proceedings at first instance were, in a case of importance, merely preliminary to those on appeal, but also that the parties' main effort in relation to proof should be reserved for the appellate stage.[66] In 1976, therefore, and as part of a wider reform intended to simplify and expedite litigation, certain rules of preclusion for the admission of proofs on appeal were introduced.[67] Even so, however, a court of appeal may still admit new proofs if it is satisfied that to do so will not cause delay in bringing the proceedings to a conclusion. The element of impurity introduced in 1976 is thus relatively slight.

It may be that in countries other than Germany in which the admission of new proofs on appeal is restricted, one of the objects of the restrictions is, as it is in Germany, to prevent a kind of degradation of the proceedings at first instance. Their effect is, however, inevitably to move the character of the appeal away from that of *novum judicium* and towards that of a *revisio prioris instantiae*. If new proofs are not admitted, a court of appeal is bound to confine itself to the appreciation of the facts as they have been proved at first instance.[68]

Common law: England

It has been stated earlier that, although the English appeal is by way of rehearing, it is nevertheless not a 'second first instance': the witnesses who testified at the trial are not heard again on appeal and, while appellate courts have power to admit fresh evidence, the power is limited and sparingly exercised.[69] In the terms of this chapter, the English appeal is unquestionably impure. Indeed, the impurity is such that the English appellate rehearing differs only in emphasis from the United States practice after trial by judge alone, notwithstanding that the latter developed out of the old proceedings for error, while in

253; Mexico, Código de procedimientos civiles para el D.F., art. 708; Spain, L.E.C., art. 862.

[66] Gilles, 'Die Berufung in Zivilsachen', pp. 150 and 154.

[67] Vereinsfachungsnovelle, 1976. See now ZPO §528.

[68] So much is spelled out in the Mexican Federal Code of Civil Procedure, art. 256, and in that country it may be that the appeal has become no more than an examination of the complaints of the appellant and of the respondent on a cross-appeal against the decision at first instance: H. Fix-Zamudio and Ovalle Favela, 'Derecho procesal' in *Introducción al derecho mexicano*, Vol. II (1981), p. 1251 at p. 1320.

[69] Chap. 14, p. 277.

England the appeal was introduced in substitution for them. There is little real difference between the English view that an appellate judge can substitute his own decision on questions to the solution of which the trial judge's ability to observe the witnesses' demeanour is not important,[70] and the American view that a Court of Appeals may substitute its own decision on questions that do not turn on the credibility or reliability of witnesses.[71] In other respects the English appeal is certainly wider than the American,[72] but, in the nature of things, it can be a true *novum judicium* only in those cases in which no oral testimony was given at first instance and such cases, though not today inconsiderable in number, make up only a small proportion of the whole.

Public and private purposes

It seems reasonably clear that procedures in the nature of cassation – procedures in which the proceedings and decision at first instance are attacked and which can result only in the affirmation or the annulment of the decision, not its replacement – emerge earlier in the development of a legal system than do procedures in the nature of appeal. So far as the English common law is concerned, there was no appeal, only proceedings in error, until the reforms of the nineteenth century, but even before the writ of error came the writ of attaint, a procedure whereby the jury itself was charged with dishonesty.[73] Maitland has pointed out that the concept of a complaint against a judgment that is not an accusation against the judge is not easily formed.[74] In France where, perhaps because of the greater influence of Roman law, the appeal came earlier, it was not until the seventeenth century that the judge of first instance ceased to be a necessary party to subsequent proceedings.[75]

That this should be so is natural enough, at least if it is accepted that the original and fundamental purpose of the entire structure of civil

---

[70] Above, p. 305.   [71] Above, p. 313.

[72] The English Court of Appeal will not normally alter the decision of the judge of first instance reached in the exercise of a discretion, but it can and does substitute its own decision on a wide variety of questions not only of law but of mixed law and fact and of fact alone. Unlike the American rule (above, p. 313) English law contains no formal requirement that the judge's findings be 'clearly erroneous'.

[73] See Holdsworth, *History of English Law*, Vol. I, pp. 337–42.

[74] F. Pollock and F. W. Maitland, *History of English Law before the Time of Edward I*, 2nd edn, Vol. II (1898), p. 668.

[75] A. Esmein, *Histoire de droit français*, 4th edn (1901), p. 428, citing R. Pothier, *Traité de procédure civile*, nos. 352, 353. In the Mexican *amparo-casación* the court whose decision is attacked is still, at least theoretically, a party to the proceedings: Ley de Amparo, art. 5; Fix, p. 388.

litigation was to replace violent by non-violent methods for the settlement of disputes. On this basis it is essential that there should be the widest possible confidence in the process of adjudication, and, while this must be principally achieved through the design of the process itself, more is likely to be required. So, for example, it is one thing to entrust decisions of fact to a jury – as happened in England – and to insist that the jury's verdict be accepted as final; it is an altogether different thing to deny the right of challenge even on the ground that the jury deliberately gave a false verdict: the writ of attaint enabled the jury's honesty to be put in question.[76] A similar point can be made about the writ of error and other forms of pure cassation, most obviously when complaint is made of error *in procedendo*, but also when complaint is made of error *in judicando*: a decision should no more be forced upon the parties and publicly upheld if it was reached by the erroneous application of the law than if it was reached following a defective procedure; only through correct, or at least consistent, application of the law can equality of treatment be secured and be seen to be secured.

If this is right, then it may well be that the original reason for giving some scope to the private initiative of the disappointed party to litigation was, as Calamandrei said,[77] to put it to the service of the wider interest of society – in this case, the maintenance of confidence in the process of adjudication. The later inclusion of other public interest purposes – such as securing consistency in the interpretation and application of the law, the clarification of the law and even the development of the law – is not inconsistent with that.

The appeal, on the other hand, is not at first sight directed to such public purposes at all but to the private purpose of improving the quality of the decision itself as it affects the actual parties to the litigation before the court. It has, indeed, even been suggested that the appeal may reduce rather than promote confidence in the system of adjudication: 'to put before a second judge a case which has already been decided by a first is deliberately to cast suspicion on the administration of justice'.[78] It is not, however, necessary to go so far as this to see something new in

---

[76] The earliest juries, composed of neighbours, were expected to reach their verdicts on the basis of their own knowledge of the circumstances. Only gradually did it become the rule that juries must decide exclusively on the evidence presented to them in open court: Holdsworth, *History of English Law*, Vol. I, pp. 330–7.

[77] Above, p. 306.

[78] Esmein, *Histoire de droit français*. Esmein asks, 'if the first judge could have made a mistake, why should not this also be true of the second?' Even so, it may be suggested that the availability of an appeal today contributes more than it detracts from public confidence in the administration of justice. See, e.g. Evershed, no. 473, where it was recognised that abolition of the right of appeal would reduce costs but the idea was nevertheless dismissed out of hand; Woolf Final, p. 153.

the emergence of the appeal, namely, recognition by a legal system that the decisions of its courts should not only be accepted as finally determinative of the disputes litigated before them, but that those decisions should in some, no doubt ill-defined, sense be correct.[79]

This makes it appear not only that cassation and appeal are different and distinct procedural institutions, but that each exists to serve a different social purpose – the one public, and the other private. Such is, indeed, the classical opinion, confirmation of which is not difficult to find even in some modern legislation. The Italian law on court organisation, for example, states that, as the supreme court, the Court of cassation 'assures the exact observance and the uniform interpretation of the law, the unity of national law . . .',[80] but it says nothing of the rights of the parties: those are the concern of the courts of first instance and of appeal. It is, however, doubtful whether this simple view was ever completely accurate, and certainly it is not so today; matters are more complex.[81]

A major source of this complexity is the impurity that now infects both cassation and appeal so widely. Cassation, even where there is also appeal, now enters into the facts of the cases under consideration and looks to the private interests of the parties – a 'humane' conception of the court of cassation, which can no longer allow a perceived error to go uncorrected[82] – while the appeal, by its restrictions on new evidence and, in common law countries, by limiting itself to a transcript instead of having the witnesses before it in person, is correspondingly less of a *novum judicium* concerned only with the correct resolution of the parties' dispute. Indeed, in most common law countries, where the highest as well as the intermediate level of jurisdiction is a jurisdiction of appeal, and where the decisions of the courts are themselves recognised as authoritative sources of law, the need for the appeal to meet the public purposes of unifying, clarifying and developing the law is manifest.[83] The House of Lords, for example, decides only about fifty civil

[79] See, e.g. Gilles, 'Die Berufung in Zivilsachen', 150.

[80] Law on court organisation, art. 65, transl., M. Cappelletti *et al.*, *The Italian Legal System* (1967), p. 152.

[81] It is of interest to compare Vincent and immediately preceding editions of the same work, with the 19th edition of 1978. The earlier edition gives the traditional account of the Court of cassation: its role is to achieve unification in the interpretation of the rules of law; it does not examine the facts but must accept them as they appear in the judgment under attack; having no power to substitute its own decision, when it quashes a decision it remands the case elsewhere. The later editions, in contrast, state that the court does not have as its sole objective the interests of the parties but is concerned also with the general interests of society: 22nd edn, nos. 1023–1.

[82] Mazeaud, p. 473.

[83] So, for example, while it has been provided that the Court of Appeal may sometimes be constituted by two judges instead of the traditional three (Supreme Court Act 1981, s.

cases in each year and its proceedings are elaborate, time-consuming and expensive: no one could sensibly suggest that the appeal to the House of Lords exists only to protect the private interest of the parties to the few cases that come before it.[84]

So much is not infrequently acknowledged, though rarely in legislation, and the position of the House of Lords from this point of view is not in practice so different from that of the Supreme Court of the United States, which, today, will give extensive consideration only to cases held to involve important questions of law.[85] There is, however, no need to labour the point. In many countries, if not in all, it is impossible to continue to insist that what is called 'appeal' and what is called 'cassation' are totally different kinds of legal institution, each serving or seeking to serve different purposes in society. The public and the private purposes of the entire legal system are served indiscriminately by both, and if it continues to appear in some systems that cassation looks more to the public purpose than does the appeal, this is because the procedure in the highest court is there a procedure of cassation. It is the level in the judicial hierarchy, rather than the description of the procedure employed, that most affects the proportions in which the public and the private purposes are combined.[86]

As already suggested, many of the changes that have produced the impurity of cassation and of appeal have been introduced with no more profound an intention than that of reducing the time and cost involved in taking litigation through all its stages to final judgment. The achievement of procedural economy is important, but consideration must also be given to the question – a question usually asked and answered in the vaguest of terms, if at all – just what is it that should be done more cheaply and more quickly?[87]

That question goes wider than the subject matter of this chapter, for it extends also to proceedings at first instance and to the current tendency in many countries to enhance the powers of the judge at the expense of

54), it is recognised that a three-judge court should sit if the questions raised include a point of law of some importance: *Coldunell Ltd* v. *Gallon* [1986] Q.B. 1184, 1202, *per* Oliver L.J. See also *Practice Note (Court of Appeal: New Procedure)* [1982] 1 W.L.R. 1312, 1319; Bowman, p. 58.

[84] Since the Administration of Justice (Appeals) Act 1934 leave to appeal to the House of Lords is always necessary. No criteria for the grant of leave are laid down, but in general leave is only granted if a point of law of importance is raised: *Re Wilson* [1985] A.C. 750, 756, *per* Lord Roskill.

[85] Exceptional cases apart, the Supreme Court of the United States will hear an appeal from a Court of Appeals only if there are 'special reasons': Supreme Court Rules, rule 19(1). This means, in practice, that it will do so only if, in the opinion of at least four justices of the Supreme Court, there is an important question of law involved.

[86] See above, chap. 14, p. 297.

[87] Below, chap. 17, p. 359.

the dispositive powers of the parties. It is, however, also necessary that thought be given to the role of proceedings subsequent to those that led to the original adjudication, whether they be in the nature of appeal or cassation or a mixture of the two. No longer can it be assumed that the roles of appeal and cassation are distinct. Exceptional cases apart, the initiation of any form of legal proceedings subsequent to an initial decision, involves the exercise of a right – a procedural right – possessed by a person affected by the decision in question, and that person is far more likely than not to be motivated by self-interest. Even if future reform is directed primarily to the achievement of economy, the reasons why that self-interest should be indulged, and the objectives and limitations of the various forms of recourse which that self-interest may set in motion, must be examined and kept under review.

Some general observations

The variables

The developments mentioned in this chapter indicate that between pure cassation, on the one hand, and pure appeal, on the other, there lies not a sharp cleavage but a range of intermediate positions. The place of a particular procedure within this range depends essentially upon two factors, namely, first, the nature of the outcome to which it may lead and, secondly, the nature of the questions to which the court's attention may be directed. The first reflects the line between a procedure which allows the replacement of a decision found to be defective and one which allows only its annulment. The second is conventionally linked to the distinction between questions of fact and questions of law, but that distinction has proved itself in practice to be a most uncertain guide: it has become, in effect, little more than a form of words used to distinguish between questions that, in a given procedure, may be reopened after decision at first instance and questions that may not.[88] In the actual structure of a legal system both these factors operate in conjunction, but it has been convenient to separate them for the purposes of discussion.

The right to decide

It is widely agreed that the right to decide, which is necessarily possessed by a court of first instance or other adjudicating authority, must be

---

[88] Above, p. 303.

respected, at least to the extent that subsequent proceedings should be the exception rather than the norm. Even where a pure appeal is open, the appellant must normally show some reason why the original decision should not be left intact.[89] Further, and more importantly for present purposes, it is almost invariably the case that where a serious procedural error has occurred, the original decision is quashed, not replaced, and the case remanded whence it came for fresh decision: this is so whether the error is established in a court of appeal or a court of cassation. The conclusion is not that the original decision was wrong but rather that it was invalid: a fresh decision must be made by the jurisdiction whose right or duty it is to make it.

Error *in procedendo* does not, therefore, ordinarily deprive the original jurisdiction of its right to decide. Error *in judicando*, on the other hand, may do so, and does do so whenever the erroneous decision is replaced in the superior court. Conversely, where the superior court can do no more than quash a decision for error *in judicando*, the consequence is to preserve the original jurisdiction's right to decide.

It is no longer possible to regard such an outcome as a mere byproduct of the distinction between courts of cassation and courts of appeal: too many courts of cassation now have extensive power to replace defective decisions with decisions of their own. It is, however, still true in certain categories of case that the only available form of recourse for error *in judicando* is the annulment of the erroneous decision, and this notwithstanding the economies that would be achieved if a final decision could be given there and then. Is any explanation available of the value that is thus apparently placed, where this is so, on preservation of the right of the original jurisdiction to decide the substance of the cases that come before it?

Within the compass of this chapter no more than a tentative answer to this question is possible, but it does appear as a general rule that it is only when litigation starts and finishes within a single judicial hierarchy that the decision of a lower court can be replaced at a higher level; when the decision emanates from an external adjudicative authority – as is the case, for example, with an administrative decision – the decision may be quashed, but then the case must be remanded to the jurisdiction from

---

[89] This is without prejudice to the question whether the court is or is not restricted to consideration of the points raised by the parties as grounds of appeal or cross-appeal. In England an appellant must state the grounds of his appeal, but the Court has a discretionary power to admit additional grounds as well. R.S.C., Ord. 59, rr. 3(2) and 3(3). In Mexico only the stated grounds of appeal and cross-appeal will be considered: Fix-Zamudio and Ovalle Favela, *Introducción al derecho mexicano*, Vol. II, p. 1320. In Germany action has had to be taken to try to restore the authority of first instance decisions: above, p. 315.

which it came. So, notwithstanding the absence of the word from English legal terminology, the English procedure of the application for judicial review retains the essential characteristics of pure cassation: the court may quash, but it may not replace, the decision of an administrative authority. Similarly, in Mexico the federal jurisdiction, seised by amparo of the decision of a state court, may quash that decision for error *in judicando*, but if it does so the new decision is made by the state, not the federal, court.

The existence in Mexico of a power in the federal court to annul the decision of a state court has been justified by the need for a central judicial power to unify the decisions of local courts since Mexican federalism is, or is said to be, 'artificial'.[90] But this is not to say that Mexican federalism is non-existent: the Supreme Court may exercise control over state courts, but it is not their direct hierarchical superior. It is, as is acknowledged by the relative purity of the *amparo-casación* against their decisions, for the state courts to pronounce the final judgment in litigation started in those courts; their right to decide is preserved.

A similar point can be made for the English application for judicial review and probably also for procedures in other countries which enable administrative decisions to be brought under scrutiny in the ordinary courts: it is the administrator, not the judge, on whom the power of decision has been conferred by the legislature, and this, it may be supposed, is because it is the training and experience of an administrator, not that of a judge, which is thought to be appropriate – appropriate not only for determining what are the basic or primary facts but also for drawing any necessary inferences of fact and for the evaluation of the facts. The administrator's right of decision must be and is preserved.[91]

Matters stand differently, however, where the case is confined within a single hierarchy, for then the judges at all levels have had similar education, training and professional experience. Except for cases tried by jury in common law countries – in which case a superior court may quash but may not replace the verdict – there is no obvious advantage in preserving the right of the court of first instance to decide. On the contrary, to the extent that the judges of the superior courts are as well placed, in relation to the materials upon which the decision must be

[90] Fix, p. 127.
[91] So for example, while the French court of cassation may determine for itself the qualification of the facts, the Conseil d'Etat, when acting as a court of cassation, may not: above, n. 11. A similar point can be made with reference to any specialist tribunal, especially if, as may be the case, an appeal lies to an equally specialist appellate body. See, e.g. *R. v. Chief Constable of the Merseyside Police, ex parte Calvely* [1989] Q.B. 424.

based, as are those of the inferior to form their own opinions on the matters in dispute, their greater experience provides an additional advantage, over and above the economies that are realised if they are permitted to dispose finally of the case. To insist that a court of cassation must always remand for no other reason than to preserve the right to decide of a lower court in the same hierarchy is, in modern conditions, little more than pedantry.

The nature of the questions

In a pure appeal all the questions raised at first instance are capable of being reopened, whether they are classified as questions of law or of fact. In a pure cassation, on the other hand, it is accepted dogma that only questions of law may be reopened. As a technique for defining the limits of different forms of recourse, however, the distinction between questions of fact and questions of law conceals more than it reveals.[92] It might be better to approach the matter by separate consideration of those forms of recourse which do, and those which do not, include as one of their objectives preservation of the right to decide of the original adjudicative authority.

The right to decide preserved

Errors *in procedendo* apart, the right to decide is, of course, best preserved by allowing the original decision to stand. It should not be annulled unless there are cogent reasons for doing so. Such reasons include, but are not restricted to, simple instances of disregard or misinterpretation of the applicable law. In particular, while both the determination and the appreciation of the facts belong to the original adjudicator, his decisions of fact or of mixed fact and law may be so extreme, so unreasonable, that they must be annulled. In England, for example, an administrative decision will be quashed if it is 'so unreasonable that no reasonable authority could ever have come to it',[93] and in France an administrative decision will be annulled for 'manifest' error or lack of 'proportionality'.[94] The question of the unreasonableness of a

---

[92] Above, p. 303.

[93] *Associated Provincial Picture Houses Ltd* v. *Wednesbury Corporation* [1948] 1 K.B. 223. A more modern statement is that a decision is 'unreasonable' if it is one 'which no reasonable authority acting with due appreciation of its responsibilities would have decided to adopt': *Secretary of State for Education* v. *Tameside Metropolitan Borough Council* [1977] A.C. 1014. See, e.g. Wade, pp. 387–459. Note also the rule that a jury's verdict may be quashed if it is perverse: p. 310, above.

[94] J. M. Auby and R. Drago, *Traité des recours en matière administrative* (1992), nos. 348 and 349.

decision may be equated to a question of law by a variety of technical devices, but to do this is to do no more than restate in different words that the question is open in the superior court. What is of practical importance is that that court will annul a decision in extreme cases, but will not do so merely because its judges, had the right of decision belonged to them, would have come to a different conclusion.

Right to decide not preserved

Here, if what has been said earlier is correct, there is no reason of principle why the opinions of the superior court should not replace those of the inferior where there is a difference between them. The important qualification is that the superior court should be as well placed in relation to the materials on which the decision is to be based as was the inferior. This qualification is met where the question at issue is of pure law, but otherwise it depends on a number of factors, of which two are particularly important. First, it must be asked whether the superior court receives the evidence or proofs in the same form as did the inferior, and if not whether the difference in form is significant in the circumstances. Secondly, it must also be asked whether the superior court is entitled to receive new evidence.[95]

The extent to which either or both of these factors operate in a given system is, no doubt, in part a result of history and tradition. It is, for example, the emergence of the jury that is ultimately responsible for the common law's preference for oral testimony at the trial, and thus for the English practice that questions of fact dependent upon an assessment of a witness's credibility will not be reopened in the Court of Appeal even after trial by judge alone.[96] Similarly, given its long history as a court of pure cassation, it may be expected that the full effects of the acquisition by the French Court of cassation of power to pronounce final decisions will not be felt for some time. Subject to this, however, it seems that the extent to which a form of recourse to a particular court places that court in the same position as the court below – in relation, that is, to the materials on which a decision will be based – depends as much on pragmatic considerations as on considerations of principle.

One such consideration is, no doubt, the need to maintain the authority and the finality of the decision at first instance in all save a minority of cases and this, as the German experience shows, may be put at risk by overemphasis on the appeal as a complete reconsideration of

[95] Where new evidence is admitted, the superior court may actually be better placed than the inferior, in which case, a fortiori, it should be entitled to substitute its own decision for that of the inferior court.
[96] Above, p. 316.

the entire case.[97] Another, to which great weight is attached in many countries at the present time, is the need for economy, not only in the direct cost to litigants or to publicly funded sources of legal aid, but also in judicial resources; it is, indeed, not uncommon to find the right of appeal excluded in cases of small monetary value or that an appeal is allowed only on a question classified as one of law: this may be achieved either by explicit legislation to that effect or by excluding appeal while allowing cassation. Obviously a recourse limited to questions of law, however imprecise that terminology may be, is less expensive than one under which questions of fact are also open. It is true that some measures of reform aimed only at improved economy may be introduced without significantly changing the character of the recourse affected, as has been attempted in England,[98] but the long-term consequences of such reforms will not be known until years after their introduction. It is to be expected that comparative study will continue to show important variations from one country to another, whether such variation is the product of deliberate intervention by the legislator or not. Pure appeal and pure cassation may be nearing extinction, but as concepts they will continue to mark the two ends of a line on which different procedures of recourse will find their individual places.

Conclusion

It is, probably, only of the recourse 'in the interest of the law', where it exists, that it can be said that a form of recourse serves only a public purpose: it can be engaged only by a public official and its outcome does not affect the rights and obligations of the parties as determined by the decision that is its subject.[99] So far as is known, all other procedures depend on party initiative for their engagement and all, to a greater or lesser extent, serve both public and private purposes.

The extent to which public or private purposes predominate in a given procedure – and which specific public purposes – depends on a number of different factors. The level within the hierarchy of the court seised of a procedure of recourse has already been mentioned, as has the nature of the questions open for reconsideration: the further a procedure is removed from the pure appeal, the greater the weight apparently

---

[97] Above, p. 315.

[98] For example, by the reduction of the constitution of the Court of Appeal from three judges to two in certain categories of case (above, n. 83).

[99] France, n.c.p.c., art. 618–1; Law no. 67–523 of 3 July 1967, art. 17. México, Ley de Amparo, art. 185*bis*; Belgium, Code judiciare, arts. 1089, 1090; Italy, c.p.c., art. 363. Occasionally of great value (e.g. Ass. Plén. 31 May 1991, D.S. 1991, 417, noted [1992] C.L.J. 37) this form of recourse is little used.

attached to matters of public interest such as the interpretation, clarification and development of the law. It must not be overlooked, however, that in practice a very great deal depends also on the relative ease with which a disappointed litigant can exercise a right of recourse and on its predictable cost or financial risk.

It is probably right that there should always be some disincentive to the use of a right of recourse, even where the predominant purpose is to secure the private interests of the parties; there is a pervading public interest in the finality of litigation and the need for economy of judicial resources. Subject to this, however, the disincentive should be no stronger than necessary.[100] On the other hand, where the predominant purpose of a procedure of recourse, whether nominally of cassation or of appeal, is to serve the public interest, where, to repeat Calamandrei's words, the state makes use of the private, self-interested initiative of the disappointed party by putting it to the service of the wider interests of society,[101] choice of the right level of disincentive is critical: those interests will suffer if it is too low and also if it is too high.

In many countries the right of recourse by way of cassation to the highest court in the judicial hierarchy is valued more highly or, at least, is better protected by the positive law, than is the right of appeal. In Italy it is constitutional,[102] and in France it can be removed, if at all, only by parliamentary legislation.[103] The procedure on cassation is also relatively inexpensive and, in light particularly of the present willingness of the court to enter into the facts, the result has been to create, in some countries, case-loads of unmanageable proportion.[104] Some cases can be dealt with rapidly by use of an abbreviated form of procedure,[105] but even so there is no disrespect to the distinguished judges of those courts

---

[100] The right of appeal is now commonly denied in cases of less than a certain monetary value. This technique is unfortunate: whatever monetary limit is chosen, the sum of money in question will be significant to many litigants and potential litigants.

[101] *La Cassazione Civile*, see n. 26.

[102] Art. 113.

[103] P. Bellet, 'La Cour de cassation en France', in Bellet and Tunc, *La Cour judiciare suprème*, pp. 193, 197. Cassation is available only against decisions which are not subject to appeal, but this includes decisions at first instance against which no appeal is allowed as well as decisions of a Court of Appeal. Comprehensible when cassation was pure, this now seems paradoxical.

[104] Tunc, 'Synthèse', in *ibid.*, pp. 5 and 15. In 1997 the French Court of cassation, exclusive of its Criminal Chamber, disposed of over 20,000 cases, but notwithstanding this productivity, the number of cases pending at the end of the year was greater than at its beginning: R. Perrot, *Institutions judiciaires* (1998), no. 221.

[105] In France, if it appears to the President of the Court, or of the appropriate Chamber, that the solution of a case is clear, the case can be assigned to a court of three rather than the usual five judges: C.org.jud., art. L. 131-6.

in the suggestion that they do not always have the time for reflection that the questions they have to resolve will frequently require.[106]

A converse situation exists in some final courts of appeal such as the English House of Lords, where, for a variety of reasons including the elaborate nature of the procedure and its extremely high cost, the number of cases decided is very low.[107] This does, of course, mean that the Law Lords have adequate time for reflection, but, however high the quality of their contributions to legal development, their opportunities to make those contributions are few.[108] It is to the Court of Appeal, not the House of Lords, that English law looks for the majority of the authoritative decisions which are so important to its make-up, and this in turn has consequences for that Court by enhancing the public aspect of its proceedings at the expense of its role in securing the interests of the parties to litigation themselves.

This is an age of procedural reform in many parts of the world, and the tendency everywhere is to concentrate on pragmatic considerations. The search is for more efficient and less expensive methods for the administration of justice. The question that most engages the attention of procedural reformers today is 'How?' and that, of course, is a question no practical lawyer can ignore. It is not the case, however, that the answers to 'What?' and 'Why?' can be taken for granted: it can no longer be assumed that different forms of recourse against decisions serve clearly distinguishable purposes and that the only question is how those purposes are best and most economically achieved. Scholars interested in procedural reform must turn their minds once more to the purposes which the institutions of their legal systems actually serve in modern conditions; and where, as is so often the case, it is found that a number of purposes not easily reconciled with one another are served by a single institution, they must consider which of those purposes should predominate, before going on to tackle matters of relative detail.

---

[106] A. Tunc, 'Journées d'Etudes sur la Cour Judiciaire Suprême' 1979 Rev.int.dr.comp. 641. More time yet would probably be required by the judges if the proposal for more explicit reasoning in the judgments of the Court of cassation were implemented: A. Touffait and A. Tunc, 'Pour une motivation plus explicite des décisions de justice, notamment celles de la Cour de cassation' 1974 Rev.trim.dr.civ. 487.

[107] Leave to appeal to the House of Lords has been required since 1934, but this is not the complete explanation. The number was no higher before 1934. See J. A. Jolowicz, 'Les décisions de la Chambre des Lords' 1979 Rev.int.dr.comp. 521, 522 and authorities at n. 8.

[108] It has been suggested that 'half a century is not an unreasonable estimate of the time that is likely to elapse before a doubtful point is settled': P. Devlin, *Samples of Lawmaking* (1962), p. 14.

16   Managing overload in appellate courts: 'Western' countries[1]

The individual reports used in preparation of the original version of this chapter reveal so great a variety of appellate systems that it is difficult to find common ground on which to base a comparative account of the problem of overload and its management. There are systems which distinguish sharply between appeal and cassation; there are federal systems in which the federal supreme court acts as the final court of appeal for the whole country and others in which it acts only in federal cases; there are systems which, though unitary, have separate jurisdictions for private and for public law cases, and others with a unified hierarchy of courts: there are systems with one tier only after first instance, and others with two or even more; there are systems in which the appeal has a suspensive effect and others in which first instance judgments are enforceable as soon as given.

Even more striking than these specific differences is the difference in the volume of appellate work in countries of roughly comparable size, and in their attitudes to the right of appeal and to possible limitations of it. So, to take a dramatic example, in England the House of Lords has jurisdiction in public as well as private law, has a mere twelve full-time judges, is not divided into chambers, is a court of appeal not cassation, and delivers judgment in about fifty civil cases a year. In Italy, by contrast, the Corte di cassazione has only limited public law jurisdiction, is divided into several chambers which sit simultaneously, is a court of cassation not of appeal, and delivers judgment in several thousand cases

[1] Based on a Report to the International Congress on the Law of Civil Procedure held in Utrecht in 1987, published in W. Wedekind (ed.), *Justice and Efficiency* (1989), p. 71. For the parallel report on 'socialist countries', see J. Németh, 'Rechtsmittelgerichte in den Europäischen sozialistischen Ländern', *ibid.*, p. 95. See also J. A. Jolowicz, 'Appellate Proceedings' in M. Storme and H. Casman (eds.), *Towards a Justice with a Human Face* (1978), p. 127; P. Yessiou-Faltsi (ed.), *The Role of the Supreme Courts at the National and International Level* (1998).

   The chapter draws on the national reports listed at the end of this chapter. All are held on file by the International Association of Procedural Law and some have been independently published. For uniformity, page references in the following text are to the original versions.

every year. In England, appeal to the House of Lords is possible only with the prior leave of the court *a quo* or of the House itself, while in Italy the right of recourse to the Court of cassation is constitutionally protected. This is not sufficient by itself to explain such different case-loads, but it does illustrate a difference of attitude: in Italy recourse to the supreme court is a matter of right; in England it is exceptional.

In the light of such extremes, and in the light also of the differences in the character of the proceedings at first instance,[2] this chapter must proceed on the basis of a number of assumptions. It is necessary to ride roughshod over some of the distinctions that are built in to some systems but unknown in others, such as that between appeal and cassation.[3] To change the metaphor, a broad brush tends to conceal nice points of detail but is essential to a comparative report that crosses the dividing line between legal families. For the purposes of this chapter, therefore, and save where the context otherwise indicates, the following conventions are adopted:

(1) The word 'appeal' is used in relation to any proceedings subsequent to the decision at first instance,[4] which come before a court higher than the court of first instance,[5] whether classified internally as appeal, cassation or revision, and whether that higher court can give its own decision on the substance of the case or is limited to the affirmation or annulment of the decision *a quo*. Appeal does not, however, extend to procedures which come before the court of first instance itself such as the French *opposition*[6] or the American application to the trial judge for a new trial.

(2) Where an appellate court has criminal as well as civil jurisdiction, criminal appeals obviously form part of its case-load, but only civil appeals are directly considered. On the other hand, save by necessary implication, the distinction between appeals in civil and in administrative cases, which exists where there are separate jurisdictions but not elsewhere, will be ignored.

(3) Account will be taken only of appeals from those first instance decisions which are made within the regular judicial hierarchy.

---

[2] Chap. 15, p. 303.

[3] This is not, in itself, to diminish the importance of the distinction, but in fact it has become much less significant than it was: chap. 15, p. 306.

[4] A 'decision at first instance' includes decisions which are interlocutory or *avant dire droit*.

[5] A 'full court', such as the full court of the Australian state supreme courts, though a manifestation of the same court as the court of first instance, is here treated as a higher court. See, however, below, n. 93.

[6] N.c.p.c., arts. 571–8.

This includes appeals from judicial determinations of the validity or otherwise of decisions originally made outside that hierarchy, such as the decisions of administrative tribunals, but it does not include procedures – of which the English application for judicial review is an example[7] – whereby those decisions can be challenged in courts of first instance.

(4) It will be assumed that appeals are instituted by a party to the original litigation or, at least, by a person who has a direct interest in the outcome of the litigation.

(5) Finally, it will be taken for granted that every appellate system has a purpose or purposes, however concealed, against which the existence of overload can be determined, and against which measures taken or to be taken for the management of overload can be assessed. A court is overloaded not only if it has a growing backlog of pending cases, but also if it cannot adequately fulfil the purpose or purposes for which it exists. As used here, therefore, 'purpose' means the purpose for which a right of appeal is granted, not the purpose of the litigant who chooses to exercise it. It follows, since no procedural right is granted in order that it may be abused, that measures intended to minimise abuse of the right of appeal are inherently justifiable provided only that they do not jeopardise achievement of the purposes for which the right itself exists. This aspect of the management of overload is mentioned later, but otherwise it will be assumed that the right of appeal is exercised in good faith.

Purpose of appeal

Explanations of the great increase in the volume of litigation by comparison with the past, and thus also of increased demands on appellate courts, are beyond the scope of this chapter. To some extent this increase in demand can be met by an increase in the total number of appellate judges and by a reduction in the quorum of judges required to constitute a court or chamber for the decision of a given case. There are, however, limits to what can be done in this way, and the limits are not only economic: if the number of judges is increased by too many it may be difficult to find sufficient people of the right calibre for appointment;[8] if too many divisions or chambers of the same court exist, the risk that even supreme courts will produce decisions that conflict with one another, and thus endanger both the coherence and

---

[7] Above, chap. 8, p. 154.
[8] See Chile, p. 11; Israel, pp. 23 and 27; Uruguay, p. 17.

the comprehensibility of the law, will be increased.[9] Almost everywhere, therefore, a variety of procedural techniques has been adopted or is under active consideration with a view to keeping the case-loads of appellate courts within bounds.

By and large, these techniques fall into two main groups. In the first place there are techniques which are intended to control the number of cases in which an appeal is instituted, of which an obvious, widely adopted, and rather crude, example is the simple denial of all right of appeal in certain kinds of case. In the second place there are techniques intended to enable appellate courts to dispose more expeditiously of the cases that actually come before them. This chapter looks at some of these techniques, but, since there is a danger that their adoption may affect adversely the capacity of an appellate court to fulfil the purposes for which it exists, it is necessary to set out briefly, and somewhat superficially, the purposes for which appellate systems exist.[10] They can be divided into two broad categories, which are here called the private and the public. Each is separately outlined below, but they are not, and cannot be, kept rigidly apart in practice.

The private purpose

The private purpose behind the grant of a right of appeal is two-fold, but its two parts coalesce. First, it is to respond to the natural desire that failure at first instance may inspire a litigant to have his case reconsidered at a higher level, and, secondly, it is to ensure so far as possible that justice is done between the parties. To fulfil the private purpose to the maximum possible extent, therefore, an appellate court needs jurisdiction to entertain questions of fact as well as of law, it needs the right to substitute its own decision for that of the court *a quo* – not merely to declare that decision right or wrong – and it needs the right to receive evidence that was not available and arguments that were not submitted to that court.

The extent to which appellate courts satisfy these requirements – the requirements of a pure appeal – varies greatly, not only from one legal system to another but between different levels within a single legal system, especially when one level is of appeal, the other of cassation. The further a particular appellate procedure departs from the theoretical concept of a complete *novum judicium*, the less well equipped it is to fulfil the private purpose in any given case. Nevertheless, if the private purpose is to be even reasonably met every time that the right of appeal

[9] USA, p. 18.   [10] Chap. 15, p. 308.

is invoked, some such departure is inevitable; in few, if any, appellate courts today is a complete *novum judicium* available.[11] On the other hand, however ill-equipped a given court may appear to be to meet the private purpose, since no court is seised of an appeal except on the initiative of a party,[12] it is almost inevitable that the judges will pay some regard to the interests of the parties before them whatever the nature of the procedure. To a greater or lesser extent, the private purpose is always there.

The public purpose

In theory as well as in practice there is overlap between the public and the private purposes, if only because a legal system that fails adequately to meet the latter will forfeit public confidence: it is an essential public purpose of every institution or procedure of a legal system that it should help to maintain public confidence in the administration of justice.

More specifically, appellate courts serve a public purpose in at least two different ways. First, and most obviously, when an appeal is brought on the ground of an alleged procedural error in the court below, they act in a supervisory capacity to ensure that courts of first instance act in accordance with the law. Secondly, the decisions of appellate courts – especially, but by no means exclusively, those of supreme courts – make essential contributions to the development and clarification of the law itself. In common law countries, which formally recognise the rule *stare decisis*, this is obviously the case, but even where judicial decisions are denied the status of sources of law, as in countries whose law is codified, there are few, if any, who would still deny that judicial decisions as such contribute to the content of the law.[13] Overload of an appellate court can have serious adverse effects on its ability to fulfil at least this aspect of its public purpose; if its case-load is too great, its judges will not be able to devote the time necessary for the proper consideration and discussion of cases which raise difficult and important questions of law. Paradoxically, this problem is more serious in courts of cassation where, in principle, questions of fact are not open and the public purpose is supposed to predominate, than it is in common law supreme courts whose procedures and formal powers resemble those of the intermediate courts of appeal, and whose role as 'guardian' of the law is not often acknowledged in the legislation.

[11] Chap. 15, p. 314.
[12] The recourse 'in the interest of the law' (chap. 15, p. 325) is an exception but is rarely used.
[13] Chap. 3, p. 73.

Restriction on right of appeal

This section examines some of the techniques which are used to keep cases out of the appellate courts by restricting the right of appeal or by qualifying it in some way. It must not be overlooked, however, that the initiation of an appeal is a voluntary act, and if an unsuccessful litigant is content to allow the judgment against him to stand, there will be no appeal. The risk of incurring an additional liability for costs is, no doubt, a factor of importance,[14] and may explain in part the extremely low case-load of some courts, but, while an element of disincentive through the costs sanction may be justifiable, it must not be carried too far.[15] In any event, if the defeated litigant at first instance normally accepts the decision as final, recognising that justice has been done, there will be relatively few appeals. Conversely, if the appeal is regarded as little more than a continuation of the proceedings at first instance, if it comes to be the general opinion that a 'real' decision is given only in the appellate court, then the burden on that court is obviously increased. Different attitudes are found in different countries to the place of the (first) appeal, and these must be mentioned before turning to more detailed matters.

The finality of the first instance

It was not until the nineteenth century that the English common law came to have a true appeal.[16] Even today, although an extensive right of appeal exists and is recognised as essential to the due administration of justice, it continues to be insisted that all rights of appeal are 'statutory', the significance of which is that if specific provision for appeal is not made then no right of appeal exists. It follows that, both in the past and at the present time, the decision at first instance is usually taken as final, and the same is true, by and large, in other common law countries. The appeal has no suspensive effect, and first instance judgments are enforceable as soon as given unless a stay of execution is ordered. As an Australian judge observed, if the substantial issues between the parties were not ordinarily settled at trial, 'the main arena for the settlement of disputes would move from the court of first instance to the appellate court, tending to reduce proceedings in the former to little more than a preliminary skirmish'.[17]

---

[14] See, e.g. Germany, p. 3; Israel, p. 18; Netherlands, pp. 17–18; Spain, p. 4.
[15] Chap. 15, p. 326.   [16] Chap. 15, p. 299.
[17] *Coulton v. Holcombe* (1986) 60 A.L.J.R. 470, 473, *per* Gibbs C.J.; chap. 14, n. 30. See also, the opinion of Professor Denti, cited Italy, p. 7.

A similar attitude prevails in Austria, in accordance with the opinion of the architect of its code, Franz Klein,[18] but elsewhere the principle of double instance is usually held to be an essential guarantee of justice. In most civil law countries,[19] subject to limited exceptions,[20] no judgment is enforceable until the time for appealing has expired or the appeal has been determined.[21] There must, therefore, be at least a risk that the degradation of the first instance mentioned above may become a reality as, apparently, occurred in Germany.[22] In that country reforms introduced in 1976 were intended, amongst other things, to improve the status of first instance decisions, and it appears that the measures taken succeeded for a time. Subsequently, however, the number of appeals entered rose once more.[23]

Exclusion from appeal

Small claims

In many countries no right of appeal exists from decisions in cases of less than a certain value.[24] Most of these, however, are countries in which the appeal is sharply distinguished from cassation, and, generally, the exclusion of the appeal does not involve the exclusion also of cassation.[25] This is not the case in Chile,[26] however, while in the Netherlands cassation in small cases is available only on the ground of violation by the court below of procedural requirements.[27] A similar

---

[18] Austria, p. 2.

[19] Italy is now an exception: below, p. 347.

[20] E.g. Uruguay, p. 12; France, n.c.p.c., art. 514. The possibility that provisional execution may be ordered is increasingly common.

[21] Belgium, p. 3; Chile, para. 2.1.1; France, p. 3; Germany, pp. 5, 24; Greece, pp. 3, 5, 6–7, 8; Japan, pp. 12, 13; Netherlands, pp. 4, 6; Spain, p. 3; Sweden, p. B18; Uruguay, p. 3. See Jolowicz, 'Appellate Proceedings', pp. 160–2. Usually, commencement of cassation proceedings has no similar suspensive effect.

[22] See P. Gilles, 'Die Berufung in Zivilsachen und die zivilgerichtliche Instanzordnungs', in P. Gilles (ed.), Humane Justiz (1977), pp. 150 and 154; Germany, p. 24; Greece, p. 3; Jolowicz, 'Appellate Proceedings', p. 145.

[23] Germany, pp. 21 and 22.

[24] Belgium, p. 9 (appeal is, however, available against all decisions of industrial tribunals); Chile, p. 5; France, p. 3; Germany, p. 2; Greece, pp. 34 and 21 where, however, the exclusion of appeals is relatively easily overcome; Italy, c.p.c., art. 339, which excludes the decisions of the conciliatore from appeal; Netherlands, p. 4; Uruguay, p. 5. A similar exclusion of appeal for cases of low value exists in some provinces of Canada (Canada, p. 16) and some states of the United States (USA, p. 8). For the difficulties that may be experienced in determining the value of a case, see Belgium, pp. 10–11.

[25] Belgium, Part II, p. 5; France, p. 5. In Italy, the exclusion from appeal of the decisions of the conciliatore is achieved by the positive statement that they are subject to cassation: c.p.c., art. 339.

[26] Chile, p. 5.   [27] Netherlands, p. 6.

emphasis on procedural requirements is found in Austria where, in principle, all first instance judgments are appealable, but the admissible grounds of appeal are restricted in small cases.[28]

No doubt, the removal of small cases from the appellate system provides a measure of relief, and the absence of a relevant rule of exclusion has been said to be one of the causes of congestion in Spain.[29] At this point, however, an obvious conflict of policy arises; a rule excluding small cases from appeal is subject to criticism as reducing the guarantee of justice, especially for the less well-endowed litigants.[30] The conflict can, however, be avoided, though not without the introduction of other difficulties, if the exercise of the right of appeal is conditional on the prior grant of leave; this is the preferred method of control in some common law countries[31] and also in Sweden.[32] In England, appeal to the Court of Appeal is now only exceptionally available without leave.[33]

Interlocutory decisions

In countries in which the principle of double instance is held to be an essential guarantee of justice, any exclusion of a right of appeal, even against a relatively insignificant interlocutory decision, requires special legislation, and legislation of this kind tends to receive a restrictive interpretation.[34] Nevertheless, interlocutory appeals hold up the progress of the litigation and may be introduced purely for the purpose of causing delay.[35] It is not uncommon, therefore, that specific legislation excludes altogether appeals from those interlocutory decisions that can affect the final outcome only indirectly if at all.[36] A rule of more general application is, however, adopted in a number of countries, namely that an appeal against an interlocutory decision is available only in conjunction with an appeal against the final decision of the case at first

---

[28] Austria, p. 13. The new English rule for the small claims track (up to £5,000) is similar; appeal is allowed on the ground of serious procedural irregularity or mistake of law: C.P.R., r. 27.11.

[29] Spain, p. 3.

[30] Ibid., p. 4; Austria, p. 19. Cf. Netherlands, pp. 6–7, where it is suggested that even the limited right of recourse to the Court of cassation allowed for small cases should be removed because of its disproportionate cost. In Japan, the *Jokuku* appeal, which is similar to cassation, comes before the High Court, not the Supreme Court, in small cases, with a possibility that the case may still reach the Supreme Court: Japan, pp. 14–15.

[31] Australia, pp. 31–2; England, p. 2.

[32] Sweden, p. B9.   [33] Chap. 14, p. 271.

[34] E.g. Belgium, pp. 6–7.

[35] Chile, para. 3.7.a; Italy, pp. 11–12.

[36] Austria, p. 15; Belgium, p. 7; Chile, para. 1.3.b; Germany, p. 3; Uruguay, p. 6. In France certain decisions such as those ordering an expertise or to stay proceedings can be appealed as soon as given, but only with the prior authorisation of the Premier Président of the Court of Appeal: n.c.p.c., arts. 272 and 380.

instance.[37] This has the advantage of preserving the right of appeal while preventing its exercise from delaying a decision, but it also has the disadvantage of requiring a definition of an interlocutory decision, which can cause difficulty.[38]

The postponement of interlocutory appeals as just described is not really possible in the common law systems; an interlocutory appeal must be disposed of before the trial of the action for the simple reason that the main purpose of interlocutory proceedings is to prepare the case for trial.[39] Nowhere, however, is there any longer an absolute right of appeal against interlocutory decisions:[40] appeal lies only with leave.[41] Here too, difficulty sometimes arises in determining whether a particular decision is interlocutory for the purposes of the rule requiring leave,[42] and decision of the question whether leave should be granted always involves the use of judicial time.[43] Unless interlocutory appeals were to be forbidden altogether, however – and that seems nowhere to be in contemplation – the requirement of leave provides the only possible control.

Appeal subject to leave (supreme courts)

Interlocutory appeals apart, the requirement that an appellant first obtain leave to appeal is now widely used to control the case-load of the supreme court. In common law countries, it is only where there is no intermediate court of appeal, so that the first and only appeal is to the supreme court, that no prior grant of leave is required.[44] In South Africa, since 1983, leave is required for an appeal to the Supreme Court

---

[37] Austria, p. 15; France, p. 3; Germany, p. 3; Greece, p. 4; Spain, but only in specified categories of litigation, p. 4; Uruguay, pp. 5–6. For the slightly different Italian rule, see c.p.c., art. 340.

[38] See, e.g. France, p. 4.

[39] But see above, chap. 14, p. 295.

[40] In England, where interlocutory decisions in the High Court are usually made by a Master, his decision is, for historical reasons, subject to appeal as of right to a judge, and from the judge, but only with leave, appeal lies to the Court of Appeal.

[41] Australia, p. 14; Canada, p. 15, where it is stated that in Ontario, at least, leave may be granted only for specified reasons; England, p. 2; Israel, p. 2; USA, p. 9.

[42] E.g. Canada, p. 15. In England, until the generalisation of the requirement of leave, an elaborate and detailed rule of court was necessary to distinguish between final and interlocutory orders: R.S.C., Ord. 59, r. 1A.

[43] See, e.g. USA, pp. 9 and 18 and the discussion in Netherlands, p. 20. In England many applications to the Court of Appeal for leave to appeal to that court are dealt with, in the first instance, on paper by a single judge of the Court, but an oral hearing may be ordered: *Practice Note (Court of Appeal Procedure)* [1995] 1 W.L.R. 1191.

[44] E.g. some American states (USA, p. 2); Israel, except when the case was decided at first instance in a magistrates' court, in which case appeal lies to the District Court and a further appeal is then possible, but only with leave, to the Supreme Court: Israel, p. 2.

– the Appellate Division – even though there is no intermediate appeal.[45] Leave to appeal to the Supreme Court is now also required in Sweden,[46] in Germany[47] and in Austria.[48] No such requirement exists, on the other hand, in countries whose legal systems follow the French model,[49] but there, in principle, appeal to the supreme court is limited to questions of law, and this limitation is considered in the next section.

In England, application for leave to appeal to the House of Lords is made, first, to the Court of Appeal and, if there refused, a further application may be made to a committee of the House of Lords;[50] and in Germany the application goes to the Court of Appeal or the Supreme Court according to the value of the case.[51] In Australia,[52] Canada,[53] the United States[54] and Sweden,[55] on the other hand, the supreme court alone controls the cases that come before it.

There is also a good deal of variation in the procedure for dealing with applications for leave to appeal. Where these are dealt with by the court *a quo*, the matter can be quickly and informally disposed of, since the court already has full knowledge of the case; but where they come before the supreme court something more elaborate is required. To take just two examples, in England applications come before a committee of three judges of the House of Lords and the procedure is initially written: if the members of the committee agree unanimously, leave may be granted or refused; otherwise an oral hearing may be ordered.[56] In Canada there was formerly an oral hearing before three Supreme Court judges, but now applications for leave are dealt with in writing unless an oral hearing is specifically ordered.[57] Written procedures have, however,

---

[45] South Africa, p. 6.   [46] Sweden, p. B9.

[47] Germany, pp. 2–3 and 17. Under current legislation, leave is not required in cases involving more than DM60,000.

[48] No appeal to the Austrian Supreme Court is possible in cases involving less than AS50,000.

[49] See, e.g. Netherlands, p. 20. The old Chambre des Requêtes of the French Cour de cassation, which was abolished in 1947, might be regarded as a body which, in effect, granted or withheld leave to appeal since it could reject but could not allow an appeal, and the same might be said of the *formations restreintes* as originally created in 1979. Since 1981, however, the *formations restreintes* have had power in appropriate cases to allow as well as to dismiss the appeal: below, p. 344.

[50] Administration of Justice (Appeals) Act 1934. The position since 1983 is similar in South Africa: South Africa, p. 6. In Austria also, both levels of jurisdiction may be involved: Austria, p. 14.

[51] Germany, p. 2.   [52] Australia, p. 10.

[53] Canada, p. 5. Prior to 1975, leave to appeal to the Supreme Court was not required if the amount at stake was more than Can. $10,000.

[54] USA, p. 18.   [55] Sweden, p. B9.

[56] Practice Directions and Standing Orders applicable to Civil Appeals Directions: *Supreme Court Practice* (1999), paras. 19A-21–19A-24.

[57] Canada, p. 6. Supreme Court Act, s. 45, as amended in 1987 (c. 42, s. 4).

been rejected in Australia on the ground that it is an important part of the Court's business to decide what cases it will hear.[58]

One final variation must be mentioned, namely the extent to which, if at all, the grounds upon which leave to appeal may be granted is specified by law. In Germany only questions of law may be entertained.[59] In Canada the legislation makes it clear that leave will not be granted if the case is of interest only to the parties: there must be an important issue of law or at least a question of public importance.[60] In most common law countries, however, there is little legislative control and the grant of leave is left to judicial discretion. In the United States, for example, the Supreme Court will hear an appeal only if there are 'special reasons'[61] and in England no formal criteria are stated.[62] Whatever the legislation, however, and exceptional cases only apart, appeals to supreme courts are in practice admitted only if there is a point of importance calling for decision at that level; the number of cases admitted for full consideration is kept low enough to enable the judges to give to each the attention necessary for its fully motivated decision.

This is not to say that some supreme courts are not under pressure but, at least, their case-loads are light by comparison with courts of cassation. In England, as has been noticed, the House of Lords decides only about fifty civil cases per year;[63] in Australia, Canada and Sweden the number is similar,[64] while in the United States it is under 200.[65] Of the countries so far mentioned, only the supreme courts of Austria and Germany have case-loads much in excess of that,[66] and in those countries the supreme court sits in more than one chamber.

Appeal limited to questions of law (supreme courts)
A rule that an appellate court shall not entertain questions of fact is not inconsistent with a requirement that leave to appeal be obtained. In

---

[58] Australia, p. 42.

[59] Germany, p. 24. See also Austria, pp. 13–14; Sweden, pp. B9–10, cf. p. B20.

[60] Canada, p. 5.

[61] For full discussion, see W. E. Wright, A. R. Miller and E. H. Cooper, *Federal Practice and Procedure*, Vol. 16B (1996), §4004.

[62] The Practice Directions (above, n. 56) state that leave may be refused if a petition does not reveal an arguable point of law of general public importance.

[63] In 1997 it disposed of fifty-two civil cases in all, of which eleven were from Scotland and one from Northern Ireland. In the same year it dealt with 180 civil applications for leave to appeal: Judicial Statistics, 1997.

[64] Australia, p. 9; Canada, p. 5 (but applications for leave are numerous); Sweden, p. C.3.6.

[65] USA, p. 14 (but there are some thousands of applications for certiorari; *ibid.*, p. 18, where it is suggested that 150 cases a year is about the maximum that the court could manage consistently with fulfilment of its purpose).

[66] In both countries the load is over 2,000 cases; Austria, p. 24; Germany, p. 14.

courts that are recognised as courts of cassation rather than courts of appeal or revision, however, the litigant's unfettered right of access is jealously protected:[67] even small cases in which no regular appeal is available may still come before the supreme court.[68]

In principle, courts of cassation must accept the facts as found below, can consider only questions of law, and, if they find legal error, cannot substitute their own decision but must remit the case elsewhere. Adherence to these restrictions, it might be expected, would suffice to limit case-loads and to ensure that the courts have to deal only with questions of law of some importance. In reality, however, the practice of cassation has become so impure in many countries – thanks, perhaps, to the judges' desire to do the best justice possible to the parties – that the restrictions have virtually ceased to apply.[69] The courts of cassation of many countries have become grossly, even grotesquely, overloaded.

A comparative excursus

A broadly based comparison between the situation of the supreme courts of the common law countries, together with Sweden, on the one hand and those which are courts of cassation, on the other,[70] reveals a paradoxical situation: the ostensible and the actual purposes principally fulfilled by each have become reversed.

Courts of cassation

Where the supreme court is a court of cassation, cassation is distinguished from appeal, and the public purpose of cassation is commonly stressed. French law, for example, states that the *pourvoi en cassation* leads to the censure of the non-conformity of a judgment with the rules of law,[71] recourse by a public authority 'in the interest of the law'[72] is available in many countries, and special chambers of the court are constituted for cases of special legal difficulty. Ordinarily, a case will only reach the court of cassation on the initiative of a party, but this is not inconsistent with the public purpose of cassation.[73] As things have developed, however the case-load of courts of cassation has almost

---

[67] Chap. 15, p. 326.   [68] Above, p. 334.

[69] This development is dealt with more fully above in chap. 15, pp. 309 and 326.

[70] Austria and Germany, whose supreme courts are courts of revision, occupy a position midway between these two extremes.

[71] N.c.p.c., art. 604; Belgium, p. 2. For the Italian legislative statement, see chap. 15, p. 318.

[72] France, n.c.p.c., arts. 618–1; Belgium, Code judiciare, arts. 1089 and 1090; Italy, c.p.c., art. 363; Netherlands, p. 9. In Germany (p. 11) and Chile (para. 2.2) the situation is not quite the same, but a similar idea exists.

[73] See Calamandrei's well-known statement, above, chap. 15, p. 306.

everywhere become so great that adequate performance of the public purpose is extremely difficult. It has been said for Italy that the *funzione nomofilattica* has become *utopistico retaggi di ordinamenti superati*,[74] and for France that 'la Cour de cassation doit désormais statuer sur plus de 16,000 affaires par an. Quelle que soit la conscience de ses membres, il est vain de prétendre qu'elle puisse faire un travail de la qualité désirable.'[75] Indeed, it has been estimated for France that of all the cases decided by the Cour de cassation, only 1.5 per cent merited the Court's attention as raising significant points of law.[76] The original, predominantly public, purpose of these courts has become submerged in the humane desire to do the best justice possible to the parties.[77]

Supreme courts of third instance

The powers of supreme courts, which are themselves courts of appeal rather than of cassation or review, are, typically, much the same as those of an (intermediate) appellate court and, at least in primary legislation, no statement is to be found equivalent to that of Italian law, which requires the court of cassation to ensure 'the exact observance and the uniform interpretation of the law, the unity of national law'.[78] On the other hand, by virtue of secondary legislation or simple practice, the cases reaching those courts will, usually, raise points of law of some importance, and care is taken to see that the judges have adequate time both to consider each case fully and to formulate the reasons for their decisions. This may be, and often is, achieved by strict application of the requirement of leave to appeal,[79] but other factors such as cost, delay, the advice of experienced advocates and widespread acknowledgment that, save in exceptional cases, the intermediate is also the final court of appeal, all operate to keep down the number of appeals. It may even be true that the case-load of, for example, the English House of Lords could usefully be increased,[80] and in Sweden consideration has been

---

[74] Italy, p. 15, citing Giuseppe Mirabelli, as president of a ministerial commission reporting in 1986. See too, Greece, p. 23: 'The Areopag is (in certain not uncommon circumstances) side tracked from considering the unified application of the law and has to concern itself with the rights and wrongs of individual cases, which is not its primary function.'

[75] A. Tunc, 'La cour de cassation en crise', (1985) 30 *Archives de la Philosophie de Droit* 157.

[76] Report of the Garde des Sceaux for 1970–71, cited Tunc, 'La cour de cassation'.

[77] Chap. 15, p. 318.

[78] Law on court organisation, art. 65, trans. Cappelletti *et al.*, p. 150.

[79] See above, pp. 336 and 338, and Canada, p. 7, where it is stated that 'the Supreme Court no longer performs the appellate function of correcting error'.

[80] Chap. 15, p. 327.

given to methods whereby the Supreme Court's contributions to the law might be enlarged.[81]

It might be suggested that the paradox derives from the fact that in common law countries the decisions of the courts, and most especially of the supreme courts, are recognised as sources of law, while this is not the case in countries whose law is codified. That, however, would be to underestimate the present importance of *jurisprudence* to the interpretation of codified law and to ignore the numerous statements which continue to be made that courts of cassation act as guardians of the law. For better or for worse, those courts have come more and more to concern themselves with the rights and obligations of the parties and, because of their huge case-loads, have difficulty in fulfilling their public purpose. Supreme courts that are ostensibly courts of appeal, which are ostensibly no more concerned with the public purpose than are the courts below them in the judicial hierarchy, have become almost exclusively devoted to the development and clarification of the law.

Restriction on content of appeal

The fullest possible appeal, which is also the most costly and time-consuming, involves a complete rehearing of the case – a 'second first instance'. The extent to which different systems of appeal (not cassation) depart from this, the importance to the enquiry of the character of the procedure used at first instance, and the extent to which new matter may be introduced on appeal, have been discussed elsewhere.[82] In those countries which adhere as a matter of principle to the rule of double instance, and especially where it is held that a principal function of the appeal is to ensure so far as possible that the facts are correctly found,[83] it is unlikely that any question will be regarded as falling outside the purview of the appellate court. Things are different, however, in common law countries, and two examples of questions on which appellate courts act with particular restraint must be mentioned. Though there is nothing here of strict legal rule, knowledge that questions of a particular character will not ordinarily be reconsidered on appeal, obviously affects the advice given by his lawyer to a disappointed litigant contemplating an appeal. Appeals that might otherwise be brought will be excluded.

[81] Report of the Judicial Procedure Commission, 1986, summarised in Sweden, Appendix D. See P. H. Lindblom, 'Scandinavian Countries', in P. Yessiou-Faltsi (ed.), *The Role of the Supreme Courts at the National and International Level* (1998), p. 223 at p. 263.

[82] Chap. 15, pp. 303 and 314.

[83] E.g. Belgium, p. 4; Chile, pp. 2–3; France, pp. 5 and 9; Germany, p. 4; Greece, p. 8; Italy, p. 10; Japan, p. 23; Netherlands, p. 18; Spain, p. 3; Uruguay, p. 3.

Questions of fact

In the United States the procedure of appeal is 'a review concerning whether prejudicial error occurred'.[84] Elsewhere it is a procedure of rehearing.[85] Under neither form of procedure are questions of fact excluded from appeal, but witnesses are not heard over again and the appellate court proceeds on the basis of a written transcript of the proceedings, including, where necessary, the evidence given below. It follows that in so far as decisions of fact were based on the trial court's assessment of the relative credibility of witnesses, the appellate court will not, save in most exceptional circumstances, intervene.[86] Beyond that, the willingness of appellate courts to reconsider questions of fact varies from one country to another and within one country from one period to another.[87] It is a matter for speculation whether this reflects a reaction to awareness of overload. In Australia and England, appellate courts are relatively willing to come to their own decisions on questions such as the qualification of conduct. In Canada, on the other hand, practice has changed, and appellate courts will intervene only if it is shown that the decision in question was 'clearly wrong'. This leads to a reduction in the number of appeals.[88]

Questions of discretion

Some judicial decisions, mainly but not exclusively those relating to the actual conduct of the proceedings, are said to depend on the judge's discretion; others, such as, for example, the assessment of the relative culpability of the parties in an accident case, or the determination of what would best promote the welfare of a child in a guardianship case, cannot be the subject of precise rules. Such decisions may not be of fact, nor do they normally depend on the credibility of witnesses, but on such questions an appellate court is likely to act with restraint, giving very great weight, at least, to the view of the judge of first instance. The House of Lords has stated, for English law, that:

An appellate court ought not to substitute its own discretion for that of the judge merely because its members would themselves have regarded the balance as tipped against the way in which he decided the matter. They should regard their function as primarily a reviewing function and should reverse his decision only in cases either (1) where they are satisfied that the judge has erred in

[84] USA, p. 10; above, chap. 15, p. 310.
[85] E.g. for England, R.S.C., Ord. 59, r. 3. Chap. 14, p. 276.
[86] Chap. 15, p. 316.
[87] Australia, p. 21; Canada, pp. 17–18; Jolowicz, 'Appellate Proceedings', p. 137.
[88] Canada, pp. 17–18.

principle . . .; or (2) . . . in order to promote consistency in the exercise of their discretion by judges as a whole where there appear, in closely comparable circumstances, to be two conflicting schools of judicial opinion as to the relative weight to be given to particular considerations.[89]

Efficiency devices

The previous section has been mainly concerned with methods for controlling the number of appeals actually launched. This section concerns a different method of managing overload, namely the adoption of means intended to dispose as rapidly and efficiently as possible of the cases that actually do reach the appellate courts. Two such methods will be mentioned: first, the use of special appellate jurisdictions, that is, courts which are not part of the normal appellate hierarchy or which are composed of fewer judges than the normal; and, secondly, devices directed specifically to the actual handling of the cases.

Special appellate jurisdictions[90]

The case-loads of the regular appellate courts can be lightened if some appeals are heard by courts normally of first instance, and the cases which do come before them can be disposed of with more economical use of judge time if they can sit for some cases with less than the usual number of judges. Examples of both devices exist.

First instance court as court of appeal

Where courts of first instance exist at two levels, the lower level of court dealing with small cases, it is common that appeal from that court lies to the court of first instance of general jurisdiction.[91] In Japan this system is carried a step further so that in small cases the second appeal, the *Jokoku* appeal, which is in the nature of cassation, comes before the High Court, which is normally a court of first appeal, and reaches the Supreme Court only in rare cases; if the High Court considers that there is a point of law on which a Supreme Court decision is required then it can transfer the case to the Supreme Court, and if there is a point of

---

[89] *Birkett* v. *James* [1978] A.C. 297, 317, *per* Lord Diplock, and above, chap. 14, p. 278. See also Australia, pp. 21–7. As a general rule appellate courts will not interfere with a judge's award of damages in respect of the non-pecuniary loss suffered as a consequence of personal injury except on the ground of error of law or that the judge's estimate of the damage was wholly erroneous (*Pickett* v. *British Rail Engineering Ltd* [1980] A.C. 136). See, however, chap. 14, p. 282.

[90] For proposals for English law, see Bowman and chap. 14, above, postscript.

[91] Austria, pp. 7–8; Belgium, p. 4; Chile, p. 2; Germany, p. 1; Israel, pp. 2–3; Italy, p. 2; Netherlands, p. 2; South Africa, p. 1; Uruguay, p. 7; USA, p. 6.

constitutional law a further, special *Jokoku*, appeal to the Supreme Court is possible.[92]

It is not only in small cases, however, that courts of first instance may serve as courts of appeal. In most Australian states, for example, the state supreme court serves as both court of first instance and court of appeal, in the latter capacity sitting as a Full Court,[93] and in South Africa a similar solution is adopted, as preferable to the creation of an intermediate court of appeal, for those appeals which are not regarded as of sufficient legal importance to warrant the attention of the supreme court.[94]

Reduction in size of appellate court

The number of judges required to constitute a chamber or session of an appellate court varies from one country to another, and in some that number has been reduced as one means of making more economical use of judges' time.[95] Of greater interest here, however, is the use of reduced size courts for certain categories of case. In England, the Court of Appeal sits normally as a court of three judges, but now two judges only sit to hear interlocutory appeals and appeals from the county court.[96] Again, in France, the Court of cassation can sit in a *formation restreinte* of three judges instead of the usual five, where it appears that the solution of the case is clear. If any member of a *formation restreinte* considers that the case should be heard by a full chamber, it will be transferred.[97]

Efficiency

In the conduct of an appeal the parties will look primarily to their own interests individually and, sometimes, to their joint interests. They are

---

[92] Japan, pp. 14–15.

[93] Australia, pp. 28–31, where an interesting comparison is made between the position in Victoria, where the same judges sit as judges of first instance and, in the full court, as judges of appeal, and that in New South Wales where there is a full-time court of appeal. 'A Full Court judge may identify more closely with the trial judge; he may attach more importance to and have greater respect for, the work the trial judge has done. And, perhaps, a Full Court judge feels more strongly the restraint imposed by "the lack of overweening certainty in one's own opinions" because he is an equal of the trial judge in a way which a full time appellate judge is not. It is not wholly waggish to observe that appellate judges do not make their mark in the legal community by affirming.'

[94] South Africa, p. 18. See also Canada, p. 11 and above, chap. 14, p. 296.

[95] In France, the minimum number of judges necessary for a decision of the Cour de cassation was reduced from seven to five in 1981: Code de l'organisation judiciaire, art. L.131-6.

[96] Supreme Court Act 1981, s. 54; above, chap. 15, n. 83. Bowman (p. 57) suggests that for some cases even one judge may suffice: see chap. 14, p. 296 above.

[97] France, p. 1; Code de l'organisation judiciaire, art. L.131-6.

unlikely to take into account the interests of other litigants whose
appeals are pending or the delays caused by appellate overload. The
penalty of costs may discourage inefficient handling of an appeal by the
parties, but in some countries there is a tradition of court control of the
procedure,[98] so that the court has powers capable of being used either
to prevent one party from behaving inappropriately or to improve the
efficiency with which appeals are disposed of. The common law tradition is to allow complete freedom to the parties to conduct their
litigation as they see fit, subject only to rules of court, but, as a response
to overload and its consequences, departures from that tradition are
increasingly common. One aspect of this is the development, for
example in Australia and in England, of strict enforcement of time
limits.[99] It has been said for England, for example, that since 1982,
when a new regime was introduced, the policy has been that of an
'interventionist' court; if, for example, an appellant fails to observe
certain time limits he will be required to show cause why his appeal
should not be dismissed out of hand.[100]

In addition to such enforcement of procedural discipline on the
parties, various attempts are being made to improve the efficiency of the
actual determination of the appeal by reduction of the common law
emphasis on oral argument. Reliance on documentation and the use of
written briefs, together with strictly limited time for oral argument, has
long been a feature of American appellate procedure, especially in the
Supreme Court of the United States, but increasing use of written
procedures is becoming common elsewhere. In a number of countries
the parties must now produce skeleton arguments, which the judges will
read in advance of the oral hearing.[101] In Israel a flexible system has
been introduced whereby the court may order the parties to present
their arguments in writing on either the whole of their cases or on
specific aspects, and it may dispense with oral argument altogether or
order such argument only by way of supplement to the written submissions. Even where oral argument is to be used, written summaries must
be presented to the court, and no argument not there mentioned can be
raised at the hearing.[102]

---

[98] E.g. Germany, pp. 5–6. In France, cases under appeal come under the control of a
judge of the Court of Appeal whose powers are the same as those of his equivalent in
the court of first instance and include the power to specify time limits for the
performance of the necessary procedural acts by the parties: France, p. 6, and n.c.p.c.
arts. 910–12 and 763–87.

[99] Australia, p. 44; England, p. 1.

[100] Chap. 14, p. 273. See also Canada, p. 16.

[101] Australia, p. 44; Canada, p. 10; England, p. 4 and above, chap. 14, p. 274.

[102] Israel, p. 20.

Efficiency in the use of judge time may also be improved by the delegation of tasks, in addition to the purely administrative, to officials or others who do not hold judicial appointments. In England, for example, there is now a Registrar of the Court of Appeal who may himself settle certain questions or hold a pre-appeal review,[103] but it is in the United States that the search for this kind of efficiency has been carried the furthest.[104] There, judicial time is saved, or sought to be saved, by the widespread use of assistants to the judges, not only during the preparatory stages of an appeal but also in the formation of decisions. Attention may be drawn, for example, to the practice of leaving the preparation of the initial drafts of judgments to be delivered to lawyers on the staff of the court.[105]

It is said for the United States that there is 'no inherent incompatibility between justice . . . and the employment of mechanisms which increase judicial capacity to decide appeals and hence to cope with increasing work loads',[106] but such mechanisms must be used with care. One danger is the risk of the emergence of court-wide norms for decision which are not articulated and which may even come to be substituted for the articulated norms. Safeguards must be evolved.

The accepted standard of decision is that judges determine the result on appeal by reasoned analysis of a universe of information consisting of the record from the trial court, constitutional principle, statute, precedent, secondary authority, and underlying policy. So long as information obtained by staff is complete and accurate judicial capacity to decide is enhanced and the decision is that of the judge. If staff-supplied information is incomplete or inaccurate, the standard is not met; staff analysis then so influences the decision that it is a staff and not a judicial product. Here again the potential of departure from an expected standard is no reason to forgo the contribution to appellate efficiency of the use of supporting personnel. It is a warning that safeguards to ensure the completeness and accuracy of information reaching the judges should be employed.[107]

Is this the way ahead for other systems, or is the provision of extensive assistance to appellate judges something peculiar to the United States? Can other systems learn from the United States how to increase the efficiency – perhaps 'productivity' is the right word – of appellate judges

---

[103] England, pp. 3 and 4. For later developments, see Bowman, pp. 71–4 and P. Jamieson, 'Of Judges, Judgments and Judicial Assistants' (1998) 17 C.J.Q. 395; *Parker* v. *Law Society*, *The Times*, 8 December 1998.

[104] USA, pp. 23–44. See also, R. S. Thompson and J. B. Oakley, 'From Information to Opinion in Appellate Courts; How Funny Things Happen on the Way Through the Forum' (1986) *Arizona State Law Journal* 1.

[105] USA, p. 37.

[106] *Ibid.*, p. 40.   [107] *Ibid.*, p. 43.

without thereby sacrificing justice in any of the manifold senses of that word?

Abuse of the right of appeal

The danger of abuse of the right of appeal seems to have attracted relatively little attention[108] but, like the danger of abuse of any other procedural right, it is ever present. To take just two obvious examples, the entry of an interlocutory appeal by a defendant before final judgment at first instance, may be intended simply to delay judgment; the entry of an appeal against final judgment may be intended simply to delay its execution.

Interlocutory decisions

In common law procedure interlocutory appeals must usually be disposed of before trial,[109] but there is no longer an absolute right of appeal against an interlocutory decision. An appeal lies only with leave. In a number of civilian countries, on the other hand, an appeal can normally be brought against an interlocutory order only after the final decision has been given and in conjunction with an appeal against that decision.[110] This, however, is not the case everywhere, and to meet the problem of interlocutory appeals entered solely for the purpose of delay, the modern tendency is to reduce the suspensive effect of the appeal.

Final decisions

In common law countries, judgments are enforceable as soon as given unless a stay of execution is granted;[111] an unsuccessful defendant thus has no incentive to appeal simply in order to delay execution. The traditional rule in the civilian systems, on the other hand, is to accord a suspensive effect to the appeal. This means that, unless provisional execution is granted, execution of a first instance judgment is postponed until the time for appealing has expired or the appeal is determined.[112] In some countries provisional execution can be granted even *ex officio* in many categories of case,[113] but in Italy the suspensive effect of the appeal has been effectively removed; provisional execution is automatic unless the contrary is ordered.[114] This should help to eliminate appeals brought solely for the purposes of delay.

[108] See Jolowicz, 'Appellate Proceedings', pp. 160–2. French law provides a sanction for an abusive or dilatory appeal: n.c.p.c., art. 559.
[109] Above, p.336.   [110] Above, p. 335.
[111] Above, p. 333.   [112] Above, p. 334.
[113] E.g. France, n.c.p.c., art. 515. In certain cases it is automatic: *ibid.*, art. 514.
[114] C.p.c., arts. 282 and 283, as amended in 1990. The change was implemented despite

Conclusion

The problem of overload in appellate courts is one of the most intractable, not least because the measures that have been, or might be,
adopted all have disadvantages which must be balanced against their
advantages, and what may appear to be a satisfactory balance at one
time or place will not necessarily so appear at another.

(1) Techniques such as the requirement of leave to appeal which are
    used in common law supreme courts and some others, and which
    are intended to allow the judges of those courts the time they
    need to fulfil the public purpose, effectively deny access to the
    majority of litigants and so tend to prevent those courts from
    fulfilling adequately or at all the private purpose. They tend also
    to cast upon the intermediate court of appeal a major role in the
    achievement of the public purpose, and thus generate a need that
    those courts also should not receive an excessive number of
    appeals.[115] Conversely where, as in many countries whose
    supreme court is a court of cassation and there is no effective
    barrier to access, the number of cases that reach the court is so
    great that its capacity to fulfil the public purpose is compro-
    mised.

(2) At the opposite end of the spectrum, the absolute denial of a
    right of appeal in some cases can be advantageous only in easing
    the passage of others, while the introduction of a requirement of
    leave to appeal for small cases makes increased demands on
    judicial time. Where leave is denied, the private purpose is
    defeated; where it is granted, both the cost and the time involved
    are increased.

(3) Increases in the number of appellate judges or reductions in the
    size of collegiate courts risk diluting the quality of decision
    making and, which is potentially even more serious, risk encoura-
    ging the demand for yet more instances as public confidence in
    the intermediate courts declines.[116]

---

fears that the result would be to remove much of the value of the appeal in genuine
cases: Italy, p. 8.

[115] An Ontario appellate judge is quoted as saying that 'the appellate function of
correcting error ends with our court [i.e., to the exclusion of the Supreme Court of
Canada] and to some extent, so does the function of clarifying and developing the law
so far as Ontario is concerned': Canada, p. 8. In common law countries generally, the
intermediate court of appeal, where there is one, contributes far more, quantitatively,
to the law than does the supreme court. In England, for example, 96 per cent of the
cases that reach the Court of Appeal go no further: England, p. 1.

[116] The Bowman proposals for appeals in 'fast track' cases create a similar risk where such

(4) Efficiency devices designed to reduce the time taken by individual cases – such as rigid adherence to time limits sanctioned
by dismissal of an appeal unheard, or the refusal to have regard
to arguments not stated in a written notice of appeal – may
adversely affect the quality of decision and, even more serious,
may give rise to the idea that litigants are denied justice because
of the shortcomings of their lawyers. Efficiency devices, such as
those used in the United States, carry the greatest risk, especially
because they seem partially to prevent litigants from making their
cases directly to the judges, but no efficiency device can work
except by making less than complete the appellate judges'
personal consideration of their cases.

If it is right that the problem of overload cannot be alleviated, let
alone resolved, without compromise and the sacrifice of some of the
traditional values of a legal system,[117] it is obvious that each legal system
must find its own compromises, and it is at least likely that its choices
will be largely controlled by what is regarded, or what is silently
assumed, to be fundamental to it. It is, for example, easier for common
law countries than for others to restrict the right even of a first appeal
simply because those countries have never accepted the principle of
double instance as fundamental. Conversely, given the strength of the
adversary tradition of their procedure, it is more difficult for common
law countries than for others to strengthen the hands of the court itself
in controlling the parties during the preparatory stages of appellate
procedure and in the presentation of their cases. Nevertheless, three
suggestions may be made by way of conclusion.

(1) While it is not suggested that cases should be positively selected
for hearing by supreme courts for their particular legal interest,[118] there does seem to be room in many countries for
greater emphasis to be placed on the public purpose which those
courts fulfil and for the development of techniques whereby the
time of supreme court judges is not unduly diverted from it. If, as
seems to be the case, the introduction of a requirement of leave

cases raise an important point of principle or practice: leave to appeal to the Court of
Appeal might be given in the course of the hearing of the ordinary appeal: Bowman,
pp. 45–6 and chap. 14, above, p. 297.

[117] As the American reporter to the 1977 Congress observed, 'A trial, a meaningful
appeal, and an opportunity to present a novel point of law to the highest court, taken
together, may be regarded as the fullest form of adjudicative justice. If so, most
litigants will have to be given less than that': cited in 'Appellate Proceedings', Jolowicz,
p. 159.

[118] See Jolowicz, 'Appellate Proceedings', p. 157.

to appeal is out of the question where the supreme court is a court of cassation, other techniques such as the French *formation restreinte* are necessary; only those cases that merit the attention of the fully constituted supreme court should receive it. Supreme courts whose humanity has led to grotesque case-loads should be de-humanised.[119]

(2) Even where the principle of double instance is not accepted as a basic principle of justice, there is general agreement that a litigant dissatisfied at first instance should be entitled to an appeal of some kind not limited to questions of law alone,[120] and the exclusion of small cases from appeal, where it exists, is generally regarded as unsatisfactory. Save for appeals from interlocutory decisions, legal rules denying altogether a right of first appeal are justified only as a crude response to a critical situation; for the sake of individual justice and of the reputation of the legal system as a whole, such restrictions must be kept to a minimum. This does not mean, however, that any and every question that was or might have been raised at first instance must be open on appeal, a point which goes beyond simple exclusion of new demands and strict control on the admissibility of new evidence or proof. On many matters decided at first instance the decision of appellate judges is little more than 'another view', and it is permissible to ask why a litigant should be entitled to that.[121] The distinction between questions of fact and questions of law should not be used as the criterion, but a more sophisticated and more flexible approach can come through the case law or *jurisprudence*. Is there a better way of reducing the number of appeals by litigants who simply hope that the appellate court will disagree with the decision reached at first instance, than for them to be advised that their appeals are almost certain to fail?

(3) The present era has everywhere seen a great increase in litigation and therefore a similar increase of pressure on appellate courts. Much of this litigation concerns the rights and obligations of individuals as consumers, as employees and as subjects of the

---

[119] Jolowicz, 'Appellate Proceedings', p. 158.

[120] As pointed out by Bowman (p. 29), the requirement of leave to appeal secures consideration of the dissatisfied litigant's complaint against an adverse judgment, while preventing appeals without prospect of success from reaching an actual appellate jurisdiction.

[121] This point is, probably, of greater weight where the judiciary is appointed from the ranks of practitioners, so that first instance as well as appellate judges are persons of experience at the time of their appointment, than where there is a judicial career so that some judges of first instance are likely to be young and inexperienced.

welfare state. It has been suggested elsewhere that, from the humane point of view, the best appellate system is one which neither party to a first instance decision feels it necessary to invoke.[122] There will, no doubt, always be litigants who seek to use their right of appeal for ulterior purposes, and in some countries it appears that there is an actual enthusiasm for litigation and for appeal.[123] Such enthusiasm will prove difficult to contain, at least in the short term, but ultimately, and however difficult it may be, it is only by strengthening the courts of first instance and ensuring their high repute in public consciousness that the problem of appellate overload can be met. Only a reduction in the demand for appeals can provide a satisfactory solution; supply side controls can be nothing but a palliative.

[122] Jolowicz, 'Appellate Proceedings', p. 154.
[123] E.g. Germany, pp. 19 and 21; Greece, p. 4; Israel, pp. 9–12.

The following national reports were received:
Australia: E. W. Wright,
Austria: E.-M. Bajons,
Belgium: J. van Compernolle and G. Closset-Marchal,
Canada: G. D. Watson,
Chile: Pecchi Croce and Ortiz Sepulveda,
England: J. R. D. Adams,
Federal Republic of Germany: P. Gottwald, *German National Reports for the Eighth World Congress on Procedural Law* (1987), pp. 141–59,
France: F. Grivart de Kerstrat,
Greece: P. Kargados,
Israel: S. Shetreet,
Italy: R. Vaccarella,
Japan: A. Ishikawa,
Netherlands: H. J. Snijders, *Dutch National Reports for the Eighth World Congress on Procedural Law* (1987), pp. 43–68,
South Africa: J. Taitz,
Spain: V. Fairén-Guillén,
Sweden: A. Bruzelius,
United States of America: R. S. Thompson.
Uruguay: Jardi Abella and Graciela Barcelona,

Part VI

Procedural reform

17 'General ideas' and the reform of civil procedure[1]

The Royal Commission on Legal Services, which reported in 1979,[2] was not called upon to review procedure or the administration of justice. It nevertheless received so much evidence on these subjects that it saw fit to publish a summary of that evidence and to recommend that 'a full appraisal of procedure and the operation in practice of our system of justice, in particular in all civil courts' should be carried out.[3] Since then, extra urgency has been given to the reform of civil procedure, both generally and in some of its more specialised aspects,[4] and in 1985 the then Lord Chancellor set up the Civil Justice Review which, after wide consultation, produced its Report in 1988.[5] Following on that, numerous changes of practice in the High Court and the Court of Appeal were introduced by legislation, by Practice Direction and simply by change in judicial practice. Even this was not enough, however, and in 1994 the Lord Chancellor appointed Lord Woolf to review the rules and procedures of the civil courts with a view, principally, to improvement in 'access to justice'.[6]

It is unnecessary to look further for evidence of continuing dissatisfaction with the administration of justice in England; it appears that when Pound said, in 1906, that 'dissatisfaction with the administration of justice is as old as law',[7] he could have added 'and will continue until law ceases to exist'. Paradoxically, however, Pound's famous address on

[1] Based on an article with the same title in [1983] *Legal Studies* 295.
[2] Report of the Royal Commission on Legal Services, Cmnd 7648, (1979), iii–iv.
[3] *Ibid.*, para. 43.3 and Appendix 43.1.
[4] For example, the report of the Committee on Procedure and Practice in the Chancery Division, Cmnd 8205 (1981). For the Commercial Court, a Commercial Court Committee was set up in 1977. The Committee meets regularly and has produced a Guide to Commercial Court Practice, which has judicial approval and should be followed: *Practice Direction (Commercial Court: Practice Guide)* [1994] 1 W.L.R. 1270.
[5] Report of the Review Body on Civil Justice, Cm 394 (1988).
[6] Woolf Interim and Woolf Final. Lord Woolf's proposals and the C.P.R. which resulted from them are mentioned from time to time elsewhere in this book and are discussed generally in chap. 19.
[7] 'The Causes of Popular Dissatisfaction with the Administration of Justice' (1906) 40 Am.L.R. 729.

'The Causes of Popular Dissatisfaction with the Administration of Justice' was delivered at a time when there seems to have been a high level of satisfaction in this country, thanks to the reforms achieved by the Judicature Acts 1873–5 and to the development of the county courts since their institution in 1846.

A few grumbles can, of course, be found in the literature of the time,[8] but the general euphoria that prevailed at the end of the nineteenth and beginning of the twentieth century can be seen in an essay by Lord Bowen in 1887 and a lecture by Blake Odgers Q.C. in 1901. Lord Bowen was prepared to assert 'without fear of contradiction that it is not *possible* in the year 1887 for an honest litigant in her Majesty's Supreme Court to be defeated by any mere technicality, any slip, any mistaken step in his litigation', and he considered that the county court legislation and those who carried out its provisions in the provinces had furnished the population of the country 'at their very doors with justice, cheap, excellent, and expeditious'.[9] Blake Odgers, while conceding that perfection had not yet been achieved, repeated Lord Bowen's sentiments in words not very different and concluded, 'Litigation in 1800 was dilatory and costly; now it is cheap and expeditious. To borrow the language of Lord Brougham, the procedure of our courts was in 1800 "a two-edged sword in the hands of craft and oppression; it is now the staff of honesty and the shield of innocence".'[10]

Considered as objective assessments of the administration of justice in late-Victorian England, such observations as these may be unconvincing, and Sir Jack Jacob has described Lord Bowen's assertion as an 'extraordinary claim'.[11] Unless they are unrepresentative of then prevailing opinion, however, it is difficult to avoid the conclusion that the level of satisfaction with the administration of justice was higher at the beginning of the century than it is today. This would not be surprising if

---

[8] E.g. the criticism by T. Snow of the extension of the originating summons on the ground that this broke up the unity of the originating process established by the Judicature Acts: (1893) 9 L.Q.R. 31, and see R. B. P. Cator's reply, *ibid.*, 238. For further critical observations by Snow and a proposal for a 'Master Machine' for law reform, see his 'The Near Future of Law Reform' (1900) 16 L.Q.R. 129. Comparisons unfavourable to English procedure were drawn with that of France and Belgium in a lecture delivered to the Solicitors Managing Clerks Association under the chairmanship of Scrutton J. in 1913: (1913) 134 L.T. 347.

[9] 'Progress in the Administration of Justice during the Victorian Period' in *Select Essays in Anglo-American Legal History* (1907), Vol. I, pp. 516, 541 and 543.

[10] 'Changes in Procedure and in the Law of Evidence' (a lecture delivered at the request of the Council of Legal Education on 17 January 1901) in *A Century of Law Reform* (1901), p. 203 at p. 240.

[11] 'The Judicature Acts 1873–1875, Vision and Reality' in Jacob, *Reform*, p. 301 at p. 309. Elsewhere Sir Jack describes it as a 'rather exuberant remark': 'Civil Procedure since 1800', *ibid.*, p. 193 at p. 214.

nothing, or nothing beyond the competence of the rule committees, had been done in the meantime to identify and meet changing demands upon the system, but in fact since long before the Royal Commission on Legal Services began taking evidence – indeed, since before the First World War – there have been numerous committees and commissions on the subject, and many of their recommendations have been implemented.[12] The situation seems to be worse than on the other side of the looking glass, where 'it takes all the running you can do, to keep in the same place'.[13] If reforms capable of producing even a few decades of satisfaction with the administration of justice are to be introduced as, evidently, the reforms effected by the Judicature Acts succeeded in doing, it should perhaps be asked not only what is wrong with our system as it is, but also what is wrong, by comparison with what was done in the last century, with our approach to its improvement.

If one looks at the reports dealing with the administration of justice that have so far appeared during this century, it will be found that, almost without exception, they concentrate directly on the twin perceived evils of cost and delay.[14] If excessive, these are serious evils, and it is not intended to suggest that it is wrong to continue to look for acceptable modifications of judicial organisation or of the rules of procedure which may tend to their reduction. If we look back to the progress of reform between, say, the Uniformity of Process Act 1832 and the Judicature Acts, however, it is apparent that, although the motivation of the reform then lay largely in the desire to eliminate costly and time-wasting procedures and unnecessary multiplicity of proceedings, it came to be realised that it was not enough simply to tackle the defects of the system one by one. Though superficially attractive, that approach is essentially negative in character and, as shown by the

---

[12] A list, not complete, of relevant reports published before that of the Royal Commission would include: The Report of the County Courts Committee 1909 (The Gorrell Committee); the two Reports of the Royal Commission on Delay in the King's Bench Division (Cd 6761, 1913; Cd 7177, 1914); the three Reports of the Business of the Courts Committee (Cmd 4265, 1933; Cmd 4471, 1933; Cmd 5066, 1936); the Report of the Royal Commission on the Despatch of Business at Common Law (Cmd 5065, 1936); the two Reports of the Committee on County Court Procedure (Cmd 7468, 1948; Cmd 7668, 1949); the four Reports of the Committee on Supreme Court Practice and Procedure (Cmd 7764, 1949; Cmd 8176, 1951; Cmd 8617, 1952; Cmd 8878, 1953); the Report of the Committee on Personal Injuries Litigation (Cmnd 3691, 1968); the Report of the Royal Commission on Assizes and Quarter Sessions (Cmnd 4153, 1969).

[13] Lewis Carroll, *Alice through the Looking Glass*, chap. 1.

[14] The most notable of the exceptions is, probably, the Report of the Committee on Legal Aid and Legal Advice (Cmd 6641, 1945) which led to enactment of the Legal Aid Act 1949.

disastrous results of the Hilary Rules of 1834,[15] can actually make things worse. A positive and principled objective was required.

Such an objective was eventually found in the concept of 'complete justice', which had emerged, at the latest, by the time of the second report of the Common Law Commissioners in 1853; in that report the opinion was expressed that 'every court ought to possess within itself the means of administering complete justice within the scope of its jurisdiction'.[16] The concept of 'complete justice', as eventually realised by the Judicature Acts 1873–5, is examined below, but at this stage two observations may be made:

(i) In the address already referred to, Pound identified, as one of the causes of dissatisfaction with the administration of justice 'lying in our peculiar legal system', 'the lack of general ideas or legal philosophy, so characteristic of Anglo-American law, which gives us petty tinkering where comprehensive reform is needed'.[17] Comprehensive reform was certainly achieved by the Judicature Acts thanks, it is suggested, to the existence of a 'general idea' which, if witnesses such as Lord Bowen and Blake Odgers are to be believed,[18] was one well adapted to the perceived needs of the time. The truth of Pound's proposition is proved by the demonstration of its converse.

(ii) The 'general idea' that is conveyed by the phrase 'complete justice' involves an understanding of the relationship between substantive law and procedure which, when it emerged, was new for England. It also enshrines, in a way which was not altogether new but which was given a new form, an understanding of the process of litigation itself and of the respective roles of the parties, on the one hand, and the judge or judge and jury on the other. Neither of these elements of 'complete justice' has been

---

[15] These Rules were introduced by the judges with the agreement of Parliament, following the recommendations of the Commissioners appointed to consider the practice and procedure of the Courts of Common Law (Second Report, 1830). They had the objectives of eliminating unnecessary expense in the parties' preparation for trial and of removing some of the occasions on which a new trial might have to be ordered. They sought to achieve these objectives by reducing the scope of the 'general issue' in favour of an extension of special pleading. The result was to produce a substantial increase in the number of cases decided on points of pleading: W. S. Holdsworth, *History of English Law*, 3rd edn (1944), Vol. IX, p. 325, citing Whittier 'Notice Pleading' (1918) 31 Harv.L.R. 501. See also W. S. Holdsworth, 'The New Rules of Pleading of the Hilary Term, 1834' (1923) 1 C.L.J. 261.

[16] Parliamentary Papers 1852–3, XL, pp. 34 *et seq.* The germ of the idea may be seen in Lord Mansfield's attempts to give effect to equitable principles in a court of common law: e.g. *Weakly* v. *Bucknell* (1776) 1 Cowp. 473. Cf. *Doe* v. *Clare* (1788) 2 T.R. 739.

[17] 'Causes of Popular Dissatisfaction', p. 736.

[18] Above, p. 356.

subjected to critical analysis since the Judicature Acts came into operation. Only in the allocation of certain kinds of litigation to specialist tribunals rather than to the ordinary courts, and, perhaps, in the recent movement to case management, has there been even tacit acknowledgment that the 'general idea' that informed those Acts may no longer have the value, as a guide to procedural reform, which it had more than a century ago.

It may be harsh – and at a certain level of generalisation it is wrong – to classify as 'petty tinkering' all of the many changes in judicial organisation and in the conduct of civil litigation that have occurred in this century. It is, nevertheless, difficult to avoid the conclusion that a great deal of effort has been directed to the reduction of costs and delay, but little, if any, to an understanding of what it is that should be done more cheaply and more expeditiously. The nineteenth-century concept of 'complete justice' has become the unspoken premise from which conscious thought begins.

'Complete justice' and the Judicature Acts

Seen through the eyes of one to whom the enactment of the Judicature Acts is part of history, the most important of the ideas contained in the phrase 'complete justice' is the creation of a single jurisdiction for the administration of both law and equity so that, in a single set of proceedings, the remedies of both should be available and the need for the parties to have recourse to more than one court should be eliminated.[19]

It is not intended to suggest that the achievement of savings of time and expense was absent from the minds of those who reported on various aspects of civil litigation during the 1850s. On the contrary, much was done during that decade to avoid multiplicity of proceedings; in particular, the Common Law Procedure Act 1852 gave certain equitable powers to the courts of common law and the Chancery Amendment Act 1858 (Lord Cairns' Act) empowered the Court of Chancery to award the common law remedy of damages in certain cases. Nevertheless, two distinct jurisdictions continued to exist and it is clear, for example, that the latter Act was not intended – or was not interpreted as intended – to confer concurrent jurisdiction on the courts of common law and the Court of Chancery even in cases of tort or breach of contract.[20]

---

[19] Judicature Act 1873, s. 24(7).
[20] *Wicks* v. *Hunt* (1859) Johns 372. See J. A. Jolowicz 'Damages in Equity – A Study of Lord Cairns' Act' [1975] C.L.J. 224, 226–7.

If, in the unreformed legal system, multiple proceedings might be necessary because of the separate administration of law and equity, so also might they be necessary in a case involving nothing but the common law because of the possibility that the plaintiff's choice of form of action might prove incorrect: following a non-suit he must either bring fresh proceedings or abandon his claim. Here, too, there was change in the 1850s, for by the Common Law Procedure Act 1852 extensive joinder of causes of action was permitted, and the court was given wide power to allow amendments in the course of the proceedings so that the danger of a non-suit was reduced. The danger was not, however, eliminated altogether, for the forms of action, as such, were not 'abolished'. In *Bracegirdle* v. *Hinks*[21] in 1854, for example, the plaintiff declared that the defendant was indebted to him in the sum of £4 for the carriage of timber and other goods and the defendant pleaded 'never indebted'. The jury awarded the plaintiff £2 because the defendant had failed to fulfil his obligation under the contract – which was to perform a service for the plaintiff, not to pay a price – but leave had been reserved to enter a non-suit. It was held that the non-suit must be entered: the case was not one of debt and, although an application to amend could have been made even at the trial, once leave had been reserved to enter a non-suit it was too late.

Though they did a good deal to remove some of the worst features of the old system, therefore, and though they may be seen as important steps on the road to 'complete justice', even after passage of the Common Law Procedure and the Chancery Amendment Acts, the English legal system remained essentially what it had always been – 'a conglomeration of procedures'.[22] Though it had become possible to combine in one set of proceedings more than one element of that conglomeration, the elements themselves remained distinct until the Judicature Acts.

In his first lecture on the 'Forms of Action', Maitland warned against the notion that 'from the beginning it was the office of the king's own court or courts to provide a remedy for every wrong',[23] and it is trite history that the courts of common law extended their jurisdiction piecemeal by development of and within the forms of action. As for

---

[21] (1854) 9 Ex. 361. Cf. *Ellston* v. *Deacon* (1866) L.R. 2 C.P. 20, where an amendment was allowed after verdict.
[22] R. David and J. E. C. Brierly, *Major Legal Systems in the World Today*, 3rd edn (1985), p. 318. In explaining the position to civilian readers, David observes that, until 1875, the English courts remained, in theory, 'juridictions d'exception': David, *Grands Systèmes*, p. 259.
[23] A. H. Chaytor and W. B. Whittaker (eds.), *Equity, also The Forms of Action at Common Law* (1916), p. 304.

equity, to quote Maitland once more, it was not a self-sufficient system 'but a collection of appendixes, between which there was no very close connexion'.[24] Though the scope of certain of the forms of action had become so great by the early nineteenth century that the rules applied under them for the solution of litigated questions could be regarded as rules of general substantive law, adherence to the forms of action and to the separation of law from equity still meant that substantive law was 'secreted in the interstices of procedure':[25] only abolition of all the procedural implications of the forms of action, and the creation of a single jurisdiction administering law and equity conjointly, could alter that.

Probably the most significant achievement of the Judicature Acts, and the most fundamental aspect of 'complete justice', was, therefore, the ultimate separation of substantive law from procedure,[26] for this alone made possible the belief, now almost universally accepted as self-evident, that legal rights and obligations are one thing, the machinery and procedures for their recognition and enforcement, another. It is difficult, in the late twentieth century, to see as other than the deliberate obstruction of justice, or as the love of form for form's sake, decisions in which plaintiffs failed to obtain judgment for no better reason than that they had chosen the wrong form of action or the wrong court for their claims. So accustomed are we to the idea that a body of coherent and self-consistent substantive law 'exists', and is itself determinative of all legal relationships, that the idea has become part of our unspoken assumptions.[27] We tend, therefore, to think of Collins M.R.'s well-known statement that 'the relation of rules of practice to the work of justice is intended to be that of handmaid rather than mistress'[28] as little more than an elegant truism. Earlier generations of judges and practitioners who knew only the separate administration of law and equity, and for whom the distinctions between the forms of action were integral to the system in which they had been trained and in which they practised, might not have declared this statement to be wrong, had any of their contemporaries been capable of making it, but they might well have found it difficult to understand.

Fact pleading

Adoption by the Judicature Acts of 'complete justice', and with it the separation of substantive law from procedure, made possible a propo-

---

[24] *Ibid.*, p. 19.
[25] H. S. Maine, *Early Law and Custom* (1869), p. 389.
[26] Chap. 4, pp. 82–5.   [27] Chap. 4, pp. 85–6.
[28] *Re Coles and Ravenshear* [1907] 1 K.B. 1, 4.

sition that we now take for granted – namely, that it is the task of the court to decide what are and were the rights and obligations of the parties to litigation by the application of 'the law' to 'the facts'. Legal argument on behalf of the parties may be helpful to the judge, and the provision of an opportunity for such argument is essential to procedural fairness, but, so far as the actual process of litigation is concerned, the determination of the facts to which the law is to be applied becomes the most important matter: the law is there and it is the court's business to apply it.[29]

This is not to say that under the old system the facts were unimportant, but each form of action covered, at least theoretically, a distinct type of factual situation or set of circumstances, and if the plaintiff failed to allege or prove facts falling within the scope of the form of action he had chosen, his action failed. Once the strait-jacket of the forms of action has been removed, however, and the objective of doing 'complete justice' by applying 'the law' to 'the facts' is adopted, there ceases to be any defined limit to the facts that the court may be required to take into account. 'Facts' began with the Creation, and it is difficult to see how anything that has occurred since then can be declared a priori to be irrelevant. It is no wonder that the Commissioners on the Courts of Common Law in 1831,[30] though they were willing to propose special arrangements to meet the particular difficulty caused by uncertainty about the boundaries of 'trespass' and 'trespass on the case', urged retention of the forms of action for the avoidance of confusion.

The solution adopted by the Judicature Acts was to substitute for the old forms of pleading the system known as 'fact pleading', in accordance with which 'every pleading shall contain as concisely as may be a statement of the material facts on which the party pleading relies, but not the evidence by which they are to be proved'.[31] Elaborate provisions were made in the Rules brought into operation by the Acts – rules which have been modified and improved over the years but which have not significantly changed their character – to ensure that each party's

---

[29] For the view that the maxim *curia novit legem* is not part of English law, see chap. 10, p. 189.

[30] Third Report of the Commissioners on the Courts of Common Law, 1831, Parliamentary Papers 1831, X.

[31] This is the original form of the rule in Ord. XIX, r. 4 of the Rules scheduled to the Judicature Act 1875. It incorporates the proposal of the Judicature Commission to combine 'the comparative brevity of the simpler forms of common law pleading, with the principle of stating, intelligibly and not technically, the substance of the facts relied upon as constituting the plaintiff's or the defendant's case, as distinguished from his evidence': First Report (1869), Parliamentary Papers 1868–9, XXV. The rule in force until 1999 (R.S.C., Ord. 18, r. 7) was little different, and C.P.R., r. 16.4 is to similar effect. 'Fact pleading' made its first appearance in New York in 1848: chap 2, p. 35.

pleading should convey to his opponent the case he would have to meet on the facts and, above all, to clarify what issues of fact are in controversy between the parties.[32]

The essential feature of fact pleading was and is that the parties allege the facts – what Erle C.J. called the *allegata probanda*[33] – which in their contentions justify the claim or defence as the case may be.[34] That a fact is not in controversy does not mean that it need not be pleaded but, conversely, if a fact is alleged by one party and admitted by the other, the case will be decided on the unproven assumption that the allegation is true. The parties had, and have, substantial possibilities of amending their pleadings as the litigation proceeds,[35] and the court may sometimes remove matter from a pleading by the exercise of its power to strike out.[36] On the other hand, it will not require to have put in issue an allegation made by one party that the other is willing to admit, and it will not, though it apparently had power to do so after 1880,[37] bring into the litigation facts that no party has chosen to allege:

---

[32] Rules of 1875, Ord. XIX, rr. 17, 22, 23. These rules were strictly applied: e.g. *Thorp* v. *Holdsworth* (1876) 3 Ch.D. 639; *Byrd* v. *Nunn* (1877) 7 Ch.D. 284. Cf. *Tildesley* v. *Harper* (1878) 10 Ch.D. 393, where leave was granted by the Court of Appeal to amend an evasive denial, reversing Fry J. ((1877) 7 Ch.D. 403), who had refused leave and treated the evasive denial as an admission. Cf. the criticism of modern pleading practice in Winn, paras. 266–70 and Woolf Interim, pp. 153–5. See now C.P.R., r. 16.5, which should improve the quality of defence pleading.

[33] Notes to Ord. XIX, r. 4 in the *Annual Chancery Practice* 1882; *Philipps* v. *Philipps* (1878) 4 Q.B.D. 127.

[34] Rules of 1875, Ord. XIX, r. 18.

[35] *Ibid.*, Ord. XXVII; R.S.C., Ord. 20; C.P.R., r. 17.

[36] Rules of 1875, Ord. XXVII, r. 1; R.S.C., Ord. 18, r. 19; C.P.R., r. 3.4.

[37] What became R.S.C., Ord. 20, r. 8, was introduced into the Rules of 1875 in 1880, and may originally have been intended to do no more than enable one party to obtain an order that the other party amend his pleading so as to give it greater particularity. In its original form the rule provided that 'The Court or a Judge may at any time, and on such terms as to costs or otherwise as to the Court or Judge may seem just, amend any defect or error in any proceedings; and all such amendments may be made as may be necessary for the purpose of determining the real question or issue raised by or depending on the proceedings.' For a case where difficulty occurred before the rule was introduced, see *Harbord* v. *Monk* (1878) 9 Ch.D. 616, and for a case in which a party was ordered to amend his pleading to give particulars, see *Spedding* v. *Fitzpatrick* (1888) 38 Ch.D. 410. Although the R.S.C. 1883 included specific provision for the giving of particulars (Ord. XIX, r. 6), the rule was retained as Ord. XXVII, r. 12 but attracted no attention in the notes to the Annual Practice until the edition of 1888–9; it was then stated that under this rule the court might act without an application from a party. The following year a query was added to this statement, but in 1901 and in subsequent years it was said, with the emphasis shown, that 'every Judge and Master has full power *of his own motion* to make any amendment which he deems necessary for the purpose of determining the real questions at issue between the parties'. If this had been taken at face value it might have transformed civil litigation in England, but it was not. The latest note to R.S.C., Ord. 20, r. 8 (*Supreme Court Practice 1999*, para. 20/8/3) is much more cautious. C.P.R., r. 17, which deals with amendment, has no equivalent.

as Fry L.J. said in 1884, 'I do not think that it is the duty of the Court to force upon a party . . . an amendment for which he does not ask.'[38]

The system of pleading introduced under the Judicature Acts, and continued until now, is thus a system that confers almost total freedom on the parties to fix 'the facts' to which the law is to be applied, leaving it to the court only to resolve, on the evidence produced by the parties, those issues which are in controversy between them. In other words, 'the facts' were and are none other than the facts alleged and admitted or proved by the parties; from this it follows that, however extensively 'the law' is understood, the question that the court must answer is effectively formulated by the parties as they jointly see fit.[39]

Under the original rules of 1875, pleadings might be dispensed with, generally speaking, only if the defendant stated at the time of his appearance that he did not require delivery of a 'statement of complaint'.[40] From time to time, however, in the interests of economy, various devices have been tried for the conduct of litigation without pleadings,[41] or their equivalent under another name,[42] but the only one of these to have achieved lasting success has been the originating summons, the scope of which has been greatly extended since it was rescued from oblivion in 1883.[43] It is, however, of the essence of the procedure by originating summons that a question is formulated for the court to answer, and the procedure is acknowledged to be inappropriate for use when facts are seriously in dispute between the parties.[44] Since

---

[38] *Cropper* v. *Smith* (1884) 26 Ch.D. 700, 715. See also the note by Lord Asquith on *Dann* v. *Hamilton* [1939] 1 K.B. 509 in (1953) 69 L.Q.R. 317. The only reported example of the exercise of the power conferred by R.S.C., Ord. 20, r. 8. that the editors of *The Supreme Court Practice* are able to cite dates from 1883: *Nottage* v. *Jackson* (1883) 11 Q.B.D. 627: *Supreme Court Practice 1999*, para. 20/8/3.

[39] Chap. 10, p. 198.   [40] Ord. XIX, r. 2.

[41] Provision for trial without pleadings was made in 1893 by what was then R.S.C., Ord. XVIII A, which survived until 1917, and again in 1954, by what was then R.S.C., Ord. XIV B, and this survived until 1962, when it was replaced by R.S.C., Ord. 18, r. 21, the note to which explains that where pleadings are to be dispensed with 'it is of vital importance that . . . it should be made absolutely clear what is the controversy between the parties': *Supreme Court Practice 1999*, para. 18/21/2. In 1897, a summons for directions was required to be taken out after appearance and before any further steps were taken, and this meant that, until 1934, pleadings were delivered only by leave: R.S.C., Ord XXX, r. 1. See A. S. Diamond 'The Summons for Directions' (1959) 75 L.Q.R. 43 and I. H. Jacob 'The Present Importance of Pleadings' in Jacob, *Reform*, p. 243. See now, C.P.R., r. 16.8.

[42] See the note by Blake Odgers Q.C. to Ord XXX, *Annual Practice* 1913.

[43] No equivalent to the originating summons appears in the Rules of 1875, but the *Annual Chancery Practice* 1882 incorporated the earlier practice used in Chancery Chambers. These were absorbed into the Rules of 1883 in Order LV, the scope of which was expanded in 1893. An equivalent to the originating summons, though not so called, is provided by C.P.R., r. 8.

[44] This was clear from the beginning; e.g. *Re Giles* (1890) 43 Ch.D. 391: *Nutter* v. *Holland*

no case can be decided save in relation to its facts, it follows that when an originating summons is employed the facts are, for all practical purposes, only those which the parties jointly decide to place before the court.

As already suggested, despite all the changes in the rules of procedure since 1875, nothing has occurred since then to alter the basic understanding of 'complete justice' which informed the Judicature Acts. Civil litigation was then understood to be a process whereby the parties submitted, for resolution by the court in accordance with law, *their* dispute as they elected to formulate it and, in so far as there has been any departure from this, the tendency has been – in the interests of economy – to try to narrow the area of dispute by pressing for greater agreement on the 'facts'.[45] Indeed, far from moving away from the notion that the court should take into account only facts which have been pleaded, it has actually been proposed that the parties should be required to include in their pleadings an 'offer of proof'[46] – that is, an indication of the evidence to be adduced in support of the allegations of fact in the pleadings, such offer to be binding – and also their 'theories of law'.[47] If these proposals were adopted, the 'private' character of civil litigation would be reinforced, and so too would be the idea that the 'justice' the court is required to administer, while justice according to law, is nevertheless no more than justice between the parties; wider considerations would have no place.

In its report, *Going to Law*, Justice stated that

the court has always seen itself as furnishing a public service to litigants, which they are free to use if they wish, and to leave unused if they do not. The court does not regard it as its function to force parties to conduct their disputes in any particular fashion: provided they agree on what is to be done, and it falls within the rules, the court will agree also.[48]

Written in 1974, these words accord well with the system for the administration of civil justice that was instituted in 1875. It is an open question whether they accord equally well with the kind of system needed on the threshold of the twenty-first century.

[1894] 3 Ch. 408, 410, *per* Lopes L.J. Under modern procedure, an action begun by originating summons may be ordered to be continued as if begun by writ, which will normally involve pleadings: R.S.C., Ord. 28, r. 8; C.P.R., r. 8.1(3).

[45] E.g. the proposals for a more 'robust' summons for directions in Evershed, paras. 225–33; see the former R.S.C., Ord. 25 and Diamond, 'Summons for Directions'. The modern rules governing the use of hearsay evidence under the Civil Evidence Act 1995 and those dealing with expert evidence under C.P.R., r. 35 have a similar tendency.

[46] Justice, *Going to Law*, paras. 165–70. C.P.R., r. 16, Practice Direction, 11.3; Woolf Interim, p. 161.

[47] Justice, *Going to Law*, para. 171. Woolf Interim, p. 159.

[48] Justice, *Going to Law*, para. 57.

The role of civil litigation

It was appreciated by the architects of the Judicature Acts that one of the purposes that a system for the administration of civil justice must fulfil is that of enabling a plaintiff with an unanswerable claim to obtain an enforceable judgment by summary process; Order 14, as it has always been until now, found a place in the rules of 1875 in a form not essentially different from that which it retained throughout its life.[49] The availability of summary judgment against a defendant with no substantial defence does not, however, detract from the assumption that civil proceedings are essentially 'private', and it is principally this, and the associated idea that 'complete justice' means no more than justice between the parties and their privies, that call for reconsideration.

It is not intended to suggest that the courts should no longer see it as part of their function to resolve private disputes between private parties.[50] The assumption that this is all that the civil courts are required to do should, however, no longer be left unquestioned. For this, many reasons may be suggested, of which only a few can be mentioned here. For convenience these are subdivided into two categories, namely, first, those which relate to litigation in which the actual concern of the parties is to promote or to protect only their own interests – which may be called 'selfish litigation' – and those in which it is not – 'unselfish litigation'. It should be noted, however, that considerations advanced in relation to selfish litigation may also apply to litigation that is unselfish.

Selfish litigation

It is inherent in the combination of the declaratory theory of judicial precedent[51] and the procedure of fact pleading that the judge should have the last word on the law to be applied to the facts before him. Some of the difficulties to which this gives rise are discussed in an earlier chapter,[52] and it emerges that by their choice of allegations of fact – and especially if one of them declines the judge's suggestion for an amendment of pleadings – the parties can actually oblige the judge to give a decision which he believes to be wrong in the light of the facts as they have emerged in the course of the proceedings.

---

[49] See *Wallingford* v. *Mutual Society* (1880) 5 App.Cas. 685. The scope for summary judgment has been expanded under the C.P.R., but, sadly, the number 14 has gone: the relevant rule is now C.P.R., r. 24. See Woolf Interim, pp. 37–8; Woolf Final, pp. 123–4.

[50] Cf. O. M. Fiss 'The Supreme Court, 1978 Term; Foreword: The Forms of Justice' (1979) 93 Harv.L.R. 1, 30.

[51] Chap. 3, p. 66.   [52] Chap. 10.

This may, not unreasonably, be thought to be an abuse of the dignity, if not of the process, of the court, which should, so far as possible, be prevented. If the parties do not want a decision in accordance with the law as the judge believes it to be, they should not submit their dispute for resolution by the court.[53]

The point just sought to be made may appear to some to be overly theoretical and without practical importance, but that must be refuted. Even leaving aside the fact that many people may be directly affected by a decision to which they were not party,[54] for the purposes of the doctrine of precedent there is no way in which it can be known, when litigation is in its early stages, whether the decision ultimately reached will or will not become significant as an authority for the decision of future cases. More important than their role as authorities, however, is the role played by judicial decisions as sources of information essential to those in the business of giving legal advice.[55] So important is it that the proportion of cases that proceed to judgment in relation to those which are settled, or stifled at birth on professional advice, should not rise, that Sir Jack Jacob has actually proposed that 'it should be regarded as a rule of professional conduct that the lawyers of the parties should engage in serious and meaningful negotiations to settle their cases on as reasonable, favourable and fair terms as possible'.[56]

The fair settlement of claims[57] should, in general, be encouraged, but it is, necessarily, the right of anyone who propounds a justiciable claim against another, and of that other, to have a court of competent jurisdiction pronounce upon it if agreement cannot be reached between them. It follows that one of the most important factors in any negotiation for a settlement is the parties' prediction of the consequences if no settlement is reached, and to this prediction information about comparable cases which have proceeded to judgment is essential.

The contribution of courts to resolving disputes cannot be equated with their resolution of those disputes that are fully adjudicated. The principal contribution

[53] In arbitration, for example, it is now recognised that finality may be more important than insistence on the 'meticulous legal accuracy' of arbitral awards: *Pioneer Shipping* v. *B.T.P. Tioxide* [1982] A.C. 724; *Antaios Compania S.A.* v. *Salen A.B.* [1985] A.C. 191. Similarly, legal accuracy is not a necessary or even, always, a desirable feature of other forms of 'alternative dispute resolution' to which the parties are at liberty and, indeed, encouraged, to resort.
[54] Chap. 7, p. 122.
[55] See M. Galanter, 'Justice in Many Rooms' in M. Cappelletti (ed.), *Access to Justice and the Welfare State* (1981), p. 147 and authorities there cited: chap. 3, above, p. 72.
[56] 'Accelerating the Process of Law' in Jacob, *Reform*, p. 91 at p. 117.
[57] The very idea of a 'fair' settlement involves a relationship between the terms of the settlement and what would have transpired if the case had proceeded to judgment. See Winn, section V.

of courts to dispute resolution is providing a background of norms and procedures against which negotiations and regulation in both private and governmental settings take place. This contribution includes, but is not exhausted by, communication to prospective litigants of what might transpire if one of them sought a judicial resolution. Courts communicate not only the rules that would govern adjudication of the dispute, but also possible remedies as well as estimates of the difficulty, certainty, and costs of securing particular outcomes.[58]

Whatever definition of civil proceedings may be adopted, the commencement of proceedings is normally the voluntary act of the plaintiff:[59] however grievous the wrong done to him, he cannot be compelled to sue. It apparently follows from this – and some may see it as an independent principle in its own right – that since a person is entitled to abandon his rights against another absolutely, he must be entitled also to abandon them in part in the course of litigation. When the compromise settlement of a claim is in question, this may be unexceptionable, but matters may stand differently when a claim comes before a court of law for judicial determination.

A problem of potentially far-reaching importance arises, namely, whether the rules of that part of the substantive law known as civil are no more than rules for the guidance of decision makers charged with the settlement of individual disputes, or whether they have a wider purpose. So far as the rules of the common law are concerned, it can be argued with some force, both on historical grounds and because they evolved through the process of adjudication, that they are directed primarily to decision makers and so are capable, public policy exceptions apart, of being excluded by the parties from consideration. On the other hand, litigation is a public act, performed in the courts of justice of the realm, and it is no longer sensible to dismiss, unconsidered, the thought that 'there stands over and above the parties a benefit in law (*Rechtsgut*) to which they are both subordinated, that their declarations, therefore, are only a means of attaining this benefit and that such attainment would never come to pass if they were left free to exercise their dispositive power and thus to pursue their own aims independently'.[60] Of course this statement goes too far if taken at face value, but should we not now admit that there is something in it?

Unselfish litigation

The importance, for present purposes, of litigation brought for the purpose of protecting diffuse interests, which is by definition unselfish,

---

[58] Galanter, 'Justice in Many Rooms', p. 153.
[59] Chap. 1, p. 21.
[60] A. Engelmann, *Der Civilprozess: Allgemeiner Teil*, cited in R. Millar, *History*, pp. 3, 13.

is obvious and the topic has been considered earlier.[61] Two points only call for mention here.

First, it is generally held today that an award of damages is intended, exceptional cases apart, to do no more than provide compensation to the injured plaintiff. As matters now stand, actions for damages are probably amongst the most private and apparently selfish of all forms of litigation. Even so, the idea that deterrence is a factor in the law of liability in damages is not completely dead, and, notwithstanding the severe limitations on the award of punitive damages,[62] such damages may still be awarded in some circumstances, as where it is necessary 'to teach a wrongdoer that tort does not pay'.[63] Since the plaintiff benefits personally from an award of punitive damages, his action in suing for them may not be subjectively unselfish, but, where punitive damages are available, should it not be recognised that the plaintiff is given an incentive to bring proceedings that should, in the wider interest, be brought?

Secondly, it is a common occurrence that a doubt arises as to the interpretation or effect of a particular statutory provision which, though not of general application, nevertheless bears directly upon the interests of a substantial number of people. This was the situation, for example, in *Allen v. Gulf Oil Refining Ltd.*[64] In that case, the question whether the defendant company was protected against liability for 'non-negligent' nuisance under a private Act of Parliament was raised as a preliminary point of law in an action brought by one of a number of householders who were adversely affected by its activities. There being, at that stage, no findings of fact, the answer to the question would not necessarily dispose finally of the action, and for this reason the House of Lords was reluctant to deal with it. Lord Wilberforce went so far as to say that, although the procedure of bringing a preliminary point of law is sometimes useful, in many cases of which the case at Bar was an example, its use does not serve 'the cause of justice'.[65] If, indeed, the object of the proceedings had been purely and simply to obtain for the plaintiff such redress as she personally might have been entitled to from the defendant, so that nothing was at stake but the private interests of the parties, the criticism would have been justified. The question raised was,

---

[61] Chaps. 5, 6 and 7.
[62] *A.B. v. South West Water Services* [1993] Q.B. 507.
[63] *Rookes v. Barnard* [1964] A.C. 1129, 1221–31, *per* Lord Devlin; *Cassell and Co. Ltd v. Broome* [1972] A.C. 1027. The Law Commission has recommended that punitive damages should be available for any tort: Law Com. No. 247 (1997).
[64] [1981] A.C. 1001. J. A. Jolowicz, 'Should Courts Answer Questions?' [1981] C.L.J. 226.
[65] [1981] A.C. 1001, 1011.

however, of immediate practical importance to a substantial number of other people – not only householders in the position of the plaintiff but others also, such as the employees of Gulf Oil. It was 'ripe'[66] for decision, it was important that it should be answered, and the House of Lords' reluctance to supply the answer came, it is submitted, from undue adherence to the idea that civil litigation is nothing but the private affair of the parties.

Conclusion

It has been the object of this chapter to suggest, first, that the success of the Judicature Acts 1873–5 in securing a period of satisfaction with the administration of justice owed much to the adoption of a 'general idea', known as 'complete justice', and, secondly, that that idea – or, rather, one particular aspect of it – should no longer continue unquestioned in the role it seems to have acquired, namely, that of unspoken premise on which procedural reform is based. Even if attention is directed, as it has been in this chapter, only to certain kinds of litigation in the High Court, it cannot still be supposed that the only function of the civil courts is to resolve particular disputes in the form and on the evidence selected by the parties. If attention is directed also to other kinds of litigation in the courts, especially litigation involving the relations between the individual and the state, litigation relating to matrimonial and other personal relationships, to the problem of 'small claims', and to proceedings before the many tribunals that are 'properly regarded as machinery provided by Parliament for adjudication',[67] the inadequacies of the nineteenth-century concept of 'complete justice' for the conditions of today are clear.

Nothing that may be done by way of reform should be allowed to undermine the separation of substantive law from procedure: that was the greatest achievement of the Judicature Acts in terms of general principle. On the other hand, everything possible should be done to encourage and sustain public confidence in the 'correctness' of judicial decisions. Whether it is true or not that, for every case whether litigated or not, there is a uniquely correct legal solution, the judges should do their best to find it, for they have the privilege of the last word – unless

---

[66] The concept of the 'ripeness' of a question for judicial determination has acquired importance in the Supreme Court of the United States. See, e.g. *Duke Power Co.* v. *Carolina Environmental Study Group* 438 U.S. 59 (1978).

[67] Report of the Committee on Administrative Tribunals and Enquiries, Cmnd 281 (1957), p. 9.

and until their 'errors' are detected and rectified on appeal by other judges.[68]

Appreciation that judicial decisions do more than settle private disputes carries with it, therefore, the requirement that the judges and other judicial officers concerned with litigation should do whatever is possible to satisfy themselves that the decisions of the courts in those cases that proceed to judgment are as nearly correct as they can reasonably be, however strenuous may be the efforts to keep the number of such cases to a minimum. In the High Court, at least, it might theoretically be sufficient for this that the courts routinely exercise the powers over the constitution of the litigation, and over the evidence presented, that they apparently already have or could acquire without legislation; but even if this is so, no real change can come without a change in attitudes of mind.[69]

In the address referred to earlier in this chapter, Pound castigated the American 'exaggeration of the common-law contentious procedure'. His principal target was the 'sporting theory of justice', which led, amongst other things, to 'vested rights in errors of procedure', but he insisted that the question which the judicial process should seek to answer is 'what do substantive law and justice require?'[70] No doubt 'justice' includes procedural justice, and the principle of contradiction must retain its paramountcy. Neither that principle nor any other should, however, be held to debar the judge from receiving or obtaining information that he considers necessary to his decision. There is nothing inherently wrong in the settlement of a dispute on the parties' terms by an arbitrator or in some other form of alternative dispute resolution. On the other hand, to insist on their unlimited freedom to control the matters to be taken into account by a judge whose task it is to pronounce

---

[68] To explain the existence of rights of appeal on the ground that judges are fallible (e.g. Evershed, para. 473) is to assume that a 'correct' solution exists. Cf. A. Esmein, *Cours élémentaire d'histoire du droit français*, 4th edn (1901), p. 257, see chap. 15, above p. 317. See chap. 16, p. 330, for discussion of the purposes of appellate courts. Even in 'selfish litigation', those purposes obviously go beyond the mere resolution of private disputes. Though not directly applicable to the manner in which English appellate courts announce their decisions (chap. 14, p. 281), there is much to be learned from the discussion in A. Touffait and A. Tunc 'Pour une motivation plus explicite des décisions de justice, notamment de celles de la Cour de cassation' 1974 Rev.trim.dr.civ. 487. See also P. Bellet and A. Tunc (eds.), *La cour judiciaire suprême. Une Enquête comparative* and J. A. Jolowicz, 'Appellate Proceedings' in M. Storme and H. Casman (eds.), *Towards a Justice with a Human Face*, p. 127.

[69] Such a change in attitudes of mind may, in the long run, result from extensive use of case management. See J. A. Jolowicz, 'The Woolf Report and the Adversary System' (1996) 15 C.J.Q. 198 and below, chap. 19.

[70] 'Causes of Popular Dissatisfaction', pp. 738–9. See also Pound, 'A Generation of Improvement in the Administration of Justice' (1947) 27 N.Y.U.L.R. 369.

in public, and according to law, the *judicial* solution to a problem, may actually deprive his decision of its judicial character.

In a lecture delivered on the centenary of the passing of the Judicature Act 1875, Sir Jack Jacob suggested that we might now need a new Judicature Commission 'whose report will lead to a new Judicature Act'.[71] Elsewhere he expressed the opinion 'that we stand today once again at the threshold of great and far-reaching reforms and improvements in the field of procedural law'.[72] Only the future will tell whether Lord Woolf's Report and the reforms that have proceeded from it match up to Sir Jack's expectations.

[71] Jacob, *Reform*, p. 302.
[72] *Ibid.*, p. vii (Preface dated 1982). The Supreme Court Act 1981 he regarded as 'a staging point in the development and reform of procedural law'.

18 Reform of English civil procedure: a derogation from the adversary system?[1]

Introduction

In an earlier chapter it was said to be almost an article of faith on the part of common lawyers that, because their civil procedure is 'adversarial', it is therefore superior to the 'inquisitorial' system which they believe to exist elsewhere.[2] In this chapter, following a brief account of the legacy of the jury as the source of our enduring loyalty to the adversary system, attention will be directed to a number of developments which occurred before, and are not superseded by, the Woolf reforms and which, it is believed, have a tendency to undermine the tenets of the adversary system as traditionally understood. The final chapter considers the impact of the reforms following that report.

Three legacies of the jury[3]

The great period of reform of the nineteenth century reached its culmination on 1 January 1876, when the Supreme Court of Judicature Acts 1873–5 came into force. Those Acts laid the foundation of the judicial organisation and created the structure of civil procedure which have endured to the present time, but they did not mark a complete break with the past. Certainly our civil procedure was cleansed of its worst technicalities and some elements of the old equity procedure found a place in the new uniform procedure, but the underlying idea on which the new procedure was constructed was that of the old common law, with its insistence that questions of fact must be decided by a jury. What is more, when the use of the jury did begin to decline and cases were decided by judge alone, the pretence was for a time maintained

---

[1] Based mainly on an article entitled 'La réforme de la procédure civile anglaise: une dérogation au système adversatif?', published in P. Legrand (ed.), *Common Law d'un siècle l'autre* (1992), p. 233.
[2] Chap. 9, p. 175.
[3] See S. Goldstein, *The Anglo-American Jury System as seen by an Outsider (Who is a former Insider)*, Leiden University, Clifford Chance Lecture (1994).

that, in performing his role as judge of fact as well as law, the judge split himself in two and fulfilled separately the distinct roles of judge and of jury.[4] The pretence is maintained no longer, but the ghostly presence of the jury is still felt: the structure of English civil procedure remains much as it was when juries were in regular use.

A procedure in two stages

The practical impossibility of calling on the members of a jury to attend for a number of hearings, each, perhaps, very short, led to the idea of the *trial* – a single, uninterrupted hearing at which all the evidence is presented and argument heard, and at the end of which the jury delivers its verdict. Obviously, if a trial of this kind is to be conducted with even reasonable efficiency, there must be a pre-trial stage, and the clear-cut division into two stages, typical of the common law, was born. During the pre-trial stage, the proceedings must be started, the parties must prepare themselves for trial, and, most importantly, as much precision as possible must be given to the questions that the jury will have to answer. That is the principal objective of the pleadings. In the past the process of pleading became excessively technical, but today it consists of the exchange of documents between the parties in which each sets out the allegations of fact on which he wishes to rely and, for the defendant, any necessary denials of allegations made by the plaintiff. Comparison of the parties' pleadings should then show what are the questions of fact that are actually in dispute between them.[5]

The use of oral evidence

It cannot be expected of most ordinary people that they are accustomed to making decisions on the basis of documents, and this is most obviously true at a time of widespread illiteracy. If satisfactory results are to be achieved from a procedure in which a jury of twelve ordinary people must decide questions of fact, therefore, it is necessary that the materials on which they are to base their decisions – the evidence – should be presented to them by word of mouth. This simple fact is sufficient in itself to explain the marked preference of the common law for oral evidence, a characteristic which it did not, and still does not, share with other systems.

---

[4] A decision may be criticised, for example, on the ground that the judge had 'misdirected himself'.
[5] Chap. 2, p. 34.

The dominant role of the parties

The members of a jury, brought together for the first and only time when the proceedings have reached the stage of trial, can know nothing of the evidence, or even of the nature of the case they are to try, before the opening of the trial. It is, however, their duty to reach their conclusion on the evidence given at the trial, and that evidence can only be collected and produced by others. The judge presides at the trial and, when the advocates of the parties have been heard, he sums up the evidence and directs the jury on the applicable law, but he takes no part in the jury's deliberations. More importantly, for present purposes, if the judge were to interfere before the trial either in the drawing up of the pleadings, and thus in the determination of the questions to be answered by the jury, or in the collection and presentation of the evidence, he would infringe the sovereignty of the jury. It is thus inevitable that the judge remains passive and that all procedural activity falls to the parties. It is for them to determine not only the subject matter of the action but the precise questions at issue between them. It is also for them to determine on what evidence the jury will come to its conclusion. In other words, because the role of the jury is necessarily a passive one, the procedure itself cannot fail to recognise that it is the parties who have the dominant role.

Of these necessary features of a system placing such reliance on the jury, English legal thinking has made virtues, not always wrongly. That all the evidence is presented at a single-session trial, for example, ensures two of the goals sought by every procedural system – concentration and immediacy. That evidence presented orally at the trial is preferred to written records, even to a written and authenticated account of what had occurred or been said on an earlier occasion, ensures not only that the witness testifies in the presence of the judge of fact but that he can be cross-examined by the advocate of the party whose interests are damaged by his testimony.

There are, no doubt, other necessary byproducts of use of the jury that could be considered advantageous for the administration of justice. The important thing is, however – and whether to its advantage or not – that English civil procedure has for long taken the dominant role of the parties for granted and has used it as a point of departure. It is not so long ago that the view was taken that it was positively desirable, and not merely unavoidable, that the jury or the judge alone, as the case might be, entered the court room knowing nothing or virtually nothing of the case that was to be tried. That way the parties could be confident that only the evidence they wished the court to hear would be taken into account.

It is not difficult to believe that some increase in the powers of
initiative of the judge during the pre-trial stage could have been made
without infringing the sovereignty of the jury, but, until recently, no
tendency to examine such a possibility can be detected. It might be
suggested, for example, that even if he could not control the claims and
assertions of the parties, the judge could at least play a part in the
formulation of the issues to be resolved by the jury. A rule of court in
existence for many years[6] actually enabled him to do so, but the cases
hold that the judge may not order an amendment to the pleadings of his
own motion.[7] And, if the judge comes to think, in the course of the
proceedings, that it would aid the discovery of the truth that a certain
witness should be heard, practice, as enshrined in a well-known decision,[8] denies that the judge has power to summon a witness not called
by one or other of the parties unless they both agree: whether they might
occasionally wish to do so or not, judges do not call witnesses.

The dominant role of the parties and the willing acceptance of its
consequences are well illustrated by the *Air Canada* case, decided in
1982,[9] in which the plaintiff had demanded sight of certain documents
held by the defendant. Under the discovery rules in force, each party
had to disclose to his opponent all relevant documents in his possession
or control, and if he did not do so the court, on request, might order
disclosure of the documents. Such an order could be made, however,
only if disclosure was necessary for the just determination of the
litigation or to avoid unnecessary costs.[10]

At first instance the judge concluded that the documents in question
could be useful to him in discovering the truth; he ordered that they be
disclosed to him personally[11] even though the plaintiff had not been able
to show that disclosure of the documents would actually assist his case.
According to the judge, it did not matter which of the parties would be
assisted by disclosure: it was his duty to discover the truth regardless of
which of the parties would benefit thereby.

The Court of Appeal and the House of Lords both held that the judge
was wrong. In the words of Lord Wilberforce:

the task of the judge is to do, and be seen to be doing, justice between the
parties . . . There is no higher or additional duty to ascertain some independent

---

[6] R.S.C., Ord. 20, r. 8; chap. 17, p. 363.
[7] *Cropper v. Smith* (1884) 26 Ch.D. 700.
[8] *Re Enoch and Zaretzky, Bock and Co.'s Arbitration* [1910] 1 K.B. 327.
[9] *Air Canada v. Secretary of State for Trade* [1983] 2 A.C. 394.
[10] R.S.C., Ord. 24, r. 8. See now C.P.R., r. 31.3.
[11] [1983] 1 All E.R. 161, 167. This procedure may be used under certain conditions
    when it is or may be necessary in the public interest to preserve a document's
    confidentiality: *Conway v. Rimmer* [1968] A.C. 910; C.P.R., r. 31.19(6).

truth. It often happens, from the imperfection of evidence or the withholding of it, sometimes by the party in whose favour it would tell if presented, that an adjudication has to be made which is not, and is known not to be, the whole truth of the matter: yet if the decision has been in accordance with the available evidence and with the law, justice will have been fairly done . . . There is no independent power in the court to say that, nevertheless, it would like to inspect the documents, with a view to possible production, for its own assistance.[12]

In the Court of Appeal, in the same case, Lord Denning M.R. stressed that 'when we speak of the due administration of justice this does not always mean ascertaining the truth of what happened. It often means that, as a matter of justice, a party must prove his case without any help from the other side.'[13]

Here, in its essentials, is the philosophy of the adversary system, and, as is shown by the words of Lord Wilberforce just cited, it is a system for the settlement of disputes in which justice is equated with procedural justice between the parties. Today the judge sits without a jury in the vast majority of cases, but he may still only resolve the controversy as it is put before him by the parties. He may take account only of the allegations that the parties have included in their pleadings, and of the evidence that they have chosen to put before him at the trial. He has no power to act of his own motion to order an investigation of fact, to require an amendment of the pleadings,[14] to hear a witness whom the parties would prefer he did not hear, or to summon the parties to appear before him for interrogation if they do not choose to give evidence.[15] He may, in theory, raise a point of law, provided that he allows it to be argued,[16] but in practice the possibilities are limited: no matter who does the research, the law applicable in a given case is only that which applies to the facts as alleged in the pleadings.[17]

Five developments in the law

The decline of the jury

Before 1876 the common law scarcely admitted that a question of fact might be decided by a judge alone. Almost without exception, whenever a question of fact arose, a jury had to be convened.[18] The Acts of

---

[12] [1983] 2 A.C. 394, 438–9.
[13] *Ibid.*, at 411.   [14] Above, p. 376.
[15] In countries such as France, where the parties are not competent witnesses, they may be summoned to appear before the judge to respond to interrogation: chap. 11, p. 215.
[16] Chap. 10, p. 194.   [17] Chap. 10, p. 198.
[18] Until entry into force of the Common Law Procedure Act 1854, the use of a jury was mandatory in the common law jurisdictions. Equity never used a jury, but important

378   Procedural reform

1873–5 left the rule of jury trial intact, but a new rule of procedure of 1883[19] introduced some flexibility by allowing the court a discretion to order trial by judge alone, and this led to a reduction in the use of the jury from 90 per cent to 50 per cent of cases.[20] There followed a number of minor changes until a law of 1933[21] clarified the situation: in a limited number of specific cases trial by jury remained the norm, but otherwise the mode of trial was in the court's unfettered discretion. By this time the percentage of cases tried by jury had fallen to 10 per cent.

In 1965, although jury trials had by then fallen to 2 per cent, the Court of Appeal held that, except where the right to a jury was statutory, a jury should be used only in exceptional cases,[22] and this was confirmed by the House of Lords in 1973.[23] Under the law now in force,[24] an application by a party for trial by jury must be granted in cases of defamation or where fraud is alleged against the applicant party, but even in those cases a jury will be refused if the court considers that the trial will involve serious examination of documents or if it considers that, for any reason, use of a jury would make the trial long and expensive. For the rest, it is now the rule that a jury will not be used unless the court otherwise decides – and that very rarely happens. Today, the civil jury is scarcely ever used outside actions for defamation.

Documentary evidence and the hearsay rule

The rule against hearsay evidence never was, in itself, a rule against the use of documentary evidence. In the first place, the rule applied as much to oral testimony as to evidence in writing. In the second place a document has always been admissible as proof of its own existence, subject only to independent proof or the admission of its provenance. The rule did, however, prevent the use of a document as evidence of the truth of statements contained within it. In 1943 it was held that a conviction for driving without due care and attention was not even admissible, as evidence in civil proceedings arising out of the same events, to prove that the convicted driver had been negligent.[25]

Plainly, therefore, abolition of the rule against hearsay would make a

questions of fact which arose in a court of equity could be transferred to a common law court and there put before a jury.

[19] R.S.C. 1883, Ord. XXXVI.
[20] See R. M. Jackson, 'The Incidence of Jury Trial during the Past Century' (1937) 1 M.L.R. 132 for an analysis of jury trial and of the relevant legislation down to 1935.
[21] Administration of Justice (Miscellaneous Provisions) Act 1933, s. 6.
[22] *Ward v. James* [1966] 1 Q.B. 273.
[23] *Williams v. Beesley* [1973] 1 W.L.R. 1295.
[24] Supreme Court Act 1981, s. 69.
[25] *Hollington v. F. Hewthorn and Co.* [1943] K.B. 587. Convictions (but not acquittals)

great variety of documents admissible as evidence – police reports, medical and hospital records, records of hearings, written statements of the parties and others, and so on. In legislation of 1968 and 1972, Parliament moved substantially in the direction of abolishing the rule against hearsay for civil cases,[26] but refrained from outright abolition and introduced a complex procedure for the use of hearsay. Now, however, by the Civil Evidence Act 1995, it is simply and shortly enacted that 'in civil proceedings evidence shall not be excluded on the ground that it is hearsay'.[27]

This does not mean that the distinction between hearsay and direct evidence has itself been abolished. Lingering doubts about the ability of judges to appreciate that hearsay evidence may be unreliable have led to inclusion in the Civil Evidence Act of statutory guidance for assessing its weight and, to preserve so far as possible the right of cross-examination, a party proposing to adduce hearsay evidence must give sufficient notice of the fact to other parties: where the written statement of a person is adduced and that person is not called as a witness, any other party may, with leave of the court, call and cross-examine him on his statement as if it were his evidence in chief. Nevertheless, it is unquestionable that much evidence that could, previously, have been put to the court only by direct oral evidence, may now be given in documentary form.

Expert evidence[28]

In principle, if technical or scientific questions arise in the course of litigation, each party is entitled to call the experts of his choice to be heard as witnesses at the trial. As witnesses, they are subjected to examination and cross-examination like any other.

Notwithstanding a party's normal right to call such witnesses as he chooses, it has long been possible[29] for the court, during the pre-trial stage, to restrict the number of expert witnesses to be heard at the trial, usually to two on each side. In addition, expert witnesses may be called upon to produce, if possible, an agreed written report for use at the trial. Obviously, if the experts are to come to an agreement, they must communicate with one another, and the main purpose of the rule is to avoid the waste of time and money involved in calling expert witnesses

---

were made admissible as evidence in civil proceedings by the Civil Evidence Act 1968, ss. 11 and 13.

[26] Civil Evidence Acts 1968 and 1972.

[27] Civil Evidence Act 1995, s. 1(1).

[28] For fuller consideration of this topic and for changes under the Woolf reforms, see chap. 12.

[29] R.S.C., Ord. 38, r. 4; C.P.R., r. 35.4.

only for it to emerge after their examination and cross-examination at the trial that there is no difference of opinion between them.

In 1974, a more far-reaching provision was brought into effect. Now, the oral evidence of an expert may, as a general rule, be given at the trial only if the parties agree or the court grants leave, and, normally, leave will be given only on the condition that the party seeking leave informs his opponent, through a written expert's report, of the substance of what the expert will say at the trial.[30] It is still open to a party to refuse disclosure of this kind, but if he does so his expert will not, save exceptionally, be heard at the trial. It follows that, in the ordinary way, all parties know in advance what will be the evidence in chief of their opponents' expert witnesses; in effect, that evidence is available in documentary form before the trial.[31]

Ordinary evidence

The rule requiring the exchange of written expert reports may be seen as a departure from a party's traditional right to prepare himself for trial independently of his opponent and of the court itself. Each party is free to inform himself of the circumstances of the case, to carry out such investigations as he sees fit, to question potential witnesses and, for his own use, to reduce their statements to writing. No communication to his opponent or to the court of the evidence a party intends to adduce at the trial used to be required. Indeed, in 1953, an important reform committee even rejected the modest proposal that the parties should disclose the names of their intended witnesses before the trial.[32]

Lying behind the rejection of so apparently harmless a proposal lies the common law's traditional insistence that oral evidence is presented at the trial for the first and only time: the freedom of the parties to prepare themselves for trial, independently of each other and of the court, is consistent with, and stems from, the philosophy of the adversary system. Nevertheless, criticism has been directed at the secrecy of the parties' preparations for trial since 1968 at the latest. First, it was said that such secrecy leads to long and costly trials and that a degree of candour would eliminate much unnecessary expense. Secondly, it was argued that settlements would be more easily reached if each party were in a position to evaluate the strength of his opponent's case in advance

---

[30] R.S.C., Ord. 38, rr. 36–44. Under the Woolf reforms no expert evidence, written or oral may be adduced without permission: chap. 12, p. 240.

[31] Only rarely will it be necessary for an expert witness to attend the trial unless his cross-examination is required.

[32] Evershed, paras. 299–302.

of the trial. A number of reform proposals have therefore looked for ways to ensure that the parties do more to disclose their hands before the trial.[33]

The kind of disclosure envisaged was eventually achieved by a new rule of procedure, introduced in restricted form in 1986 and completed in 1988.[34] This gave the court a discretionary power to order a party to communicate to other parties, in written form, the substance of what a witness would say at the trial. Since 1992 an order for the exchange of witness statements is ordinarily required to be made in all actions started by writ, and, now, witness statements may be used at the trial as the witnesses' evidence in chief so that, if a witness is not required for cross-examination, he need not attend the trial. Though a party is not actually obliged to provide witness statements to his opponent, if he does not do so he can only adduce evidence to which an order relates if he obtains the leave of the court.

Skeleton arguments

The development and nature of skeleton arguments in the Court of Appeal has been described in an earlier chapter.[35] The practice of submitting similar written arguments also grew up in complex cases at first instance and is now compulsory in the High Court.[36] At both levels, skeleton arguments form part of the documentation available to the parties and to the court before the hearing.

An unintended outcome of the reforms

It was, probably, at least part of Lord Donaldson's purpose in introducing skeleton arguments that judges should be provided, in advance of the hearing, with the means to inform themselves of the questions they would be called upon to resolve and even to engage in preliminary reading of the authorities with a view to saving time at the hearing. The virtual abolition of the hearsay rule, though obviously significant beyond the confines of procedure, helps procedural economy by avoiding the need to call witnesses whose evidence, though necessary, is not in

---

[33] E.g. Winn, para. 132.

[34] R.S.C., Ord. 38, r. 2A, as amended. See also *Practice Note (Civil Litigation: Case Management)* [1995] 1 W.L.R. 262. Though acknowledged by Lord Woolf to be a source of expense and in need of minor modification, there is no suggestion that use of witness statements should be abandoned: Woolf Interim, pp. 175–80; Woolf Final, pp. 128–30; C.P.R., rr. 32.4 and 32.5.

[35] Chap. 14, p. 274.

[36] *Practice Direction (Civil Litigation: Case Management)* [1995] 1 W.L.R. 508.

controversy. The achievement of economy also lies behind the requirement for exchange of experts' reports and witness statements. The second and third of these reforms only became possible with the decline of the jury, but the objective of all of them was the saving of time and costs, rather than increasing, for its own sake, the amount of information available to judges in advance of a trial or other hearing.

Be that as it may, however, their combined result has been that a far more elaborate and complete documentation is brought into existence before the trial than was the case before and, even if that documentation is primarily intended for exchange between the parties to make their preparation for trial more of a collaborative than a competitive activity, it is also available to the judge.

Throughout the long history of English civil procedure, even after the virtual disappearance of the jury and until very recently, the judge who, exceptionally, wished to inform himself before the trial about the case he was to try, was not really in a position to do so. He had at his disposal only the pleadings, documents disclosed on discovery and, perhaps, an agreed bundle of correspondence between the parties. Now, in contrast, numerous documents – written reports of experts and witness statements in particular – are available for the judge to read in advance of the trial if he wishes to do so. Whether intentionally or not, the reforms have created a situation in which the judge can prepare himself in advance of the trial and become acquainted, not only with the nature of the case he is to try, but, to a substantial extent, with the evidence on which the parties propose to rely.

A derogation from the adversary system?

The adversary system is the product of the use of the jury as judge of fact, and so too is the denial of the judge's power to act *ex officio* 'to ascertain some independent truth'.[37] Only those issues that the parties have put into controversy through their pleadings can be resolved by the court: only the evidence that the parties choose to adduce can be heard or taken into account by the judge: for so long as the judge – or the jury – is not in a position to have knowledge, in advance of the trial, either of the dispute itself or of the evidence to be adduced, nothing else is possible. After centuries of familiarity with the restraints imposed by use of the jury, English legal thinking has come to see them as virtues. The conviction that the adversary system is the best adapted for the good administration of justice in England is still with us.

[37] Above, p. 376.

Now that the civil jury has virtually disappeared and so much documentation is available for the judge to study before the trial begins, it is time to ask whether the English attachment to the adversary system can survive indefinitely. Will the judges not come, in time, to recognise that they should be involved in the preparation of the cases they are to try with a view to ensuring, not only that they are conducted with economy, but also that the evidence made available, should, so far as possible, reveal the truth?

There is nothing in the legislation mentioned in this chapter that obliges the judge to read in advance the documentation which it requires the parties to produce; still less is there anything which requires active judicial participation in trial preparation.[38] Abolition of the rule against hearsay only indirectly affects procedure, the requirement of skeleton arguments related until recently only to appeals,[39] and the new rules about experts' reports and witness statements look to mutual disclosure between the parties; they contain nothing that is overtly inconsistent with the philosophy of the adversary system. Taken together, however, these changes created the possibility that the judge, after reading the documents, might form the view that the evidence was incomplete, and, having formed such a view, might be inclined to do what he could to see that the gap was filled.

In the past, it was impossible for the judge actually to detect deficiencies in the evidence brought by the parties until presentation of their evidence at the trial had been completed. Abrogation of the rule forbidding the judge from calling a witness himself[40] would not, therefore, have had much effect: for an additional witness to be heard by the judge's order, or even at his suggestion to counsel, would have required the adjournment of the trial with all the delays and costs that that involves. Now, however, abrogation of the rule could have practical as well as theoretical consequences.[41]

No such change has so far been suggested, but there are signs of dissatisfaction with the situation as it is. First, in two of its reports,[42] the Review Body on Civil Justice observes that it would be useful if judges were to read before the trial, or 'pre-read', the documents available to

[38] It is a major purpose of the C.P.R. to bring fundamental change to this aspect of English procedure. See chap. 19, below.
[39] Above, p. 381.   [40] Above, p. 376.
[41] From the technical point of view of the doctrine of precedent, abrogation of the rule would not be difficult. The decision on which it rests is not strong, and the rule itself is more a matter of practice and the result of traditional habits of thought than an entrenched rule of law.
[42] Civil Justice Review, Report of the Review Body on Civil Justice, Cm 394 (1988), para. 264; Civil Justice Review, General Issues (1987), para. 202.

them, including the witness statements. It also envisages that, in many cases, such pre-reading would enable the judge to identify at an early stage what are the questions to be answered and what evidence should be adduced at the trial.[43] In succeeding paragraphs, the report points out that the trial as we know it finds its origin in the use of the jury, notes that the jury is no longer used in civil cases except in actions for defamation and concludes that the pride of place traditionally given by English law to orality is no longer justified.

This has no more weight than belongs to the opinion expressed by a committee, which opinion was not explicitly directed to the advantages and disadvantages of the adversary system as such. Nevertheless, the suggestion that the judge should form an opinion before the trial, for example on the evidence to be presented, would be pointless if it were not intended that he should act on his opinion, at least to the extent of making suggestions to the parties as to the conduct of the trial.[44]

Secondly, and perhaps more immediately indicative of changing judicial attitudes, it is possible to detect in some judgments a sense of discomfort with that particular aspect of the adversary system which was reaffirmed by the House of Lords in the *Air Canada* case,[45] namely that it is no part of the judge's business to search for an independent truth. There is, for example, the clearly expressed view of the judge of first instance in that case,[46] and there is also the judgment of Sir John Donaldson M.R. in a case of 1987 when he used words not easily reconcilable with those of the House of Lords in the *Air Canada* case. He said, 'Litigation is not a war or even a game. It is designed to do real justice between opposing parties and, if the court does not have *all* the relevant information, it cannot achieve this object.'[47] It is unlikely that Donaldson M.R. would admit to a desire to confer inquisitorial powers on English judges, but his words mark at least a partial retreat from the underlying philosophy of the adversary system.

This may be little more than a straw in the wind, but the wind is blowing in the direction of a modernised understanding of the role of civil litigation in the modern world. Edouardo Couture's observation that the civil action is civilisation's substitute for vengeance[48] is of great

---

[43] Civil Justice Review, *General Issues*.

[44] In the past the legislature has several times attempted to enable the court to give substantive directions for the future conduct of the trial, but without success. See, e.g. Jacob, *Fabric*, pp. 102–9 and, for the future, below, chap. 19.

[45] Above, p. 376.   [46] Bingham J.

[47] *Davies* v. *Eli Lilly and Co.* [1987] 1 W.L.R. 428, 431; emphasis in the original. See D. A. Ipp, 'Reforms to the Adversarial Process in Civil Litigation' (1995) 69 *Australian Law Journal* 705 and 790, at pp. 714–15.

[48] 'The Nature of the Judicial Process' (1950–1) 25 Tulane L.R. 1. See chap. 3, p. 71.

value to an understanding of the history of legal institutions. It is, however, inadequate to account for the realities of life in industrialised countries at the end of the twentieth century. The philosophy of the adversary system, if it looks to justice between the parties and not just to the avoidance of violence, must presuppose a contest on equal terms, and that cannot always be guaranteed even today. It also requires of the advocates not only that they act honestly and in fair competition with each other, but that they each do their best to ensure that the court does indeed have '*all* the relevant information', whether favourable to the interests of their clients or not. But that is scarcely the role of an advocate in an adversary process.[49]

This leads to one final point. We are beginning to recognise that however narrow the application of *res judicata*, it is not always or even generally true that litigation concerns only the parties to it. We recognise, in effect, that the judgments in many cases will have consequences not only for the parties but for numerous other persons and even for the community at large. If the judge does not concern himself with those interests at least to the extent that they are not the same as the interests of the parties, no one can do so. Does this not mean that the judge himself should use his best endeavours, in the preparation of the case, to ensure that he is adequately informed?

Conclusion

English civil procedure will, no doubt, continue for the indefinite future to distinguish sharply between the pre-trial and the trial stages of an action. It is, however, difficult to believe that the old philosophy of the adversary system and the refusal to acknowledge that there may be value in a judicial attempt to find the truth, can survive much longer. The reforms already implemented give the judge the opportunity to inform himself during the pre-trial stage and so to form a view as to the evidence that should be adduced. Is it too far-fetched to suggest that future judges will take advantage of the opportunity thus provided to play a more active role in the preparation for trial, over and above the management role that is to be cast upon them?

---

[49] It is generally agreed that an advocate must not conceal from the court a legal authority that runs counter to the interests of his client, but is he obliged to call a witness whose evidence will assist his opponent and of whose existence his opponent is unaware?

19   The Woolf reforms

In March 1994, Lord Woolf, a senior Law Lord, was appointed by the then Lord Chancellor to carry out a review of the current rules and procedures of the civil courts in order 'to improve access to justice and to reduce the cost of litigation; to reduce the complexity of the rules and modernise terminology; to remove unnecessary distinctions of practice and procedure'.

In little more than a year, Lord Woolf published an interim report,[1] and his final report was published in July 1996.[2] Such was the Government's desire to make progress on the recommendations of the report that in February of the following year the Civil Procedure Act 1997 received the Royal Assent. The Act sets up a new Civil Procedure Rule Committee with power to make rules governing the practice and procedure of the Court of Appeal (Civil Division), the High Court and the county courts.[3] The old Supreme Court and county court rule committees disappear and a new, unified, set of comprehensive Civil Procedure Rules replaces both the old Rules of the Supreme Court 1965 and the County Court Rules 1981.

Following the change of Government in May 1997, the new Lord Chancellor asked Sir Peter Middleton, a former Treasury official, to report on the proposals for reform and to do so within an extremely short period in order that momentum might not be lost.[4] In the meantime, in October 1996, Sir Jeffery Bowman, an accountant with a law degree, was appointed to chair a review of the Court of Appeal (Civil Division) and his report appeared in September 1997.[5] In the course of preparation of all three reports, their authors consulted widely, and there was much further consultation as drafting of the new Rules proceeded. Since April 1999 there has been a completely new set of

[1] Woolf Interim.   [2] Woolf Final.
[3] The Act also creates a Civil Justice Council with a continuing review and advisory role.
[4] Sir Peter Middleton's report (hereafter 'Middleton') was published in September 1997.
[5] Bowman.

Rules of procedure, a new language and, if Lord Woolf's intentions are realised, the beginnings of a new legal culture.[6]

This is no 'petty tinkering', and it is certainly intended to be 'comprehensive reform', but does it have the 'general ideas or legal philosophy', the absence of which from Anglo-American law Roscoe Pound bemoaned almost a century ago?[7] Certainly the whole is focused on reduction in the cost and delay of civil litigation, which gives it a 'general', if not an original, idea, but the likely success or failure of the reforms in achieving such a reduction will not be considered here.[8] The object is, rather, to ask about their 'legal philosophy', or, to be more prosaic, to enquire whether the reforms themselves, and the expository parts of the reports on which they are based, take us any further towards recognition and, where appropriate, promotion of the purposes that are served by the institution of civil litigation and its use – purposes which must not be confused with the purposes of the litigants who use it. This distinction, which is seldom taken explicitly and is commonly overlooked, is of fundamental importance: even dispute resolution, though one of the purposes of litigation, is unlikely to be the purpose of either party: the claimant's purpose in instituting proceedings is to obtain, and the defendant's purpose in defending them is to resist, the award of a remedy.[9]

The original purpose of what we now know as civil litigation was to provide a non-violent procedure for the resolution of disputes, and to this day civil proceedings cannot normally be instituted if there is no dispute.[10] On the other hand, no one can any longer suggest that the civil action is still no more than civilisation's substitute for vengeance.[11] Especially when it comes to procedural reform, the resolution of disputes must not be treated as if it were the only purpose served by civil litigation: the procedure of our courts is too important for that, not least because it is 'the practical way of securing the rule of law'.[12]

[6] Woolf Interim, p. 18. See Middleton, pp. 18–19.
[7] 'The Causes of Popular Dissatisfaction with the Administration of Justice' (1906) 40 Am.L.R. 729. See above, chap. 17, p. 358.
[8] See, e.g. A. A. S. Zuckerman, 'Lord Woolf's Access to Justice: Plus ça change . . .' (1996) 59 M.L.R. 773; M. Zander, 'The Woolf Report: Forwards or Backwards for the New Lord Chancellor?' (1997) 16 C.J.Q. 208; H. Woolf, 'Medics, Lawyers and the Courts' (1997) 16 C.J.Q. 302; M. Zander, 'The Government's Plans on Civil Justice' (1998) 61 M.L.R. 382 and references there given; S. Flanders, 'Case Management: Failure in America? Success in England and Wales?' (1998) 17 C.J.Q. 308. A number of the contributions to A. A. S. Zuckerman and R. Cranston (eds.), *Reform of Civil Procedure* (1995) also bear on the question.
[9] Calamandrei's statement about cassation (chap. 15, above, p. 306) provides a rare example of convincing instructive use of the distinction.
[10] Chap. 1, p. 21.   [11] Chap. 4, p. 92.
[12] Jacob, *Fabric*, p. 66, cited above, chap. 3, p. 59.

The question to be considered in this chapter falls into two parts. First, it will be asked whether the reports reveal an intention on the part of their authors to do more than try once more to reduce the costs and delays of dispute resolution through litigation. Secondly, and more importantly, it will be asked what are the foreseeable consequences of the reforms, taken with those mentioned in the previous chapter, for the character of civil litigation in England and for the future perception of its purposes.

The reports

In the first two pages of his report Lord Woolf acknowledges that a system of civil justice is essential to a civilised society. He then goes on to state, without elaboration, a number of principles that should be met by a civil justice system, but, with one exception, these relate only to matters internal to the litigation process.[13] The report then turns to dispute resolution, and thereafter does little to dispel the impression that civil litigation is envisaged as no more than a particular method of achieving that end. Though he blames the 'adversarial process' for the evils he seeks to remedy,[14] and though the remedy proposed is a 'fundamental shift in the responsibility for the management of civil litigation from the litigants and their advisers to the courts',[15] Lord Woolf rejects concerns that his proposals will undermine the 'adversarial nature of our civil justice system'.[16] He is, indeed, anxious to reassure his readers that he has no intention of abandoning 'our adversarial and oral tradition' – the tradition which most clearly sustains the dispute resolution model of litigation.[17]

Sir Peter Middleton, in his report, does acknowledge that benefits wider than mere dispute resolution 'flow from the existence of an effective civil justice system'. Unfortunately, however, he seems to believe that the cases which provide such benefits are few in number and capable of being considered as test cases. He does not see, or at least he does not mention, as benefits the messages that come, for example, from the courts' handling of a number of similar cases, none of which would qualify by itself as a test case,[18] and he suggests that test

---

[13] Woolf Interim, pp. 2–3; Introduction, above, p. 3. Lord Woolf also cites with approval a number of 'objectives' set out by the Review Body on Civil Justice in its report (Cm 394 (1988), para. 220) but these are no more far-reaching: Woolf Interim, p. 28. For the exception see below, p. 397.
[14] Woolf Interim, p. 7.   [15] *Ibid.*, p. 18.
[16] Woolf Final, p. 14.
[17] Woolf Interim, p. 29.
[18] See above, chap. 3, p. 72.

cases might be subjected to special procedures.[19] If this were not sufficient to indicate his view that the way in which the great majority of cases pass through and are decided by the courts is of no general interest, he actually states that, for him, 'civil justice' is essentially concerned with the resolution of disputes. Justice, as he defines it, is 'the satisfactory resolution of disputes' and, as such, forms part of the service sector of the economy.[20]

Consequences of the reforms

The adversary system[21]

Lord Woolf's protestations to the contrary notwithstanding, the first casualty of the reforms is likely to be the adversary system, at least as it is traditionally understood. Under the adversary system, the parties dictate at all stages the form, content and pace of proceedings; one author lists no less than twelve matters that are under the control of the parties.[22] Some of these, such as the initiation of the action, are under the control of the parties in any system of civil litigation,[23] but the list covers virtually every feature of litigation prior to judgment and so includes matters both of procedure and of substance. Included in the parties' control there is, on the one hand, for example, the pre-trial progress of the action and, on the other, the evidence on which the judgment will in due course be founded.

Some items in the list could be dropped without danger to the adversary system, at least as it is explained in the *Air Canada* case, namely as a system according to which the court has no duty to discover an independent truth; the judge must decide, and decide only, the dispute as defined by the parties, and he must base his decision exclusively on the evidence supplied by them: 'If the decision has been

---

[19] Middleton, pp. 9 and 69.

[20] *Ibid.*, p. 9. This view, which overlooks the distinction referred to earlier (above, p. 387), is reflected in the statement of the Lord Chancellor in 1997 (see Access to Justice, Discussion Papers on Civil Court Fees, February and November 1998) that court fees should be so fixed as to cover, subject to exemptions and remissions, the full costs of the system. See also Middleton, pp. 70–1.

[21] See chap. 9 and chap. 18, p. 377.

[22] N. H. Andrews, 'The Adversarial Principle: Fairness and Efficiency: Reflections on the Recommendations of the Woolf Report' in A. A. S. Zuckerman and R. Cranston (eds.), *Reform of Civil Procedure*, p. 169 at p. 171. See also Andrews, *Principles of Civil Procedure* (1994), chap. 3; D. A. Ipp, 'Reforms to the Adversarial Process in Civil Litigation' (1995) 69 *Australian Law Journal* 705 and 790, at p. 712.

[23] Chap. 1, p. 21.

in accordance with the available evidence and with the law, justice will have been fairly done.'[24]

Such an approach equates justice with procedural justice; it restricts the court to a decision between the rival contentions of the parties and encapsulates the dispute-resolution purpose of civil litigation. In theory, therefore, the introduction of judicial management of the pre-trial procedures under the Woolf reforms is compatible with retention of the adversary system. If all that is involved is a shift from 'party prosecution' to 'judicial prosecution' of the progress of proceedings, depriving the parties of the opportunity to procrastinate, then a shift to case management is consistent with retention of the principles of 'dispositive election' and of 'party presentation', principles which, together, form the core of the (substantive) adversary system.[25] In reality, however, even case management limited to management of the progress of the action through its procedural stages would be unlikely to leave the adversary system untouched.

In the preceding chapter it was pointed out that the developments and reforms there considered, beginning with the decline in use of the civil jury, lead to conditions in which, during the pre-trial stages, judges can be far better informed about the facts and circumstances of the cases they are to try than was previously possible, and that this could result, to put it no higher, in some discomfort on their part when faced with the rule that it is not for the judges to look for an independent truth.[26] None of those reforms, however, actually required the judges to read the documentation produced by the parties in advance of the trial.[27] Effective case management, on the other hand, demands that the judge is adequately informed about the substance of the case he is to manage, and under the new Rules there are numerous provisions to ensure that he has the necessary information.[28] Lord Woolf himself proposes that time should be allocated to enable judges to 'pre-read the papers'.[29]

It has been suggested elsewhere that, in France, the introduction of an effective form of judicial case management in 1965 resulted eventually in recognition that the judge has a part to play in seeking the best approximation to the truth that can be achieved;[30] there is no reason to

---

[24] [1983] 2 A.C. 394, especially 438–9, *per* Lord Wilberforce, cited in chap. 18, above, p. 376.

[25] The phrases used are Millar's translations of the German *Parteibetrieb, Offizialbetrieb, Dispositionsprinzip* and *Verhandlungsmaxime*: R. Millar, 'The Formative Principles of Civil Procedure', *History*, 3, pp. 11–21.

[26] Chap. 18, p. 384.   [27] Chap. 18, p. 383.

[28] For example, C.P.R., rr. 26.3 and 26.5 and Woolf Final, p. 61 (Allocation questionnaire); C.P.R., r. 28.5 and 29.6 (Listing questionnaire).

[29] Woolf Final, p. 29.

[30] J. A. Jolowicz, 'The Woolf Report and the Adversary System' (1996) 15 C.J.Q. 198.

suppose that, as case management establishes itself and becomes routine, the same will not happen in this country. It is, after all, at best an awkward notion that the judge has no business with the truth: it is a notion that runs counter to a non-lawyer's idea of what a judge's role should be, and it is one which the Lord Chancellor's Department has actually rejected in a revealing aside. The definition of the 'Overriding Objective' of the Rules, which is to 'enable the court to deal with cases justly', refers only to procedural matters, and that, so far as it goes, is consistent with the adversary system. In a footnote, however, the Department explains that, after consideration, it was finally decided not to include a provision to the effect that dealing with a case justly also includes trying to find out the truth about the matters in issue because, amongst other reasons, 'seeking the truth is so obviously part of the court's role that it does not need to be stated expressly in the Rules'.[31]

Over and above the psychological undermining of the adversary system that comes from the increase in information available to the judges during the pre-trial stage, case management under the Civil Procedure Rules directly curtails the freedom of the parties to present the substance of their cases as they choose. The judge is expected to be more than what has elsewhere been called a 'calendrier parlant',[32] and his role in case management creates an additional and more direct threat to survival of the adversary system. One of the more dramatic examples is that the court may dispose summarily of a case, not only on application but on its own initiative, if it considers that the claim or defence, as the case may be, has no 'real prospect of success'.[33] Expert witnesses, for all practical purposes, will cease to take part in an adversary process since, first, no party may call an expert witness or put in an expert's report without the court's permission, secondly, the court may direct that expert evidence be given by one expert only, and, thirdly, it is made the overriding duty of the expert to help the court impartially even at the cost of his duty to the person instructing or paying him.[34] Clearest of all, however, and potentially the most far-reaching, is the rule which gives explicit power to the court 'to control evidence'; this it may do by giving directions on the issues on which it requires evidence, on the nature of

[31] C.P.R., r. 1.1 and footnote to the Third Revision (footnote omitted from later Revisions). See also G. A. Lightman, 'Civil Litigation in the 21st Century' (1998) 17 C.J.Q. 373, 388–91; Ipp, 'Reforms to the Adversarial Process', pp. 714–15.

[32] G. Oberto, 'L'administration judiciaire de la preuve dans le procès civil italien' [1998] R.I.D.C. 779, 786.

[33] C.P.R., r. 2. Woolf Interim, p. 37; Woolf Final, p. 123. This extends to the facts as well as the law. See also C.P.R., r. 3.4.

[34] C.P.R., r. 35.4(1), 35.7(1) and 35.3, respectively. See chap. 12, postscript. The most that Lord Woolf claims here is that a neutral expert would function 'within a broadly adversarial framework': Woolf Final, p. 140.

the evidence which it requires to determine those issues and on the way in which the evidence is to be placed before the court.[35]

Out of court dispute resolution

It is, and for long has been, widely accepted that it is in some general sense 'better' if the parties to a dispute can settle their differences by agreement. The reports and the Rules adopt this view, but they do more than before to promote dispute resolution otherwise than through civil litigation. First, the old system of payments into court is enlarged so as to enable claimants as well as defendants to make offers in such a way as to bear on the allocation of costs.[36] Secondly, it is a declared objective both of the new 'pre-action protocols',[37] and, indeed, of the whole process of case management, to assist and encourage settlement at the earliest appropriate stage.[38] Thirdly, and of particular interest here, official encouragement is given to the avoidance or curtailment of civil litigation through recourse by the parties to alternative dispute resolution ('ADR').

There is nothing new about ADR as such.[39] In 1994, however, it attracted the attention of the commercial judges and led them to give active encouragement to its use by the parties to commercial cases.[40] This, so far as is known, was the first time that the courts have sought actively to turn away business in favour of what might formerly have been considered a rival institution,[41] but the Commer-

---

[35] C.P.R., r. 32.1. The court may use this power to exclude evidence which would otherwise be admissible: *ibid.*, r. 32.1(2). See also, *ibid.*, r. 3.1, which, amongst other things, allows the court to exclude an issue from determination if it can do substantive justice between the parties on other issues. If freely used by the judges, this rule will greatly reduce the parties' freedom to control the substance of their litigation.

[36] R.S.C., Ord. 22. See Woolf Interim, chap. 24; Woolf Final, chap. 14; C.P.R., r. 36.

[37] Woolf Final, p. 107; *Practice Direction – Protocols*, para. 1.4.2.

[38] Woolf Interim, p. 38.

[39] See, e.g. W. Twining, 'Alternative to What? Theories of Litigation, Procedure and Dispute Settlement in Anglo-American Jurisprudence' (1993) 56 M.L.R. 380; N. Fricker and J. Walker, 'Alternative Dispute Resolution – State Responsibility or Second Best?' (1994) 13 C.J.Q. 29; K. Mackie (ed.), *A Handbook of Dispute Resolution* (1981); M. Palmer and S. Roberts, *Dispute Processes* (1998). For convenient accounts of various methods of dispute resolution, including ombudsmen (public and private), advice agencies and mediation, see Woolf Interim, pp. 137–43; Middleton, Annex C. For a comparative discussion, see H. Kötz and R. Ottenhof, *Les Conciliateurs, La Conciliation* (1987).

[40] *Practice Note (Commercial Court: Alternative Dispute Resolution)* [1994] 1 W.L.R. 14; *Practice Statement (Commercial Cases: Alternative Dispute Resolution) (No. 2)* [1996] 1 W.L.R. 1024.

[41] 'There must be no Alsatia in England where the King's writ does not run': *Czarnikow v. Roth, Schmidt and Co.* [1922] 2 K.B. 478, 488, *per* Scrutton L.J.

cial Court's lead was soon followed for most other kinds of High Court proceedings.[42]

In his report, Lord Woolf devotes an entire chapter to ADR,[43] and, in keeping with his view that disputes should, wherever possible, be resolved without litigation,[44] the Rules provide that the court may, at an early stage and either on application or of its own motion, order a stay of the proceedings to enable the parties to resort to ADR.[45] Sir Peter Middleton seems to hold a view of the merits of ADR similar to Lord Woolf's, but he prefers to see the 'civil justice system' as including ADR and encompassing 'all the ways in which people can legitimately resolve disputes and enforce their rights and the obligations of others under the law'.[46]

Despite his enthusiasm for ADR, Lord Woolf accepts that it would be wrong in principle to erode the citizen's existing entitlement to seek a remedy from the civil court, and it has already been remarked that the existence of a dispute is normally a prerequisite of any judicial activity. Nevertheless, the development and encouragement of the use of ADR,[47] together with the expansion of techniques for promoting settlements, reflect a view that disputes should be resolved whenever possible outside the courts and by methods other than actual litigation.

Number of cases

It is impossible to know how many potential or even actual disputes get no further than a boardroom, a family discussion, or at most a solicitor's office. It is known, however, that of all the civil actions that are started in England and Wales, only a tiny proportion reach trial.[48] The proportion becomes even smaller if cases decided by arbitration in the county court or, now, on the small claims track, are discounted, as would not be unreasonable: given their flexibility and freedom from procedural and evidentiary formalities, those procedures may be thought closer to ADR

---

[42] *Practice Note (Civil Litigation: Case Management)* [1995] 1 W.L.R. 508, Pre-trial Checklist, points 10–13.

[43] Woolf Interim, chap. 18, 'Alternative approaches to dispensing justice'.

[44] Woolf Final, p. 107. See also *ibid.*, p. 15.

[45] C.P.R., r. 26.4. See also *ibid.*, r. 1.4(2)(e).

[46] Middleton, p. 9. The trouble with this is that, while successful use of ADR resolves disputes, it is as likely as not to do so by finding a compromise solution agreeable to the parties rather than one which enforces their rights and obligations 'under the law'.

[47] Middleton proposes a Government role and even, in appropriate cases, Government funding to encourage and facilitate the development of ADR: Middleton, p. 68.

[48] Taking the Chancery and the Queen's Bench Divisions of the High Court together, and ignoring county court and small claim cases, it is under 1 per cent: Judicial Statistics 1997. See chap. 3, above, p. 72.

than to ordinary civil litigation.[49] If such measures as pre-action protocols and case management succeed in increasing the number of settlements, if the expanded power of summary disposal brings more cases to
early termination, and if the encouragement of ADR by the courts
proves to be effective, the proportion will be yet further reduced.[50]

A changing character and a new perception of civil litigation?

One of the points sought to be made in various places in this book has
been that the purposes of civil litigation should no longer be seen as
limited to the resolution of disputes.[51] That the institution of civil
litigation in fact serves other purposes is, of course, perfectly understood
as much by those concerned with reform of its procedures as by
others,[52] but reform is still presented as concerned only with simplification and the reduction of the costs and delays of dispute resolution in
the courts; the object is to improve 'access to justice'. The other
purposes served by civil litigation are either overlooked or taken for
granted as mere byproducts.

That may have been a reasonable attitude to have adopted in the past.
Now, however, the changes that have been and are being put in place
seem destined to bring about, in course of time, not only a change in the
character of civil litigation but also a more realistic perception of its role
in society.

One major factor will be increasing awareness of the extremely small
number of disputes, by comparison with the whole, which are actually
resolved by litigation. The fact is not new, but attention is now drawn to
it by the further reduction in numbers sought by the Woolf reforms. The
increased pressures on the parties to settle and the promotion of the use
of ADR may be subjectively intended by the authors of the reforms to
do no more than encourage parties to resort, in their own interests, to
methods of dispute resolution that are less expensive than civil litigation.

---

[49] Beldam L.J. comes close to saying this: *Afzal* v. *Ford Motor Co. Ltd* [1994] 4 All E.R.
720, 733–5. And, see, e.g. J. Baldwin, 'Small Claims Hearings: The "Interventionist"
Roles played by District Judges' (1998) 17 C.J.Q. 20. For procedure on the small
claims track, see C.P.R., r. 27. The present general limit for the track is £5,000:
C.P.R., r. 26.6.

[50] Even before introduction of the Woolf reforms, the number of civil actions started in
1997–8 was substantially less than the number for 1993–4: J. Frenkel, *Law Society
Gazette*, 16 December 1998, p. 33.

[51] See, in particular, above, chap. 3 (*passim*); chap. 7, p. 123; chap. 9, p. 179; chap. 17,
p. 366.

[52] See, for example, the opening remarks in Lord Woolf's article, 'Judicial Review – The
Tensions between the Executive and the Judiciary' (1998) 114 L.Q.R. 579.

Viewed objectively, however, the same developments appear to be calculated to promote a policy that as many disputes as possible should be resolved outside the courts. And if it is asked what lies behind such a policy, an answer which comes readily to mind is that an attempt should be made to avoid wasting the time of the judges – or at least of the senior judges – on cases whose decision will do nothing other than bring an individual dispute to an end.

In a system in which the contribution of the courts to dispute resolution is quantitatively insignificant but qualitatively of the highest importance, such a policy must appeal. It makes sense that the time of the judges should be devoted, so far as possible, to cases in which the proceedings and the decisions will, for one reason or another, bear on interests over and beyond those of the nominal parties to them,[53] or at least will provide guidance for the future administration of the law and for the resolution of other disputes wherever, and to whomsoever, either task may fall. If reasoning of that kind comes to be accepted it will mean, at the same time, that dispute resolution through civil litigation comes to be recognised to be as much a means to other ends as an end in itself.

The demise or, if that is too strong a word, the evisceration of the adversary system leads in the same direction. A product of civil trial by jury, the adversary system, as it was, might have been custom designed to attract disputants away from violent, and towards non-violent, procedures. It comes closest of all non-violent procedures to a duel in which the combatants behave as such but use words as weapons instead of swords. There are, of course, rules for the conduct of the forensic, as of any other, duel, but, subject to the rules, each side fights as best it can, and at the end of the day the judge (or jury) – acting more as a referee than as a representative of the state dispensing justice – declares the winner.[54]

In such a system, any attempt by the judge to look for an 'independent truth' is out of place, and so too is any attempt by him to redress inequalities in arms or skills between the parties. Protection of the weak against the strong is unnecessary if the only object of the exercise is the avoidance of violence, for the weak cannot resort to violence against the strong.[55] Today, of course, no one would exclude the protection of the weak against the strong from the business of civil litigation, and there is

[53] The interests in question range from those of society as a whole, for example in the clarification and development of the law, through the competing interests of sections of Government and of the governed, to the interests of even relatively small numbers of persons not parties to but liable to be affected by the outcome of an action.
[54] See Cappelletti and Jolowicz, pp. 167–8.
[55] The advent of legal aid to supply a 'white knight' to the weaker of the parties, so as to

unlikely to be dissent from the proposition that the civil action must be civilisation's substitute for injustice as well as for vengeance. That is not itself a consequence of the Woolf reforms, but it must be realised that even so small a step beyond what is necessary to preservation of the peace, involves a departure from the purities of the dispute resolution model.

In an earlier chapter, reference was made to the 'demand for correct decisions',[56] a demand which can be met only by a system that accepts that the judge has a duty in relation to the truth, and that aims at substantial as well as procedural justice. No one today is likely to deny that our system should pursue both aims. Indeed, Lord Woolf himself places at the head of his list of principles that should be met by a civil justice system, that 'it should be *just* in the results it delivers'.[57]

Lord Woolf's statement may be open to more than one interpretation, but if the judge does not believe his own decision to be just, then it is more than ordinarily unlikely to be so. It follows, as a minimum, that the judge's decision must be based on findings of fact that he believes to be the best approximation to the truth that can be achieved.[58] The same is even more obviously the case where the interests of non-parties, or of those who are parties only by representation in a class or multi-party action, are affected.[59] Perhaps the courts can make their contribution to the clarification and development of the law itself through decisions based on a version of the facts which is some way off the truth, but, if so, it is so only when the decision turns on a pure point of law. When it comes to the 'messages' that come from the handling of numbers of similar cases, or the application of flexible principles of law, then, unless efforts have been made in all of them to discover the truth in so far as it can be discovered, there is bound to be a risk that any grouping of 'similar' cases will in reality be nothing of the kind, and the message therefore falsified.

None of this is intended to suggest that dispute resolution, as such, will cease to be a purpose of civil litigation. The jurisdiction of the court will always have to be invoked where dispute resolution requires use of a coercive power such as only the courts possess; some of the cases which are brought to an end only by judgment after trial run their course simply because of the obstinacy of the parties or the sheer magnitude of the sums of money at stake. For those cases, civil litigation as a court-

redress the disparity between them, undermines the adversary system much less than does judicial intervention.

[56] Chap. 4, p. 85.
[57] Woolf Interim, p. 2. Emphasis in the original.
[58] Chap. 4, p. 86; chap. 18, p. 385.
[59] Chap. 7, above.

based dispute resolution system and nothing else, remains essential, but they do not represent the whole. Except where one party deliberately seeks delay, most of the cases that resist settlement, or other disposal without trial, do so because they raise one or more issues on which neither party is willing to compromise and on which each believes he has a reasonable prospect of success after a full hearing before a judge. Where such an issue exists, the manner of its resolution is likely to be of interest to the future application or administration of the law.

Once the new Civil Procedure Rules have been applied in everyday practice for a number of years, they will take on a life of their own. They will take root, and the resulting system of civil litigation will become as much part of the familiar, given, world for future judges, practitioners and academics as is the system introduced by the Judicature Acts to those of today. The new system, it is believed, will then be seen to be different from the present, not only in form but in its underlying principles; the notion that a judge has no business to look for an 'independent truth' will vanish.

As contemplated by Lord Woolf, and as provided by the Civil Procedure Rules, different cases will call for and receive different degrees of 'hands-on' case management,[60] and in many it will be neither necessary nor possible for the judge to do much more during the pre-trial stage than he did before. On the other hand, it will be for the judge to decide the extent of his intervention in each case, and that is yet another departure from the adversary system. It may be true that civil litigation achieves its purposes through the resolution of disputes, but, while ADR can achieve nothing but dispute resolution, the purposes of civil litigation are much wider. Whether by accident or design, the Woolf reforms and the Civil Procedure Rules, once absorbed into the system, will give us an institution better adapted to the achievement of those purposes than was its predecessor. Paradoxically, an important element in the justification of this prediction is the fact that implementation of the Woolf reforms, which were introduced in order to improve the performance of litigation as a process for the settlement of disputes, will ultimately make it impossible for informed people to continue to think of litigation in the civil courts as just that and no more.

---

[60] E.g. Woolf Final, p. 16. H. Woolf, 'Medics, Lawyers and the Courts' (1997) 16 C.J.Q. 302, 315–16.

Index

Note: For the purposes of the Index, 'civil proceedings' has normally been used in the abstract sense where the discussion in the text is about whether something is or is not 'civil proceedings'. 'Civil litigation' deals with subject-matter where that issue is taken as decided. It also covers 'civil justice'. 'Procedural law' relates to 'civil procedural law' except where otherwise indicated.

Wherever possible, issues have been dealt with by way of principle, with the application in individual jurisdictions dealt with separately under country headings. Where this would have overloaded a country heading (e.g., England and Wales, experts) the entries have been given their own heading (i.e., Experts (England and Wales)). In a few cases where all entries relate to a single jurisdiction (e.g., judicial review), these entries are grouped under single heading indicating that jurisdiction (i.e., Judicial review (England and Wales)).

CAMBRIDGE STUDIES IN INTERNATIONAL AND COMPARATIVE LAW

Books in the series

Lightning Source UK Ltd.
Milton Keynes UK

177324UK00001B/77/P